S0-FBC-022

Medieval Archaeology

medieval & renaissance
texts & studies

Volume 60

Medieval Archaeology

*Papers of the Seventeenth Annual Conference
of the Center for Medieval and Early Renaissance Studies*

EDITED BY
Charles L. Redman

medieval & Renaissance texts & studies
State University of New York at Binghamton
1989

© Copyright 1989
Center for Medieval and Early Renaissance Studies
State University of New York at Binghamton

Library of Congress Cataloging-in-Publication Data

State University of New York at Binghamton. Center for
Medieval and Early Renaissance Studies. Conference (17th:
1983)

Medieval archeology / edited by Charles L. Redman.
    p.   cm. — (Medieval & Renaissance texts & studies ; v.
60)
  Includes index.
  ISBN 0-86698-044-X (alk. paper)
  1. Archeology, Medieval.   2. History—Methodology.
I. Redman, Charles L.   II. Series.
D125.M43 1988
940.1—dc19   88-24158
                                                        CIP

This book is made to last.
It is set in Baskerville, smythe-sewn,
and printed on acid-free paper
to library specifications.

Printed in the United States of America

Contents

Preface   vii
    CHARLES L. REDMAN, *Arizona State University*

Section I: Society and Economy

Archaeology and the Pirenne Thesis   3
    DAVID WHITEHOUSE, *Corning Museum of Glass*

Viking Raiders: The Transformation of Scandinavian Society   23
    KLAVS RANDSBORG, *University of Copenhagen*

The Vikings Versus the Towns of Northern Gaul:
    Challenge and Response   41
    MICHEL ROUCHE, *University of Lille III*

Emporia, Monasteries and the Economic Foundation
    of Medieval Europe   57
    RICHARD HODGES, *University of Sheffield*

Section II: Materials of the Archaeological Record

Ceramic Technologies of Medieval Northern Morocco   75
    EMLEN MYERS, *Smithsonian Institution*

Diversity in Ceramic Production: A Case Study from
    Medieval North Africa   97
    NANCY BENCO, *SUNY-Binghamton*

Numismatics and Medieval Archaeology 119
  ALAN M. STAHL, *American Numismatic Society*

Novgorod Birchbark Documents: The Evidence for
  Literacy in Medieval Russia 127
  EVE LEVIN, *Ohio State University*

Underwater Archaeology and Medieval Mediterranean Ships 139
  GEORGE F. BASS, *Texas A&M University*

Beowulf and the Language of Hoarding 155
  ROBERT PAYSON CREED, *University of Massachusetts, Amherst*

Section III: Rural Community Studies

The Role of Cemeteries in the Formation of Medieval Settlement
  Patterns in Western France 171
  ELIZABETH ZADORA-RIO, *Centre National
  de la Recherche Scientifique*

Hillfort Reuse in Gloucestershire, A.D. 1–700 187
  JANICE B. KLEIN, *University of Pennsylvania*

Zooarchaeology at Early Anglo-Saxon West Stow 203
  PAM JEAN CRABTREE, *University of Pennsylvania*

Historical Archaeology of Medieval Muslim Communities
  in the Sierra of Eastern Spain 217
  KARL W. BUTZER AND ELISABETH K. BUTZER,
  University of Texas, Austin

Section IV: Urban Community Studies

Urban Archaeology in Douai (Nord, France) 237
  PIERRE DEMOLON, *Service Archaeologique du Muses de Douai*

Early Medieval Florence: Between History and Archaeology 261
  FRANKLIN K. TOKER, *University of Pittsburgh*

Rewriting an Urban Text: The Ottomanization of Cretan Cities 285
  DONALD PREZIOSI, *University of California, Los Angeles*

Preface

CHARLES L. REDMAN

One thousand years spans the end of the Classical World and the beginning of Modern European history. During that enormous period of time, circa AD 600 to AD 1600, empires rose and fell, great inventions appeared, the social order was transformed, and the economic foundations of today's world were laid. How well understood are the events and social processes of these seminal thousand years? Like the times themselves, the study of medieval society is a matter of extremes. Medieval art, literature, religion, architecture, and history are among the traditional scholarly pursuits, especially strong at European universities and actively conducted in America. Despite a long and productive tradition of scholarship in the individual fields, medieval studies, as a composite, is undergoing a revolution in our times. More than anything else, this upheaval and extraordinary rate of advance is caused by a new era of interdisciplinary cooperation and the application of modern technology and intellectual approaches to the age-old questions that pervade medieval studies.

Among the new approaches being applied to this period is increasingly systematic and scientific archaeology. Whereas, until recently, documents and monuments had been considered the only avenues to knowing medieval history and society, archaeology is rapidly making noteworthy contributions. The studies represented in this volume provide testimony to the achievements of medieval archaeology, and more than anything else, its close cooperation with scholars in the historical disciplines.

The great literature of the era has been preserved and widely read since its creation. To that have been added archival texts, records, and maps that recent scholars have rediscovered and interpreted for our use. These sources offer a truly rich data base to the traditional medieval scholarly disciplines. But it is an incomplete data base: incomplete in terms of inclusion of all communities and all walks of life, and incomplete in terms of the alternative forms of evidence that archaeologists can reveal.

To rely on historic documents alone to illuminate this crucial episode in the human career would be narrow sighted. It is through archaeology that one can learn about the poorly described aspects and the inadequately recorded places of the historic past. Specific descriptions of all but the largest communities are scarce, leaving them to be fully understood only with the aid of archaeology. Rather than strictly being used to fill the gaps in historic records, archaeological techniques can reconstruct certain patterns of past behavior better than textual evidence. These include patterns that leave preserved material remains, such as layouts of cities and their civic structures, systems of fortifications, building technologies, and traded goods that reflect both distribution of luxury items within a community and the existence of trade routes linking the investigated community to the external world. Even more than this, the archaeologist brings a new perspective and new source material to the study of past societies. At a time when many historians have become more interested in social process, the diversity of lifeways, and the full range of community forms, the serious archaeologist has come to their rescue, providing them with just the kind of information that they require.

The above comments should not be taken to mean that the exchange between archaeology and history only flows one way; to the advantage of the historian. Quite to the contrary, this is a truly symbiotic situation. The study of historic civilizations offers a series of unique opportunities to the archaeologist that equal and sometimes surpass those provided by the more commonly studied prehistoric cultures. First, the existence of historical documentation often facilitates the formulation of absolute chronologies for excavated material. By correlating archaeology episodes with historically dated events, one can formulate an absolute chronology for the remains, and it is frequently possible even to assign lengths or duration to particular occupations. Second, the architectural and artifactual remains of historic civilizations are usually abundant in quantity and more readily identifiable than prehistoric material. Since many of the excavated tools, decorated objects and important building types are known from texts, art work or their continued use in recent times, identification and functional interpretation are more reliable, having been made by homology rather than by analogy. Relatively sophisticated behavioral questions can be addressed because of the above interpretative advantages and the fact that the historic record often provides general insights into the political and economic patterns of the era that aid in model building.

In European countries the archaeological study of medieval monuments and other remains is as old as archaeology itself. What is changing today is the application of newer, more systematic techniques of archaeology and the expansion of interpretive perspectives beyond that of local histories. This volume reflects the philosophy that medieval society can best be understood in a geographic perspective broader than the confines of a single country, or even of all Europe. Chapters on the Viking adventures abroad and the Islamic Mediterranean world provide insight into many of the forces at work in the heartland of Europe.

The mutual interest of scholars in history, art, literature, anthropology, and archaeology in the development of medieval society offers a unique opportunity for meaningful interchange. Although scholars in each of these disciplines work from different perspectives and with largely different empirical data, the areas of overlap make this a workable intellectual venture. The need for this type of interdisciplinary cooperation and its potential benefits parallels the rewards realized from joint investigations into the origins of agriculture in the years following World War II. It is through this type of long-term cooperative effort that new levels of understanding may be achieved.

Medieval archaeology, while among the oldest and most respected branches of archaeology in Europe, is only beginning to gain recognition in the United States. Those who practice it in American universities, lacking departments of their own, often have their primary affiliation with departments of English, comparative literature, romance languages, art history, or anthropology. This has hindered communication among practitioners. Notwithstanding, medieval archaeology has taken hold in America and is growing rapidly. This can be attributed partly to the availability of medieval remains and the pressure from host countries to see systematic research performed on them, and partly from the growing intellectual excitement generated by recent research in the field.

During recent years, however, as the number of people in the field of medieval archaeology has mushroomed, the lack of forums particularly in North America, for effective communication has become a serious problem. Attempts are being made by different individuals to improve this situation. My own efforts began with a conference on the contributions and new directions in medieval archaeology held at Binghamton, New York in October 1983. Sixty-five papers were presented and over three hundred scholars and students attended. The conference was a great success with many of those in attendance citing the need for increased communication. It is because of this need that I have assembled this volume of 16 of the most important papers presented at the conference.

In selecting the papers for *Medieval Archaeology* I made a special effort to include articles on interpretive issues of special interest, methodological issues that span the discipline, and examples of research from diverse countries and as applied to diverse material. Although no volume can ever be totally comprehensive, this one does attempt to demonstrate the scope and vitality of this emerging field.

Chapter Contents

The diversity of topics investigated in this volume is a reflection of the range of subject matter, perspectives, and geographic foci that typifies the recently revitalized field of medieval archaeology. At this point in the growth of the field, I believe it is more important to provide the reader with examples of this diversity, than to limit the chapters to a single theme. Because of that decision this volume attempts to stimulate interest and indicate potentially profitable directions of study, rather than to answer a specific set of questions about the past.

The first section of this volume, "Society and Economy" is comprised of four chapters, each examining the impact of Viking conquest and trade on the growth of medieval Europe. "Archaeology and the Pirenne Thesis," by David Whitehouse, re-examines the impact of both the Mediterranean Islamic world and the Viking north on the growth of the Carolingian empire on the continent. The next chapter, "Viking Raiders: The Transformation of Scandinavian Society," by Klavs Randsborg examines the same time period, but focuses on the Scandinavian homeland and demonstrates how alternative patterns of Viking raiding and trading transformed a largely rural economy into a hierarchical society. Michel Rouche's chapter, "The Vikings Versus the Towns of Northern Gaul: Challenge and Response," relates the nature of Viking influence and how it contributed to the growth of population centers in this particular region. In the final chapter of this section, "Emporia, Monasteries and the Economic Foundation of Medieval Europe," Richard Hodges discusses how new information provided by archaeology now allows scholars to reassess the origins of the market economy. Hodges' use of evidence on the movement of goods during the early medieval period and archaeological means for dating these trading patterns provides a transition from chapters concerned with broad, almost continent-wide processes to the actual materials examined by individual archaeologists.

The second section, "Materials of the Archaeological Record" contains six chapters on a selection of the materials and approaches used by archaeologists. The first two chapters, Emlen Myers' "Ceramic Technologies of Medieval Northern Morocco" and Nancy Benco's "Diversity in Ceramic Production: A Case Study from Medieval North Africa," are both concerned with alternate modes of ceramic production and how they reflect the broader economy and societal organization at the time. Myers examines the later centuries of the medieval period and utilizes his own ethnographic observations of pottery producers to formulate models on the relationship of production and societal organization. Benco, who deals with the early medieval period, employs measures of diversity, used by other anthropological archaeologists, to indicate the level of specialization of production and what that means about the society. Alan M. Stahl, in his chapter, "Numismatics and Medieval Archaeology," reviews the diversity of ways the study of coins may aid the archaeologist and illuminate the society in question. In "Novgorod Birchbark Documents: The Evidence for Literacy in Medieval Russia," Eve Levin uses a relatively unusual set of material to provide insight into an otherwise difficult question. George Bass' chapter, "Underwater Archaeology and Medieval Mediterranean Ships," provides examples of the value of underwater archaeology, and also serves as a review of merchant ship technology in the Mediterranean from antiquity through the medieval period. Beyond the wealth of beautiful objects that Bass and his colleagues have recovered, they are able to provide new information on the economy and interaction of Mediterranean countries. The final chapter of this section, Robert Creed's "Beowulf and the Language of Hoarding," views the meaning of potential archaeological material from a literary perspective. Archaeologists increasingly are using burial evidence they discover to indicate the nature of the society that produced it. In this chapter, the oral traditions surrounding the epic of *Beowulf* are examined for what they reveal about possible meaning for burial goods.

Section Three, "Rural Community Studies" begins with a chapter by Elizabeth Zadora-Rio on "The Role of Cemeteries in the Formation of Medieval Settlement Patterns in Western France." Instead of treating the burial goods, as the previous chapter has done, Zadora-Rio looks at the cemetery as a node for human settlement. Janice Klein, in "Hillfort Reuse in Gloucestershire, AD 1–700," monitors the use of abandoned Iron Age forts as a locus for new settlements. Pam Jean Crabtree's chapter, "Zooarchaeology at Early Anglo-Saxon West Stow," discusses the way one learns about local economies from the remains of animal bones recovered in archaeological excavations. A major element of understanding why settlements were located as they were and how markets and manors evolve is the changing nature of agrarian production. Karl and Elisabeth Butzer, in "Historical Archaeology of Medieval Muslim Communities in the Sierra of Eastern Spain," look at a different form of medieval settlement, the village. Their chapter provides insight into the range of archaeological information that is recovered from the excavation of a small community.

The final section of this book, "Urban Community Studies" is comprised of three chapters that attempt to reveal the beliefs and organization of societies from the form of their cities. "Urban Archaeology in Douai (Nord, France)" by Pierre Demolon begins this section with a description of the activities of an urban archaeological service. Through scattered, but precise excavations one gains an overall view of the growth of this city. Franklin Toker, in his chapter "Early Medieval Florence: Between History and Archaeology," shows how, in even the best of historically documented cities, there is much to be learned from archaeological work. Beyond this lesson we are given a fascinating view of the growth of the core of Florence and some of its main buildings. In the final chapter, Donald Preziosi moves up in time to examine how several late medieval cities on the island of Crete were transformed by their new overlords in "Rewriting an Urban Text: The Ottomanization of Cretan Cities." The central issue here, repeated so many times throughout Europe and the Mediterranean, is how do conquerors of a city rebuild it to symbolically conform to their own ideology and culture?

This volume would not have been possible without the energies of numerous people, foremost among them the conferees, both those who presented such stimulating papers, and the others in attendance who added immeasurably to the scholarly interchange. The conference itself, as well as this volume, was a creation of the Center for Medieval and Early Renaissance Studies at the State University of New York at Binghamton. It was their executive board that approached me with the original idea and the Center that provided the necessary financial and logistical support to make the conference a reality. Beyond the many others, Paul Szarmach, CEMERS Director, and Dorothy Huber, secretary for the Center, deserve a special thank you. I was aided in the editorial process by Jane Peterson and Joyce Hitchcock. It is to all of these people that this volume is dedicated.

SECTION I
Society and Economy

Archaeology and the Pirenne Thesis*

DAVID WHITEHOUSE

Among the most positive developments in the archaeology of the Mediterranean region in the last twenty-five years has been its application — sooner in some areas than in others — to the material remains of the Middle Ages. In Italy, for example, medieval archaeology was almost unknown in 1960, but today it is taught in universities and it has its own scientific journal, *Archeologia Medievale*. A similar development is taking place in Western Asia, where formerly the archaeology of the Islamic period was neglected in favor of older civilizations. Archaeologists in both the Mediterranean and Western Asia, therefore, are now providing evidence for the cultural history of the Middle Ages. Indeed, we have at our disposal a new, almost inexhaustible source of information. This paper attempts to illustrate the central importance of archaeology for the medievalist by examining one of the milestones of twentieth-century historiography — the Pirenne Thesis — in the light of excavations in Europe, the Mediterranean, and Western Asia (figs. 1 and 2).

When he died in 1955, Henri Pirenne had just completed the first draft of *Mohammed and Charlemagne*. Although rough-hewn, it is the most ample expression of an argument advanced first in 1922 and elaborated in the opening chapters of *Medieval Cities* (1925). This argument, now known as the Pirenne Thesis, concerns the origin of the Carolingian state. It is summed up in two sweeping statements at the end of *Mohammed and Charlemagne*:

> 1. The Germanic invasions [of the Migration Period] destroyed neither the Mediterranean unity of the ancient world, nor what may be regarded as the truly essential features of Roman culture as they still existed in the 5th century.

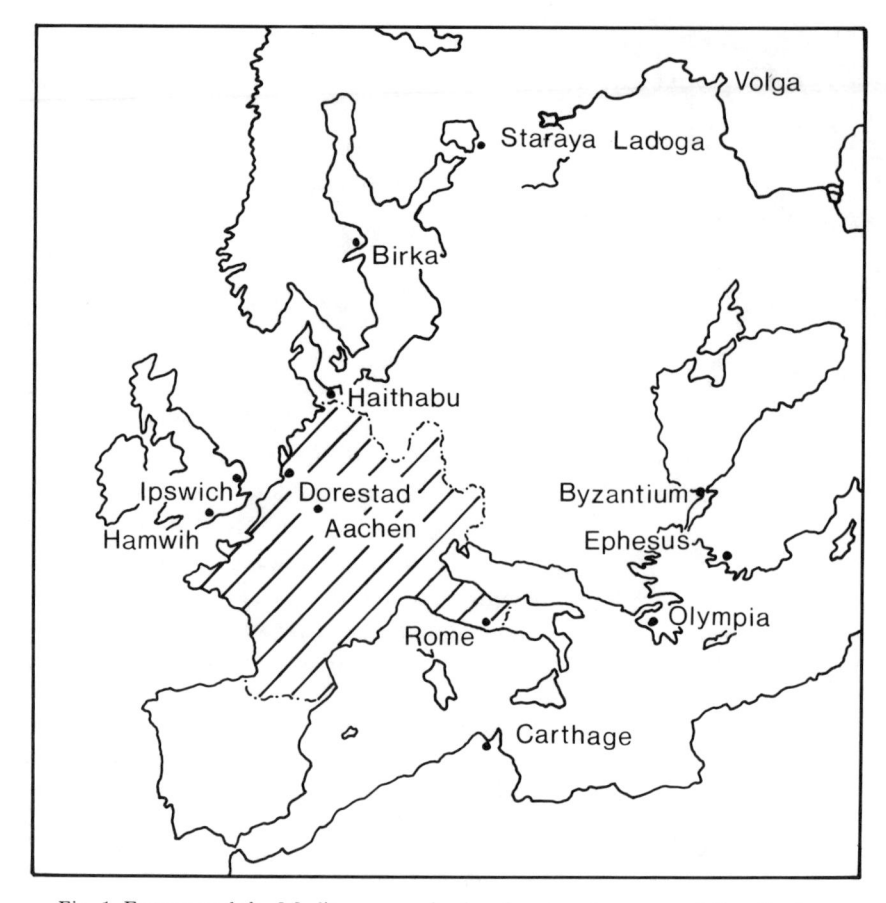

Fig. 1. Europe and the Mediterranean basin, showing the extent of Carolingian Empire (hatched) and places mentioned in the text.

Despite the resulting turmoil and destruction, no new principles made their appearance . . . what civilization survived was Mediterranean. . . .

The Orient was the fertilizing factor: Constantinople the centre of the world. In 600, the physiognomy of the world was not different in quality from that which it had revealed in 400.

2. The cause of the break with the tradition of antiquity was the rapid and unexpected advance of Islam. The result of this advance was the final separation of East from West, and the end of Mediterranean unity. Countries like Africa and Spain, which had always been parts of the Western Community, gravitated henceforth in the orbit of Baghdad. . . . The

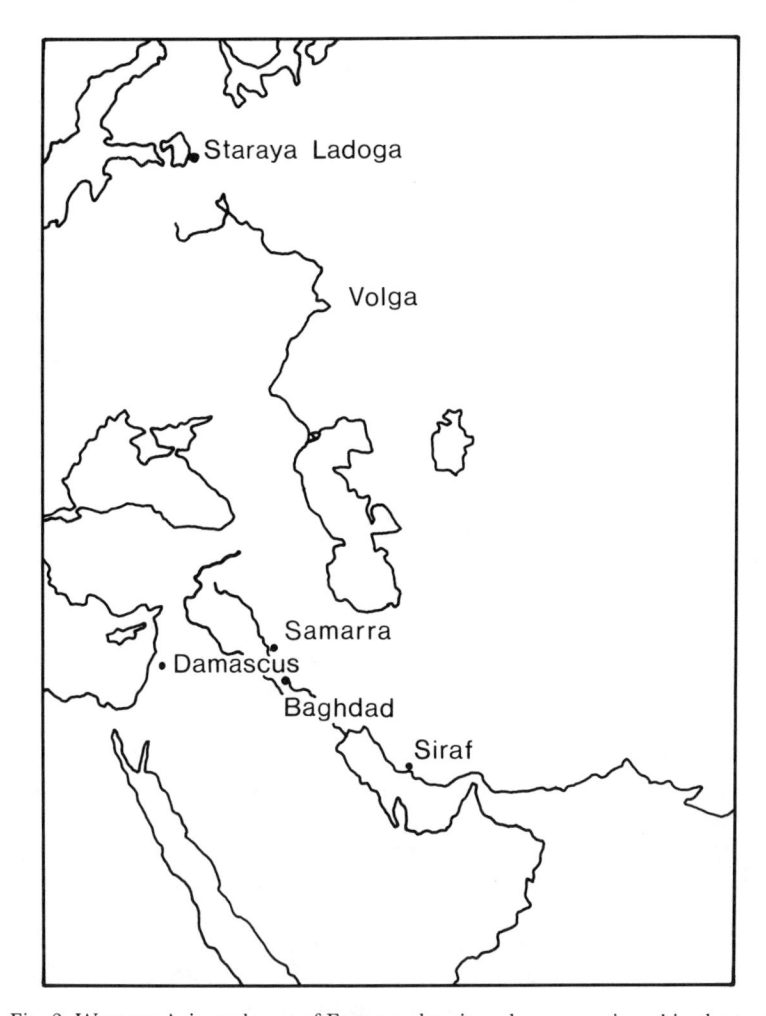

Fig. 2. Western Asia and part of Europe, showing places mentioned in the text.

Western Mediterranean, having become a Musulman lake, was no longer the thoroughfare . . . which it always had been.

The West was blockaded and forced to live upon its own resources. For the first time in history the axis of life was shifted northwards from the Mediterranean. The decadence into which the Merovingian monarchy lapsed as a result of this change gave birth to a new dynasty, the Carolingian, whose original home was the Germanic North. . . .

This development was completed in 800 by the constitution of the new Empire, which consecrated the break between the West and the East, inasmuch as it gave the West a new Roman Empire—the manifest proof that it had broken with the Old Empire, which continued to exist in Constantinople.[1]

In northwestern Europe, archaeology had begun to generate information relevant to the Pirenne Thesis while the author was still alive. The first result of excavations at Dorestad, an early medieval port-of-trade in Holland, appeared in 1930. A little later, excavations began at another medieval entrepôt, Haithabu, in north Germany. In 1937, two years after the death of Pirenne, the Swedish archaeologist Holgar Arbman published *Schweden und das Karolingische Reich*, in which he explored relations between Scandinavia and the Carolingian Empire. Later, he published the finds from the 19th century excavations at Birka, in Sweden, which furnished a wealth of information about the commercial activities of the Vikings. After World War II, Joachim Werner and others transformed our knowledge of early medieval exchange through studies of particular types of artifacts, such as "Coptic" ewers and bowls. Today, research in the field proceeds at an ever-increasing rate, with the result that our perception of the foundations of Charlemagne's Europe is derived not only from the written word but also from the material remains.[2]

Thus, for some time it has — or should have — been impossible to ignore the archaeological data in the study of early medieval Europe, and it is becoming progressively more difficult to do so in the Mediterranean basin and Western Asia. Indeed, today we possess a reasonable amount of archaeological information from all the regions involved in the Pirenne Thesis and the debate that it provoked. I propose to use this information to discuss three issues: (1) Pirenne's view that the "physiognomy" of Mediterranean civilization was the same on the eve of the Arab invasion as it had been, two hundred years earlier; (2) the emergence of the Carolingian state; (3) the Abbasid Caliphate, which may have been a source of the silver, with which Charlemagne reformed his currency. Each discussion is self-contained, in the sense that the conclusions reached in one do not depend in any way on the conclusions reached in another. In the final paragraphs, however, I shall attempt to unite all three sections in a hypothesis concerning the origin and development of the Carolingian Empire.

1. *The Mediterranean in Late Antiquity*

Pirenne concluded that civilization in the Mediterranean region was essentially the same in the early seventh century as in the fifth; the break between antiquity and the Middle Ages was caused by the Arabs, who severed the trade routes between the Mediterranean and Europe. Recent excavations compel us to see things differently. Instead of a catastrophic break after the mid-seventh century, we find that the political fragmentation of the Roman Empire was accompanied by a long process of economic decline and urban decay, which began at least two centuries before the arrival of the Arabs.

The collapse of urban life is apparent now from one end of the Mediterranean to the other. The five most important cities of late antiquity—Rome, Carthage, Constantinople, Antioch, and Alexandria—all contracted; indeed, Carthage and Antioch virtually ceased to exist.

In the first few centuries AD, Rome possessed the greatest concentration of monumental architecture and the largest urban population that had ever existed in the West. Such information as we possess suggests that the population may have been a million under Augustus and possibly of the same order in 367. In the late fourth and early fifth centuries, the population seems to have declined, although it may have been stable (or even increasing) between 419 and 452, at a time when the city enjoyed a revival of large-scale construction. After the Vandal invasion of 455, however, the situation deteriorated. By the 530s, the importation of foodstuffs from distant provinces had ceased. Following the long and debilitating Gothic War, in which the city changed hands repeatedly, only one of the aqueducts was functioning and the presence of cemeteries within the walls points to the existence of areas without inhabitants. By 750, even the palace of the popes was in disrepair. At the beginning of the ninth century, after three generations of gradual recovery, the inhabited area was still confined to the Fora, the Palatine and Campus Martius, the Esquiline, the papal enclave at the Lateran, and the Borgo. Rome never ceased to be a city, but the difference between the imperial metropolis and its Dark Age successor could hardly have been greater.[3]

Elsewhere in Italy, excavations have shown that the port of Luna, near Carrara, collapsed in the fifth century, and before 600 the area of the forum was dotted with wooden huts—a far cry from the civic pride and comfortable town houses of the first and second centuries. The fate of Rome (a special case by virtue of its role as the capital of an empire) and of Luna (arguably a special case by virtue of its dependence on the marble trade), should not lead us to suppose that *all* urban life became extinct. At Ravenna, Milan, Verona and elsewhere in the Po Plain, it is argued, some form of continuity existed, and the same may have been true of Naples. Nevertheless, no town in Italy was populated on the same scale in about 600 as it was two centuries earlier, and few (even if they were occupied) functioned *as towns*.[4]

A similar decline in urban life occurred in North Africa, where not a single city emerged from the Dark Age with the population, economic activity, and amenities it possessed in the fourth century. The most fully documented example is Carthage, which in its heyday had been the second Roman city in the West. Beginning in 1972, teams from nine countries, working under the aegis of UNESCO, excavated at Carthage on a massive scale. The excavations transformed our knowledge of its fortunes in late antiquity. Despite variations between one part of the city and another, three general conclusions emerged. First, the prosperity which Carthage enjoyed in the third and fourth centuries continued until the Vandal conquest of 439. Second, despite some signs of continuing wealth (such as restoration in the "House of the Greek Charioteers"), the general impression of conditions under the Vandals is one neglect; public buildings decayed, suburbs began to decline. Third, the Byzantines, who conquered the city in 533, invested heavily in renovating the defenses, the harbors, public buildings and churches. Even so, repairs to the Circular Harbor were never completed and, in the suburbs, the decline continued. Thus, the suburb known as Centuria A was gradually abandoned and by about 600, the Rectangular Harbor was choked with silt.[5]

Even in the heart of the Byzantine Empire, which Pirenne regarded as "the centre of the world," a similar transformation was taking place. In 1977, using both archaeological and documentary evidence, Clive Foss published a study of the "twenty cities of Asia" named by Constantine Porphyrogenetos in the tenth century. They include Ephesus, Miletus, Pergamum, Sardis, and Smyrna, all of which were excavated on a large scale in the last century. While early excavators might have missed ephemeral timber buildings like those at Luna, surely they would have found substantial structures of brick or stone; as far as the seventh century is concerned, there are none. Take the case of Ephesus, the subject of a separate monograph by Foss (1979). In the fifth century, a program of urban renewal took place. Under Justinian, the magnificent church of Saint John was erected; about this time, the area round the Embolos, an elegant boulevard in the city center, was thronged with the houses of wealthy citizens. At the beginning of the seventh century, however, everything changed. The Sasanians invaded the Byzantine Empire, damaging an already weakened political and economic system. Ephesus, which also suffered an earthquake in about 614, declined—as did every other city about which we are informed, with the possible exception of Smyrna. At Byzantium itself, public works virtually ceased; the principal aqueduct, cut by the Avars in 626, was not repaired until 768 and the Theodosian harbor, like the Rectangular Harbor at Carthage, became filled with silt. In the words of Cyril Mango, "If one were to draw a graph of the fortunes of Constantinople, one would find that it showed a sharp dip at the same time when provincial cities came almost to the zero line."[6]

Indeed, the only areas in which urban life may have continued on anything approaching the scale of the Early Empire were parts of Syria, Palestine, and Egypt—and here, too, there are signs of decay.

As cities declined, so did the infrastructures that supported them. By the early centuries AD, the largest cities had far outgrown the carrying capacities of their territories and were supplied with surpluses of cereals, wine, and olive oil from other regions. Some of these foodstuffs were transported in amphorae, and a study of the distribution and numbers of amphorae from known places of production provides a glimpse of the shifting patterns of interregional exchange. Throughout the western Mediterranean, the overall trend is a reduction in the volume of imported amphorae in late antiquity. The trend is most apparent in the largest cities, Rome and Carthage. Early Imperial Rome, for example, had devoured commodities and manufactured goods from all over the Mediterranean and beyond. An excavation at the Schola Praeconum (between the Palatine and the Circus Maximus) revealed thousands of fragments of fifth-century amphorae from Africa and the East Mediterranean. By the seventh century, however, the volume was much diminished. Some trade, of course, continued, but the number of sailings and the volume of cargo were no more than shadows of what had existed in the first few centuries AD.[7]

The decay of urban life and the collapse of interregional exchange may well have been accompanied by widespread changes in rural settlement. In certain areas, the pattern of scattered farms gave way to defended villages: "isles of refuge" in Greece, "strategic hamlets" in Italy. Even today, however, after two decades of excavation and survey, the data are difficult to interpret. The problem is this: written sources are scarce and the number of rural sites of the sixth or seventh century identified by the archaeologist is very much smaller than the number of sites of the first or second century. However, since most of these sites are identified on the basis of imported pottery, such as African red slipware, we do not know the extent to which the shortage of sites is due to the demonstrable collapse of long-distance trade and the consequent shortage of imports. In other words, the sites may exist but we cannot recognize them, although the fact remains that intensively surveyed areas such as the Roman Campagna contain few, if any, major sites that have yielded exclusively nondescript finds and can be attributed, therefore, to the period after importation ceased.[8]

In any case, a definite hint that something may have happened on a pan-Mediterranean scale exists in the form of the geological phenomenon known as the Younger Fill. This is a deposit of alluvium laid down by streams and rivers, sometimes in a dramatic fashion: Olympia in the Peloponnese literally was buried by earth and gravel dumped by the river Kladeos. Radiocarbon dates and historical records show that much, but not all, of the Younger Fill belongs to the period between AD 400 and 900.

Two hypotheses have been advanced to explain this phenomenon.[9] The first, proposed by the geologist Claudio Vita-Finzi, attributes the Younger Fill to climatic change. An increase in rainfall would produce a greater volume of water in the rivers, and this would cause more rapid erosion and a greater capacity to transport the resultant alluvium downstream. This hypothesis, however, fails to explain the deposits of Younger Fil that are older or younger than the period in question. Moreover, there is no independent evidence of greater rainfall in the Mediterranean region at the end of the Roman period; indeed, recent research in Libya suggests that no such increase occurred.

The second hypothesis regards the alluvium as a by-product of human activity. At any rate, over-grazing or the destruction of forests to extract mature timber encourages erosion. In the period which concerns us, failure to repair cultivation terraces as the great urban markets for oil and wine diminished would have enlarged the process, and the same would have happened if drainage ditches were no longer maintained. The Younger Fill, therefore, might be seen as an indication of a change not in climate, but in landuse — an attractive hypothesis which has the merit of explaining why deposits accumulated at different times in different places.

What, one may ask, in this welter of dying cities, economic crisis, and alluvium-filed valleys, has become of Pirenne? Precisely this: for Pirenne in the 1930s, the physiognomy of the Mediterranean world in 600 was essentially the same as it had been two centuries earlier and it was the Arabs in the seventh century who cut the links between the Mediterranean and Western Europe, isolating the Franks and so compelling them to work out a new, self-sufficient political and economic system. For the archaeologist in the 1980s, Mediterranean civilization experienced a long process of change, in the course of which the old political and economic unity disintegrated. This process of disintegration was well advanced long before the seventh century; thus, when the Arabs arrived, the Mediterranean and Western Europe already were poles apart.

2. Northwest Europe

Two aspects of the origin of the Carolingian Empire about which the archaeologist has something to say are towns and trade, and the extent to which they existed before and after the time of Charlemagne. In Western Europe, as in most of the Mediterranean, the construction of prestigious public monuments in towns ceased in the late Roman period. Where evidence of fifth or sixth century occupation has been found, the buildings are often of wood, as at Luna. Manufacturing and regular long-distance trade collapsed and coins went out of use as the medium for everyday transactions. Excavations of settlements and cemeteries show that the Merovingians and their neighbors had access to a much more restricted range of manufactured goods than their Roman predecessors, and most of these were made locally. In a nutshell, the period between the fifth and the seventh centuries saw the re-emergence of a wholly agrarian society, in which most of the population lived in small rural communities. The town- and market-oriented economy of the Roman provinces had collapsed and the archaeological data point unequivocally toward an almost total dependence on local production.[10]

Centers of power, of course, survived both in the countryside and in the former cities. Those in the towns-the residences of kings or bishops—were small enclaves surrounded by abandoned suburbs. Aethelberht, king of Kent, for example, was living in the ruins of the former city of Canterbury, when he received Saint Augustine in 597. There is no suggestion, however, that the towns themselves still functioned. Indeed, urban excavations are beginning to reveal the sorry condition of these enclaves, such as the bishop's palace at Tours.[11]

Indeed, we should not be misled be the fame of such centers into overestimating their grandeur, even under the Carolingians. The imperial palace at Aachen—the most important administrative center in Western Europe—occupied scarcely five acres (most of which was empty), while the ideal monastery described in the Plan of Saint Gall (ca. 820) was designed for only 270 permanent residents—the population, I suppose, of a single *insula* in imperial Rome.[12]

Commercial exchange virtually ceased, but from time to time exotic objects reached even the farthest parts of Western Europe: bronze vessels from Egypt, wine from Palestine, fine pottery from Tunisia. A paradox? I think not, and prefer to interpret these rare and costly items as objects of non-commercial exchange. Two of the founding fathers of social anthropology, Malinowski and Mauss, explored the concept of gift exchange, a means of rendering homage or reinforcing social and political bonds. Following their lead, and that of the numismatist Philip Grierson, I suspect objects such as the Byzantine silver vessels from Sutton Hoo represent the fruits, not of commerce or warfare, but the exchange of gifts on an extraordinarily lavish scale.[13]

It is a small step, well documented by the anthropologist, from occasional gift exchange to the establishment of long-term partnerships reinforced by regular exchanges of presents. An essential element in any such system is the creation of emporia: official ports-of-trade, where the exchanges are supervised. It may appear far-fetched to think of early medieval Europe in these terms, but the correspondence between Charlemagne and the Anglo-Saxon king Offa shows it to be justified. Indeed, the emporia themselves are beginning to emerge. Eight miles from Sutton Hoo, excavations have revealed that Ipswich was already a port in the seventh century. The kings of Wessex had Hamwic, the forerunner of Southampton. On the continent, there were Quentovic and Dorestad.[14]

In the course of the eighth century, the emporia experienced a dramatic change. They grew (Dorestad came to occupy some 600 acres); they became not only ports of call for traders but also the permanent homes of artisans; the quantity and range of material culture increased. Coins, previously scarce, became more common. The expansion of the emporia reached a peak in the early ninth century, after which they declined.[15]

Fig. 3. Denier of Charlemagne, struck at Aachen in 806–814.

The culmination of the emporia coincided with a turning point in the history of monetary systems in Western Europe: Charlemagne's reform of 793 or 794, when the silver content of the penny was increased by one-third (fig. 3). Evidently, the king was doing everything in his power to make the use of money attractive, in order to stimulate the economy and facilitate the collection of taxes. The success of the reform is shown by the adoption of similar measures by two of Charlemagne's contemporaries, Offa and the pope.[16]

The North Sea was not the only region in which ports were particularly active in the years around 800. Just outside the Carolingian frontier, after a raid which saw the destruction of one of Charlemagne's towns and the abduction of its merchants, the Danes established their own entrepôt, Haithabu, where (according to tree-ring dating) construction was under way by 810 (fig. 4). Their motive, it seems, was to gain control of the new commercial relations between the Carolingians and the Baltic, where the archaeological record charts the emergence of an economic system every bit as active as that of the North Sea. A hundred years ago, the excavation of the cemetery at Birka revealed the wealth and long-range contacts of this Swedish community in the ninth century. More recently, excavations at Staraya Lodge, near Leningrad, have shown us that here, too, a commercial center began to emerge in, or just after, 800.[17]

While Haithabu grew rich as the go-between for the Carolingians and the merchants of the Baltic, Staraya Ladoga played a similar role in the relations between the Baltic and the East. It is well known that the Vikings exploited

Fig. 4. Haithabu (Photo K. Schietzel, reproduced from R. Hodges and D. Whitehouse, "Archeologie en de stelling van Pirenne," *Spiegel Historiael*, February 1984, 69–75).

a network of long-range contacts with Russia, Byzantium, and the Islamic countries of Western and Central Asia. This network, I suggest, was a vital ingredient in the economic expansion of Charlemagne's Europe.

3. The Abbasid Caliphate

In 750, the last caliph of the Umayyad dynasty was deposed. The new rulers of the Islamic realm, the Abbasids, decided to abandon Damascus and create a dynastic capital outside Syria (which was full of Umayyad supporters), nearer their power base in the East. Twelve years later, after much indecision, the caliph al-Mansur decided to establish the new capital, Baghdad, on the river Tigris, at a point where the Tigris and Euphrates are less than twenty-five miles apart and where they were already connected by canals. With the benefit of hindsight, ninth and tenth century writers were unanimous in praising the choice from the commercial point of view. Al-Muqaddasi (writing in about 985) maintains that the caliph was told, "The caravans of Egypt and Syria will come by way of the desert, and all kinds of goods will reach you from China on the sea, and from the country of the Greeks [i.e. the Byzantine Empire] and Mosul by the Tigris." Ya'qubi (in 842) states that al-Mansur chose the site because "the Tigris to the east and the Euphrates to the west are the waterfronts of the world." Tabari (d. 923) makes the caliph exclaim, "This is the Tigris. There is no distinction between us and China. Everything on the sea can come to us."[18]

Baghdad was well placed to exploit not only riverine (and consequently maritime) trade but also communications on land. The "Khorasan road" arrived from Iran and Central Asia, bringing among other things silver from the mines of Afghanistan and Uzbekistan. As al-Muqaddasi remarked, other routes led westward to Syria and south or southwest to Arabia and Egypt. Abbasid Iraq, therefore, became the core of a vast empire.

Abbasid Baghdad is buried beneath the modern city, and the most dramatic illustration of the wealth at the disposal of the caliphs is Sāmarrā, another new capital, 65 miles to the north. Sāmarrā was begun *ex novo* in 836 and was abandoned by the court in 882. In only 46 years, the Abbasids constructed a city which extended intermittently along the Tigris for more than 20 miles — more than the length of Manhattan. It was an astonishing achievement. Consider just four of the principal buildings: the founder, at-Mutasim, erected a palace (the Jausaq al-Khaqani) that was larger than Versailles; his successor, al-Mutawakkil, built another (the Balkuwara) almost as large. He also erected two mosques, both of which occupied areas larger than Saint Peter's, in Rome (fig. 5). Admittedly, building materials (mostly mud brick) and labor were cheap, but the palaces and mosques were adorned with marble, mosaics,

Fig. 5. Sāmarrā. The Great Mosque, built by al-Mutawakkil between 848 and 852.

paintings, and stucco. In any case, regardless of the character of the materials, the construction in fewer than 50 years of the second largest city in the world (only Ch'ang-an was larger) must have required colossal resources.[19]

An important aspect of the Abbasid economy was maritime trade, which brought commodities and luxury goods from beyond the frontiers. For millennia, long-distance exchange was a determining factor in the cultural development of communities on the shores of the Arabian Sea and Persian/Arabian gulf. At the beginning of the Christian era, the *Periplus of the Erythraean Sea* (probably written in Egypt) revealed a network of communications connecting East Africa, Western Asia, India and Sri Lanka, and a vague knowledge of ports farther east. By the tenth century, the horizons were even wider. Abbasid merchants, we are told, were voyaging regularly from the Gulf to China and to African ports south of the equator.[20]

Fifteen years ago, excavations at Siraf, on the Iranian coast of the Gulf, suggested the date at which maritime trade suddenly expanded. Siraf stood in a region of poor soil and low rainfall, ill-suited to supporting an urban community. Nevertheless, occupation extended along the shore for 2 1/2 miles, and at least 270 acres were densely packed with buildings, some of which were several stories high (fig. 6). The surpluses invested in the city, its aqueducts, and its irrigated fields came exclusively from the sea, and the development of Siraf was a direct reflection of the development of maritime trade.[21]

Fig. 6. Siraf. The courtyard of a ninth- or tenth-century house, seen from the entrance.

The key to understanding this development is the largest public building in the city, the Congregational Mosque. The mosque was built on an earth-filled platform, which concealed the remains of a fort and other structures of the Sasanian and early Islamic periods. Not long after the mosque was constructed, it was enlarged. In the terminology adopted in the final reports on Siraf, the fort and the other early buildings belong to periods B1-4; the mosque was erected in period B5 and enlarged in B6. It was surrounded by an extensive bazaar, laid in period B5 or B6.[22]

Among the pottery associated with periods B1 and B2 are sherds of red slipware from Gujarat. The first Far Eastern fragments occur in period B3 and consist of green- ("Dusun") and black-glazed storage jars. In period B5, the quantity and variety of Chinese ceramics increased dramatically. Instead of comprising only 0.2 percent of all the pottery, as in period B4, Chinese vessels now account for 0.7 percent. Furthermore, instead of consisting solely of storage jars, they now include tableware such as bowls with painted decoration or plain greenish glaze. A Dusun jar from period B6 bears two names, Maymun and Mansur, scratched in Arabic letters before the vessel was fired; in other words, it was intended for a destination where Arabic was understood.[23]

The finds may be interpreted as follows:

Periods B1-2.	Siraf was trading with Gujarat.
Periods B3-4.	Siraf received Chinese ceramics, but on a small scale.
Period B5.	The mosque was built, as perhaps was the bazaar. The availability of Chinese ceramics rose by 350 percent.

The evidence for the date of period B5 consists of coins lost during the construction of the mosque. The latest legible coin from the filling of the platform was struck in 188/803-4. The latest legible coin from the core of the steps by which one reached the platform (which do not necessarily survive in their original form) was struck in 199/814-5. If the existing steps are original, the mosque probably dates from the period ca. 815-25; if (as I suspect) they are secondary, the suggested date of construction is ca. 805-15.[24]

The implications are clear. At the beginning of the ninth century, Siraf and the pattern of its overseas trade were transformed. The construction of the Congregational Mosque and the bazaar coincided with a sharp increase in the availability of Chinese ceramics, and the discovery of a storage jar inscribed in Arabic *in China* underlines one of the reasons for the boom: the establishment of direct communication by sea between Western and Eastern Asia. The creation of Baghdad was followed by the flowering of Siraf, and I conclude that the establishment of one (an avid consumer) made possible the growth of the other (an adventurous supplier). Quang-zhou, the largest port in southern China, had been closed to foreigners in 758. It reopened in 792 and Western merchants were quick to take advantage of the opportunity that this afforded. Indeed, the evidence from Siraf demonstrates that maritime trade between the Abbasids and China was well under way in the first quarter of the ninth century.

4. *Mohammad and Charlemagne: A New Revision*

As I remarked at the beginning, each set of observations—on conditions in the Mediterranean, northwestern Europe, and Western Asia—is independent of the others. Thus, regardless of the origins of the Carolingian Empire, the archaeological evidence points to the collapse of civilization in may parts of the Mediterranean basin before the Arab invasion. And, regardless of the economic development of the Abbasids, Charlemagne's empire was the culmination of a long, indigenous process of state formation in Western Europe. Nevertheless, one is struck by the virtual simultaneity of Carolingian expansion, the development of the Baltic economy, and the rapid extension of Abbasid trade routes. This simultaneity prompts me to ask whether we are dealing with coincidence, or whether the phenomena were related.

The case for believing that events in Western Asia, the Baltic, and Western Europe *were* related was stated not long after the publication of *Mohammed and Charlemagne* by the Swedish numismatist Store Bolin.[25] In 793-794, Charlemagne reformed the Frankish monetary system, increasing the weight of the silver denier from 1.3 to 1.7 grams. Where did he obtain the metal to do this? There are several possibilities: booty, the opening of new mines, and trade with the Baltic.

The silver, Bolin claimed, came from the Baltic, which has yielded numerous hoards of silver coins, jewelry, and bullion amassed by the Vikings. And they, he continued, obtained their silver in the East; indeed, a high proportion of the coins from the Baltic hoards is Islamic. A recent analysis of 71 hoards from the western republics of the Soviet Union suggests that Bolin was right, for it revealed that the volume of Islamic silver coins exported to the Baltic reached an unprecedented level in the years 790-820. This was the period in which the Abbasid economy was at its peak and the Carolingians became capable of receiving, and converting for internal use, large quantities of bullion.[26]

To sum up: the Abbasid caliphs ruled an empire ten times larger than Western Europe, with a huge economic capacity. In the south, the ship-owners of Siraf were initiating regular maritime trade with China; in the north, Moslem and Viking merchants were trading with Western Asia and the Baltic. At the same time, Charlemagne gained access to sufficient silver to increase the weight of his coins by a third. If Charlemagne's silver did come from the Baltic, the spurts of growth at Siraf, Staraya Lodge, Haithubu, and Dorestad were related. Indeed, in this respect, the towns and trade of the Carolingians, far from developing in isolation, as Pirenne believed, owed much to external stimuli. These stimuli came, not from Rome or Byzantium, but from the Baltic and, indirectly, the world economy of the Abbasids.

Notes

*This paper is based, with the permission of my co-author, on R. Hodges and D. Whitehouse, *Mohammed, Charlemagne and the origins of Europe* (London and Ithaca, 1983). The arguments advanced in section 1 are discussed at length in D. Whitehouse, *The Collapse of Civilisation* (London, in press). Section 2 owes much to R. Hodges, *Dark Age Economics* (London, 1982).

1. H. Pirenne, *Mohammed and Charlemagne* (London, 1939), 284-85.
2. H. Holwerda, "Opgravingen van Dorestad," *Oudheidkundige Mededeelingen* 9 (1930): 32-93; H. Arbman, *Birka, Sveriges aldsta handelstad* (Stockholm, 1939); J. Werner, "Fernhandel und Naturalwirtschaft in östlichen Merowingerreich nach archäologisches-

numismatischen Zeugnissen," *Bericht der Römish-Germanisch Kommission* 42 (1961): 307-46.

3. R. Krautheimer, *Rome: Profile of a City, 312-1308* (Princeton, 1980), gives an incomparable general account. For the size of the population, G. Hermansen, "The Population of Imperial Rome: The Regionaries," *Historia* 27 (1978): 129-68. For the interruption of imports of food, Cassiodorus, *Variae* II, 39. For aqueducts, Procopius, *BG* V.xix.13. For cemeteries within the walls, J. Osborne, "Death and Burial in Sixth Century Rome," *Echos du Monde classique/Classical Views* 28 (NS 3), (1984): 291-99. For the papal palace, *Liber Pontificalis*, vol. I, 432. For inhabited areas in the ninth century, R. Vielliard, *Recherches sur les origines de la Rome chrétienne*, 2nd ed. (Rome, 1959). See also D. Whitehouse, "Rome and Naples: Survival and Revival in Central and Southern Italy," in *The Rebirth of Towns in the West*, ed. B. Hobley (London: Council for British Archaeology, in press).

4. The case for continuity is well stated by B. Ward-Perkins, *From Classical Antiquity to the Middle Ages. Urban Public Buildings in Northern and Central Italy AD 300-850* (Oxford, 1984).

5. For Carthage in general, J. G. Pedley, ed., *New Light on Ancient Carthage* (Ann Arbor, 1980). For Centuria A, A. Carandini, et al., "Gli scavi italiani a Cartagine. Rapporto preliminare delle campagne 1973-1977," *Quaderni di Archaeologia delle Libia* 13 (1983): 7-60. For the Rectangular Harbor, W. van Zeist and S. Bottema, "Palaeobotanical Studies of Carthage," *CEDA Carthage Bulletin* 5 (1983): 18-22. See also H. R. Hurst in H. R. Hurst and S. P. Roskams, *Excavations at Carthage: The British Museum, vol I, 1: the Avenue du President Habib Bourguiba, Salammbo: The Site and Finds Other Than Pottery* (Sheffield, 1984): 42-47. J. H. Humphrey, "Vandal and Byzantine Carthage: Some New Archaeological Evidence," in Pedley, 85-120, takes a more optimistic position: in about 600, there was still "reconstruction and a moderately high standard of living. . . . [Nevertheless] at some time after the middle of the seventh century, there seems to have been a marked downturn in the fortunes of the city, perhaps to be associated with an exodus of some of the wealthier members of the community."

6. C. Foss, "Archaeology and the 'Twenty Cities' of Byzantine Asia," *American Journal of Archaeology* 81 (1977): 469-86; *Ephesus after Antiquity: A Late Antique, Byzantine and Turkish City* (Cambridge, 1979); C. Mango, *Byzantium: The Empire of New Rome* (New York, 1980), 81. Cf. H. Thompson, "Athenian Twilight, AD 267-600," *Journal of Roman Studies* 49 (1959): 61-72; Athens, he wrote, is a " 'case history' for the study of the actual way in which ancient civilization went to pieces."

7. For amphorae, M. Fulford, "Carthage: Overseas Trade and the Political Economy, c. AD 400-700," *Reading Medieval Studies* 6 (1980): 68-80; C. Panella, "Le anfore di Cartagine: nuovi elementi per la ricostruzione dei flussi commerciali del Mediterraneo in età imperiale romana," *Opus* 2 (1983): 53-73. For importation to Rome, D. Whitehouse, et al., "The Schola Praeconum I," *Papers of the British School at Rome* 50 (1982): 53-101; D. Whitehouse, et al., "The Schola Praeconum II," *Papers of the British School at Rome* 53 (1985): 163-210. For a comparable decline in long-distance trade in red slipware, J. W. Hayes, *Late Roman Pottery* (London: The British School at Rome, 1972), esp. 453-65, maps 1-37. For the decline in the number of sailings, A. J. Parker, "Shipwrecks and Ancient Trade in the Mediterranean," *Archaeological Review from Cambridge* 3, pt. 2 (1984): 101-13. My conclusion is flatly denied by C. R. Whittaker, "Late Roman Trade and Traders," in *Trade in the Ancient Economy*, ed. P. Garnsey, K. Hopkins, and C. R. Whittaker (London, 1983), 163-80, esp. 179: "The aim of this paper was to follow in the footsteps of Pirenne and Fustel de Coulanges by showing that the institutions and even the practice of trade did not alter radically between the later Roman Empire and the Merovingian period."

8. S. Hood, "Isles of Refuge in the Early Byzantine Period," *Annual of the British School at Athens* 65 (1970): 37–45; T. S. Brown, "Settlement and Military Policy in Byzantine Italy," in *Papers in Italian Archaeology* I, ed. H. McK. Blake, T. W. Potter and D. B. Whitehouse (Oxford: British Archaeological Reports, 1978): pt. 2, 323-28. For two regional studies in Italy, T. W. Potter, *The Changing Landscape of South Etruria* (London, 1979): 138–46 and R. Hodges, G. Barker and K. Wade, "Excavations at D85 (Santa Maria in Città): An Early Medieval Hilltop Settlement in Molise," *Papers of the British School at Rome* 48 (1980): 70–124. For warnings against exaggerating the degree of change, C. R. Whittaker, "Agri deserti," in *Studies in Roman Property*, ed. M. I. Finley (Cambridge, 1976): 137–65 and C. J. Wickham, "Historical and Topographical Notes on Early Medieval South Etruria: Part II," *Papers of the British School at Rome* 47 (1979): 66–95, esp. 86. And for a skeptical comment on "isles of refuge," T. E. Gregory, "A Desert Island Survey in the Gulf of Corinth," *Archaeology* 39, pt. 3 (1986): 16–21.

9. C. Vita-Finzi, *The Mediterranean Valleys* (Cambridge, 1969); J. M. Wagstaffe, "Buried Assumptions: Some Problems in the Interpretation of the 'Younger Fill' Raised by Recent Data from Greece," *Journal of Archaeological Science* 8 (1981): 24–64; G. Barker and G. D. B. Jones, *The UNESCO/Libyan Valleys Survey: report on three years of fieldwork, 1979–1981* (Manchester, 1983), 56. For a recent case study, T. H. van Andel, C. N. Runnels and K. O. Pope, "Five Thousand Years of Land Use and Abuse in the Southern Argolid, Greece," *Hesperia* 55, pt. 1 (1986): 103–28.

10. R. Hodges *Dark Age Economics* (London, 1982). See also G. Astill, "Archaeology, Economics and Early Medieval Europe," *Oxford Journal of Archaeology* 4, pt. 2 (1985): 215–29.

11. Galinié, "Archeologie et topographie historique de Tours – Ivème–XIème siècle," *Zeitschrift für Archäologie des Mittelalters* 6 (1978): 33–56. P. A. Février, "Permanence et héritages de l'antiquité dans la topographie des villes de l'occident durant le haut moyen âge," *Settimane di studio del Centro Italiano di Studi sull'Alto Medioevo* 21 (Spoleto, 1974): 41–138, shows conclusively that Tours was by no means exceptional.

12. W. Horn and E. Born, *The Plan of St. Gall* (Berkeley, Los Angeles, and London, 1979) vol. 1, 342.

13. The pioneer studies of gift exchange are B. Malinowski, *Argonauts of the Western Pacific* (London, 1922) and M. Mauss, *Essai sur le don* (Paris, 1925). For a translation of the latter, Marcel Mauss, *The Gift: Forms and Functions of Exchange in Archaic Societies*, trans. Ian Cunnison with intro. by E. E. Evans-Pritchard (London: Cohen and West, 1954; repr. with corrections, London and Henley, Routledge and Kegan Paul, 1966, 1969). For Western Europe, P. Grierson, "Commerce in the Dark Ages: A Critique of the Evidence," *Transactions of the Royal Historical Society* 23 (1941): 71–112. And for Sutton Hoo itself, R. L. S. Bruce-Mitford, *The Sutton Hoo Ship Burial*, 3 vols. in 4 (London, 1975–84).

14. P. Holdsworth, 'Saxon Southampton: A New Review," *Medieval Archaeology* 20 (1976): 26–61; R. Hodges, *The Hamwih Pottery* (London, 1980) W. A. van Es and W. J. H. Verwers, *Excavations at Dorestad I The Harbour: Hoogstraat I*. (Amersfot, 1980).

15. Hodges, *Dark Age Economics*. For Dorestad, van Es and Verwers, *Excavations at Dorestad I*; for its dendrochronology, D. Eckstein, W. A. van Es and E. Holstein, "Beitrag zur Datierung der frühmittelalterlichen Dorestad," *Berichten van de Rijksdienst voor het Oudheidkundig Bodemonderzoek* 25 (1975): 165–76.

16. P. Grierson, "Money and Coinage under Charlemagne," in *Karl der Grosse* (Dusseldorf, 1965): vol. I, 501–36.

17. H. Jankuhn, *Haithabu, ein Handelsplatz der Wikingerzeit*, 6th ed. (Neumunster, 1976); K. Randsborg, *The Viking Age in Denmark* (London, 1980).

18. K. A. C. Creswell, *Early Muslim Architecture* 2nd. ed. (London, 1968), vol. 2, 1-5.

19. Astonishingly, no detailed description of the site exists, although work is now under way to map the site from air photographs: see A. Northedge, "Planning Sāmarrā: A Report for 1983-84," *Iraq* 48 (1985): 109-28. For early air photographs, E. Herzfeld, *Ausgrabungen von Samarra, VI: Geschichte der Stadt Samarra* (Berlin, 1948); for the principal monuments, Creswell, *Early Muslim Architecture*. J. M. Rogers, "Samarra: Study in Medieval Town Planning," in *The Islamic City*, ed. A. H. Hourani and S. M. Stern (Oxford, 1970); 119-55, discusses the foundation and construction of the city; it was, he wrote, "an act of folly on a vast scale."

20. D. Whitehouse, "Maritime Trade in the Arabian Sea: The 9th and 10th centuries AD," *South Asian Archaeology 1977* (Naples, 1979), vol. 2, 865-85.

21. Interim reports on the excavations at Siraf appear in *Iran* 6 (1968): 1-22; 7 (1969): 39-62; 8 (1970): 1-18; 9 (1971): 1-17; 10 (1972): 63-87; and 12 (1974): 1-30.

22. D. Whitehouse, *Siraf III: The Congregational Mosque and Other Mosques from the Ninth to the Twelfth Centuries* (London, 1980); R. Hodges and D. Whitehouse, *Mohammed, Charlemagne and the Origins of Europe*, 143-49.

23. D. Whitehouse, "Excavations at Siraf: Third Interim Report," *Iran* 8 (1970): 1-18, esp. 5 and pl. XIIc-d.

24. D. Whitehouse, *Siraf III*, 8-9.

25. S. Bolin, "Mohammed, Charlemagne and Rurik," *Scandinavian Economic History Review* 1 (1952): 5-39.

26. T. S. Noonan, "Ninth-Century Dirhem Hoards from European Russia: A Preliminary Analysis," in *Viking-Age Coinage in Northern Lands*, ed. M. A. S. Blackburn and D. M. Metcalf (Oxford: British Archaeological Reports, 1981): 47-118. I do not dissent from the view that the wealth of the Carolingians owed much to the immense booty captured from the Avars in 795. This, however, cannot explain the monetary reform, which took place at least a year before the seizure of the treasure.

Viking Raiders: The Transformation of Scandinavian Society

KLAVS RANDSBORG

The Vikings have recently attracted much attention. Their rustic material culture has been exposed to the international public and, once again, their raids have been evoked, like the famous attack on Lindisfarne, England on June the 8th, AD 793.

However, the Viking phenomenon of the period c. 800–1050 cannot be understood without dealing with the Scandinavian homelands of the Vikings and in particular with their societies and economies (Randsborg 1980; also for the following). The written historical evidence for this is meager, leaving aside the much later Icelandic Sagas. But archaeology has provided an increasing amount of data elucidating both the dramatic events and the realities overlooked by written history.

A crucial factor is the inner development of the Scandinavian societies. When we first encounter the Vikings, around the time of the sack of Lindisfarne, they come from rural, yet sophisticated kingdoms, pagan and relatively loosely organized. At the end of the Viking Age, around 1000, at least Denmark had developed into a state with towns, royal fortresses, manors, highroads, taxation of various kinds, etc. This meant an increase in the power of the Danish king who secured regular income and was in command of large military forces. To foreigners he was a formidable opponent. Danish kings held sway over England in the first half of the eleventh century. Most famous of the Danish-English kings was Canute who was even portrayed in a contemporary painting kneeling at the altar of Winchester (with his queen).

The early ravage of Lindisfarne was actually a rare act of violence in the decades around 800, the start of the Viking Age. Most Viking raids, both in England and on the Continent, take place somewhat later in the second half of the ninth century, stopping around 900. Why did the Vikings become hooligans? In fact, their acts of violence can be explained in terms of a crisis that hit the Scandinavian societies in the first half of the ninth century.

A few decades earlier, at the end of the eighth century, international trade had suddenly expanded at a drastic rate throughout the entire Old World (Hodges & Whitehouse 1983). China was opened to Muslim merchants. In turn, the Islamic world was trading weapons, slaves and furs with Scandinavians, mainly Swedes, sailing down broad Russian rivers, the Dniepr, Volga, to the trading cities at estuaries such as Itil on the Caspian. There the Vikings met Jewish and Muslim traders from the Middle East who were opening up trade via Rayy (the later Teheran) and Baghdad (by sea through the Persian Gulf, and overland by the Old Silk Road [Lombard 1975, 23 f. and 33 ff.]) These routes were the gateways to India, China and the Far East. The Vikings were reaching the Near East also by way of other routes stretching south down the east coast of Africa and west into the Mediterranean.

The Muslims also had contact with Christian Western Europe. For instance, Haroun-al-Raschid, the famous Caliph of Baghdad, described in the *Arabian Nights,* sent an elephant to Charlemagne, the Frankish emperor. (The beast actually died of flu when it was brought north to participate in the fighting against the Danes.) At Viking courts silk and peacocks were found. More importantly, Islamic silver flowed from Russia into Scandinavia and from there into Western Europe. It has been suggested that this was the financial basis for the so-called Carolingian renaissance: the remarkable cultural development around 800. A historical parallel would be the 16th century Spanish silver fleets from the New World. In the decades around 800 a small-scale world system of trade and politics was created, a phenomenon usually confined to the centuries between Columbus and our own era.

Thus, in a short time, the Norsemen became actively engaged in the world around them, mainly through trade. Incidents like the sack of the monastery of Lindisfarne in, by many historians considered the start of the Viking Age, were still rare. However, this international trade network broke down in the second quarter of the ninth century, due to economic recession, social unrest and war in the Near East and Russia. In Mesopotamia, for example, center of the Islamic world, the population of the fertile flood plain dropped to only a fragment of its previous size to judge from the archaeological surveys of settlements carried out in the area (Adams 1981) (fig. 1).[1] In Russia warring and migrations by Magyars and other peoples were taking place. With the eastern trade routes severed, the Viking magnates began to look for other sources of income. But why were raiding parties organized, as risky as they were?

The explanation basically lies in the nature of the Viking society. In the period after the collapse of the west Roman Empire in the fifth century, Scandinavia was marginal to the European development. The North was made up

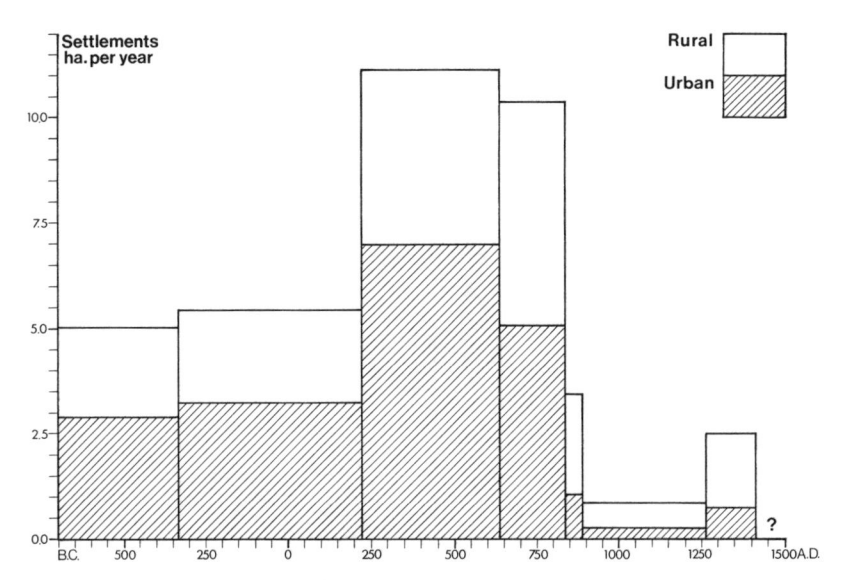

Fig. 1. Development of settlements in an area of the Mesopotamian floodplain. Data McAdams 1981.

of tribal societies, organized in petty kingdoms or chiefdoms. Land and wealth were important, but the kings were not powerful, and the economy lacked incentives.

At the beginning of the Viking Age, however, when the international luxury trade expanded, the kings gained substantial incomes. They set up market-towns on the coast, like Ribe and Hedeby in Denmark and Birka in Sweden, and started to use their income to gain further power. When the trade dwindled, the incomes disappeared and the kings were left with obligations they could not fulfill. Throne-pretenders, younger members of the royal dynasties, and others constituted a real threat to the power of the kings. Expeditions organized by any party may have been a means to avoid further conflict.

We now meet the loathed "Danes" (generic term for Norsemen or Vikings) of, say, the Anglo-Saxon Chronicle. Moving around quickly, these gangs or armies in their superb long ships could enter even small rivers and yet withstand high waves on the open sea. Thus the Norsemen, along with the Magyar horsemen and the Muslims in the Mediterranean, became the terror of Europe. Seemingly these groups of Scandinavian warriors soon were quite independent of their homeland. In France, for instance, we know that the Vikings received at least 50,000 pounds of silver in tribute in the later ninth century, but hardly a single French coin of this period has been found in Scandinavia (Albrectsen 1976). The Viking armies, led by so-called "kings," also began to interfere in the local politics of Britain and France. This resulted in Viking

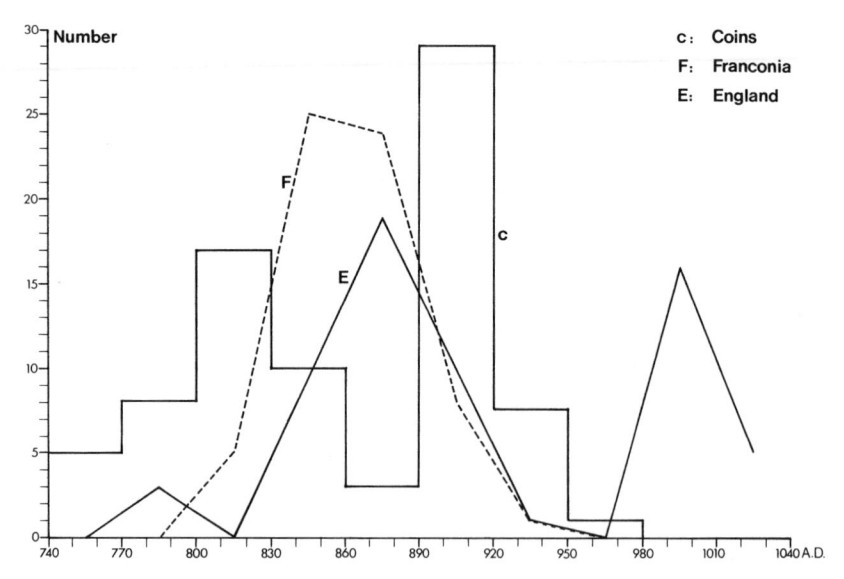

Fig. 2. Frequencies of foreign (in the main Islamic) coins in the graves of the emporium of Birka in Sweden (near present-day Stockholm) contrasted with frequencies of years with Viking attacks on England and on the Frankish Empire. Coins after Arbman 1943. Historical information after Whitelock 1955 (The Anglo-Saxon Chronicle) and Albrectsen 1976 (various continental sources).

political domination over large parts of England. In France, Normandy was given as a fief. It also resulted in settlements of large numbers of Danes, in particular Danish Vikings, for instance in eastern England, first the armies, then other settlers.

But not only the Danes moved permanently out from Scandinavia to free themselves from social troubles and constraints. At the beginning of the Viking Age the Norwegians had already landed in Scotland, where they established themselves on the Northern Isles and the Hebrides. A little later the Vikings colonized the Faroe Islands and Iceland and, at the end of the Viking Age, even the southern tip of Greenland. A few intrepid explorers extended the boundaries of the then known world when they reached the coast of North America and founded the short-lived settlement at L'Anse aux Meadows, Newfoundland (Ingstad 1970). Clearly Viking ship technology and seamanship still improved as the wide stretches of open sea were crossed. Ironically, the main body of settlers in the North Atlantic seems to have been Celtic slaves under their Norwegian masters. The blood type percentages of the present day Icelandic population differ substantially from those of the present day Norwegian population, while they are identical with those of western Scotland and Ireland (Frydenberg and Spärck 1963, 145 f.). This shows how careful we must be not to confuse Scandinavian lordship with pure Scandinavian settlement.

In a graph, the period of raiding in the ninth century and the trading period around 800 can be more precisely contrasted (fig. 2). To reflect the long-distance trade we use the number of foreign coins in the graves of the Swedish market-town of Birka near Stockholm, at the beginning of the route towards Russia and the east. The raids in the west are recorded in English and Frankish chronicles (Randsborg 1981a). We see how the frequency of trade and the one of raid in the early Viking Age are mutually exclusive. We also see that raiding or warring by the Vikings almost disappears at 900 when a second boom in trade took place and once again sent very large amounts of Islamic silver into Scandinavia through Russia.

The reason for this second peak is found in the establishment of the new Samanid dynasty of Turkestan and Afghanistan, that was very rich and largely supported by trading (Lombard 1975, 46 f.). The Samanids controlled the very crossroads between Europe, the Near East and the Far East. In addition they controlled some extremely rich silver mines. From the Near East Islamic merchants and diplomats now reached as far as the middle Volga where they again established contacts with the Viking traders.

We will, however, leave the Viking expansion at this stage and turn to Scandinavia itself. This enables us to understand more fully both the ninth century, the first Viking Age, and the happenings to come at the end of the tenth century, the second Viking Age. The two Viking Ages were, as previously indicated, very different: the first one was characterized by international trade, raids, wherever opportunity offered, settling abroad, and comparatively loosely organized societies in Scandinavia; in the second Viking Age an economic and social development takes place, especially in Denmark. Trade on an international scale is relatively unimportant whereas local and regional markets are created to serve the growing state systems. When expansion does take place, it is in the form of conquest. Denmark, the crucial country in the second Viking Age, was also very populous and closely linked with Britain in the West.

In the first Viking Age and before, Denmark was covered with regular villages and hamlets with streets and greens (Hvass 1978 and 1979; Stoumann 1979). The farms were big and situated on spacious, square crofts surrounded by palisade fences. The private space of each single farmstead in the village was, thus, large. The main structure was a well-built wooden longhouse with separate living quarters, stables, barns, magazines, etc. This longhouse was surrounded by smaller buildings with other living quarters (perhaps for slaves), workshops, etc. Such compounds would reflect a well-organized social structure with individual control of basic resources.

On the political level the country was, as were its Scandinavian neighbors, made up of rather petty kingdoms. The farmers and rulers were also warriors and only in times of war did powerful kings emerge, like king Godfred, Charlemagne's opponent in crucial encounters shortly after AD 800. King Godfred had his troops erect a new frontier wall immediately to the South of the main market place of Hedeby. This enlargement was founded as an emporium to accommodate international trade. Trade incomes enriched kings and nobility but, in general, life went on much as in the previous late Iron Age period.

In the ninth century AD there were only a couple of towns in Denmark, situated at the border and on the North Sea. The best known is Hedeby, near present day Slesvig, that has produced a splendid archaeological picture (Jahnkuhn 1976; Schietzel 1975 and 1981). In the harbour area all land was registered. Between the plank-covered streets and lanes lay narrow plots with lightly built wooden structures in one story. The houses were constantly renewed. Typically they consisted of a main room and a couple of smaller workshops or storage areas. There was very little free space around the buildings. The impression is one very different from the later permanent towns with much more room for both habitation and outdoor activities. The occupants of each dwelling changed at fairly short intervals and there is no special quarter for any of the trades. Birka's layout was probably less structured, more in the style of Kaupang, the major South Norwegian trading site, with small houses in irregular clusters.

These towns were not provincial centers but were geared to international trade. They were, in other words, marketplaces rather than normal towns. Significantly, judging from the sizes of the many shoes found and the skeletons in the burial yards, men, as traders, craftsmen and workers, made up the largest part of the population. Hedeby was connected with Birka near Stockholm in Sweden, Birka with trading-centers in Russia, and so on. (It was also through these emporia that the Christian missionaries reached the North.) Since Hedeby and Birka, the gateways to the West and East respectively, were primarily market places, they ceased to exist when the periods of long-distance trade were over and when provincial towns were established.

The arts, or at least those of the aristocracy, were highly abstract or ornamental, almost completely lacking in content (Foote and Wilson 1970, 286 ff.). Actually this art style continues even into post-Viking times, thus postulating continuity and hiding social and ideological changes. The society was pagan, which, in this case, meant believing in a number of gods whose behavior resembled an idealized version of the life of the magnates: travelling, feasting, and seeking excitement. In addition the Vikings, to judge from the Saga literature, believed in lesser, often evil, supernatural beings, resembling the commoners. Also venerated were the forces of nature. As in Islam, the death of a warrior could mean a ticket to Valhalla, the hall of the slain, in Asgard, the home of the gods. But in the stories the Vikings told about their gods there is also a feeling of aimlessness, that all this activity has no deeper aim. Do we detect the same ideology in the arts of the Viking aristocracy, highly abstract or ornamental as they are, but almost completely lacking in content?

Earlier we discussed the world trade of the period around AD 800 which quickly dwindled and was followed by decades of unrest, raids and settling abroad. In Scandinavia a second wave of trade with the East started, as mentioned, in the 890s, and almost overnight the Viking raids in western Europe ceased (fig. 2). Taxation of the trade created new wealth, and the Scandinavian turned from warfare to trade. But again this second wave of trade with the Islamic world quickly dwindled. In the 920s Viking merchants were still on the Volga in Russia, and hundreds of thousands of Arabic silver coins, minted in the fabled cities of Buchara and Samarkand, flowed into the North in exchange for slaves and furs. But by AD 950, at the time of the powerful King Harald of Denmark, the eastern trade was only a shadow of itself, and by AD 1000 it was almost negligible. The reason was the decline of the eastern Samanid dynasty, which by AD 950 had lost control of all important trading centers, especially Teheran, conquered by another Muslim dynasty. The result being that the network could not be maintained. This had far-reaching consequences. For instance, Birka at Stockholm, which like Hedeby in Denmark did survive the first decline in spite of its dependence on the trade with Russia, crumbled and never rose again. Thus the second wave of eastern trade collapsed.

The interesting thing is that the Danes did not resume raiding during the second crisis, around AD 950. If stress was felt in the Danish society for this reason, it did not find the same expression not outlet as a century before. This is most probably a clear indication that the Scandinavian societies of the late Viking age were different from those of the early Viking Age, especially in Denmark.

In the late Viking Age in Denmark we suddenly see a novel type of farm, the magnate farm or rather, the manor. Three such magnate farms are found at Vorbasse in Central Jutland, two smaller and one larger (Hvass 1979). The croft of the largest magnate farm measures 120 by 215 meters, or more than two and a half hectares. There is no reason to believe that this farmstead was exceptionally large since it is situated on rather poor soils. In the middle of the crofts of the manors was a splendid hall, rivalled only by those of the royal fortresses. The hall was the landlord's living quarters. Along the periphery of the croft were the stables with room for about 100 animals, magazines, other living quarters (for servants), workshops, etc. As at Vorbasse, several such magnate farms may lie next to one another, shadowing the property of the ordinary farmers. On the manors were also watermills for grinding cereals, a most important novelty. Such finds clearly show how, in the late Viking Age, wealth in rural resources was amassed on a scale not known before. And the economic basis for the magnates and rulers such as Canute, the Danish and English king of the early eleventh century AD, is understood.

At the royal fortress of Fyrkat in Jutland, built in the later tenth century AD, was found a huge cache of rye (most probably seedcorn) (Helbaek in Olsen et al. 1977). This particular high-grade, with unusually big grains, was imported from southeastern Poland or even the Ukraine. It reflects the very strong interest that the leading echelons of Danish society showed in subsistence agriculture at this time. In the periods before the Viking Age, ranching was dominant, but in the late Viking Age there was a surge of growing cereals, accompanied by the introduction of new and more sturdy types of ploughs and the harrow. In this period private property became paramount as is evident from the memory runestones, the Viking charters (Randsborg 1980, 22 ff.). With private land came taxation of this same land and a permanence of settlement location that has lasted until the present day (Grøngård Jeppesen 1981).

This fundamental change in agricultural practice resulted in an ability to feed a very large population. Consequently, there were no serious attempts to expand settlements abroad in the late Viking Age. On the contrary, the new types of subsistence and settlement became the basis for the State of Denmark, more stable than the various earlier kingdoms in the country.

The Danish state was founded in Jutland where the links with Western Europe were also very strong. The first direction of expansion of the state was towards the east, however. At the royal center of Jelling in Jutland, around AD 960 King Harald erected a huge stone to commemorate his parents and underline his own position and power (cf. Krogh 1982). The stone, a masterpiece of Viking ornamental art, carries an image of Christ and a huge animal fighting a snake. The monument was erected next to Harald's large wooden church and between the two largest burial mounds in Denmark. One of them probably held the bodies of the king's parents, mentioned in the runic inscription of the stone:

> King Harald bade be made this monument after Gorm his father and Thyra his mother — that Harald who won for himself Denmark all, and Norway, and made the Danes Christian.

Obviously, King Harald must have been hailed as supreme lord in Norway as well as in Denmark. He also accepted Christianity as the state religion, a move to identify his state with the West European societies to keep the German emperor at bay. A few years earlier the emperor had nominated German bishops for pagan Denmark in an attempt to gain political control over the country.

The core of King Harald's realm, western Denmark, was secured with fortifications (fig. 3). To the south, fourteen kilometers of ancient Jutland border walls were reinforced (Andersen et al. 1976). To the north and east, King Harald "bade be made" some magnificent circular fortresses of the famous

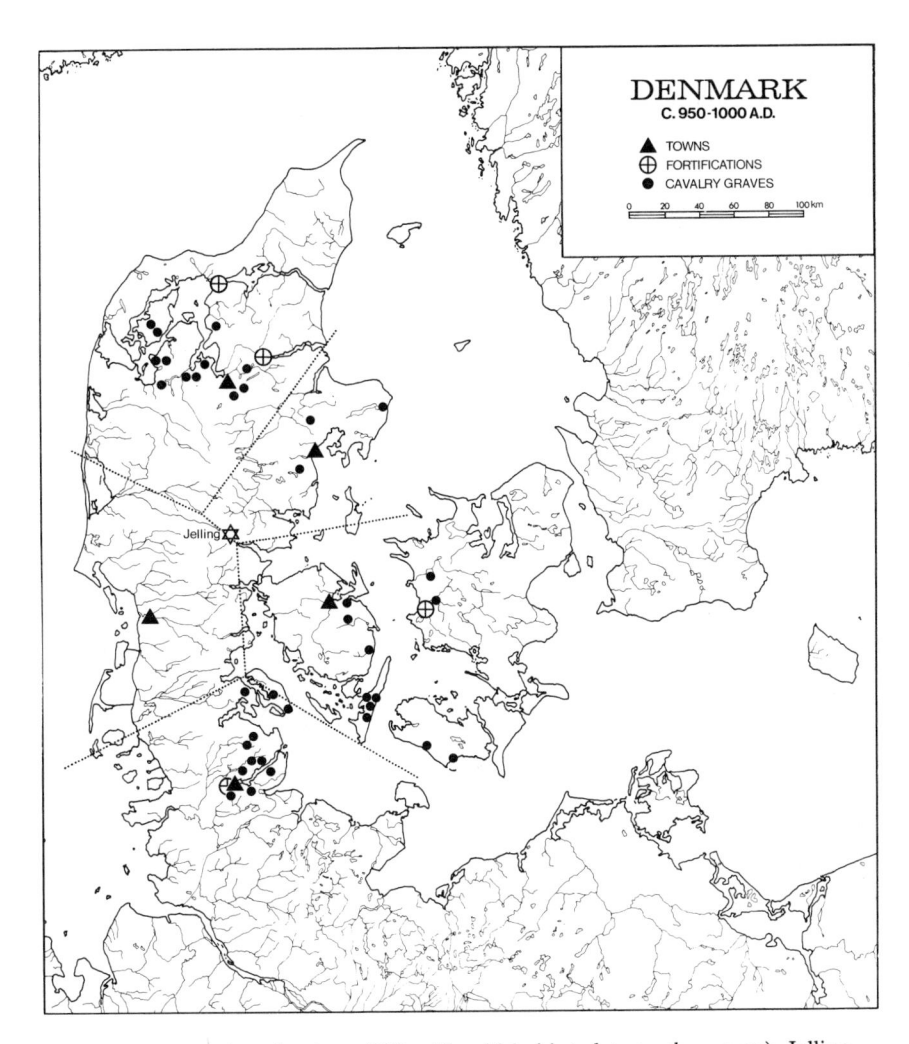

Fig. 3. Denmark at the time of King Harald (mid- to late tenth century). Jelling = Royal center. Fortifications = The fortresses of Trelleborg type plus the Danevirke walls on the frontier with Germany. The broken lines indicate the borders of the theoretical catchment areas of the (larger) towns. Cavalry graves after Randsborg 1980.

Trelleborg-type, modelled over symmetrical plan and housing only halls (Olsen et al. 1977; Roesdahl 1977). The largest of these fortresses was more than 250 meters across and had 48 identical thirty-two-meter-long wooden halls. These halls were arranged in blocks of four within a grid system of six streets, three going north-south and three east-west. The earthen wall and the streets were covered with planks. Even the smallest of these fortresses (with only sixteen halls plus additional structures) required an enormous amount of wood, labor and provisions for its construction. Around the core of the kingdom a number of cavalry men was settled to further secure the center (Randsborg 1981b). We identify them from their rich burials with weapons, heavy bits and stirrups. For centuries burial wealth was almost unknown in the country, all valuables being inherited. Its appearance now underlines the special status of these royal warriors. The trappings are of Magyar type allowing an AD 900 novelty in warfare, the fighting of cavalry battles in formation.

In the core area of the state we find the earliest provincial towns, regularly spaced in the country. These towns were still very small by our standards but they occupied a crucial position in a new type of economy. The provincial towns acted as markets for produce from the surrounding areas, and as centers for increased craft manufacture for local consumption. Towns also housed the most important church institutions and royal representatives whose two-fold primary task was to collect taxes and to supervise the life of the towns. In some towns they also oversaw the mint. The archaeological picture of these towns is still meager, but is does yield massive deposits indicating continuity in settlement and a high level of activity (not to mention lack of refuse collection!) (Andrén 1976). The layout of the towns was more open than in the harbour area of Hedeby in the ninth century AD. There was sufficient space for yards and even stables. Wood was still the main building material, and remained so almost until modern times. However, shortly after AD 1000, the first churches of stone were erected with the aid of English stone-masons.

When discussing this crucial development in terms of various types of centers: towns, fortresses, etc., it should be mentioned that for the hinge and flux years around AD 1000 when Eastern Denmark was just incorporated in the State system (fig. 4), archaeology has demonstrated a considerable overlap in terms of the function of the centers of this period across the country, ignoring the terms previously given a system emerges. The larger centers[2] are equally spaced and have smaller centers on or at the borderlines between their hypothetical catchment areas. The smaller centers[3] may thus make up a secondary level in a hierarchy based on the sheer size of the sites. This archaeological picture probably shows that the new economy was still very much under royal planning and organization. A striking but earlier parallel would be the southern England of King Alfred with its fortified towns and townlike fortresses (Biddle 1976).

However, for both the earliest period of build-up (mid- to late tenth century AD) (fig. 3) and especially, for the period of stabilization of the mid-eleventh century AD (fig. 5), the usual functional distinction between the centers is the most meaningful one. In the early period the royal center of King Harald at Jelling is situated like a spider in the middle of the small West Danish web

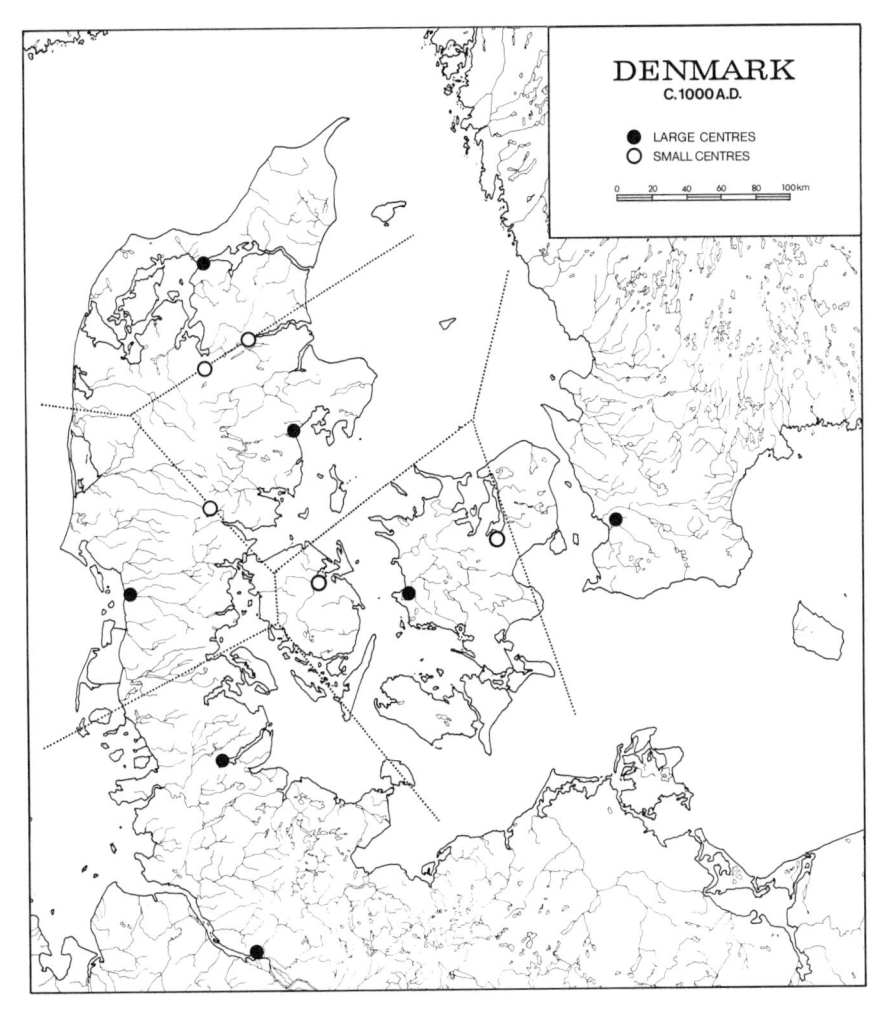

Fig. 4. Denmark around AD 1000. The broken lines indicate the borders of the theoretical catchment areas of the larger centers. Also indicated is Hamburg in Germany.

of a few provincial towns and, further out, the Trelleborg fortresses (at the same distance as the cavalry graves). Hedeby, also at the periphery and at the border with Germany, is retaining a role as a port-of-trade involved with some international traffic. For the eleventh century AD we detect a significant picture of the major provincial towns or cities, the only major centers then known, equally spaced across the country.

No doubt the social development in Denmark in the tenth century was a

34 / KLAVS RANDSBORG

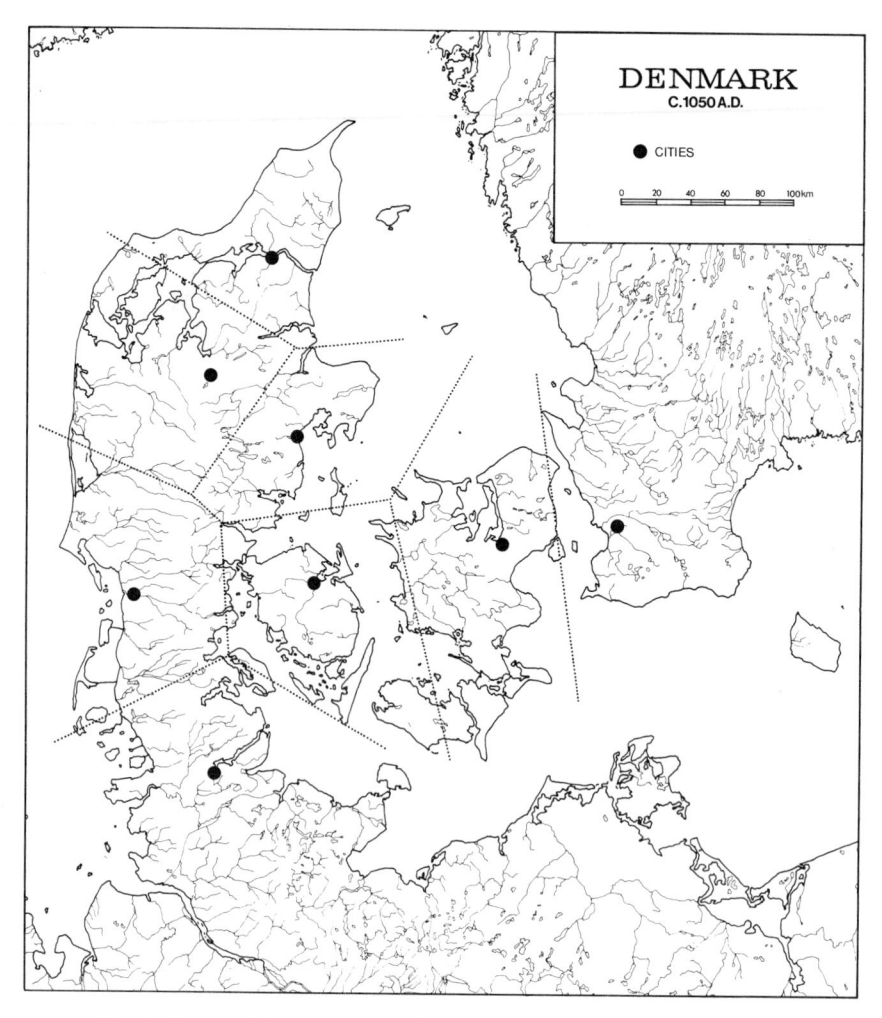

Fig. 5. Denmark in the mid-tenth century. The broken lines indicate the borders of the theoretical catchment areas of the cities.

very costly one. The military sector alone, including ships, fortifications, the Trelleborg fortresses and so on would easily have eaten up the traditional royal revenue. In addition this early Danish state and its magnates also built churches and developed what we today would call the infrastructure of the country, roads were improved and bridges built. Immediately to the south of the royal center at Jelling, a two-lane wooden bridge was built in King Harald's later years, almost one km long and carrying a load of five tons (Ramskou 1980). This bridge gives an impression of the size of the traffic and of extraordinary civil engineering. It is characteristic for such society to start expanding its power. The military instrument was at hand and fresh income was needed to maintain the new order at home.

Thus, at the same time as political control was strengthened in Denmark, the rivalry between the various Nordic societies and factions was steered for conflict. The son of King Harald of Denmark, King Sven, seems to have led a rebellion against his aging father. The uprising may even have been pagan in character. However, Sven died as a Christian king (in AD 1014), leaving his realm to his son Knud, or Canute.

Also around the year AD 1000, the eastern provinces of Denmark were, as mentioned, engulfed in the kingdom and, especially in its new economic and social system with towns, markets, bishoprics, etc. Norway, and especially isolated Sweden, seem to have been far less developed in this period when Denmark attempted to expand its power. During the reign of Canute both Norway and parts of Sweden belonged to the Danish king, who also, of course, held England with all its wealth, and parts of Scotland too.

This milieu of rivalry and social development on a large scale makes up the background of the second Viking Age, which is very much an English phenomenon (fig. 2). In the 980s and 990s Norse pirates, first apparently Norwegians, and only manning a few ships, returned to the coasts of England for booty. (I imagine this to be a side-effect of the unrest in Scandinavia in the latest years of King Harald and in King Sven's first years on the throne.) In AD 994 King Sven himself leads a direct Danish assault on England.

A few years earlier the English had, for the first time, used tribute payments to keep the Vikings off their coasts and cities. Ten thousand pounds of silver were delivered, which was only a trifle of the total payments to the Danes in this period. All in all almost 250,000 pounds of silver were paid by the English in increasingly larger portions in the period 991 to 1018. No wonder that Sven and later Canute were elected English kings; the tributes were such severe penalty that it was cheaper to pay them regular tax. Certainly the normal taxation level must have been lower than the latest tribute payments, up to more than 80,000 pounds at one time. For comparison the French payments to the Vikings in the entire ninth century AD only amounted to about one sixth of the English payments of more than a century later.

There is another important difference. The money from the raids in the ninth century AD was spent abroad. The income of Kings Sven and Canute resulted in a doubling of the silver stock in Denmark with other Scandinavian countries benefitting also. Seemingly, the Danish kings counted on large number of foreign leaders for their conquest of England. Swedish runestones, for example, laud magnates who participated in the campaigns and "received payment from Canute." Yet this Scandinavian hegemony was fragile. It was easier to create an empire by promise of booty than to maintain it across wide areas of sea.

King Canute and his son managed to maintain a North Sea empire based on England and Denmark, but only until AD 1042 when the English freed themselves from Danish rule. In reality it was never possible for the Danes to administer both England and Denmark across wide stretches of sea. Canute was, in reality more a king of England than of Denmark. Such rule was based on military power and motivated by easy gain. After the conquest it was no longer possible to extort tribute. It seems the Danes had no plans for a continued presence in England and may well have overreached themselves. For instance, after the conquest they dissolved most of the army. This made the occupation less onerous on the English, but the Danes lost a crucial instrument of power.

The fighting in Scandinavia, especially between Norwegians and Danes continued. Shortly before Anglo-Saxon England was conquered by the Normans in 1066, a Norwegian king, Harald, fell in the famous battle of Stamford Bridge in an attempt to revive Scandinavian rule in England. Ironically this was only a few days before the Norman conquest which was to establish new and lasting political order in England.

The Harald of Stamford Bridge who had been an extremely wealthy mercenary officer at the court of Byzantium, also pillaged Denmark, which by this time must have looked much the same as England: a rather prosperous state, well organized, based on a developed subsistence with towns and markets to regulate the economy. In the cities there were bishops with foreign relations, but the large-scale international trade in the Baltic was more important than across the North Sea to England, or to the Islamic East after luxuries. Denmark had turned into a small and vulnerable West European Continental state. Deprived of a major source of wealth in England it could no longer buy the support of its old barbarian allies, who now turned into raiders. But they too were to step out of antiquity and become developed and settled.

The Viking Age must be seen as a period of social transition and economic flux. Trade, raid, and social and economic development go hand in hand, and no phenomenon can be understood without referring to the others. Certainly the Viking Age does not constitute a unique stage in the development of European society. The Vikings were only active participants in a general process where they seized the opportunities offered by economic and political events to make Scandinavia one of the most dynamic societies of its time and thus to influence the entire development of Western Europe.

Did the Vikings produce a legacy? One such has been studied in terms of, for example, language, technology, relating especially to ships and navigation, and even the characteristic decorative styles that survived into later periods, referring to the ancient status of Scandinavian kings and traders. For instance, the English language has a very strong Danish component. You cannot *thrive*, be *ill*, or *die* without speaking Danish, and hundreds of English place names, by derivation American names, are Danish. In the end, however, the direction of the strongest social and cultural impact was always from the developed western Europe to Denmark and to the rest of Scandinavia. Admittedly, the Vikings also left a negative impact by such highly visible acts as the sack of Lindisfarne. In penalty for this they have to posterity become known first of all as hooligans, another Viking legacy. It is an ongoing task of social and economic history and especially of archaeology, to produce new data from this almost prehistoric age in Scandinavia, to correct and explain such legacies.

Notes

1. The figures are drawn by Poul T. Christensen.
2. I.e., the "towns" of Hedeby, Ribe, Aarhus and Lund; the "fortresses" of Aggersborg and Trelleborg.
3. I.e., the "towns" of Viborg, Odense and Roskilde; the "fortresses" of Fyrkat; the declining "royal center" at Jelling.

References

Adams, R. McC. *Heartland of Cities: Surveys of Ancient Settlement and Land Use on the Central Floodplain of the Euphrates.* Chicago University Press, Chicago.
1981.

Albrectsen, E. *Vikingerne i Franken.* Odense Universitetsforlag, Odense.
1976.

Andersen, H. H., H. J. Madsen and O. Voss
1976. *Danevirke: Jysk Arkaeologisk Selskabs skrifter XIII.* Aarhus.

Andrén, A. "Stadsbilden," in Mårtensson 1976, 21 ff.
1976.

Arbman, H. Birka I. Die Gräber, Stockholm. Kungl. Vitterhets Historie och Antikvitets Akademien.
1943.

Biddle, M. "The Towns," in Wilson 1976, 99 ff.
1976.

Chapman, B., I. Kinnes, K. Randsborg (eds.)
1981. *The Archaeology of Death.* Cambridge University Press, Cambridge.

Foote, P. G. and D. M. Wilson
1970. *The Viking Achievement.* Sidgwick and Jackson, London.

Frydengerg, O. and J. V. Spärck
1963. *Arv og race hos mennesket*. Berlingske, København.

Grøngård Jeppesen, T.
1981. *Middelalderbyens opstaaen*, Fynske Studier XI. Odense Bys Museer, Odense.

Helbaek, H. "The Fyrkat grain," in Olsen et al., [1]-[4].
1977.

Hodges, R. and D. Whitehouse
1983. *Mohammed, Charlemagne and the Origins of Europe: Archaeology and the Pirenne Thesis*. Duckworth, London.

Hvass, S. *Die völkerwanderungszeitliche Siedlung Vorbasse: Mitteljütland*. Acta Ar-
1978. chaeologica 49, 61 ff., Copenhagen.

1979. *Vorbasse: The Viking-age Settlement at Vorbasse, Central Jutland*. Acta Archaeologica 50, 137-72.

Ingstad, A. S. *The Norse Settlement at L'Anse aux Meadows: A Preliminary Report from*
1970. *the Excavations 1961-1968*. Acta Archaeologica XLI, 109 ff., Copenhagen.

Jankuhn, H. *Haithabu: Ein Handelsplatz der Wikingerzeit* (6th edition), Neumün-
1976. ster, Karl Wachholtz.

Krogh, K. J. *The Royal Viking-Age Monuments at Jelling in the Light of Recent Ar-*
1982. *chaeological Excavations: A Preliminary Report*, Acta Archaeologica 53, 183 ff., Copenhagen.

Lombard, M. *The Golden Age of Islam*. Amsterdam, North Holland.
1975.

Mårtensson, A. W. (ed.)
1976. *Uppgrävt förflutet för PKbanken i Lund*. Acta Archaeologica Lundensia VII.

Olsen, O. and H. Schmidt
1977. *Fyrkat, en jysk vikingeborg I*. Borgen og bebyggelsen, Nordiske Fortidsminder serie B., in 4to, no. 3. København.

Ramskou, T. *Vikingebroen over Vejle å-dal*, Nationalmuseets Arbejdsmark, 25-32.
1980.

Randsborg, K. *The Viking Age in Denmark: The Formation of a State*. Duckworth, Lon-
1980. don; St. Martin's Press, New York.

1981a. *Les activités internationales des vikings: Raids ou commerce?* Annales Économies Sociétés Civilisations 5, Sept.-Oct., 862-68.

1981b. "Burial, Succession and Early State Formation in Denmark," in Chapman et al.

Roesdahl, E. *Fyrkat: en jysk vikingeborg II*. Oldsagerne og gravpladsen, Nordiske
1977. Fortidsminder serie B, in 4to, no. 4. København.

Schietzel, K. *Haithabu: Ausgrabungen in Deutschland 3*. Römischgermanisches Zen-
1975. tralmuseum zu Mainz, Monographien 1; 3, 57 ff.

1981. *Stand der siedlungsarchäologischen Forschung in Haithabu — Ergebnisse und Probleme*. Berichte über die Ausgrabungen in Haithabu 16.

Stoumann, T. *Saedding: A Viking-age Village near Esbjerg.* Acta Archaeologica 50,
1979. 95–118.

Whitelock, D. (ed.)
1955. *English Historical Documents I, c. 500–1042.* Eyre and Spottiswoode, London.

Wilson, D. M. (ed.)
1976. *The Archaeology of Anglo-Saxon England.* Methuen, London.

The Vikings Versus the Towns of Northern Gaul: Challenge and Response*

MICHEL ROUCHE

When the Viking attacks were launched in the middle of the ninth century against the towns of northern Gaul, these were almost without fortifications. By the beginning of the tenth century, with few exceptions, they were almost all provided with solid ramparts. What was the cause of this fundamental change in the rural and urban landscape over a half-century? This problem has never been successfully resolved, and given the importance of this region for subsequent urban history, I would like to attempt a solution.

This study will be limited to an area largely neglected by historians heretofore, and still very little clarified by archaeological excavations: the region situated between the Aa, the Exant, the Meuse, the Oise and the Seine. It has always been believed that this zone was ravaged by the Vikings without any resistance on the part of the towns. While the Viking's invasions of the Belgian region,[1] as well as the banks of the Rhine[2] and England[3] are well known now, the territory which interests us here has been studied only in comparison with the others or only along its borders. Recent publications and work at the University of Lille III (France) will allow us to demonstrate that one of the motivating elements of this movement towards fortification was the impact of the Viking challenge on the dawning urban movement.

The state of abandon of the Roman walls in the North or the absence of walls for the new urban centers in the Carolingian period have already been discussed many times elsewhere. Jean Hubert and F. Vercauteren[4] have amply described the effort towards urbanization in Charlemagne's time, with the destruction or collapse of the Roman ramparts. In 816 and 817-826, the prelates of Langres and Reims obtained authorization to pull down their walls, and in 859, that of Sens for Melun. Beauvais followed suit.[5] Tournai saw the collapse of her walls between 845 and 855. Let us also include Lillebonne and Cassel,[6] but these cases were due, rather, to their stagnation in the face of competition from Rouen and Tournai, which replaced them. Amiens was perhaps a similar case.[7] In addition, numerous outlying communities, which appeared during the Merovingian period, were without any defense. The case of Arras is particularly clear: the suburb which had grown up around the monastery of Saint-Vaast, in the face of the Viking attack, was abandoned in 880, by the monks "struck with terror . . . the more so as the monastery territory was still without defense, not closed in with a wall, not so much as surrounded by a ditch."[8] Now these small market towns, proof of a dawning urban move-

Vikings Versus the Towns / 43

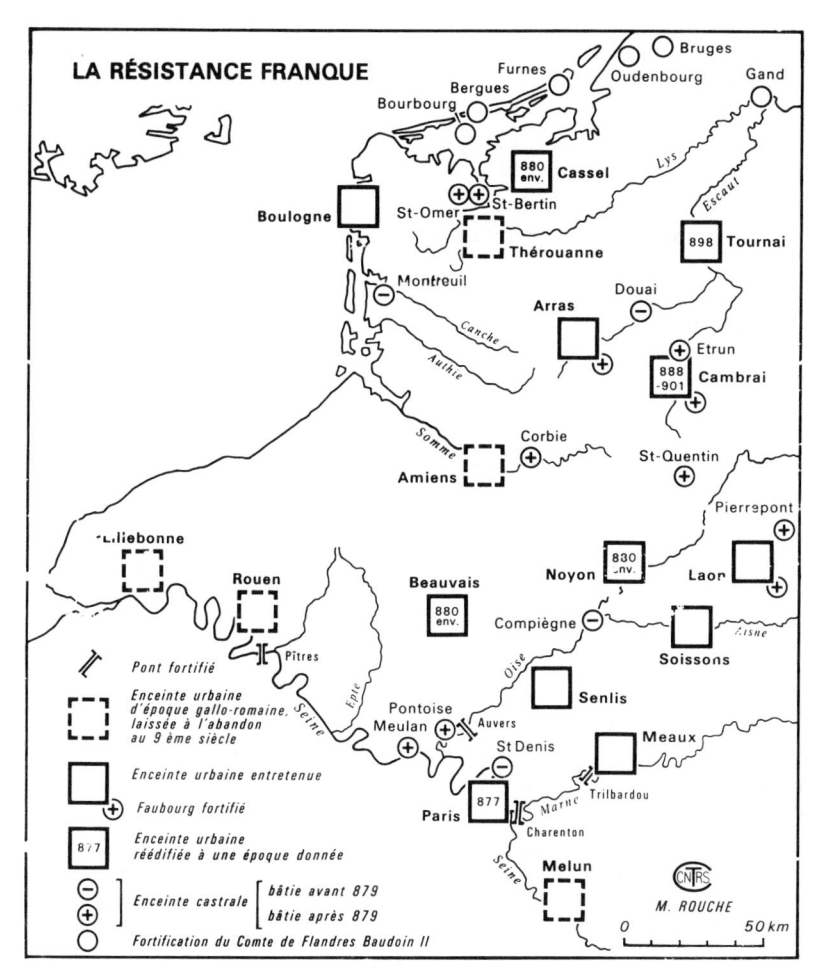

ment, were very rich and could not but attract the Danes. Finally, as Hariulf noted in around 860, "the districts of Vimeu and of Ponthieu rarely or never included small castles or fortifications and by way of these coastal territories France lay open to her enemies."[9] In fact the beaches and offshore sand bars, from Cap Gris-Nez to Bresle, were perfectly accessible to the Viking flat boats and made their landings extremely easy. Then, from 862–864 to 879, at the initiative of the king, attempts were made to build fortified bridges and strongholds, especially in the regions between the Seine and the Loire.[10] At the same time the Vikings were ravaging, unchallenged, the lands between the Seine and the Aa, and beyond. Finally, the second wave of Danish assaults, profiting from the political crisis from 879 to 884, broke loose on all the North of Gaul. Many towns were taken and pillaged: Amiens, Therouanne, Arras, Cambrai, Tournai,"[11] as well as Valenciennes, Saint-Omer, Saint-Quentin, Saint-Amand, Corbie and Saint-Riquier.[12] A dozen towns in all, including the faubourgs of Boulogne, Laon and Reims whose citadels withstood the assault (cf. General Table). According to F. Vercauteren, only this phase of assaults stimulated the construction of new fortifications between 879 and the beginning of the tenth century. He attributed responsibility for this building to the king and then to the bishops and abbots at the end of the century. This suggestion in no way explains, however, why, at the time of the first phase, after Quentovic, Rouen, Beauvais, Dorestadt, Noyon, Amiens, Ghent and Therouanne were taken, between 838 and 863, no one did anything. How could those responsible, laity and clergy, how could the people have remained passive, without resisting, for twenty years? I cannot agree with the hyper-critical Belgian author, Albert d'Haenens, when he styles, "isolated and marginal invasions"[13] an assault which Ferdinand Lot had earlier termed the great Norman invasion of 856-862, as they left the two greatest ports of the Carolingian Empire, Quentovic and Duurstede smoldering ruins.

The enemy attacks were so frequently renewed that the only response possible was military force. From the day they tried to settle an area, they first paralysed, then stimulated the conquered people to react. A. d'Haenens has already noted the importance of the Vikings camps. In fact these appear earlier and were more numerous than he says. He particularly stresses the establishment of the Danes within the urban precincts at Ghent from 879 to 880, Courtrai from 880 to 887, Amiens in 883/4 and then in 890-892, and just outside Noyon in 890-891.[15] In addition the Vikings built non-urban fortified camps: Ascloha in 881-882, Condé in 882- 883, Louvain in 884-885 and 891-892.[16] In reality there were others, much earlier. Having appeared as early as 810 in Frisia and 835 in the Loire valley, they were introduced along the Seine in 856: "after having pillaged and devastated the towns along the two banks of the river, and even the monasteries and estates located further away, they chose for a resting place a well fortified location near the Seine, Jeufosse (near Bonnières) where they passed the winter peacefully."[17] Likewise, between 856 and 858 they settled on the island of Oscelle where they constructed fortifications and remained until 862.[18] Among the other camps which served as general quarters we should note Pitres, occupied at two different times, in 856 and 865, in spite of fortifications raised by Charles the Bald in 862 and 864, in particular "a castle built of wood and stone"[19] because the site is located at a fluvial crossroad. In 887, they chose Chessy-on-the-Marne to build their camp.[20] In 896 it was Choisy au Bac on the Oise.[21] Their second route of access, the Somme, was thus lined with their fortified settlements. During 859-861, they settled in an unknown location,[22] returned at the time of the great attack of 881,[23] and then settled in Argoeuves in 890-891.[24] In short, the custom of building permanent fortifications originated with the Vikings, as much for the towns as for strategic sites.

These examples are only those found in the best known texts. A systematic study, incorporating archaeology, aerial photography, etc. would surely reveal others. For example, still looking at the banks of the Somme, at Ponthoile on the right bank of the estuary, R. Agache has discovered a perfect ringwork, whose defenses are enormously thick compared to the small size of the enclosed area.[25] It so closely resembles the plans of the great Danish circular forts, that it must be Viking. A little further up-stream, Laviers, a circular enclosure, 36 meters in diameter on the inside, with three gates and surrounded by a moat, is of the same type.[26] Still upstream, but on the left bank, the ancient oppidum Liercourt-Erondelle and probably also that of La Chaussée-Tirancourt, were reoccupied by the Danes.[27] There are still other temporary camps erected by the Vikings which are yet to be located and investigated: at Jumièges, Rouen, Charlevanne, Saint-Denis, Meaux, Melun, Pontoise and Saint-Maur-des-Fossés.[28] Only that of Etrun, mentioned in the 881 texts, is clearly visible today, but, to my knowledge, the site has not been excavated.

Moreover, the Vikings never gave up building fortifications: in 900 Rollo raised some at Pont de l'Arche, in a place today called Les Damps.[29] Later, when the Danes were officially settled in Normandy, they protected the northern border of the Duchy by building forts like the ones at Eu, in 925, and at Arques, sometime before 945.[30] Thus the apparent inactivity in the face of the Viking attack should not be blamed on passivity on the part of the people and their leaders. Rather, from 856 until 879, the Vikings were vigorously at work constructing an unassailable network of fortifications, which rendered harmless any counter-attacks. When this tactic became widespread, especially after 880, it finally provoked action on the part of Charles the Bald, whose response to the challenge had been hampered by lack of funds and support.[31]

What exactly were the Vikings' offensive methods? We have no information about the towns and ancient ramparts which they used. At Noyon they built a camp outside the new walls[32] from which they could attack the city and spend the winter. Perhaps the present Island of the Mohicans is the site of this fortified camp.[33] Contemporaries, anyway, found their methods simple but quite effective, particularly their predilection for islands or circular camps surrounded by water. For example, they decided, in 886, to settle around the Parisian church of Saint-Germain-l'Auxerrois, located outside the walls: "They encircled it with ditches a foot wide and 3 feet deep, interrupted only by the paths necessary to those coming and going. . . . The earth taken out of these ditches was mixed with stones to build up entrenchments." Likewise did they surround Saint-Germain des Prés: "they surround the meadow with entrenchments: on all sides the holy . . . is enclosed by walls." At Chessy their camp included two ditches and a double embankment.[34] At Pont de l'Arche, "Rollo and his men built a fortress with entrenchments and a redoubt, shutting themselves up behind an earthen levee and leaving, in lieu of a gate, a vast open space, traces of which can still be seen today."[35] Thus, at the least, they always dug a ditch which had to be easily floodable, and then used the dirt to make a circular rampart with openings where the gates would have been. Next, the bank was topped by a palisade. Thus, at Eu, the natural oppidum was "situated near the sea"; before it was a bank (*vallum*) topped with a wall of stakes. The Franks broke through and burned this palisade.[36] Probably built on a height, this camp must have contained a thousand warriors as well as the non-fighting population. It was apparently much larger than that on the island on which some of the Normans hid subsequently. The *munitio* or *castellum* (fortified camp) should be distinguished, therefore, from the *castrum* (temporary fort). Elsewhere Abbo uses these two terms, *castellum* and *castrum* to indicate two distinct entities: camps with garrisons and permanent buildings to lodge them, and forts or more temporary refuges, respectively. One such *castrum* was located on the rural domaine of Avaux, near Reims, where some looters took refuge in 882 to escape arrest by Carloman.[37] When the Danes abandoned their camps and forts they would burn them,[38] affording additional evidence of the importance of wood in the building of fortifications. Of particular interest to archaeologists, this suggests that the banks and ditches were not levelled and they should still be visible to surface survey.

An inventory of Viking fortifications between the Seine and the Aa, in terms of these categories, has never been done. There is as yet no equivalent in North-East France to Hague-Dyke, excavated by Michel de Bouard on the tip of Cotentin.[39] In addition, it is clear that, in comparison to Normandy, the Danish settlements were short-lived; the only permanent one was at Guines, in 925. This is not to say that such camps and forts are not there, waiting to be discovered. Indeed, at the frontier of the Duchy of Normandy, a Swedish team was excavating Le Grand Besle de Buchy which they date to the first half of the tenth century.[40] This circular enclosure has an embankment which measures between six and eight meters high from the ridge to the bottom of the ditch. Its interior diameter is about fifty meters. Clearly here is a garrisoned ringwork from the time of the first Dukes of Normandy. In addition, the term *besle* or *bel* is a Norman place name of Scandinavian origin. It comes from *bol,* which designates the tenure or holding accorded to Danish peasants.[41] So these fortified camps situated on islands or plateaux are still to be found and their presence in the countryside of Northern France points up the significance of the Viking challenge to the authorities and the people.

A response from the Franks was late in coming for political reasons which do not concern us here.[42] The kings, unable to find sufficient garrisons to man their fortifications, from 880, cede their place to the nobles and clergy who will finally evolve a solution. The Church, forced to pay a heavy tribute, or danegeld, took the initiative to refortify the ancient Roman towns and to surround the pre-urban centers with walls. Then, around 885, the Franks "begin to resist, no longer in pitched battles, but by constructing fortifications."[43] The *Miracula Sancti Bertini* reveals that, already, around 890–891, the Normans, in the maritime region of Saint-Omer, were striking upon "recently constructed castles."[44]

The first reconstructions of city walls at Noyon and Beauvais, in 880, are in fact symptomatic. The one, ravaged in 859, and the other, burned in 851, were not repaired at that time, probably because the king, Charles the Bald, had given orders to repair only those fortifications between the Seine and the Loire.[45] Once power passed to the non-Carolingian king, Eudes, the respective bishops bestirred themselves to repair the walls. Thoroughly plundered and abandoned in 882,[46] Reims had her ramparts rebuilt between 883 and 887 by Bishop Fulco.[47] In 898, Charles the Simple tried to reassert the royal prerogative on building fortifications when he authorized the people of Tournai, returning from exile in Noyon, to re-erect the walls of their city.[48]

But in other cases restoration was not enough: new construction also appears. In Lotharingia, the bishop of Cambrai, Dodilo, had built an additional wall, enclosing to the north-east the old Roman camp as well as encircling the Abbey of Saint-Aubert.[49] Likewise in Arras the monastic suburb of Saint-Vaast was transformed between 883 and 887 (possibly in 885) by a fortified enclosure, probably wooden. Here again, permission was granted by the Emperor, Charles the Fat. Eudes confirmed this new construction in 890, but it burned in 892. Reconstructed once again, Eudes then besieged the town in 895.[50] It appears that at the end of the tenth century a new enclosure had been constructed with demolition debris. Supported against the Crinchon river, but separated from the Roman citadel, it formed a rectangle, garnished with towers and surrounded by a ditch, about 300 meters long by 245 wide.[51] Here is a case in which the dawning urban phenomenon had been stopped by the Vikings, but this refortification allowed development to begin again. Let us compare this with the old Roman towns which did not develop in this way during the Carolingian period: neither Amiens, Rouen, Tournai, Reims, Noyon nor Boulogne have fortified suburbs, an indication of lesser importance. The only exception is possibly Laon. The plateau had been partially fortified by the Romans. After 882 new ramparts may have been put in, enclosing the entire eastern part of the hill, including the Abbey of Notre-Dame. For the moment, however, archaeological evidence is lacking.[52] Reims was only provided with a fortified suburb, Saint-Remi, in 923 and Lillebonne and Therouanne were abandoned completely.[53]

It is evidence of the extent to which this region was prey to a profound new movement, the fact that new communities in the Carolingian period, born around city gates and religious establishments, built up fortifications more willingly and more readily than did the older towns. The most famous examples are the two monasteries, Saint-Bertin and Saint-Omer. Thanks to orders given by the Abbot Rodolphus, the latter abbey was surrounded by a wall made of earth and stone, forming a trapezoidal enclosure measuring six hundred meters around and covering a surface area of two hectares. The construction was certainly completed by the time the Vikings appeared to ravage the surrounding countryside in 891.[54] The same defensive instinct led the people and count-abbot of Saint-Quentin to protect themselves as well. In 886, three years after the Vikings burned it, Theotricus began construction of a wall intended to enclose the monastery and basilica as well as the non-clerical quarter which had grown up around them; in all, the perimeter measured 900 meters, covering a surface area of five hectares. The wall, finished in 895, was made with large blocks of sandstone.[55] From this moment, Saint-Quentin "took off" and became, as the capital of the Vermandois facing Cambrai, one of the key fortresses in the kingdom of Northern France, withstanding seven sieges in the course of the tenth century.[56] Another new city, Quentovic, founded in the Merovingian period, tried to regain trade by withdrawing to a knoll on the left bank of the Canche, at Montreuil. Count Helgaudus built a castle around 875–880 which successfully repulsed pirate attacks in 898.[57] As for the monastery of Corbie, Abbot Franco had fortifications built in 892 on his own initiative. In 901, he obtained, from King Charles the Simple, acknowledgement of his achievement and a guarantee of immunity for the new walls.[58] So, already between 875 and 892 there were six new fortified urban complexes built.

Whether it is a question of old cities or new, the role played by the king in these developments was small. There is one clear exception: Pontiose, in 885, was entrusted to Altramnus but the Danes seized and burned it.[59] At the same time, Bishop Gauzlinus was restoring the walls of Paris, and it is well known in this case how victorious was the resistance.[60] Another royal project, Etrun-sur-l'Escaut not only suffered an identical defeat, but even served as a refuge for the Vikings. On the other hand the Bishop of Laon, Dido (883–895) organized the construction of fortifications at Pierrepont to protect the people and the relics of Saint Boetien.[61] In the end, only the initiative of the great nobles who were established in a region, men like Rodolphus, Abbot of Saint-Vaast and of Saint-Bertin, or Count Helgaudus, or, even more, the bishops, abbots and count-abbots succeeded, because their of ties to the local population.

There still remains a few particular cases of fortifications: Compiègne, as the principal royal palace, had to be protected. So it was in 877, as had been Saint-Denis, the royal funerary abbey, in 869.[62] The most enigmatic case is Cassel. On the one hand, some consider it to have been a new castle since the Danes came to grief before its walls in 891.[63] On the other hand, Folcuinus tells us, after 968, that nothing remained of the town except ruins. This was also the case with Saint-Riquier, which, defenseless, was abandoned in 881 and even lost its abbots for more than half a century.[64] So, there were new cities which were fortified, others which were not. I leave aside the case of Douai, which is especially complex, (see Demolon's article), but in general as we can see, a new urban geography resulted from this movement towards fortification against the Viking attacks.

The construction techniques, moreover, used by the Franks closely resemble those of the invaders. They had to build quickly, meaning that earth and wood were the primary materials used. More rarely, stone was employed, as at Saint-Quentin, or sometimes as part of a second building campaign, as at Saint-Vaast.[65] In general, these rapid constructions went up after a preliminary ground survey; first the timber was cut, then the ditches were dug wide enough and deep enough so there was plenty of dirt to build a turf embankment. Then stakes, either simple tree trunks whose branches had been cut off or squared timbers, were stuck into this embankment. Sometimes the enclosure wall had towers but there was never a dungeon, much less a central motte. The result, consequently, echoed the Viking strategy: to gather goods and people in the shelter of a more or less circular enclosure. In no respect does this recall a seignorial manor.[66] As temporary and flammable as these enclosures were, they were nevertheless efficient. But it was not possible to build really large ones, as Abbot Fulco dreamed, wishing to surround both the abbeys of Saint-Omer and Saint-Bertin with one single embankment. "The circumference" was so vast that he had to give up the idea. In fact, the largest diameter was more than 800 meters. Before 891, Rodolphus had to be content, therefore, with a *castellum* around Saint-Omer and as the town around Saint-Bertin also developed, it too was finally fortified around 915,[67] in this case, in stone. When we stop to consider the dimensions of these small enclosures we realize that they were very little and just barely reached 200 meters in diameter or 300 in length. Pierrepont was "a slightly bulging oval island emerging about one a half meters above the swamp, 300 meters long, 200 meters wide" surrounded by a palisaded slope.[68] Only Cambrai and Saint-Quentin surpassed these others in size, and they were built in stone. As for forts like those at Etrun, Montreuil, Pontoise, etc., they were either the same size or even smaller. In fact, all these fortifications respond to specific and well defined local circumstances: the goal was to get rid of the invaders as quickly as possible in those places where they posed the greatest threat and where the population was most exposed, in other words, on the banks of the rivers and in the towns.

A comparison between Flanders and England will help us to see more clearly exactly how temporary, disorderly and haphazard these earth and wood fortifications really were. It is today generally agreed that a network of fortresses built after 879 which spread from Schouwen to Bourbourg are due to the efforts of Count Baldwin II the Bald. Among the dozen counted, there were two former Roman forts. Built on the model of a wide ditch with an earthen embankment, they measure close to 200 meters in diameter, and they are none of them further from one another than thirty kilometers. Thus they form a veritable line of surveillance covering the coast from the estuary of the Exant to that of the Aa.[69] These castles were intended to keep guard over the countryside and had their counterparts in England, where, after his victory in 878 over the Danes, King Alfred had ordered that some thirty boroughs be fortified. Here again, each was approximately thirty kilometers from the next. Ten of them were forts, four were old Roman towns, four new centers on flat land and twelve other new centers on heights.[70] In addition, for the most part they were protected by earth and wooden ramparts, as in Flanders and Northern Gaul. Thus the characteristics particular to the latter region become more clearly evident. The isolated efforts of Charles the Bald to remedy the situation had been frustrated in the field by the presence of at least six Viking camps. Then, suddenly, after his death in 877, and especially after 880, as in Flanders and England, the movement towards fortification of the cities gained momentum (cf. General Table). The parallels are so strong as to lead to the conclusion that they are all part of a general movement. But, unlike Flanders and England, the thirty kilometer system did not exist. For lack of a strong political authority, it was not possible to set up regular surveillance zones under a central command. Even more, the proximity to the Duchy of Normandy, the frontier with Lotharingia and growing rivalries among regional powers stimulated the building of fortifications outside the towns which had managed to assert themselves. From this time on, there were about twelve major towns sharing the space between the Aa, the Oise and the Seine; four of them were new foundations, nine were ancient and among these four boasted new suburbs.[71] The response to the Viking challenge is an entirely new urban geography, destined not to change essentially again and to become the basis for urban Northern France in the twelfth and thirteenth centuries.

Outside of Flanders, essentially nothing else changed them. No new towns appeared, no other enclosures were put up before the eleventh century, except for a few outlying villages. Even those at Noyon do not seem to have been enclosed in the tenth century.[72] The fortification movement moved out towards the countryside, beginning a long period of castle construction. Always made of wood and earth, these castles were built on top of natural buttes. The Annales of Flodoardus indicate that during the years 920 to 958, the territorial princes and the chief noble leaders built at least twenty-eight *castella* and *munitiones*, all in the same territory, that is the North of France.[73] None of them can be called towns: they were clearly personal fortifications, housing only the garrisons attached to each one. Even though they were easily destroyed and burned down, they nonetheless opened the way towards a third type, the motte-and-bailey castle which appeared around 950. The clearest and earliest attested examples are Douai, in 965, and Vinchy, in 977.[74]

We are not able to assess more clearly the importance which the Viking challenge posed to Northern Gaul. With their fortified camps and circular refuges topped with palisades the Vikings scattered a multitude of new military strongholds throughout a peaceful kingdom which had forgotten the Roman military order, and thus caused the break up of political power. The kingdom fell apart and smaller units of authority replaced it. The backlash, which became very strong after 879, only strengthened what they, the Vikings, had begun. Viking and Frankish fortifications thus strangely resembled one another, because they were due to the initiative of local and regional groups. Systematic archaeological excavations and the search for traces of these wood and earthen fortifications, organized around four chronological periods, 840–879 (Vikings), 879–circa 900 (Franks), 900–circa 950 (seignorial citadels) and post-950 (feudal mottes), will allow us to shed new light on the Vikings — innovators and inventors.

Table I

TOWNS	VIKINGS RAID	RETORT
Valenciennes	circa 880	—
Tournai	880	898
Cambrai	881	post 888 (faubourg)
Arras	880–881, 883, 890, 925	post 883 (faubourg)
St-Bertin		
St-Omer	860–891	shortly before 881; 895
Therouanne	851, 879, 881, 891 (?)	abandoned
Ghent St-B	851, 870	880
Courtrai	880	—
Amiens	859, 881, 883, 925	abandoned temporarily
Corbie	859, 881	892
St-Quentin	883	883–886
Boulogne	883 (failed)	—
Quentovic	842	875–880 (Montreuil)
Beauvais	851	880
Noyon	859, 890–891	880–c. 896
Cassel		before 891
Reims		883–887
Dorestadt	835, 836, 837, 847, 857, 863	abandoned
Rouen	841, 885	—
Laon	882 (failed)	post 882 (faubourg)
St-Riquier	881	abandoned temporarily
Paris	885	887

Notes

*I wish to thank Mrs. B. Young very much for her translation and Ch. L. Redman for the organizing of this book.

1. W. Vogel. "Die Normannen und das frankische Reich," 793–911, *Gründung der Normandie*. (Heidelberg, 1906), F. Vercauteren, *Etude sur les civitates de la Belgique Seconde* (Brussels, 1934); F. Vercauteren, "Comment s'est-on défendu au IXe siècle dans l'Empire franc contre les invasions normandes?" in *XXXe Congrès de la Fédération Archéologique et historique de Belgique* (1936) 117–32; A. d'Haenens, *Les invasions normandes en Belgique au IXe siècle* (Louvain, 1967).

2. E. Ennen, "Die Entwicklung das Stadt an Rhein und Mosel von 6 bis 9 Jahrundert" and F. Vercauteren, "La vie urbain entre Meuse et Loire du VIe au IXe siècle," both in *La Citta nell'alto Medioevo*, Settimane di studio del Centro italiano di studi nell'alto Medioevo, vol. VI (Spoleto, 1959) 419–52 and 453–84, respectively.

3. M. Biddle, "The Development of the Anglo-Saxon Town," in *Topografia urbana e vita cittadina nell'alto Medioevo in Occidente*, Settimane di studio del Centro italiano di studi nell'alto Medioevo, vol. XXI (1974) 203–30; H. Jankuhn, W. Schlesinger, H. Steuer (Hrg)., *Vor- und Fruhformen der europaischen Stadt in Mittelalter*. Abhandige der Akademie den Wissenshaften in Gottingen, Philosophisch-historische Klasse Dritte Folge, Bd. 83 und 84, Teil I (1973) and Teil II (1974).

4. Derville Alain, ed., *Histoire de Saint-Omer* (Lille, 1981); L. Trénard, *Histoire de Cambrai* (Lille, 1982); H. Platelle, *Histoire de Valenciennes* (Lille, 1982); A. Lottin, *Histoire de Boulogne-sur-Mer* (Lille, 1983); See especially the following unpublished Master's Theses (under the direction of M. Rouche): M. C. Bezanger, "Les Normands de l'Aa à la Seine" (1971–72); F. Baès, "L'évolution topographique de Vermand, Saint-Quentin et Noyon, du Ve au XIe siècle (1981–82). For Douai, see M. Rouche and P. Demolon, *Histoire de Douai* (Dunkerque, 1985) 24–37.

5. Jean Hubert, "Evolution de la topographie et de l'aspect des villes de Gaule du Ve au XIe siècle," Settimane di studio del Centro italiano di studi nell'alto Medioevo, vol. VI (1959) 529–44. Maps still need to be made, but it is clear that there were at least twelve Roman urban enclosures in the northern region; Vercauteren, 1936, 120, n. 4 includes Chalon-sur Saône among those enclosures in ruins; *Anonymi Vita Hludowici*, R. Rau, ed., (Berlin, 1956), chap. 52, p. 352 proves that it was false because in 834 Lothaire spent five days besieging it; *Annales de Saint-Bertin*, F. Grat, ed. (Paris, 1966) 250, hereafter cited at *A. St.B.* Reims was not defended "by any wall, any human hand."

6. M. Rouche, "Le changement des noms de chef-lieux de cité en Gaule au Bas-Empire," *Mémoires de la Société Nationale des Antiquaires de France*, Vol. IV (1969) 53, n. 3 and 56, n. 4.

7. The current state of research tells us nothing about any enclosure around Amiens, nor about a reconstruction in 925, contrary to L. Pietri, *La topographie chrétienne des cités de la Gaule*, without date and place, p. 4. Flodoard, *Annales*, P. Lauer, ed., Paris, (1906), s.a. 925, pp. 29–30, hereafter cited as *Annales*, says that the walls were burned, not rebuilt, in 925; s.a. 950, p. 127, specifies that one tower belongs to the bishop and one to the count. We do not know when it was reconstructed, if indeed it was; *Annales Bertiniani*, R. Rau, ed., (Berlin, 1966), s.a. 885, p. 308, hereafter cited as *A.B.*, adds Rouen in 885.

8. "Sermo de relatione corporis B. Vedasti," *Monumenta Germaniae Historica, Scriptores* quoted as *M.G.H.SS.*, W. Wattenbach, ed. (Hanover, 1887), vol. XV, p. 402 ("Monachi pavore consternati . . . praesertim cum ad hic locus monasterii hujus ad foret

immunitus, nec muris esset circum septus, nec saltem vallo circumdatus"; Mgr J. Lestocquoy, *Etudes d'histoire urbaine, le développement urbain d'Arras* (Arras, 1966, passim).
  9. Hariulf, *Chronique de Saint-Riquier*, F. Lot, ed. (Paris 1894), bk. III, chap. 10, p. 118 "Pontivus vel Wimacus provinciolae tunc castella aut munitiones aut raro aut nusquam habebant et proinde per has liber ingressus ad Franciam hostibus existebat."
  10. M. Rouche, "Les Saxons et les origines de Quentovic," *Revue du Nord* 69 (1977): 457-78; Platelle, 19.
  11. Vercauteren, 1936, 128.
  12. Platelle, 21; Derville, 23; A. d'Haenens, 47-51; the chronology of the Viking expeditions has now been definitively delineated: see Bezanger, 7-23; Baes, 106 and 117 for Saint-Quentin and 104 for Noyon.
  13. d'Haenens, 43.
  14. F. Lot, "La grande invasion normande de 856-862" in *Bibliothèque de l'Ecole de Chartes* (1909), vol. 69, pp. 5 ff.
  15. d'Haenens, 46-49 and 53-55.
  16. Ibid., 50, 52, 54, 57-58 and 312-315.
  17. *A.B.*, s.a. 856, p. 92 ". . . pyratae Danorum alii mediante Augusto Sequanam ingrediuntur et vastatis direptisque ex utraque fluminis parte civitatibus etiam procul positis ac monasteriis atque villis, locum qui dicitur Fossa-Givaldi Sequanae contiguum stationique munitissimum deligunt; ubi hiemem quieti transigunt."
  18. *A.St.B.*, s.a. 858, p. 78 and a. 867, p. 85 ". . . castellum in insula quae Oscellus dicitur a Normannis constructum. . . ."
  19. Ibid s.a. 869, p. 153 ". . . castellum quod ibidem ex ligno et lapide fieri praecipit . . ."; s.a. 874, p. 195 ". . . castellum novum apud Pistas . . ." B. Elmqvist, "Les fibules de Pitres," *Meddelanden Från Lunds Universitets Historiska Museum* (1966-68, 1969), pp. 203-24; In Pitres the discovery of the tomb of a Scandinavian woman proves that this settlement lasted for some time.
  20. *Annales Vedastini*, R. Rau, ed. (Berlin, 1966), s.a. 887, p. 314, hereafter cited as *A.V.*, ". . . iterum per Sequanam Maternam fluvium ingressi Gaziaco sibi castra statuunt."
  21. Ibid., s.a. 896, p. 332 "Nortmanni vero iam multiplicati paucis ante nativitatem Domini diebus ingressi Cauciaco sedem sibi nullo resistente firmant."
  22. *A.B.*, s.a. 860, p. 102; "inani Danorum in Somna consistentium."
  23. Ibid., s.a. 881, p. 300; "sani revertuntur ad castra." "interitum suorum nuntiavere in castra," ibid.; this happened after the battle of Saucourt, so along the bank of the Somme river.
  24. Ibid., s.a. 890, p. 320 "Alstingus autem cum suis Argava super Sumnam sedem sibi firmavit." and s.a. 891, p. 322; "Qui vero Argobio, Ambianis sedem sibi firmant."
  25. R. Agache, *Détection aérienne de vestiges proto-historiques gallo-romains et médiévaux* (Amiens, 1970), Pl. 195, fig. 624.
  26. M. Peigné- Delacourt, *Les Normans dans le Noyonnais aux IXe-Xe siècles* (Noyon, 1868), p. 69; *A.V.*, s.a. 881, p. 300. Laviers had certainly been an important Viking camp since, in 881 Louis III ". . . transiens Hisam fluvium Latverum tendere coepit, quo credebat Nortmannos redire"; p. 304, in 883 Carloman ". . . in pago Withmau contra Latverum cum exercitu ad custodiam regni resedit; Northmanni vero Octobrio mense finiente Latverum cum equitibus et peditibus atque omni suppellectili veniunt"; p. 306 "Nortmanni sua castra incedunt atque ab Ambianis recedunt."
The Somme river was so bordered on both banks by Danish camps. Laviers is mastering a ford making easy the crossing of the river.
  27. Bezanger, 80.
  28. For references concerning those camps which were used for less than a single

winter, see *A.B.*, s.a. 845, p. 64; s.a. 861, p. 105; s.a. 862, p. 106; s.a. 862, pp. 108–110; s.a. 866, p. 156 (this concerns an island facing Saint-Denis); *A.V.*, s.a. 884, p. 306; s.a. 888, p. 318; s.a. 881, p. 300 for Etrun, ". . . rex quoque adunato exercitu in pago Cameracensium venit castrumque sibi statuit in loco qui dicitur Strum ad debellationem Danorum." *A.B.*, s.a. 887, p. 282 in fact, in 881, on the orders of King Louis, this camp was destroyed: "castellum materia lignea quorundam consiliarorum suorum hortato in loco qui dicitur Stromus clausit; quod magis ad munimen paganorum quam ad auxilium christianorum factum fuit quoniam ipse rex Hludowicus invenire non potuit, cui illud castellum ad custodiendum committere posset."

29. Dudon de Saint-Quentin, *De moribus* . . . ed. J. Lair, Paris, 1865, bk. II, chap. 12, p. 154: "Rollo igitur, super responsis suorum laetus a Rotomo divulsis navibus sub huc iter ad Arches quem as Dans dicitur."; II, c. 14, p. 155: ". . . interim Rollo, et qui cum eo erant, fecerant sibi munimen et obstaculum in modum castri munientes se per gyrum avulsae terrae aggere, locoque portae relinquentes spatium prolixae amplitudinis, quod apparet ad tempus usque istius dici." So, the author himself has seen this entrenchment standing up after 1015.

30. *Annales*, s.a. 945, p. 95 "Arnulfus . . . quosdam Nordmannorum qui custodias observabant apud Arcas fudit." s.a. 925, pp. 31–32 "Arnulfus quoque comes et ceteri maritimi Franci praesidium quoddam Nordmannorum aggrediuntur; quo etiam Rollo, princeps, eorum, mille Nordmannos, praeter ipsius inhabitatores oppidi, ex Rodomo transmiserat. Idem vero castrum, secus mare situm, vocabatur Auga; quod circumdantes Franci, vallum quo pro antemurali, cingebatur irrumpunt, murumque infrengentes conscedunt; et, oppido pugnando potiti, mares cunctos interimunt, munitionem succendunt. Nonnuli tamen evadentes finitimam quamdam occupant insulam; quam aggredientes Franci majore licet mora quam oppidum ceperant, capiunt."

31. Ibid., s.a. 925, pp. 31–32.

32. Vercauteren, 1934, p. 171. "Noviomagum petunt ad statuenda sibi castra hiemalia. Illis vero qui per terram iter agebant occurrit rex Odo circa Germaniacum (unidentified place-name); sed propter loci incommoditatem nil eis damni intulit. Nortmanni vero coeptum iter peragentes castra sibi adversus civitatem statuunt." *A.V.*, s.a. 890, p. 320.

33. *A.B.*, s.a. 881, p. 244 for Amiens and Corbie we know only that they were there in 881; Peigné-Delacourt, p. 80. The camp at Amiens was possibly located to the west of the city, at the confluence of the Selle and Somme, but R. Agache has found no trace of it, in spite of numerous surveys.

34. *Annales Vedastini*, B. von Simson, ed., M.G.H in usum scholarum, (Hanover, 1909), s.a. 885, p. 62 "Imperator vero cum exercitu ad castra Nortmannorum veniens quia ex utraque parte fluminis castra fixerant, eis unam fecit deserere, fluvium que transire atque in unum castra ponere." Abbo of St-Germain-des-Prés, *Le Siège de Paris par les Normands*, H. Waquet, Paris, ed. (1962), p. 28, v. 174–175 "Et castra beatum/Germanum circa teretem componere vallis/commixto lapidum cumulo glebisque laborant." II., v. 37–38, p. 68 "Circumeunt castris aequor, sed et undique vallo/ clauditur a! Dominus meus quasi carcere latro." v. 202, p. 80 "vallantes littora circum"; v. 426–427, p. 98 "Mox adhibent propriis vitam sine madere castris/vallatum geminis mortem sine tegmine prunas."

35. Guillaume de Jumièges, *De Gestis ducum Normannorum*, J. Marx, ed. (1914), bk. II, chap. 10.

36. See note 30.

37. Abbo, bk. I, v. 603, p. 60 "dardumque ferens castella petivit . . . castra petit muros ferit . . . exiliunt foras" and *A.B.*, s.a. 882, p. 250 "Maior vero et fortior pars de Nortmannis in quadam villa quae vocabatur Avallis (Avaux-le-Chateau, arr. Rethel, cant.

Asfeld) se reclusit, ubi eos illi qui erant cum Carolomanno sine periculo sui adire nequieverunt."

38. *A. V.*, s.a. 884, p. 306 "Nortmanni vero suo castra incendunt atque ab Ambianis recedunt."

39. M. de Boüard, "Quelques aspects archéologiques de la colonisation scandinave en Normandie," *Revue Historique Droit Français et Etranger*, 4e série, 33 (1955): 22–33.

40. H. Arbman, "Fortifications autour de Buchy" in *Meddelanden Från Lunds Universitets Historiska Museum* (1966–68, 1969), 47–73 and 74–84 for metal objects found at Le Grand Besle; see also in the same volume: J. Lejiksaar, "Restes d'animaux provenant de Grand Besle, 85–116; M. Okborn, "La céramique du Grand Besle," 128–162; E. Thun, "Traces de sidérurgie au Grand Besle," 117–127.

41. M. de Boüard, "Les petites enceintes circulaires d'origine médiévale en Normandie, Château- Gaillard," Colloque des Andelys, 1962, C.R.A.M., (Caen, 1964) 22–33.

42. It should be mentioned that, as until 880, the Vikings were often paid, with *danegeld*, to leave the country, the need for fortifications was less urgent.

43. *A. V.*, s.a. 885, 1965, p. 308 "Tunc Nortmanni sevire coeperunt incendiis, occisionibus sitientes, populumque christianum necant, captivunt, ecclesias subruunt, nullo resistente. Iterum Franci parant se ad resistendum non in bello, sed munitiones construunt, quo illis navale iter interdicant."

44. *Miracula Sancti Bertini*, W. Wattenbach, ed., M.G.H.SS. (Hanover, 1887), vol. XV, p. 512 "In regnum quondam Hlotharii irent (Northmanni) tractantes per maritima transire et castella ibi recens facta optinere incolasque omnes, nisi se dederent mortificare."

45. Vercauteren, 1934, pp. 171 and 272. *A.B.*, s.a. 869, p. 166.

46. See note 5.

47. Vercauteren, 1934, p. 83; *Epitaphe de Foulques de Reims*, P. de Winterdeld, ed., M.G.H., *Poetae Latini* (Berlin, 1909), vol. IV, 1, p. 176, v. 9–10 "Auxit episcopium superaddens plurima rerum. Urbis istius moenia restituit."

48. d'Haenens, 201–2, critical study of the Diploma of Charles the Simple.

49. M. Rouche, "Topographie historique de Cambrai Ve–XIe siècles," *Revue du Nord* 55 (1976): 339–47; Saint-Gery must have been protected by a ditch and a bank at a point unknown to us because it withstood the Hungarians in 953; Trénard, 24.

50. G. Tessier and R. H. Bautier, *Recueil des actes d'Eudes* (Paris, 1967), N° 20, 97 ". . . castrum propter munimen loci, Karolo imperatore petentibus monachis consentiente et permittente, in ipso monasterio ab eis constructum est."

51. Lestocquoy, pp. 171 ff. believes that the Roman walls had already disappeared but, in fact, there is no evidence to prove that this was the case; d'Haenens, 117, dates this fortification to between 885 and 890, which is too vague.

52. Lottin, 43 and 48; M. Roblin, *Le terroir de l'Oise* (Paris, 1978), 213 and 220, suggests that Senlis and Beauvais also had fortified suburbs; J. Lusse, "Occupation du sol and peuplement dans le diocèse de Laon, avant l'an Mil," unpublished thèse de 3e cycle, Université de Nancy (1983), 199–200.

53. P. Desportes, *Reims et les Rémois* (Paris, 1979), 50; G. Coolen, "Les remparts de Thérouanne," *Bulletin trimestriel de la Société Académique des Antiquaires de la Morinie* (1962), t. XIX, 545–65.

54. Derville, 24; d'Haenens, 117, nn. 127, 128; see the long story of an eyewitness, *Miracula Sancti Bertini*, vol. XV, 1, pp. 512–16; Vercauteren, 1936, p. 130 confuses Saint-Bertin with Saint-Omer. The abbey of Saint-Bertin was not fortified until the beginning of the tenth century, twenty-five years after Saint-Omer.

55. P. Heliot, "Quelques éléments de la topographie de Saint-Quentin au Moyen-

Age," *Bulletin de la Société Nationales des Antiquaires de France*, (1958) 106-13; *A.V.*, s.a. 895, p. 330.

56. Baès, 134.

57. J. Lestocquoy, "Les origines de Montreuil sur Mer," *Revue du Nord* 30 (1948): 84-96.

58. d'Haenens, "Corbie face aux Vikings," in *Corbie abbaye royale* (Lille, 1963) 187-90.

59. *A.V.*, s.a. 885, p. 308 ". . . castrum quoque statuunt super fluvium Hisam ad loco qui dicitur Ad pontem Hiserae, quod Aletramno committunt ad custodiendum. Parisius civitatem Gauzlinus episcopus munit. . . . Nortmanni vero dictum igne cremaverunt castrum. . . ."

60. Abbo, passim.

61. See note 28. M. Bur, "Vestiges d'habitat seigneurial fortifié des Ardennes et de la vallée de l'Aisne," (Reims, 1980), vol. II, 97.

62. L. Levillain, "Etudes sur l'abbaye de Saint-Denis," *Bibliothèque de l'Ecole des Chartes* (1926), vol. 87 p. 84. The *castellum*, built to shelter a garrison, was 250 meters wide at the most.

63. d'Haenens, 1967, p. 118; *Miracula Sancti Bertini*, chap. 10, p. 516 "arcem quondam opinatissimam Menapum." Given the qualifier, *quondam*, this citadel, situated on the hill of present day Cassel, could only be the old Roman fortification of the Late Empire. See note 6. There is no archaeological excavation.

64. Hariulf, bk. III, chap. 21, pp. 149-50.

65. d'Haenens, 1967, p. 119, correctly notes that the stone walls found by J. Lestocquoy could only have been raised after the burning of the first chateau in 892.

66. Ibid., 119-21; d'Haenens, *Les invasions normandes, une catastrophe*? (Paris, 1970) 65-67. I find unacceptable d'Haenens' translation of the *Annales Bertiniani* (see note 28). *Castellum* can not be translated as "dungeon," but rather is the total fortification.

67. I call attention to Alain Derville's thesis (unpublished) on Saint-Omer. His reconstruction of the chronology must now replace d'Haenens' as the definitive work on the subject. I wish to thank Mr. Derville for making his results available to me.

68. See note 51 for Saint-Vaast, note 54 for Saint-Omer and note 61 for Pierrepont.

69. d'Haenens, 1967, p. 118 and the map on p. 345; *Vita Winnoci*, M.G.H.SS. (1887), t. XV, p. 776 "Balduinus . . . Calvus fines Flandriae facile usque ad id temporis accessibiles . . . castris munierat."

70. Biddle, 221-23.

71. Saint-Quentin, Saint-Omer, Montreuil, Douai (if it was fortified), Boulogne, Noyon, Beauvais, Rouen, Amiens, Laon, Arras, Cambrai and Paris (if we take Saint-Denis to be Paris) make twelve communities with one possible exception.

72. Flodoard, s.a. 925, p. 30 indicates that Amiens, as well as Arras and the suburbs of Noyon, were burned. "The castle guards and the inhabitants of the faubourgs go out against the Normans . . . and liberate a part of the faubourg."

73. Ibid. Mention the following; p. 2, Mézières in 920; p. 9, Epernay in 922; p. 11, Chevremont in 922; p. 15, Château-Thierry in 923; p. 39, Coucy-le-Château in 927; p. 41, Gouy in Arrouaise in 928; p. 41 Mortagne in 928; p. 44, Vitry in Perthois in 929; p. 46, Mouzon in 930; p. 49, Braisne-sur-Vesle in 931; p. 55, Charleville in 933; p. 55, Roye in 933; p. 68, Montigny-Lengrain in 938; p. 68, Corbeny in 938; p. 70, Chausot in 938; p. 70, Pierrepont in 938; p. 76, Châtillon-sur-Marne in 940; p. 89, Ambly in 943; p. 92, Clastres in 944; p. 99, Omont in 945; p. 116, Montaigne in 948; p. 117, Roucy in 948; p. 124, Mareuil in 949; p. 125, Chauny in 949; p. 128, Braine in 950; p. 131, Briarne in 951; p. 131, Montfélix in 952; p. 145, La Fère in 968.

74. M. Rouche, "Vinchy, le plus ancien château à motte," *Mélanges d'archéologie et d'histoire médiévales en l'honneur du doyen Michel de Boüard* (Paris, 1982), 365-69.

Emporia, Monasteries and the Economic Foundation of Medieval Europe*

RICHARD HODGES

Archaeology is an important means of testing as well as enhancing historical models founded upon documentary research. It offers a quantifiable perspective of the past which complements contemporary, that is, medieval opinions and accounts. Since the last war a flood tide of archaeological fieldwork, to quote M. I. Finley, has made it possible to reconsider traditional frameworks of medieval history. Now, at long last, we can put some scale on the settlements and activities of the Middle Ages. In so doing, we are no longer dependent upon a monk's casual comments on the size of such-and-such a place, or passing observations of settlement density. Similarly, modern approaches to archaeological evidence enable us to ascertain the scale of production, and to crudely measure to distribution of goods and services. *Moreover*, these measurements, in theory, are not confined to the places or material culture of the literate elite. Modern archaeology aims to document — rather as modern censuses attempt to do — the spectrum of society. Such fieldwork is bound to transform our historical impressions of the Middle Ages, offering instead the opportunity to be anthropologists.[1] As might readily be imagined, the anthropology of early medieval Western Europe with its accompanying vein of historical scholarship, is an exciting field of enquiry.

I hope that this paper, in line with the conference, points the way open to medieval archaeologists as to how they may cut across disciplinary boundaries, test major issues and enhance our historical awareness of a formative epoch.

Historians and archaeologists are coming to agree that the origins of the European landscape lie in the 9th and 10th centuries, and not earlier.[2] The pattern of villages took shape in the post-Carolingian world, as did the pattern of fields.[3] Similarly, excavations in countless European towns have given material expression to a 10th- or 11th-century commercial revolution. New towns were founded in all the regions of western Europe, including many old Roman-period centers which were refurbished and flourished once more.[4] Of course, 10th- and 11th-century settlement patterns owed something to earlier Merovingian- or Carolingian-period traditions — but *what exactly* remains as intense and important a debate nowadays as it did when Henri Pirenne published his *Mohammed and Charlemagne* almost half a century ago.[5]

In this paper I wish to examine one central aspect of this debate: the origins of this commercial revolution — the beginnings of the competitive market system which is the particular mark of this revolution. It seems to me that as archaeologists we have an opportunity to explain an important historical phenomenon, one that has defied explanations by anthropologists and geographers studying modern market systems. The origins and development of competitive markets, creating a society in which the laws of supply and demand are of paramount social concern, can be analyzed as a pan-European issue towards the end of the first millennium AD. Hence archaeological fieldwork increases in all parts of Europe. The models explaining the formation of market systems can be tested in a variety of well-documented environmental and political contexts.

Two explanations have been proposed for the origins of competitive markets. First, the importance of long-distance trade between elites has been regarded by many scholars as a key factor leading to regional exchange. Trade in luxuries, it has been argued, stimulates regional exchange and periodic fairs. With growing social complexity these institutions are regularized and become permanent.[6] Rather more scholars, *however*, have stressed the importance of agricultural intensification as the factor triggering the emergence of local markets. Population growth as well as competition between the elite leads, it is argued, to increased production and increased exchange of agricultural goods. Periodic, then permanent, markets are created to meet the needs of this exchange. Historians of the early medieval period have tended to prefer this explanation when seeking to understand the foundations of the 10th-century commercial revolution. Henri Pirenne, F. L. Ganshof and George Duby, to name but three eminent historians of this era, have based their socio-economic models on the miscellaneous Carolingian documentation which would appear to lend some support to the preceding notion of agricultural intensification preceding urban expansion.[7] Yet these historians, like many anthropologists, economists and geographers who have considered this question, are hindered by an imperfect data base. First, the chronology of the transition from a partially commercialized society to one dependent on competitive markets is far from adequate in most cases. Secondly, the means of measuring this transition at all levels of society, across regions, seldom exists. For these reasons, especially in the medieval period, we must have some reservations about the traditional explanations. Medieval archaeology, though offers us grounds for a fresh appraisal of the issue.

The recent development of dendrochronological dating, ever more refined studies of Dark Age numismatics, and highly improved pottery sequences make it theoretically possible for medieval archaeologists to monitor the transition from one socio-economic pattern to another with an important degree of accuracy. Similarly, the gradual development of settlement and, in some areas, regional studies begins to cast light on regional change. In short, we have just arrived at the point where we can begin to assess, if not to test, these alternative explanations.

Let us first examine the evidence for long-distance trade as a key factor leading to regional exchange and markets.

The archaeology of long-distance trade in early medieval Europe is particularly rich. I have outlined much of the evidence for this trade in my book, *Dark Age Economics*. In that book I contended that competitive markets servicing the regions of Late Roman Europe disappeared in the 5th and 6th centuries. A far more primitive network of exchange systems took their place. This network was barely more than aboriginal in character, and focused upon the small royal, baronial, and monastic nuclei of the 7th and early 8th centuries. Towns, as such, simply did not exist. Instead as excavations in Rome, Milan, Tours, Paris, Trier, Cologne and London have shown, once great Roman market centers were occupied by royal courts numbering a few dozen persons, or by monasteries often numbering no more than tens of persons. The villages of this era — the only other class of settlement — seem to have comprised between four and eight farms, roughly 25 to 50 persons.

During the course of the 7th century, however, a trade in luxuries between the European elites grew more significant. Indeed, as many historians noted long ago, trade became focussed around the North Sea basin. The discovery of large trading sites, emporia as they were known then, along the North Sea littoral, in southern and eastern England, and around the Baltic Sea has made it possible to define the pattern of commerce during the 8th and 9th centuries, and to relate it to the development of political authority in each of the kingdoms in which such sites have been discovered. The emporia of Carolingian-period Europe were by far the largest communities of the period. Dorestad, the emporium at the mouth of the Rhine handling Middle Rhenish produce, has been shown to cover more than 50 hectares.[8] Its farmer-traders, I have argued, monopolized the trade-routes northwards to the Baltic, finding there slaves, furs and after AD 800 a vital source of silver and prestige oriental commodities. The scale of Dorestad in comparison to contemporary elite sites as well as villages covering no more than 1 or 2 ha indicates that this was an administered trading network. Comparable trade networks emanated out of other parts of the Carolingian regions: excavations in Ipswich, East Anglia, have documented a major trade connection between Flanders and the otherwise enigmatic East Anglian court between the 7th and 9th centuries. Ipswich reached about 40 hectares in area by about 800. Similarly, we must envisage a similar trade connection between the site of Quentovic in northern France and Hamwih, Saxon Southampton. Southampton was laid out c. AD 700 covering some 45 ha in area, and evidently was the point where alien, Frankish traders paused while they traded with the West Saxon elite.[9]

As yet there is no evidence of comparable trading sites around the Mediterranean. It appears that commerce was restricted to alliances made between the emergent new core of Europe, settled between the Seine and the Rhine, and the courts of certain Anglo-Saxon kingdoms as well as those on the edge of the Baltic.

Two points need to be emphasized about this administered commerce. *First*, the finely dated archaeological remains in emporia like Dorestad and Hamwih enable us to readily identify contemporary sites in their surrounding regions. As a result we can state with some certainty that exchange within these emporia did not lead to archaeologically detectable markets being generated within the region. Towns like Winchester, Dorchester, Bath and Exeter in Wessex remained dormant while 5000 persons regularly inhabited Southampton in the 8th and 9th centuries.[10] The objects of the exchange network were largely monopolized by the elite. These luxuries, were employed as an effective way of controlling competitive groups. The exchange of gifts created a network of personal alliances and obligations that stabilized power.[11] (The restricted sale of trade was seemingly sustained by very low-level taxation.)

Secondly, the well- dated sequence at Dorestad and Hamwih enable us to demonstrate that in these cases administered centers did not lead directly to a system of regionally dispersed competitive markets. In each of the regions in north-west Europe where emporia have been found it is possible to show that new markets occurred as much as one or two generations after the disappearance of the emporium. Hence for example, the port of Late Saxon Southampton owes little or nothing to the Middle Saxon emporium of Hamwih. The Middle Saxon site served the needs of the West Saxon elite, while the Late Saxon port was one of several markets in Wessex serving its immediate locality.[12]

We can conclude, therefore, that long-distance trade did not lead *directly* to the development of the 10th- and 11th-century commercial revolution. Instead, the trade in luxury goods was being channelled into the hands of the elite who used this to maintain and in some cases enhance their status.

Turning to my second theme: did the elite during the 8th and 9th centuries gradually develop their agricultural resources, thus providing the scaffolding, as Henri Pirenne saw it, on which the economic transformation of the 10th century was founded?

In Roman times there was a fluid hierarchy of rural settlements, ranging from cottages to the grandest villas, servicing a similarly complex hierarchy of markets. The same complex settlement hierarchy began to emerge in 10th-century Europe, the nature of the settlement pattern between the 7th and early 10th centuries however, remains more elusive. It is clear from the contemporary documentation that royal centers and monasteries acted as quasi-central places at the apex of the settlement hierarchy. The precise role of these elites centers, though, appears to be rather contentious. The royal sites, for example, had to accommodate peripatetic households; so a number of settlements were maintained within a region by one extended royal family. Yet, even the largest of these—the Carolingian imperial palaces at Aachen and Inelheim—were comparatively small settlements. By contrast, the monasteries were fixed points in an underpopulated landscape. Great monasteries like St. Riquier in northern France, St. Gall in Switzerland and Farfa in central Italy possessed estates the size of small kingdoms. Administrative surveys of these estates by their 9th century abbots has led George Duby to describe them as: "overpopulated islands where biological increase stimulated by agrarian prosperity pushed men to the verge of security, (and) contrasted with ocean-like stretches of country where farming was well-nigh impossible."[13] Were these monasteries in effect small towns serving their overpopulated islands? If so, does the great increase in prosperity enjoyed by monasteries throughout western Europe in the first half of the 9th century—the period of the Carolingian Renaissance—mark an attempt to generate greater income from their ever-growing estates?

Early medieval monasteries have been seldom excavated though they are frequently described by contemporary monks. Not until the Cluniac reform after the turn of the millennium do we begin to gain some impression of the scale and complexity of these places as regional centers. In the 8th century, for example, only the abbey churches offer us an insight into the scale of the settlements. Most were evidently very small. At the start of the 9th century, the period of the Carolingian Renaissance, miscellaneous excavations show the existence of new, enlarged abbey churches. From the same period there is also the schematic blueprint from the new monastery at St. Gall. This blueprint dates to the climax of the Carolingian Renaissance, either 819 or 820. Following the detailed analysis by Walter Horn,[14] it offers us a rare idea of the variety of buildings as well as the size of a major monastery at this time. In particular the plan indicates the size of the claustral zone—the ritualistic area—in relation to the zones designed for accommodation and for production. It points to increased emphasis being placed on ritual from the early 9th century onwards, and the productive capacity was being enlarged in line with this. Horn has calculated that the monastery illustrated on this plan should have accommodated just under a hundred monks, and slightly more lay brothers engaged

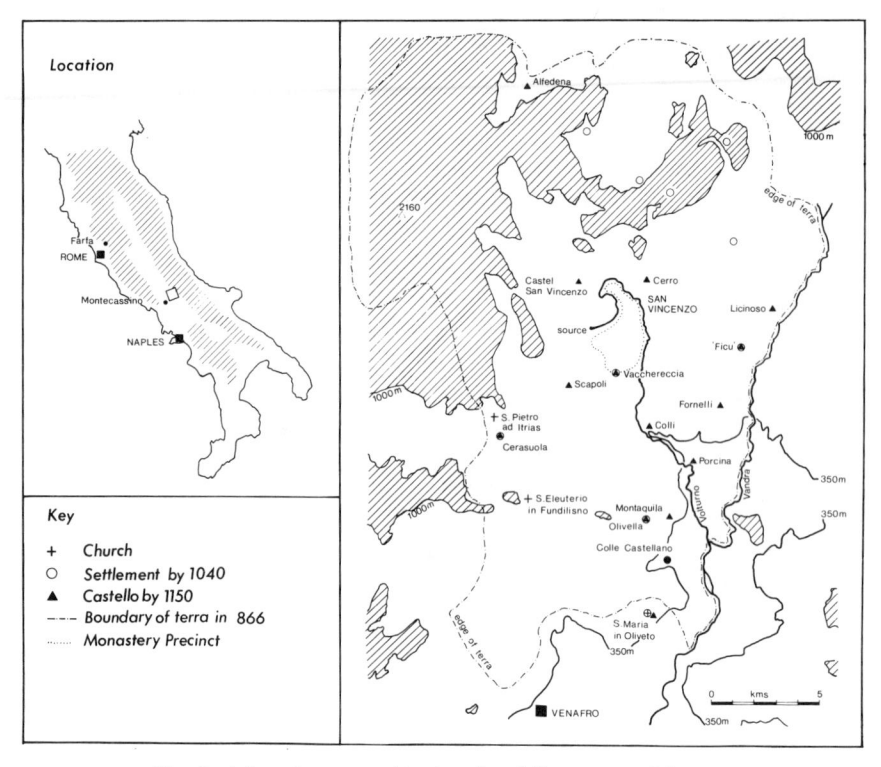

Fig. 1. A location map showing San Vincenzo and its *terra* as it was in the ninth and tenth centuries.

in maintaining the community. But is this an accurate impression of one of Carolingian Europe's more celebrated centers? If so, it suggests 1) increased emphasis on ritual in spatial *and* demographic terms, and, consequently it would seem to suggest 2) increased emphasis on the management of estates and production of agricultural goods to sustain this enlarged community.

In 1979, I was invited by the Soprintendenza Archeologica del Molise, to excavate just such a monastery in central Italy, and at the same time I was granted permission to survey the surrounding monastic estates in order to document the character of the regional production-distribution systems between the Later Roman period and the 11th century. Since 1980 in a series of six campaigns we have begun to shed new light on these issues. While it is premature to be definitive about any conclusions, there are some preliminary results which are worth drawing attention to.

San Vincenzo is situated in Central Italy, in the foothills of the Abruzzi, on the frontier of the Lombard kingdom of Beneventum (fig. 1). The abbey was founded in the early 8th century and was evidently a modest settlement until the beginning of the 9th century. Then, for half a century, with Beneventan patronage it enjoyed a great period of wealth and esteem. In 881, however, the monastery was sacked by the Arabs, and it never regained its standing. The 12th-century *Chronicon Vulturnense*[15] describes the monastery's later history in great detail. In particular, it reports the systematic foundation of villages within the *terra* of San Vincenzo in the second half of the 10th century.[16] The abbey itself gained a modest new lease of life in the early 11th century when it was rebuilt, and then in the early 12th century the old monastery was abandoned in favor of a new site. By this time local lords had forcibly stolen most of its property.

When we began our project in 1980 we assumed that the monastery would have been no larger than a hectare in area—the size of S. Gall—and we were greatly influenced by historians of the monastery who have accepted that the Carolingian-period monastery lies buried beneath the romanesque one, which still stands in a greatly refurbished form. In fact, the Carolingian-period monastery covers an area of about 5 ha along the western banks of the river Volturno, some 400 meters from the later 12th-century settlement. The excavations have uncovered a large part of this complex close to one of its entrances, and we have mapped and sampled other parts of this great settlement.

I will briefly describe the site (fig. 2) before returning to my theme.[17] First, the monks who founded San Vincenzo chose a site which had been an Iron Age (Samnite) and Republican sanctuary, and a later Roman (5th- to 6th-century) villa. The 8th-century monastery appears to have been built within the later Roman villa. So far we have only found the remains of one building, a church (possibly the abbey itself) with an altar, which belong to this first monastery. By contrast, the 9th-century ruins are extensive. Close to the entrance stood a major reception room, an *aula* similar in plan to those surviving at Aachen and Ingelheim (fig. 3). Beneath the marbled upper floors (which have collapsed) was a small crypt at one end, and three undercrofts. The central undercroft was used as a stable early in the 9th century. This grand building overlooked its own garden to the south, and a small chapel to the north. On one side of the garden was a small, finely decorated range which has been interpreted as the guests' refectory. The main monastery, however, lay to the south. Visitors progressed from the entrance passages into a large reception room with benches. Our excavations show that this room was impressively decorated with a series of paintings by north Italian, Beneventan and Roman artists (fig. 4). The paintings, it seems, give some small indication of the monastery's northern affinities and alliances and at the same time they demonstrate how the monastery wished to portray itself (fig. 5). Once in this vestibule, the visitor could choose to sit, perhaps glancing at the floors paved with inscribed tiles, or he might enter the refectory with the reader's pulpit to the right

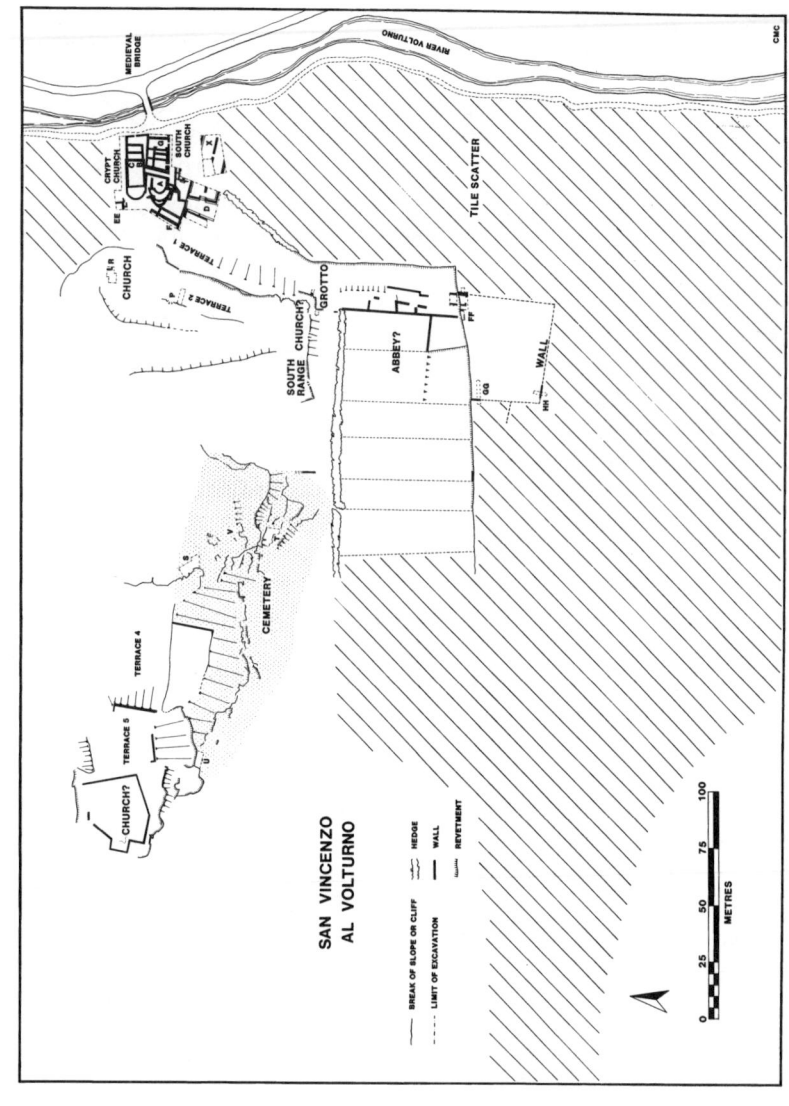

Fig. 2. A preliminary survey of the early medieval settlement at San Vincenzo al Volturno, showing the excavations between 1980 and 1983.

Fig. 3. A view looking eastward across the ruins of the "South Church"—a ninth-century aula at the entrance of the monastery which was built on top of an eighth-century church (note the remains of its altar in the foreground), and a later Roman (fifth to sixth century) funerary basilica (part of a villa). The partitioned cells were stalls and workshops concealed by a colonnaded portico and beneath the now-destroyed main hall and chapel on the floor above (i.e., at the height from which the photograph is taken).

Fig. 4. A detail of a painting of a saint, thought to have been the work of a ninth-century artist trained in Rome.

The Economic Foundation of Medieval Europe / 67

Fig. 5. A detail of the prophet Micah — part of a painting depicting several prophets in the vestibule that led either to the abbey church or into the refectory. The painting of Micah dates probably from the early to mid-ninth century and is almost certainly the work of an artist trained in the northern Lombard kingdom.

Fig. 6. A general view of the early to mid-ninth-century monastic refectory. The reader's pulpit is in the far left of the large room, tucked into the corner. The central wall would have supported an open arcade made of re-used columns and capitals. The floor tiles frequently bear the maker's mark and several have short inscriptions and graffiti. The room could have held many hundreds of persons and is a means of measuring the community at its zenith.

(fig. 6), or he might proceed down the room to the cloisters. Finally, he might pass on southwards to the great building in the vineyards which we believe to be the new abbey church erected, according to the *Chronicon* by Abbot Joshua in the early 9th century. Nestling beside these vineyards we have discovered the remains of the workshops where window, vessel and liturgical glasses were made.

On the second terrace overlooking the entrance area we have located a colonnaded corridor leading to a church, and further around the hill are the ruins of another range culminating in a fine building which may well be another of San Vincenzo's nine churches. On the central slopes of the hill is the monastic cemetery, and the hill is crowned by another of the monastic complexes.

We have located the south perimeter wall, and together with the seating capacity of the refectory we can begin to estimate the size of San Vincenzo at its zenith. The *Chronicon* tells us there were five hundred monks here when the arabs sacked the monastery in 881, but the seating capacity of the refectory indicates a figure of about 300 monks and as many lay brothers might be nearer the mark. Even so, it is an enormous complex, twice the size of St. Gall, for example—and as such ranks among the largest Carolingian-period monasteries in Europe. This may be due to its location. Like Monte Cassino it lay just beyond the southern frontier of the Empire, a day's journey from Byzantine territory. A monastery of classic Carolingian design would have been an impressive symbol of the Empire and a bastion on a vulnerable front. At the same time it would have been a powerful, stabilizing factor in the unstable Beneventan territory. But when the Empire (and Beneventum) dissolved into civil war, what then?

The excavations answer this question clearly. The 10th century settlement was once again very small. The sacked buildings remained derelict and the few surviving buildings have a temporary character. San Vincenzo was a shadow of its former self; indeed, it became a center consistent with the region rather than a center consistent with European status. The successive rebuildings of the 11th century monastery were modest by 9th century standards and far from outstanding in their age; these too were consistent with its regional rather than any international status.

Returning to my principal theme, let us see what light these excavations and the survey throw on agricultural intensification before the 10th century. The archaeological survey of San Vincenzo's territory indicate that there were no dispersed farms in this region after the 4th century AD. Instead, we have found traces of two mid-slope settlements dating to the period in question. We have carried out exhaustive excavations of one known as Vacchereccia 4kms from the monastery, and we have trial-trenched another at Colle Castellano 25 kms away at the southern end of the *terra*.[18] These were small, loosely aggregated settlements exploiting environmental niches before AD 900. Indeed, there are no signs, as far as we can tell of increased agricultural activity before the 10th century. Then, according to the *Chronicon*, these settlements were legally defined and enlarged with a complement of colonists. Late in the 10th century, not before, the monastery began to administer its lands effectively. Large-scale fortifications unearthed at Colle Castellano begin to confirm the history. This new management presumably led to increased production — we have yet to document this — and to rapid demographic growth.[19] In short, our survey suggests there were poor settlements in the region and little emphasis on agricultural management before AD 1000. We must therefore hypothesize that the large 9th-century community, like the earlier, smaller 8th-century community at San Vincenzo supported itself by cultivating the plateau on which the monastery is located. By contrast, the large 9th-century monastic ranges seem to be a symbol of the Carolingian *renovatio*, created by at least two successive abbots who had connections with the Carolingian imperial court.[20] Hence, like the St. Gall plan, the 9th-century monastery at San Vincenzo appears to roughly divide between a ritualistic zone and a zone where the workforce lived and worked to maintain the center. This investment, it seems, was designed to stabilize the region and at the same time it presented an image of wealth and authority to those potentially hostile forces in southern Italy. Obviously, the monastery collected some form of rents and services from its villagers, but to judge from our initial investigations of these sites, their management was hardly significant to form San Vincenzo's well-being until late in the 10th century. Then, after 950, when the monastery was a spent political force and the community numbered tens of persons, it was compelled to intensify its agrarian practice, like monasteries all over the western world. With declining donations and the rise of numerous competing secular lords such a policy now made economic sense.

The research at San Vincenzo is far from completed, and in any case we must evaluate whether this illustration is typical of the pattern of the European economy. If it is, we must scrutinize the historical data in the light of this study, using the measurements of this monastery and its region to put some scale on the system as a whole. Needless to say, though, more surveys (of early medieval sites) and excavations (of Carolingian-period settlements) are necessary in France and West Germany to test our results.

In conclusion, the archaeology of long-distance trade indicates that the commerce detected by historians was in fact monopolized by the elite. There was no immediate attempt to establish market systems while prestige goods could be obtained through trade. Some of these prestige goods were evidently invested in enlarging and promoting elite centers — centers like San Vincenzo where imagery stabilized a fragile political situation. Archaeology also indicates that the development of a new economy, and indeed the formation of the European states was largely a reaction to the collapse of the previous system. Economic intensification followed a period of instability, not stability.

History, of course, tends to emphasize tradition, and archaeology emphasizes change. In a sense the sources complement one another. Yet, the archaeology draws attention to a very important social and economic transformation, far more momentous than most historians have acknowledged. Europe passed swiftly from being an underdeveloped continent conscious of its Roman glory in Carolingian times to one matching in every respect the social and economic achievements of the Romans less than 150 years later. This transition undeniably owed something to the systemic evolution of the Carolingian-period kingdoms, yet it marked a radical break with the past when the new towns, for example, were founded and formed throughout Europe. If we wish to explain how such a transformation occurred, archaeology compels us to examine the role of the elite Carolingian warriors, faced with instability, in the history of those changes. Indeed, we might echo Marvin Harris' point when he says history repeats itself in countless acts of individual obedience to cultural rule and pattern, and as a result, revolutions require great opportunities as well as great men and women.[21] Archaeology, in fact, not only calls us to recognize the importance of institutionalized mechanisms of adaption—once we have regionally documented data—but it also addresses our attention, if we have finely dated remains to the existence of thinking individuals whose actions are influenced by their perception and interpretation of what goes on around them.

Medieval archaeology, I would claim, by measuring the magnitude of social and economic change between the 8th and 11th centuries, is giving us an insight into perhaps the greatest revolution and revolutionaries of the Middle Ages.

Notes

* I would like to express my gratitude to Professor Charles Redman for inviting me to the conference at Binghamton, and for arranging a teaching position within the state university at that time. I should like to thank Paula Bienenfield, Emlyn Myres, Paul Szarmach and Vincas Steponaitis for their hospitality and good company. The San Vincenzo project has been run in collaboration with the Soprintendenza Archeologica del Molise and I am especially grateful to Dott. Gabriella D'Henry, Soprintendente, for her assistance and support. The project has been funded by the British Academy, the British School at Rome, the Craven Fund, the Society of Antiquaries of London and the University of Sheffield.

1. See Richard Hodges, Method and Theory in Medieval Archaeology, *Archeologia Medievale* IX (1982): 7-39.

2. George Duby, *The Early Growth of the European Economy* (London: Weidenfeld & Nicholson, 1974); Richard Hodges, *Dark Age Economics* (London: Duckworth, 1982).

3. M. W. Beresford and J. G. Hurst, *Deserted Medieval Village Studies* (London: Butterworth, 1971); Jean Chapelot and Robert Fossier, *Le village et la maison au moyen age* (Paris: Gallimard, 1980), Chris Wickham, *Early Medieval Italy* (London: Macmillans, 1981) 92-114 all provide essential introductions to this subject.

4. Hodges, *Dark Age Economics*, 162-98.

5. Henri Pirenne, *Mohammed and Charlemagne* (London: Hodder and Stoughton, 1937); Richard Hodges and David Whitehouse, *Mohammed, Charlemagne and the Origins of Europe* (London: Duckworth, 1983).

6. B. W. Hodder and D. Lee, *Economic Geography* (London: Methuen, 1974) 137 ff; Carol A. Smith, "Exchange Systems and the Spatial Distribution of Elites: The Organization of Stratification in Agrarian Societies," in *Regional Analysis*, ed. C. A. Smith (New York: Academic Press, 1976) II: 309-74.

7. Pirenne, 236 ff.; F. L. Ganshof, *Feudalism* (London: Longman, 1964); Duby, 91-128.

8. See W. A. van Es and W. J. H. Verwers, *Excavations at Dorestad: 1-the Harbour* (R. O. B., 1980); Hodges and Whitehouse, 98-101.

9. Hodges, *Dark Age Economics*, 67-69 (Southampton), 73-78 (Ipswich); on early medieval London see Alan Vince, "London — the Anglo-Saxon Phases," in *The Rebirth of Towns in the West*, ed. B. Hobley and R. Hodges (London: Council for British Archaeology, 1987).

10. Figures based upon work of Philip Andrews and Mark Brisbane who are currently leading the excavations in Southampton for the City Museum.

11. The classic paper on this topic is Philip Grierson, "Commerce in the Dark Ages: A Critique of the Evidence," *Transactions of the Royal Historical Society* 23 (1959): 123-40. On taxation and its significance for production see Richard Hodges, *Dark Age Economics*, 130-41 and idem, "Diet in the Dark Ages," *Nature* 310 (1984): 726-27.

12. Richard Hodges, *Dark Age Economics*, 162-84; my thesis, however, challenges the more traditional historical appraisal of the evidence which is rather reductionist, for example: Martin Biddle's classic essay "The Towns," in *The Archaeology of Anglo-Saxon England*, ed. David M. Wilson (London: 1976, 99-150).

13. George Duby, *Rural Economy and Country Life in the Medieval West* (London: Arnold, 1968) 14; see also David Herlihy, "Church Property and the European Continent, 701-1200," *Speculum* 36 (1961): 81-105. The views of Duby and Herlihy are repeated and often elaborated in many of the modern histories of early medieval western Europe. To be fair it should be stressed that these two historians have been critically cautious when analyzing their data and not a little aware of the potential of archaeology to put some sense of scale upon the issue.

14. Walter Horn and Ernest Born, *The Plan of St. Gall*, (Berkeley: University of California Press, 1979).

15. V. Federici, [ed.] *Chronicon Vulturnense del Monaco Giovanni III*, (Rome: Fonti per la Storia d'Italia, 1933).

16. Chris Wickham, *La tierra di San Sincenzo al Volturno e il probleme dell'incastellamiento di Italia centrale* (Siena: University of Siena, 1985).

17. Richard Hodges and John Mitchell, *San Vincenzo al Volturno: Archaeology, Art and Territory* (Oxford: British Archaeological Reports, 1985).

18. Richard Hodges et al, "Excavations at Vacchereccia (Rocchetta Nuova): A Hilltop Settlement in the Upper Volturno Valley, Molise," *Papers of the British School at Rome*, 52 (1984): 148-94.

19. Chris Wickham, *La tierra di San Vincenzo*.

20. Richard Hodges, John Moreland and Helen Patterson, "San Vincenzo al Volturno, the Kingdom of Benevento and the Carolingians," in *The Third Italian Conference*, ed. Caroline Malone and Simon Stodart (Oxford: British Archaeological Reports, 1984): 261-85 is the first attempt by members of the project to assess the symbolism and to place it into the European ideological context brilliantly described by Walter Ullmann, *The Carolingian Renaissance and the Idea of Kingship* (London: London Press, 1969).

21. Marvin Harris, *Cannibals and Kings* (London: Fontana, 1978, 208-10).

SECTION II
Materials of the Archaeological Record

Ceramic Technologies of Medieval Northern Morocco

EMLEN MYERS

This paper describes the results and future directions of a research project on technological variation in the medieval pottery of northern Morocco. The general aim of the research is to describe and interpret the range of potting techniques employed in the medieval period in Northern Morocco. The aim of the paper, however, is to summarize what has been learned so far about the pottery at a particular medieval site in this region, the Islamic town of Qsar es-Seghir (AD 1250–1458). The pottery consists of deluxe and common wheelmade wares which are designated Hispano-Moresque wares, and handmade coarsewares. The handmade wares are of a neolithic technological level, but have no specific cultural designation. Information for the study comes from historical sources, archaeological investigations at Qsar es-Seghir, and ethnographic investigations of traditional pottery industries in the region.[1] A discussion of the pottery from other medieval sites in northern Morocco (fig. 1) will place the findings from Qsar es-Seghir in the broader setting appropriate to these investigations.

Historical and Archaeological Background

Documentary sources report that Qsar es-Seghir, a small natural harbor on the Straits of Gibraltar, was the site of an Islamic settlement by AD 711.[2] The earliest remains found at the site, however, date from the thirteenth century, during the Marinid Dynasty. Based on archaeological evidence, the span of Islamic occupation at the site has been divided in half, into an early Marinid period (AD 1285–1350), and a late Marinid period (AD 1350–1458). This chron-

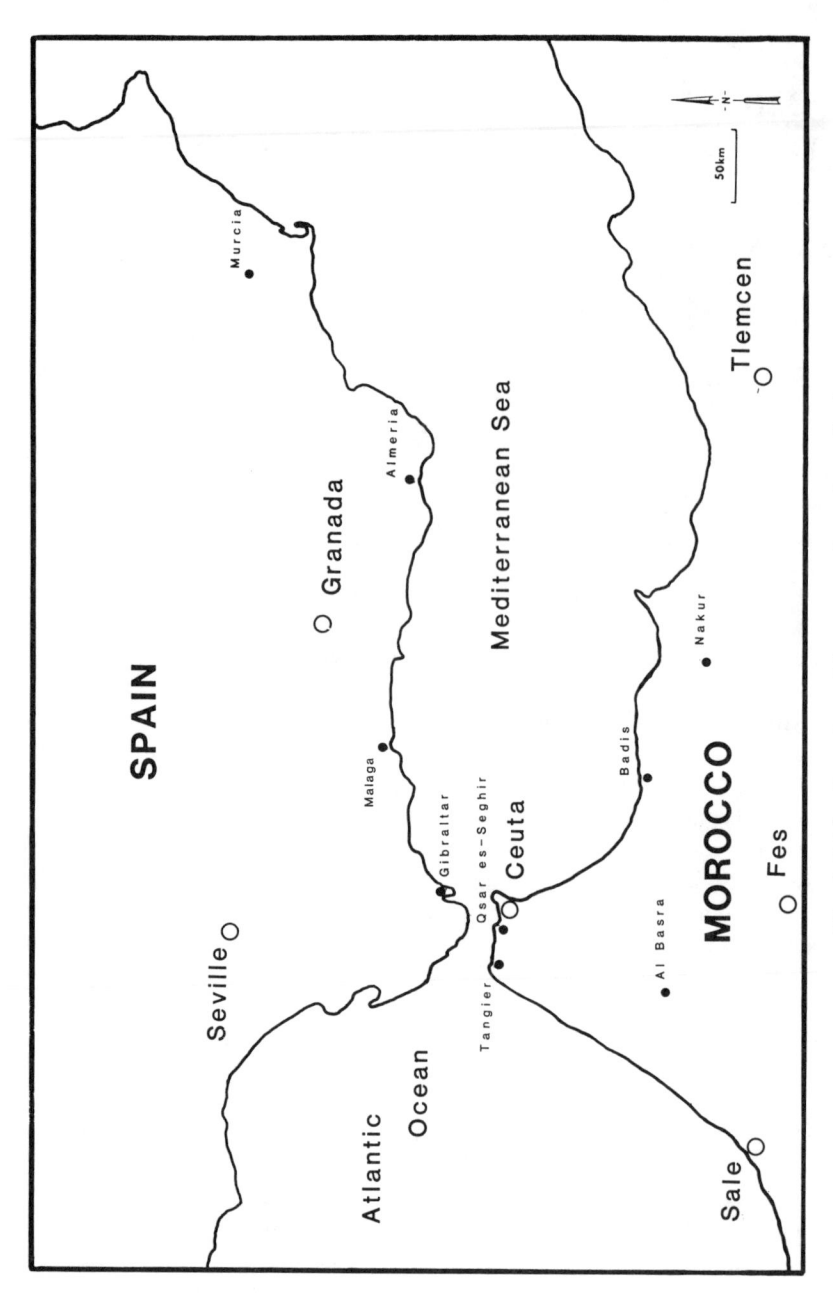

Fig. 1. Map of northern Morocco and southern Spain.

ology was developed from architectural and ceramic evidence for the purpose of comparing the pottery used over time in the Marinid occupation of the town.[3] The end of the Marinid period at Qsar es-Seghir came in 1458 when a Portuguese expeditionary force seized the town, expelled its Muslim inhabitants, and began what was to be a one-hundred year occupation.[4] The ceramic evidence of this transition is the sudden appearance of large quantities of imported Iberian maiolica.[5] Recent excavations in northern Morocco have provided direct evidence of pottery manufacture in the Islamic period at Qsar es-Seghir and have expanded investigations to include other medieval townsites in northern Morocco including Badis, Basra, and Nakur.[6] Basra and Nakur are earlier than Qsar es-Seghir, dating to the eighth through twelfth centuries, while Badis dates to the same period.

The Islamic pottery found at Qsar es-Seghir falls into three general technological categories: handmade low-fired wares (roughly 1% of the excavated assemblage by sherd counts), wheelmade commonwares (94%), and deluxe wares, including tin-glazed wares (3%).[7] The handmade wares, the crudest pottery in the assemblage, are present in small quantities throughout the Islamic occupation. Wheelmade utilitarian wares predominate over all other categories of pottery at Islamic Qsar es-Seghir, occurring in a wide variety of forms and fabrics. These include plainwares, manganese mat-painted wares, and simple lead-glazed wares. The most common vessel forms will now be described. Braziers or chafing dishes are usually unglazed and sometimes have mat-painted or incised designs (fig. 2, A). Jars are necked or neckless with one or two handles, and are usually plain (fig. 2, B–D). They vary from large vessels for water storage, to smaller ones for drinking. Large splaying-walled basins are unglazed and were probably used for food preparation tasks such as the mixing and kneading of dough (fig. 2, E). The most common cooking form is a shallow casserole that is usually lidded and glazed on the inside (fig. 2, F). These casseroles may have been used for baking or for cooking over the direct heat of an open fire or brazier. The convex-bottomed casseroles are compatible in size and shape with the braziers. Oil lamps are common and occur in glazed, plain, and mat-painted varieties (fig. 2, G–I). The glazed conical plate is the most distinctively Islamic vessel form of the assemblage, and was used for serving food (fig. 2, J). These bowls are usually decorated with curvilinear black designs under a clear lead glaze. Another common wheelmade form is the globular cooking pot (fig. 2, K), which has a collar-like vertical rim and is glazed on the inside.

The deluxe wares, which comprise the remaining 4% of the assemblage, are most easily distinguished from the commonwares by their surface treatment. The most numerous deluxe wares are lusterware, resistware or *cuerda seca*, and *sgrafito*.[8] These vessels occur most often in open bowls or plate-like forms similar to the commonwares. They frequently have pairs of small holes

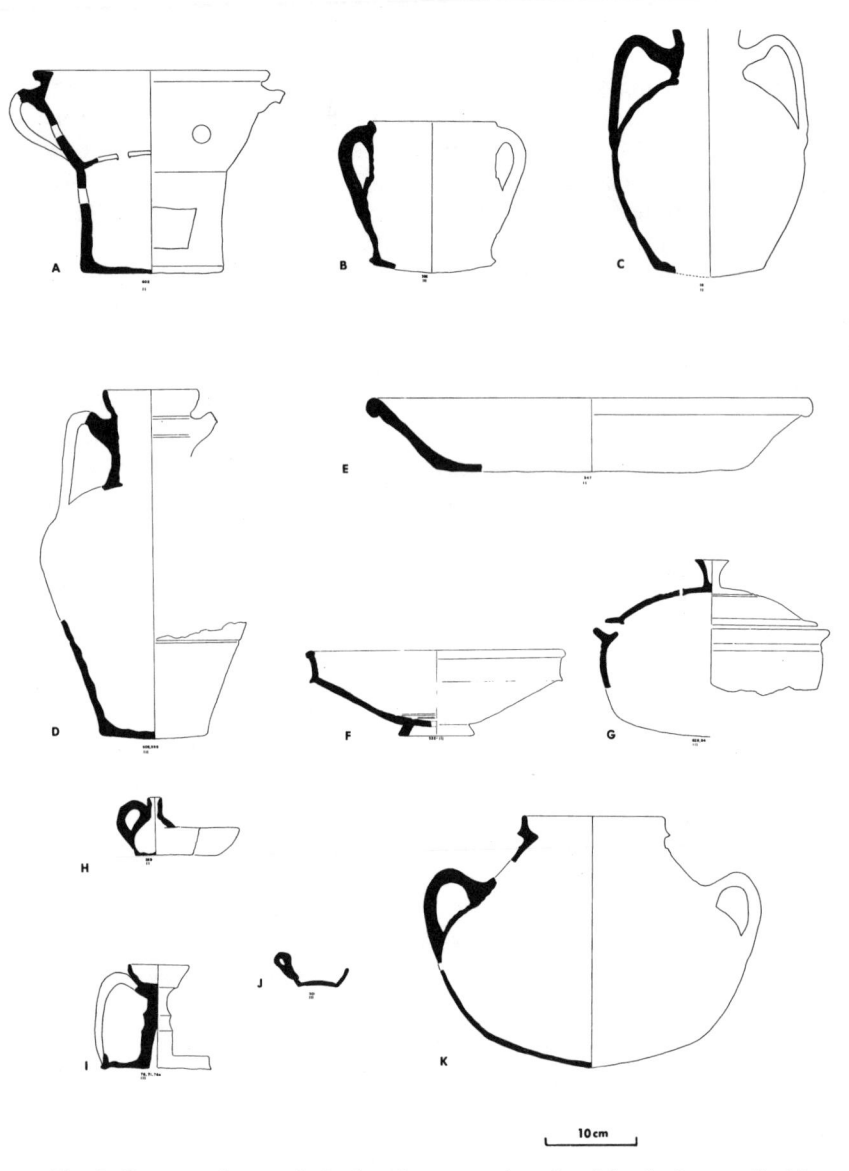

Fig. 2. Common forms of wheelmade pottery found at Islamic Qsar es-Seghir. A: brazier; B-D: jars; E: basin; F: conical plate; G: casserole; H-J: lamps; K: globular cooking pot.

in the base, indicating that they were hung up for display by a loop of cord. Lusterware is a lustrous glazeware decorated with copper oxide paint. The metallic appearance of the oxide paint was achieved through a laborious and failure-prone process involving three separate firings.[9] The examples of lusterware found at Qsar es-Seghir are most probably from either Malaga or Manises, both of which were Spanish production centers of the time. Resistware occurs in several distinctive styles, all of them having in common a manufacturing process wherein a glaze-repelling agent is applied to some part of the vessel in order to separate the glaze that is applied later. Also found at Qsar es-Seghir is a particular kind of *sgrafito* unique to late medieval Islamic assemblages in the western Mediterranean. This is an unglazed ware that occurs in thin-walled, ring-based jars. The fabric is cream-colored or cream-slipped. On these vessels a distinctive pattern of incised curvilinear design is achieved when the areas of black-fired manganese paint are scratched through with a stylus to expose the lighter clay fabric beneath it. This ware is probably a ceramic imitation of a black smudged copperware produced at the same time by Mamluk smiths in the eastern Mediterranean.[10] A well-known decorative ware relatively conspicuous in its low frequency is the blue painted lusterware pottery made in Malaga.[11]

Recent Investigations of Hispano-Moresque Pottery

Medieval Islamic pottery of Spain and northern Morocco, known as Hispano-Moresque ware, has been described in print and exhibited in museums since late in the nineteenth century.[12] Recently, considerable new information on the topic has become available from stratigraphic excavations in the region, and from detailed descriptions of museum collections.[13] A major part of these recent contributions has come from research in northern Morocco by teams of Moroccan, French, and U.S. researchers who are still at work. Related physical and chemical provenance investigations being conducted on ceramics from the Straits region are also beginning to increase our knowledge of the production sites for these materials as well.[14] Following a brief review of the pottery from the recently excavated sites mentioned above, a more detailed description of Qsar es-Seghir's pottery will be provided.

The overall pattern of change in Hispano-Moresque pottery indicated by recent research is an interesting one. Despite the varying techniques of manufacture there is no evidence for a cumulative increase in skill or for an improvement of technique in the throwing or firing process, from the earliest excavated north African examples of Islamic pottery at Nakur and Basra, to the latest Islamic examples left at Qsar es-Seghir in the 1450s. Aside from stylistic variation, the major shifts in the assemblages occur simply in the pro-

80 / EMLEN MYERS

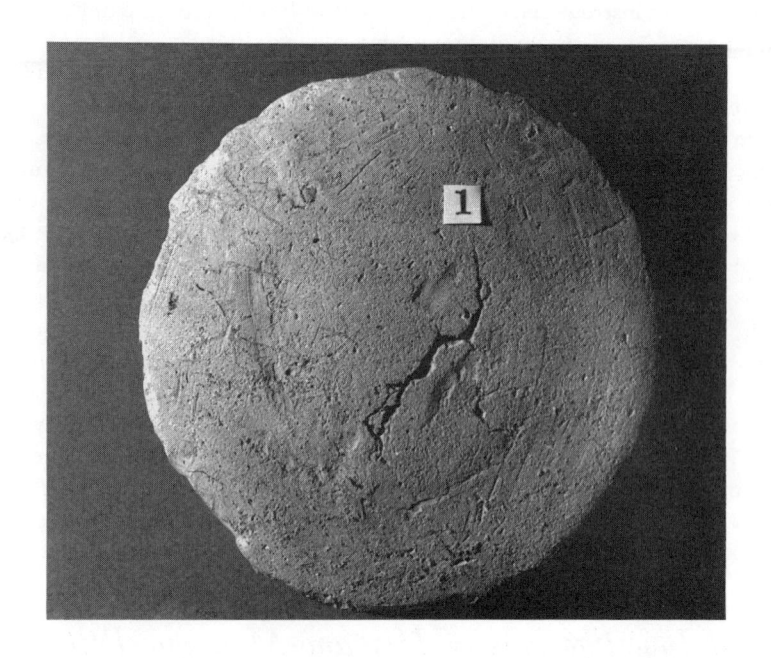

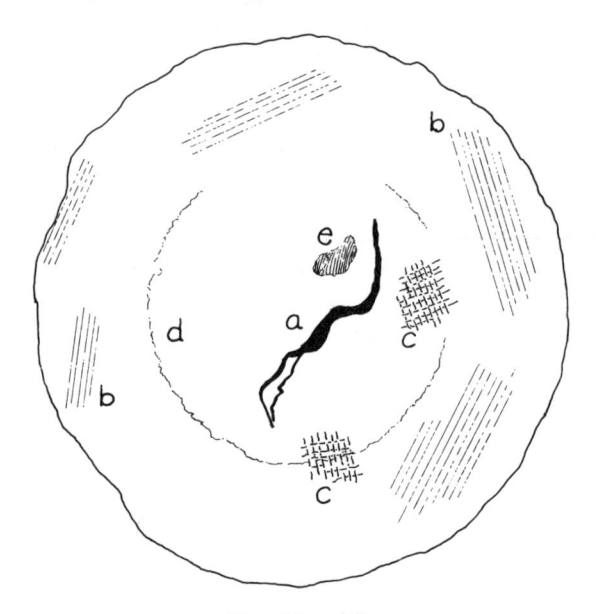

Figs. 3A and B

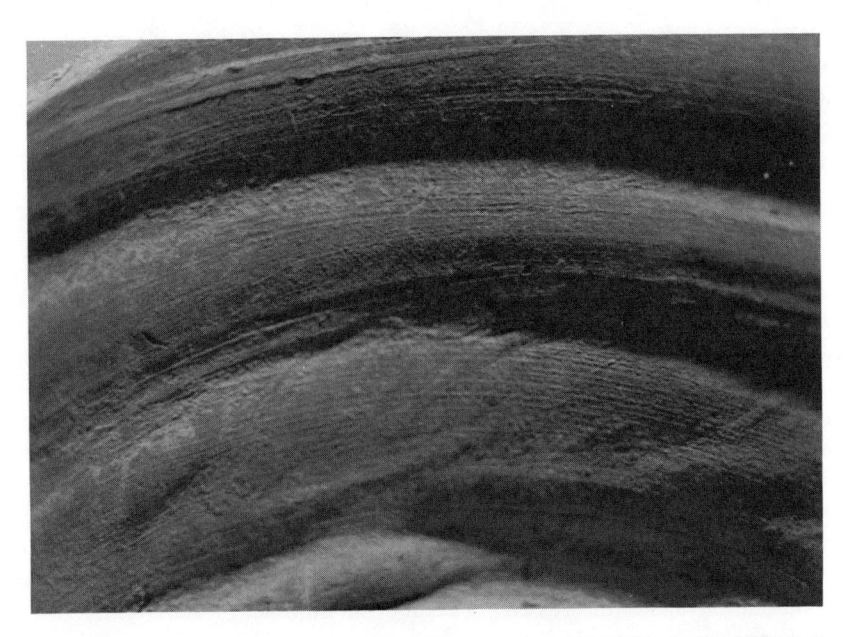

Fig. 3. Traces of the potter's work used to reconstruct manufacturing techniques. A: photograph of jar base, B: schematic drawing of the same jar base, C: photograph of jar with spiral finger grooves on interior indicating use of potter's wheel.

portions of vessels made by different techniques and the functional categories of vessels on which these different techniques were used. Glazed wares, for example, occur at the ninth through eleventh century agricultural town of Nakur, though only among the relatively rare decorative wares. The vast majority of Nakur's assemblage is unglazed wheelmade utilitarian ware.[15] Basra, a site founded shortly after Nakur in one of Morocco's major agricultural regions, also has a large proportion of wheelthrown plainware, with only a few pieces of decorative glazed wares in its earliest levels.[16] Handmade vessels, which are relatively rare at Qsar es-Seghir, occur in a wide variety of utilitarian forms at Basra. The earliest examples of wheelmade, glazed utilitarian forms occur in what are probably late thirteenth century contexts at Qsar es-Seghir and Belyounesch.[17] The frequencies of glazed utilitarian forms increase through time at both sites.

The site of Badis, located between Qsar es-Seghir and Nakur on the Mediterranean coast, is roughly contemporaneous with both Belyounesch and Qsar es-Seghir. Its ceramic assemblage shows a marked increase in the proportion of handmade vessels through time as certain vessel forms, which were originally wheelmade and probably imported from Spain, were later copied and replaced by locally manufactured, handmade functional equivalents. This description of the pottery from several medieval sites in northern Moroccan provides a background against which to present a technological analysis of changes that occurred in Qsar es-Seghir's pottery.

Reconstructing the Potting Techniques at Qsar es-Seghir

The manufacturing techniques of Qsar es-Seghir's commonwares were reconstructed by examining the traces of the vessel forming process.[18] This method is particularly useful for commonwares such as the Qsar es-Seghir materials because many of the traces of manufacture remain unobscured by subsequent finishing. The base of the jar in fig. 3 exhibits these kinds of traces and serves as a good example of this method of reconstruction. First, the large s-shaped crack in the center of the base (letter a in the fig. 3-B) is the result of uneven shrinkage during the drying process. This defect frequently results when the production technique called "throwing off the hump" is used. It is caused by an unequal degree of alignment of clay particles in the base and walls of the vessel.[19] The uneven alignment leads to differential shrinkage during the drying process, which in turn causes stress great enough to rupture the vessel. Thus, the s-shaped crack is the result of a special pottery production technique, the main advantage of which is the rapid production of pottery.

The steps of manufacture for this jar have been reconstructed as follows: First, the top portion of the mound of clay on the potter's wheel is centered and pulled up into the rough vessel shape while the wheel is in motion. This is indicated by the spiral groove on the interior of the vessel (fig. 3-C). The vessel is then cut from the mound of clay that remains on the wheel and is placed by hand on a piece of cloth for drying. Letter e in fig. 3-B is a fingerprint left by the potter when lifting the vessel off the wheel. Traces of the cloth impression are pictured as letter c in fig. 3, B. The cloth would slow the drying process, making cracking less likely. The next step was the trimming of the base with a sharp edge. Parallel scratches that resulted from the trimming are pictured as letter b in fig. 3, B. Another indication of the trimming is that fabric impressions remain only in the area around the center of the base. The circle shown by letter d in fig. 3,B marks the outer boundary of this area. It is noteworthy that this final trimming step need not have been carried out by someone as highly skilled as the person who threw the pot. This particular jar contrasts greatly in appearance with the more labor intensive wet-smoothed, convex-based jars mentioned earlier (fig. 2-D) that characterize the early period examples at Qsar es-Seghir.

Technology of Qsar es-Seghir's Commonware Through Time

The findings from the technological analysis of Qsar es-Seghir's pottery will now be summarized. The most common vessel form throughout the early (AD 1285–1350) and late (AD 1350–1458) periods at the site was a communal serving dish called the conical plate (fig. 4). The characteristic attributes of this vessel are its turned ring-foot and sharp upward carination just before the rim. Examples of the form found in the early and late periods show a consistent set of differences in manufacturing technique. Early examples are glazed inside and out, and have manganese painted designs under a clear glaze, while the late examples are glazed on the interior only, and have no painted designs. Early examples are of a fine fabric while the later examples occur in both coarse and fine fabrics. This difference in fabric is attributable either to the type of clay source used, that is primary versus alluvial clay deposits, or to different tempering or levigation procedures having been employed by the potters. A few examples have a copper-oxide green glaze and some show unsuccessful attempts at black, manganese painting under a clear glaze. Comparing the early and late conical plates on the basis of form and traces of manufacture, it is apparent that the early examples are made with more care (fig. 4). Examination of the profile and surface of the vessels for the two periods show that re-wetting followed by smoothing, as well as a greater degree of leather-hard shaving on the wheel, were involved in the manufacture of the early forms. Also, the early forms have a greater maximum diameter, both absolutely and relative to their height. In sum, this evidence indicates a lower input of labor per vessel.

Other changes in common forms distinguish the early from the late commonwares at Qsar es-Seghir, and most of these differences can also be linked to decreasing labor expenditure. For example, three kinds of lamps appear in the early assemblages (fig. 2, G–I). One is a simple pinched bowl with a strap handle (G). A second form is a pinched-disc mounted on a thrown clay pedestal (H). This form resembles a lathed wooden candlestick in shape. In the third variant a wheel-thrown jar serves as the oil reservoir (I). A strap-handle is attached to the jar and a hand-formed nose is attached opposite the handle as a wick-trough. Oil is added through the neck of the jar. All three of these types of lamps were used during the early Islamic occupation of the site, while during the late occupation, the labor intensive nosed form was no longer used. Another example of this pattern occurs among the common jar forms. Among the varying jar-bases are a smoothed convex form (fig. 2,C) and an unfinished, blade-trimmed form (fig. 2,B). As with the other forms described above, the labor intensive variant drops out of use in the late Islamic occupations. A final instance of this pattern is seen in the painted designs on the pottery. Glaze

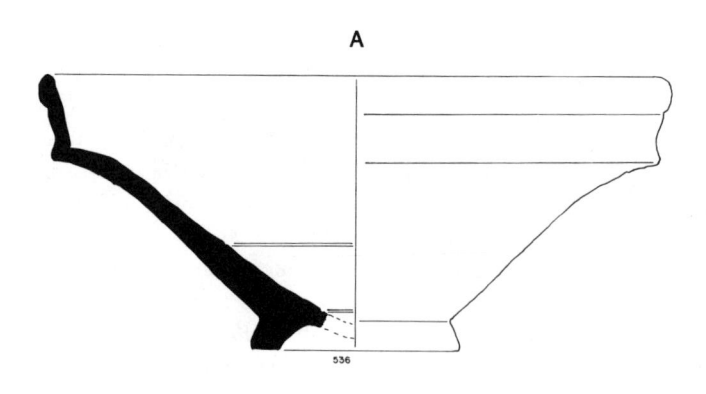

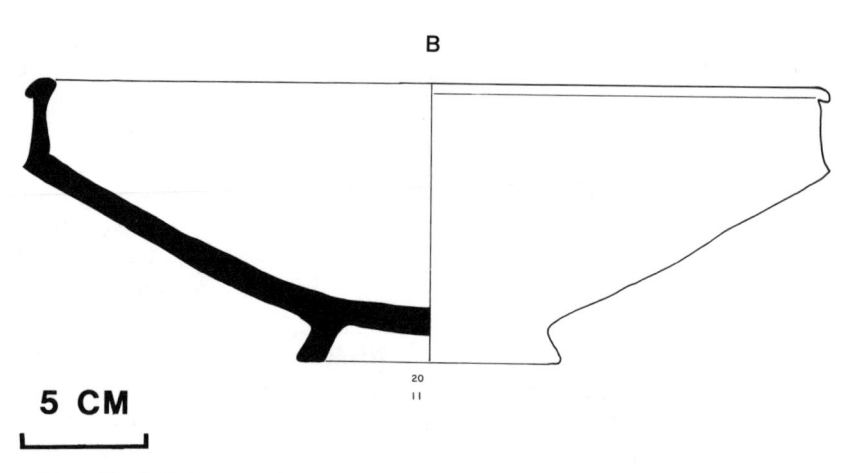

Fig. 4. Conical plates such as these examples found at Qsar es-Seghir were used as communal serving dishes in medieval Morocco. A: late period (AD 1350–1458); B: early period (AD 1285–1350).

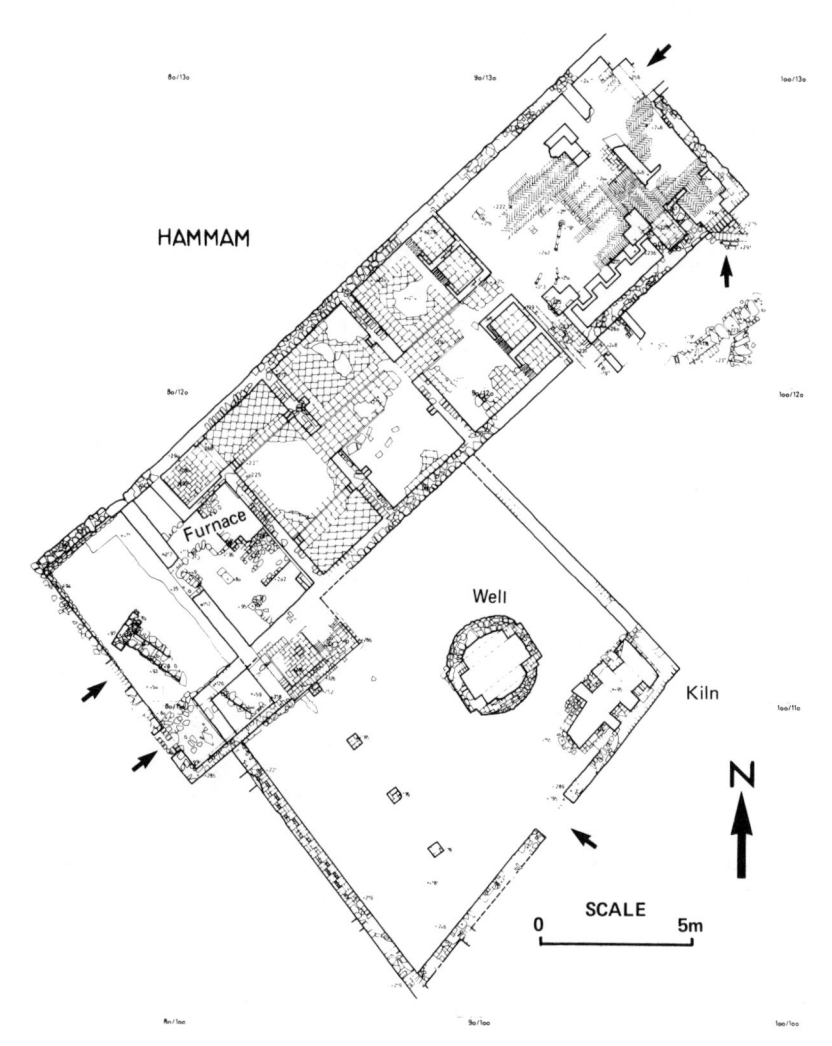

Fig. 5. Late period kiln and shop area excavated at Qsar es-Seghir (AD 1350–1458).

paint decreases in relative frequency and in its the care of application through time, and the mat-painted designs on jars decrease markedly in fineness and orderliness.

Having discussed both broad patterns of technological change in medieval Moroccan commonwares and some specific technological changes that took place among the Qsar es-Seghir commonwares, we can now summarize what is known about where and how these pots were made. To date, three medieval pottery shops have been identified in northern Morocco, one at Qsar es-Seghir and two at Basra. The pottery shop excavated at Qsar es-Seghir contains a well, the partially preserved fire-chamber of an updraft kiln, a small enclosed burning surface which may have been used for glaze preparation, and an immense quantity of wasters and other debris from pottery manufacture.[20] The shop was constructed after and adjacent to the city bath or *hammam* (fig. 5), which has been dated on stylistic grounds to around 1350.[21] The inventory of wasters found at the kiln-site has allowed us to date the kiln's products relative to the rest of Qsar es-Seghir's ceramics and also suggests which ceramic types found at the town are likely to be local products. The diagnostic wasters are all wheelmade commonware from the late period, including examples of most of the vessel forms used at that time. Details of the kiln loading procedures employed at the shop are provided by the cockspurs found scattered throughout the excavated area of the shop (fig. 5). Cockspurs are small, three-armed clay pieces used to separate glazed wares during firing, keeping them from sticking together. "Glazed bricks" were also found in the area of the shop and were apparently placed on edge between the load of pots and the perforated floor of the firing chamber, to allow for the proper circulation of heat. These bricks were probably not intentionally glazed but may have become glassy on the surface due to their having been fired a number of times. The kiln at Qsar es-Seghir appears to have been similar to the rectangular-based, updraft kilns still in use in Morocco and Spain today.[22]

Direct evidence of pottery manufacture has also been found at the site of Basra.[23] There, portions of two different probable ninth century kilns have been excavated within the city walls. The kilns resemble Roman examples known from Europe more than they do any traditional Spanish or North African kilns of today.[24] They were updraft kilns and, unlike the oblong example at Qsar es-Seghir, were more nearly square in plan. The major products of the Basra kilns appears to have been corrugated plainware jars and nosed lamps.

Economic and Social Factors Affecting Pottery Production

To understand the variation in pottery manufacture evident at Qsar es-Seghir it is necessary to examine some of the economic and social factors that may have influenced the potters. For this reason the social setting of the two broadly defined kinds of pottery, the handbuilding and the wheel-assisted industries, will be discussed.

In contemporary Morocco there are two variants of the handbuilding technique. One involves modeling the desired shape out of a single piece of clay and the other involves constructing the vessel by coiling and pinching rolls of clay into the desired shape. Vessels produced by these two methods, both now and in the medieval period, are burnished and frequently painted as well. Vessels are fired in batches of less than ten. They are primarily for food preparation, although handmade service and display forms were still common in Morocco in the early twentieth century.[25] Wheel-assisted pottery production, the other common category of manufacture, includes all those techniques that employ a fixed-pivot potter's wheel. The one variant of the potter's wheel used in contemporary Morocco is the familiar kick-wheel.[26] The potters who use the wheel also use brick and mortar constructed updraft kilns. The production level achieved with these techniques is measured in the hundreds of vessels per kiln-load.

Based on ethnographic data, it is possible to make several generalizations about the contrasting social and economic settings of the two industries. Handmade wares are produced by women in a rural household setting as a part-time or seasonal activity for home consumption or for occasional sale or exchange in weekly periodic markets. The wheelmade wares, by contrast, are manufactured in workshops by males who work full-time as potters. Within the shops themselves there is also specialization, with the work divided according to skill, seniority, and ownership of equipment. These shops operate continuously throughout most of the year and supply pottery to urban households that do not produce their own wares. With regard to the geographical distribution of the techniques, the handbuilding method is used in rural areas by a large number of potters who make a few pots at a time for home consumption, and the wheel-assisted method is employed in urban communities by a few specialists who work long hours making pottery for a large clientele.

Quantifying Pottery Production and Consumption

While these ethnographic generalizations are useful in themselves for understanding medieval pottery production, it is worthwhile taking the additional step of introducing numerical values into the discussion. For the handbuilding industry, the amount of time required to make a vessel varies considerably depending on the amount of care that goes into the shaping of the vessel after it has its initial form. The observed rate of manufacture for the coil and pinch method of handbuilding is about one and one-half to two hours per vessel including firing.[27] The craftspeople observed spent about half of the total time per vessel on the burnishing process. As a daily rate this would be six to eight vessels. As an average estimate for handbuilding techniques this is too high, since the vessels produced at this rate are quite a bit truer in shape and more carefully burnished than both nineteenth century and medieval examples.

The estimate for the wheel-assisted industries is based on field observations made in the town of Ksar el Kebir in 1980.[28] The potter observed uses a kick-wheel and employs techniques similar to those of Qsar es-Seghir's medieval potters. These include the rapid production technique called "throwing off the hump," and the throwing of large vessels in sections that are later laminated together. The modern potters at Ksar el Kebir use a kick-wheel mounted in a pit, a common ethnographically observed pattern throughout Morocco.[29] The pots are fired in a two-chambered updraft kiln. The capacity of the contemporary kiln was reported by its owner to be twelve hundred pots. This figure is based on the reported capacities of a kiln for vessels of a number of different sizes. About eighty-five percent of the pots in a kiln-load survive the firing in a usable form and a firing cycle takes about ten days to complete. This means that three firings per month or twenty-seven firings per year can be undertaken. The yearly estimate was arrived at by excluding the three month Moroccan rainy season during which potters are usually inactive. The potential production rate of any similarly equipped pottery shop would then be about twenty-seven thousand pots per year.[30]

The average life of utilitarian pots, based on reports from traditional Moroccan households, is three years.[31] In other words, at least one third of the pots in a household *must* be replaced every year. The number of earthenware vessels required at any one time by a household is about thirteen.

In discussing the question of modern-to-medieval correspondence, it is important to remember that an observed rate of production or consumption is caused by a complex combination of factors which include more than the practical limitations of a set of potting techniques. The basic non-technological determinant of the volume of production for different industries is the amount of time devoted to potting. Reasonable upper limits of a potter's work schedule might be dictated by common-sense estimation while potential lower limits are harder to define. It is also possible to use historical and technological evidence to estimate the differences, if any, between the modern and medieval rates of production.

The two major pieces of potting equipment for the wheel-assisted industries are the wheel and the kiln. There is no direct evidence for the type of wheel employed at Qsar es-Seghir. The range of techniques evident in the archaeological pottery suggest, however, that a high-momentum fast wheel was used. The relatively smooth, turned surfaces on conical plates, however, indicate that the axle bearing had to be at least as precise as those used on today's wheels. The kiln in use at medieval Qsar es-Seghir was similar to those used today at Ksar el Kebir.[32] The complete dimensions of the firing chamber of Qsar es-Seghir's kiln are not recoverable, but the similarity of its size in plan to those of contemporary kilns indicates a similar capacity. A number of ancillary activities such as fuel procurement must have absorbed the labor of medieval potters and their assistants. Today these commodities are most frequently purchased by the potters so, while these acquisitions are reflected in the cost of production, they do not require labor *per se*. This would suggest a slower production rate for the medieval period. The modern figures for household pottery use and disposal rates are applicable as a general range for the medieval period. The modern household use-rate may be somewhat lower than the medieval period due to the introduction of plastic and to the higher frequency of metal artifacts today. The similarity of archaeological and ethnographic cooking vessels, and the continuity of cooking techniques indicated by a thirteenth century Andalusian cookbook[33] suggest that changing cooking practices have not had a significant effect on the number of vessels required per household. The upper limit on the longevity of pottery is determined by the cooking practices employed and by the physical properties of the vessels themselves. Whether or not a vessel is discarded prior to mechanical failure, however, would be highly variable. It is known that fresh earthenware was considered desirable for important annual feast days in the medieval period.[34] This practice is also indicated by the fact that recipes from the period frequently specify the use of new cooking vessels for certain dishes.[35]

To summarize this assessment of production rates, we can say that a number of factors affecting the rate have been identified, and we can conclude, based on the consideration of these factors, that modern wheel-assisted industries provide a good estimate for Qsar es-Seghir's potential production rate. The medieval rate may have been slightly lower since most raw materials were probably not acquired through commerce, but by the direct efforts of the potter.

The population of Qsar es-Seghir in the late Islamic period was about 270 households.[36] This estimate is based on the proportion of the site given over to residential space in excavated areas and the average house size encountered. These two figures combined with the total town area, a little more than two hectares, were used to arrive at the household estimate. The implication of this estimate for the household pottery consumption rate of the town is as follows. Two hundred and seventy households, each requiring that about one third of their thirteen earthenware vessels be replaced every year, would need more than eleven hundred new pots per year. Comparing this estimate to the previously discussed ethnographic industry we reach the conclusion that the potential production capacity of Qsar es-Seghir's workshop was approximately twenty-five times what was needed by the community. As has been noted, it is quite possible that the per household consumption rate of pottery was somewhat higher in the medieval period. However, even if this were true and the rate was, for example, twice as high, Qsar es-Seghir's potential for production would still have greatly exceeded its consumption.

Before we consider the implications of these figures, the potential effects of transport conditions on medieval pottery production must also be discussed.

Wilkenson,[37] in his discussion of pottery from the Islamic city of Nishapur, indicates that transport conditions can have a dramatic effect on the regional organization of pottery production. He notes the contrast between Iran and Egypt. Iran, with few navigable rivers, had pottery workshops located at most medium-sized or larger towns in the medieval period. Egypt, on the other hand, had very different natural transportation routes. The Nile allowed Egyptian potters to build workshops up river from the major population centers and then ship the wares down river by boat to their customers.

The western Mediterranean is more varied than Iran or Egypt in its natural transportation routes. Major towns like Fes and Granada had no adequate routes of water transport, while at the same time most of the major commercial centers were located on the shore of the Mediterranean. The coastal locations were serviced by commercial vessels in great numbers. Unlike the Nile, the Mediterranean required larger vessels. The difficulty of land transport of goods and even land travel in Morocco and Spain are legendary. The Geniza documents contain a personal letter written in the twelfth century in which a merchant wishing to travel a few hundred kilometers westward from Libya to Tunisia is advised that the quickest way to go is to book passage to Seville and from there proceed by boat to Tunisia.[38] This letter points out what are, for this discussion, the two most important facts about medieval transport: (1) land travel was extremely difficult in comparison to sea travel, and (2) seaborne travel between nearby ports was irregular when it occurred at all.

Returning to the issue of pottery production at Qsar es-Seghir, it has already been concluded that the production capacity of a wheel-assisted full-time shop would be roughly twenty-five times the probable household demand for pottery in a town of Qsar es-Seghir's size. We can take the idea further and describe the three possibilities that follow:

1. About one year of work would supply the town with enough pots to last for twenty-five years.
2. Three weeks of work per year could supply the town with enough pots to last for one year.
3. The needs of twenty-five towns the size of Qsar es-Seghir could be supplied by a shop working on a nine month schedule.

These different ways of viewing the relationship between production and consumption capacities can also be thought of as alternative hypotheses about the patterns of pottery distribution. Number one could be called the "stockpiling hypothesis." In this hypothesis potters would produce a large surplus of pottery over a short period of time and then sell it to a go-between or market it themselves over a period of time when no new pots were being made. In what could be called the "itinerant pottery hypothesis" a single potter would travel to a number of shops in different towns, working in each long enough to replenish local supplies. The third possibility, which could be called the "distribution network hypothesis," would be a potter working a full-time schedule in one location while supplying a number of different towns or villages.

The "distribution network hypothesis" cannot account for the presence of the kiln at Qsar es-Seghir. The town was smaller than any of the other production centers in the Straits region, with Malaga, Ceuta, and Tangier all having populations at least ten times as great. Also, after survey and test excavations in the areas surrounding the site, it can be said that the ceramics attributed to Qsar es-Seghir were not distributed to the countryside.[39] Thus, the principal arguments against the "distribution network hypothesis" are (1) the lack of evidence for export to the countryside and (2) the apparent irrationality of shipping large quantities of pottery to towns with their own industries, especially since short distance sea travel between nearby locations was so irregular.

The "stockpiling hypothesis" would also appear inappropriate for several reasons. The costs of storage and the immense labor investment with no short-term compensation are the two obvious negative arguments. The "itinerant potter hypothesis" on the other hand, seems to have quite a bit to recommend it. It could be an ideal solution to the problem of slow overland transport: move the potter rather than the pot. Perhaps some mixture of multiple workshops for a single potter, under-employment, and stockpiling will, as investigations progress, provide the most reasonable explanation of the disparity in apparent production capacity and actual production levels.

An additional datum for this discussion, based on chemical analysis of pottery, is the apparent fact that the construction of the pottery kiln at Qsar es-Seghir marks the first time that a local specialist industry existed there.[40] This means that before 1350, Qsar es-Seghir's wheelmade pottery was probably imported.

In the light of all of these considerations then how are we to view the transition from the early to late manufacturing techniques evident in the pottery unearthed at Qsar es-Seghir, the primary aspects of this change being the decrease in labor expenditure per vessel among the common-wares wares? First let us consider the evidence provided by the sixteenth century chronicler Leo Africanus. He writes that quantities of timber were exported from Qsar es-Seghir to southern Spain[41] which itself had been deforested by the eleventh century. He provides no precise dates for the beginning and end of the trade. It is possible that the changes in Qsar es-Seghir's pottery assemblage that occur at around 1350 were a secondary effect of the discontinuation of the timber trade. The availability of transportation on boats coming from Andalusian ports to load on the wood and naval stores could explain the lack of locally produced, wheelmade commonwares in Qsar es-Seghir's early period (AD 1285-1350). The thousand or so vessels needed at the site each year could have been brought along on the Andalusian timber boats. The end of the trade in timber would account for the start of local commonware pottery production. A potter may have seen the opportunity and set up shop at Qsar es-Seghir, or he may have been induced to start the industry by more direct means, possibly government fiat.

If this account is accurate, then how do we explain for the late-period production techniques that required less labor input per vessel? First of all, the shift in techniques must have been the result of circumstances, perhaps an expanding market, that existed somewhere other than at Qsar es-Seghir. The late period production techniques clearly did not evolve in response to local conditions at the diminutive port town. For, as consumption rate estimates indicate, it is unlikely that there was pressure on the potter(s) to increase the rate of production at Qsar es-Seghir itself. Thus the explanation of the change must be sought through the consideration of regional economic and political events. It is this approach that is taken in a longer work by the author on the same subject.[42]

Technological Conservatism and the Handmade Tradition

An additional point must be made, one concerning the handmade pottery tradition that has been so persistent through time in rural areas of northern Morocco. The conventional suggestion that peasant conservatism is the main cause of this long duration of "primitive" techniques in pottery and other handicrafts[43] seems improbable. It can be suggested rather, that the handbuilding technique represents a compromise or balance between the need for a functionally adequate ceramic product, and the low labor and capital inputs dictated by a subsistence economy. Frequently, in the medieval period and before, this technique must have provided a small-scale alternative source of pottery to the rural and urban settlements which either had no need of or access to wheelmade wares. This better accounts for the technique's survival than does the hypothesis of generalized technological conservatism. A brief discussion of the assemblages of Nakur and Badis that follows will further illustrate this point. At Badis, new wheelmade forms were introduced to an isolated coastal area of the Rif region in the late medieval period. A variant of the waterwheel or *noria* jar and the brazier were introduced as wheelmade forms and were later copied in handbuilt wares, apparently after the supply of wheelmade pottery had ceased. Thus the hand-building technique facilitated the adoption of a new cooking technique and new water transport technology rather than indicating conservatism. Nakur, the earliest excavated Muslim settlement in Morocco, located east of Badis in a more populous agricultural region, shows another interesting pattern in its pottery assemblage. There, wheelmade forms predominate in all functional classes, though surviving pre-Islamic burial rites employ pots of Muslim introduced technology as grave goods.[44] These examples indicate that conservatism regarding material culture can be a very selective phenomenon.

Conclusion

A detailed knowledge of pottery production and distribution patterns in northern Morocco has yet to be achieved. Physical and chemical studies already begun by Qsar es-Seghir project members and Moroccan and French researchers working in the area will shed further light on these issues. Craftspeople who may have been itinerant, and the southward migration of Muslim craftspeople in response to the advancing Christian Reconquista provide an interesting challenge to stylistic and technical studies of ceramics of the area since when potters travel they will leave their trace elements behind them, but will surely take their techniques with them.

In concluding this discussion, which has briefly considered both coarse- and fine-grained shifts in pottery technology through time, we are in a position to make an important methodological point. This is that in the attempt to determine the labor and material requirements of techniques employed in the past, we develop a useful body of predictions and hypotheses that concern questions such as when it is that we can expect certain kinds of techniques to be employed by a society and, conversely, what it may indicate about a society when such techniques are adopted.

Notes

1. Emlen Myers, "The Political Economy of Pottery Production: An Archaeological Study of the Islamic Commonware Ceramics of Medieval Qsar es-Seghir." Ph.D. diss., State University of New York at Binghamton, 1984.
2. Henri Terasse, *Histoire du Maroc I* (Casablanca: Editions Atlantides, 1975).
3. Emlen Myers and M. James Blackman, "Conical Plates of Medieval Qsar es-Seghir: Petrographic and Chemical Investigations," *Proceedings of the Third International Colloquium on Medieval Ceramics in the Western Mediterranean* (Florence: Edizioni all'Insegna del Giglio, 1986): 55-68.
4. Charles Redman and James Boone, *Qsar es-Seghir: A 15th and 16th Century Portuguese Colony in North Africa*, Centro de Estudos Historicos Ultramarinos Da Junta De Investigacoes Cientificas Do Ultramar (Lisbon, 1975).
5. James Boone, "Majolica Escudillas of the 15th and 16th Centuries: A Typological Analysis of 55 Examples from Qsar es-Seghir," *Historical Archaeology* 18 (1984): 76-86;

Charles Redman, "Description and Inference with Late Medieval Pottery from Qsar es-Seghir, Morocco," *Medieval Ceramics*, 3 (1979): 63-79; Carla Sinopoli, "The Blue on White Majolica of Qsar es-Seghir," Manuscript available from author, University of Michigan Museum of Anthropology.

6. Charles Redman, "Comparative Urbanism in the Islamic Far West," *World Archaeology*, 14 (1983): 357-77.

7. Ibid.,375.

8. Idem.

9. Frank Hamer, *The Potter's Dictionary of Materials and Techniques* (New York: Watson-Guptill Publications, 1975) 187.

10. Esin Atil, *Renaissance of Islam: Art of the Mamluks* (Washington, D.C.: Smithsonian Institution Press, Washington, D.C., 1981) 98-99, n.32.

11. Emilio Fernandez-Sotelo, *Arqueologia Catalogo* (Ceuta: Guia, 1980).

12. Charles D.E. Fortnum, *Maiolica* (New York: Garland, 1979); Fernandez-Sotelo, *Arqueologia Catalogo*, plate 54.

13. Dorethea Duda, *Spanisch-Islamisch Keramic aus Almaria von 12-15 Jahrhundert* (Heidelberg: Kerle, 1970); Michelen Grenier de Cardinal, "Recherches sur la ceramique medieval marocain X-XV Siecles," *Proceedings of the First International Colloquium on Medieval Ceramics in the Western Mediterranean* (Paris: Editions CNRS, 1980) 227-49; Myers, *Islamic Commonware of Qsar es-Seghir*; Redman, *Medieval Ceramics* (1979); Patricia Rubertone, "Social Organization in an Islamic Town: A Behavioral Explanation of Ceramic Variability," Ph.D. diss., State University of New York at Binghamton, 1978.

14. Myers and Blackman, *Medieval Ceramics in the Western Mediterranean* (1986).

15. Redman, *World Archaeology*.

16. Ibid. See article by Benco in this volume.

17. Grenier, *Medieval Ceramics in the Western Mediterranean* (1980).

18. H. J. Franken and J. Kalsbeek, *Potters of a Medieval Village in the Jordan Valley* (Amsterdam: North-Holland Elsevier, 1975); S. E. van der Leeuw, *Studies in the Technology of Ancient Pottery* (Amsterdam: 1976).

19. Hamer, *Potter's Dictionary*,294.

20. Charles Redman and Emlen Myers, "Pottery Manufacture at Qsar es-Seghir: Interpretation and Classification," *Production and Distribution: A Ceramic Viewpoint*, ed. Hilary Howard and Elaine L. Morris (Oxford: BAR International Series 120, 1981) 285-307.

21. Henri Terasse, "Trois Baines Merinides du Maroc," *Melanges William Marcais* (Paris: Editions C.-P. Maisonneuve, 1950) 311-20.

22. Daniel Rhodes, *Kilns* (Radnor, Pennsylvania: Chilton, 1981) 19, 23.

23. Nancy Benco, "Organization and Technology of Pottery Production in Early Medieval Morocco." Ph.D. diss., State University of New York at Binghamton, 1986.

24. D. P. S. Peacock, *Pottery in the Roman World* (New York: Longman, 1982).

25. Arnold van Gennep, "Recherches sur les Poteries Pientes de L'Afrique du Nord," *Varia Africanus, Harvard African Studies* II (1918): 235-97.

26. Alfred Bel, *Industries de la Ceramique a Fes* (Paris: A. Leroux, 1918).

27. Myers, *Islamic Commonware of Qsar es-Seghir*.

28. Ibid.

29. Bel, *Ceramique a Fes* (1918); R. Joly, "L'Industrie a Tetouan," *Archives Marocaines* (1906): 265-324.

30. Myers, *Islamic Commonware of Qsar es-Seghir*, 211.

31. Ibid., 212.

32. Redman and Myers, *Production and Distribution*; Myers, *Islamic Commonware of Qsar es-Seghir*, 69.

33. Mohammed B.A. Benchekroun, *La Cuisine Andalou-Marocaine au XIIIe Siecle d'apres un Manuscrit Rare* (Rabat: F.A.N.N.A, 1981).

34. S. D. Goitein, *A Mediterranean Society, Volume I Economic Foundations* (Berkeley: University of California Press, 1967) 169.

35. Benchekroun, *La Cuisine Andalou-Marocain*.

36. Charles Redman and Ronald Anzalone, "Discovering Architectural Patterning at a Complex Site," *American Antiquity* 45 (1980): 284-90.

37. Charles Wilkenson, *Nishapur, Pottery of the Early Islamic Period* (New York: The Metropolitan Museum of Art, 1973) 292.

38. Thomas F. Glick, *Islamic and Christian Spain in the Early Middle Ages* (Princeton: Princeton University Press, 1979): 26.

39. Myers, *Islamic Commonware of Qsar es-Seghir*.

40. Myers and Blackman, *Medieval Ceramics in the Western Meidterranean*, 1986.

41. Jean-Leon L'Africain, *Description De L'Afrique* (Paris: Librarie de l'Amerique et d'Orient, 1981) 271-72.

42. Marvin Mikesell, *Northern Morocco: A Cultural Geography* (Berkeley: University of California Press, 1961).

43. Ernest Rackow, *Beitraege zur Kenntnis der Materiellen Kultur Nordwest Marokkos: Wohnraum, Hausrat, Kostuem* (Weisbaden: Otto Harrassowitz, 1958); John L. Myres, "Collateral Survival of Successive Styles of Art in North Africa," *Man* II (1901): 102-5.

44. Redman, *World Archaeology*.

Diversity in Ceramic Production: A Case Study from Medieval North Africa

NANCY L. BENCO

In the past decade, archaeological research has become increasingly concerned with the evolution of craft specialization in prehistoric societies. Such research has focused primarily on the investigation of factors that caused a transition from domestic to specialized craft production in ancient times.[1]

Much less effort, however, has been directed toward a study of the organization of specialized craft production in complex societies, in particular the relationship between craft manufacture and political/administrative structures,[2] despite its importance in understanding the development and maintenance of early societies.

In this paper, I present a theoretical framework for viewing specialized craft production in state and imperial societies and describe an archaeological situation from medieval Islamic Morocco where this model is being tested. The approach used to examine the model involves measuring the diversity, or heterogeneity, of pottery assemblages excavated from the early medieval Islamic site of al-Basra in order to reconstruct the nature of the local pottery industry.

Theoretical Framework

The theoretical framework is derived from the work of several social scientists concerned with the relationships between political and economic structures in regional social systems.[3] On the basis of historical and contemporary situations, this research suggests that political and economic hierarchies overlap in regional systems and that the degree of overlap varies through time and across space. In other words, the degree of political and economic integration differs among centers in a region, depending on each center's relative position and role within the system. For example, in a study of late imperial Chinese society, G. William Skinner found that cities located near regional or imperial frontiers exhibited a higher degree of political and administrative influence than cities located in regional or imperial core areas.[4] Furthermore, Skinner's work suggested that the degree of political and economic overlap in one center varied over a period of time as that center's position *vis à vis* the larger regional system changed.[5]

This research also has shown that the degree of overlap in political and economic structures appears to affect the production and distribution activities within a system. Strong political-economic integration seems to inhibit competition among producers, which results in fewer economic choices for producers and consumers. On the other hand, weak administrative-economic integration seems to encourage competition, which leads to an increased number of economic choices for producers and consumers. For example, in a study of Chinese cities Skinner found that "in general, both merchants and officials preferred to sojourn in cities whose economic central functions overshadowed their administrative importance and to avoid whenever possible cities whose administrative level was disproportionately high in relation to their economic importance."[6] Carol Smith observed a similar pattern in modern-day Guatemala, where an administratively controlled economy was "most efficient for urban-based bureaucrats or monopolists who were attempting to control a region—it is not well suited from the point of view of the consumers, for the distribution of any economic commodities."[7] In an administratively controlled economy, Smith found, competitive forces were minimized.[8]

To summarize, the work of these social scientists suggests the following: (1) that political and economic systems may overlap in regional social systems; (2) that the degree of overlap may vary through time and across space; and (3) that the degree of political and economic integration may affect economic competition, i.e., that strong integration seems to lead to lower competition among producers and fewer choices for consumers or vice versa.

History of al-Basra

This model is being tested with documentary and archaeological material from the early medieval town of al-Basra in northern Morocco. Located in the foothills of the Rif mountains about 40 kilometers from the Atlantic coast (fig. 1), the town served as an administrative, commercial, and agricultural center during its 300-year history.

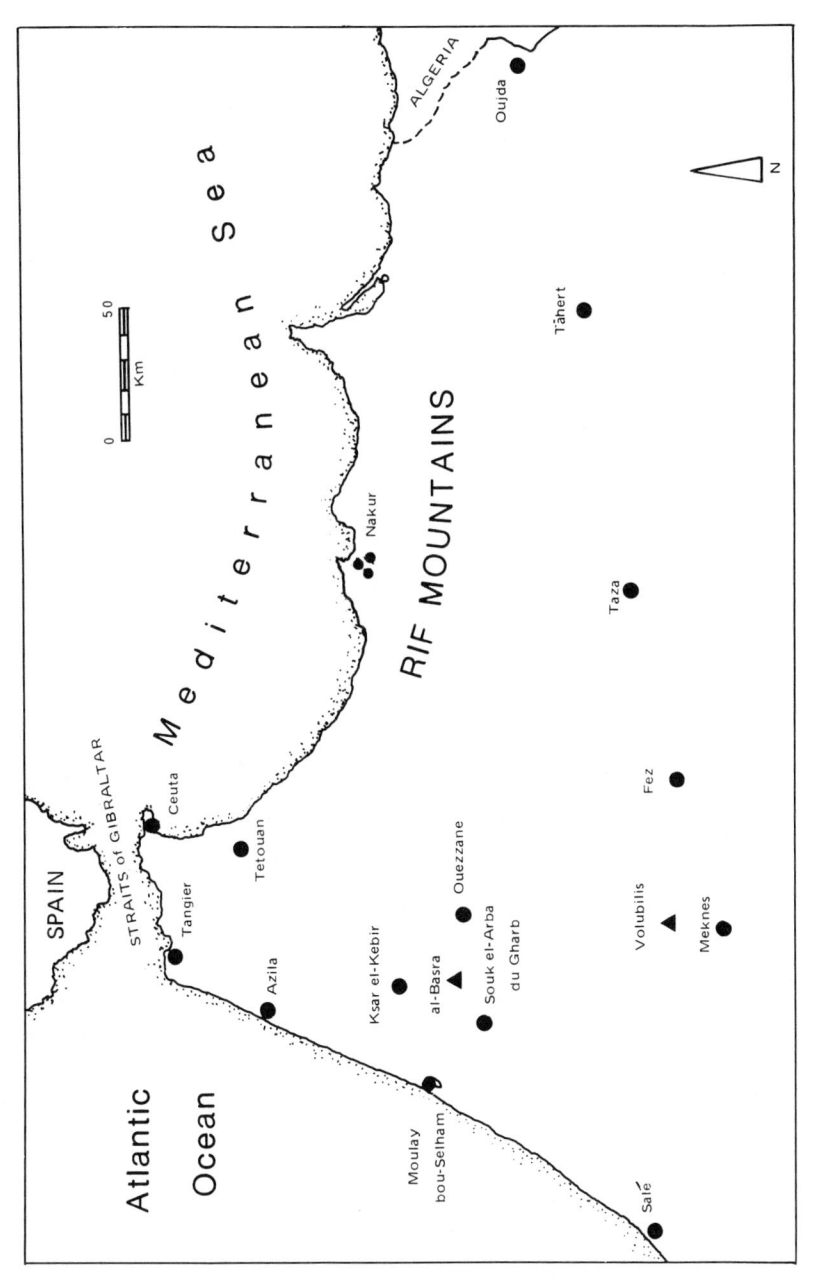

Fig. 1. Map of Northern Morocco.

The history of al-Basra is known primarily from the chronicles of Arab travelers who journeyed through the region between the ninth and twelfth centuries.[9] While these documents occasionally reflect the biases of their authors—e.g., the account of Ibn Hawkal, who may have traveled through the area in the tenth century as a Fatimid spy, shows an unusual interest in the strength of city walls and the location of urban water supplies—the documents remain a major source of information on the political and military events in the Maghreb during the early Islamic period.

According to the chronicles, al-Basra was founded at the beginning of the ninth century by the Idrisids, who established one of the earliest Arab states in North Africa. In addition to al-Basra, the Idrisids established several other cities, including Fez, which became an important entrepôt in the gold and slave trade between sub-Saharan Africa and the Mediterranean. After Idris II died in AD 835, the state was partitioned into many small kingdoms, which were governed independently by various descendants of the Idrisids for the next 80 years.

In AD 917, the Fatimids of Tunisia extended their empire across North Africa, taking control of most of the Maghreb. Sometime in the middle of the tenth century, the Fatimids named the city of al-Basra as a regional capital, apparently making it a center of administrative and military activities for their empire in northern Morocco. According to the chronicles, it was during this period that al-Basra shipped agricultural products, such as flax, to cities along the Mediterranean coast. At the end of the tenth century, al-Basra was destroyed, although the exact circumstances and the extent of the destruction are left unclear in the chronicles. By the eleventh century, however, the city had been rebuilt, and it continued to serve as a minor commercial center under the Umayyad Caliphate of Spain and the Zenata Berbers in Morocco. Sometime during the eleventh or twelfth century, al-Basra was permanently abandoned.

In terms of the theoretical model, then, administrative involvement in economic affairs at al-Basra would be expected to be relatively weak during most of the Idrisid period, because of regional political fragmentation and the lack of a centralized government (see Table 1). Political/administrative control of economic activities would be expected to be relatively strong during the Fatimid period, when the empire extended its control across North Africa and established al-Basra as a regional capital, presumably drawing Fatimid bureaucrats and military contingents into the area. Finally, political/administrative involvement in the economy would be expected to be relatively weak during the final period of Zenata and Umayyad hegemony; the Zenata tribes had little centralized power and the Spanish Umayyads maintained only a brief interest in northern Morocco. If these expectations hold true, then, economic competition among producers would be higher in the early and late periods at al-Basra when political involvement in economic activities was low; according to the model, greater competition among producers would lead to a higher diversity of consumer goods. On the other hand, competition among manufactur-

Table 1
Model of Ceramic Diversity at Al-Basra

Occupation Phase	Regional Political Events	Political Control of Production	Economic Competition	Expected Technological Diversity
5 Post-urban	—	—	—	—
4 Late	Fragmented Umayyad-Zenata confederacy	Weak	Strong	High
3 Middle	Fatimid imperial hegemony	Strong	Weak	Low
2 Transition	Collapse/reconstruction of Idrisid city	Weak	Strong	High
1 Early	Fragmented Idrisid state	Weak	Strong	High

ers would be lower during the middle period when Fatimid control of the area was strong; this would result in a lower diversity of manufactured products.

Archaeological Excavations at al-Basra

Because of its importance to the early history of Morocco and its potential for investigating questions concerning the development and organization of complex societies, archaeological excavations were conducted at the site of al-Basra in 1980 and 1981 by Dr. Charles L. Redman, director of the Moroccan-American Archaeological Project.[10]

Located on the road between Ouezzane and Souk-al-Arba, the site of al-Basra covers an area of about 30 hectares. It extends across the slopes of two hills and the valley between them. The only visible remains of the ancient city are a small portion of the 2-meter-thick wall that once encircled the city for about 2.5 kilometers and an ancient cemetery outside the walls on a promontory overlooking the Mda River valley. The present-day village of Jouana-Basra is situated on part of the northern slope and villagers' gardens, orchards, and threshing fields extend across the rest of the site.

During the course of two field seasons, a total of 18 soundings were excavated within the walls of the ancient city in order to assess the extent and depth of architectural remains below the surface and to collect a representative sample of artifacts for analysis (fig. 2). The excavations revealed substantial architectural features, particularly in the valley portion of the site. These remains included a series of superimposed stone walls, which represented three major con-

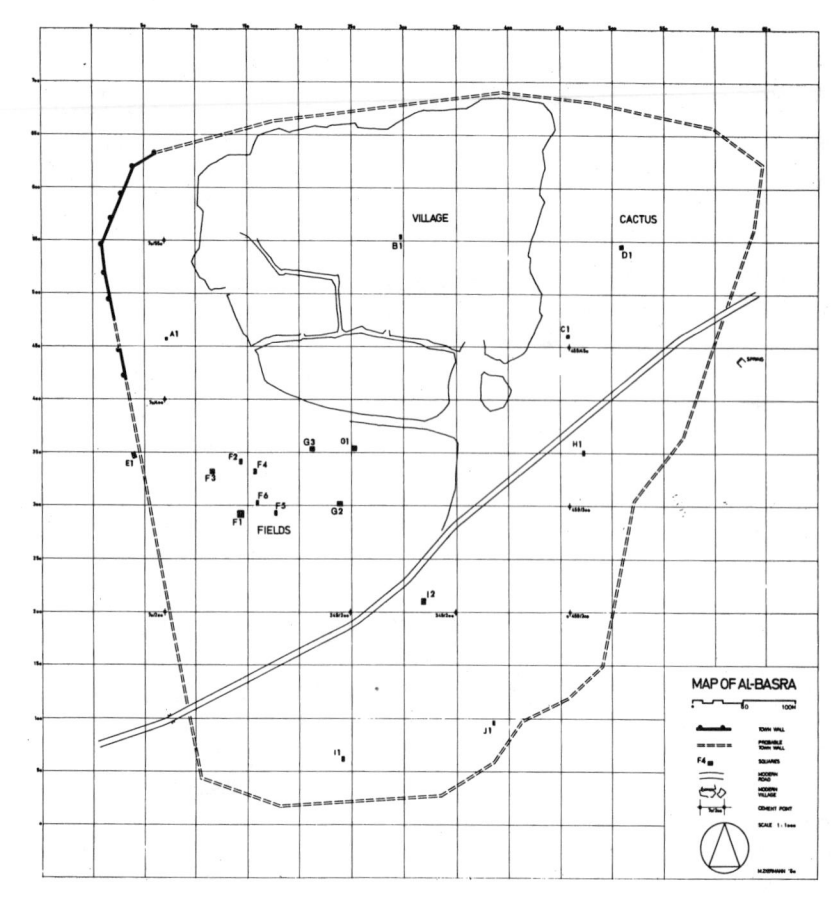

Fig. 2. Map of al-Basra, showing the location of soundings excavated in 1980 and 1981.

struction and occupation phases in the city's history. Among other important discoveries were two updraft kilns located about 50 meters apart near the western walls of the city in an area probably devoted to industrial activities. Although, on the basis of stratigraphic evidence, the kilns appear to have been in operation at different periods of time, i.e., one during the earliest occupation and the other during the middle occupation, they are similar in construction. Both are about 4 by 4 meters in size and built of mud brick; a series of transverse brick arches support the flue-lined floors of the firing chambers. The presence of these kilns, along with numerous ceramic wasters distributed across the site, strongly indicates that al-Basra served as a pottery production center during most of its 300-year history.

The large quantity of pottery found at al-Basra, which totals nearly 100,000 fragments, consists almost entirely of undecorated, wheelmade utilitarian vessels. Most of the pottery (80% of the total collection) is made from a buff-firing clay, which contains varying amounts of quartz inclusions; these have been classified as sandy, fine, and very fine buff-firing wares and likely represent the use of different clay resources and/or clay preparation techniques by local potters. Smaller proportions of pottery are made from a highly calcareous, cream-firing clay (12%) and from a buff-firing clay containing large quartz and calcite inclusions (2%). According to a mineralogical and chemical study of the pottery and local clays, buff- and cream-firing vessels were very likely produced at the site and fired in one of the kilns.[11] The remainder of the collection consists of glazed pottery (2%) that was made at other production centers in North Africa or Spain, and handmade pottery (5%) that was likely produced by domestic potters for their own use.

A number of different forms were made from the local buff- and cream-firing clays. Distinguished by variations in rim and neck morphology, these forms include band rim jars, grooved band rim jars, triangular rim jars, carinated jars, pitchers with a simple lip, large jars with triangular rims, tall-necked jars, and nosed oil lamps (fig. 3).

A total of 21 combined ware-form types were commonly made at al-Basra (Table 2). In this paper, these are referred to as technological types because they are characterized primarily by attributes that are related to manufacturing processes, such as choice of clay materials, clay preparation techniques, and forming and firing procedures. The 21 technological types can be assigned to six functional vessel classes that are distinguished by general size and shape. The functional classes are small storage jars, large storage jars, water storage jars, serving vessels, pitchers, and oil lamps (Table 3).

Diversity in the al-Basra Pottery Assemblages

The research that is in progress is an attempt to determine if changes in the degree of administrative/political involvement in economic activities implied in the historical record can be detected in the archaeological record, specifically in the nature of pottery assemblages. The site of al-Basra provides an exceptionally good case study because of the availability of documentary data, the unambiguous evidence of pottery production at the site, and the presence of well-defined stratigraphic sequences.

Although several indicators eventually will be employed to assess the degree of political/administrative control of craft production at al-Basra,[12] this paper discusses the results of only one: the diversity of locally produced pottery. As it is used here, the concept of diversity refers both to the number of different

A

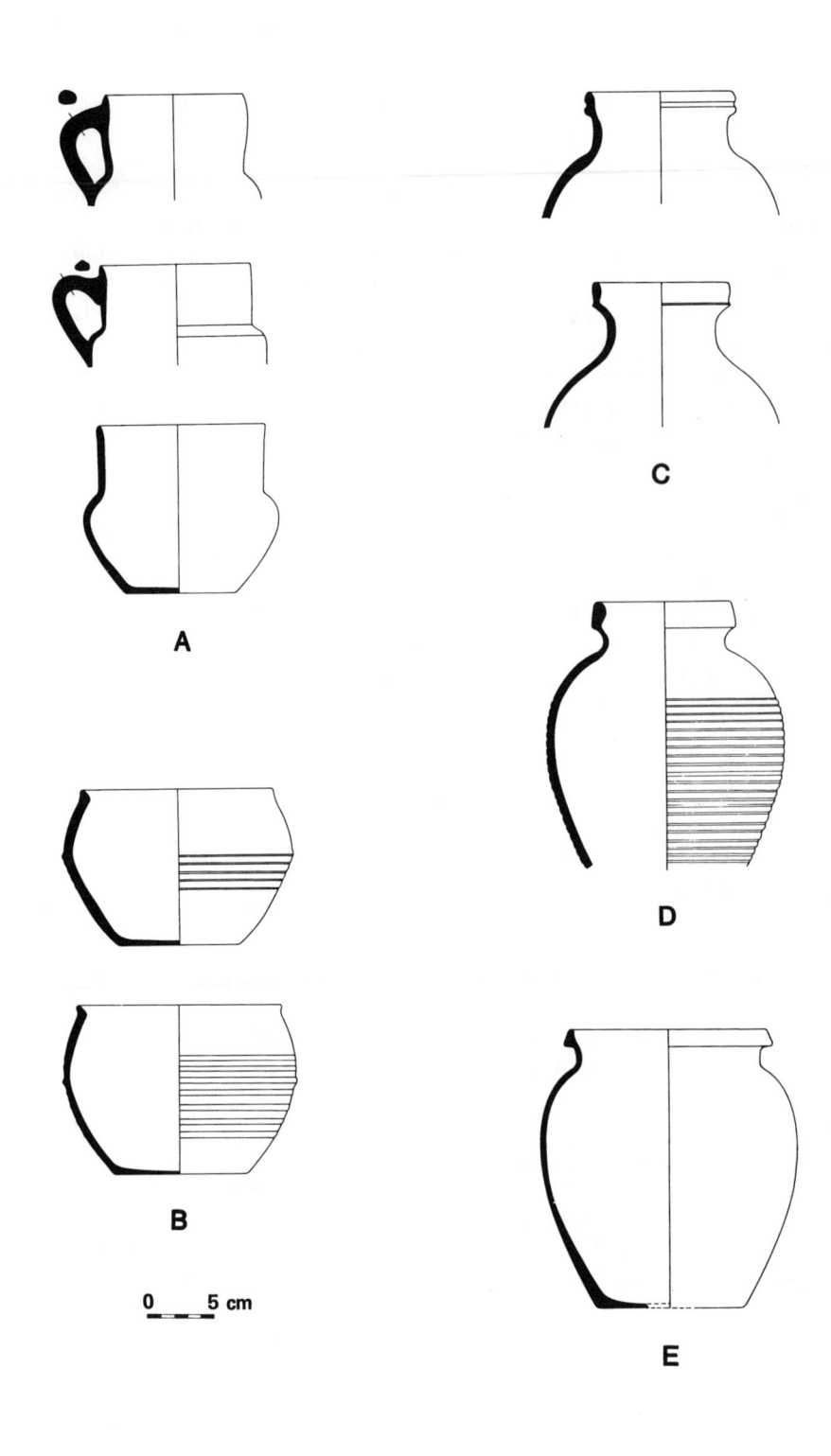

B

0 5 cm

C

D

E

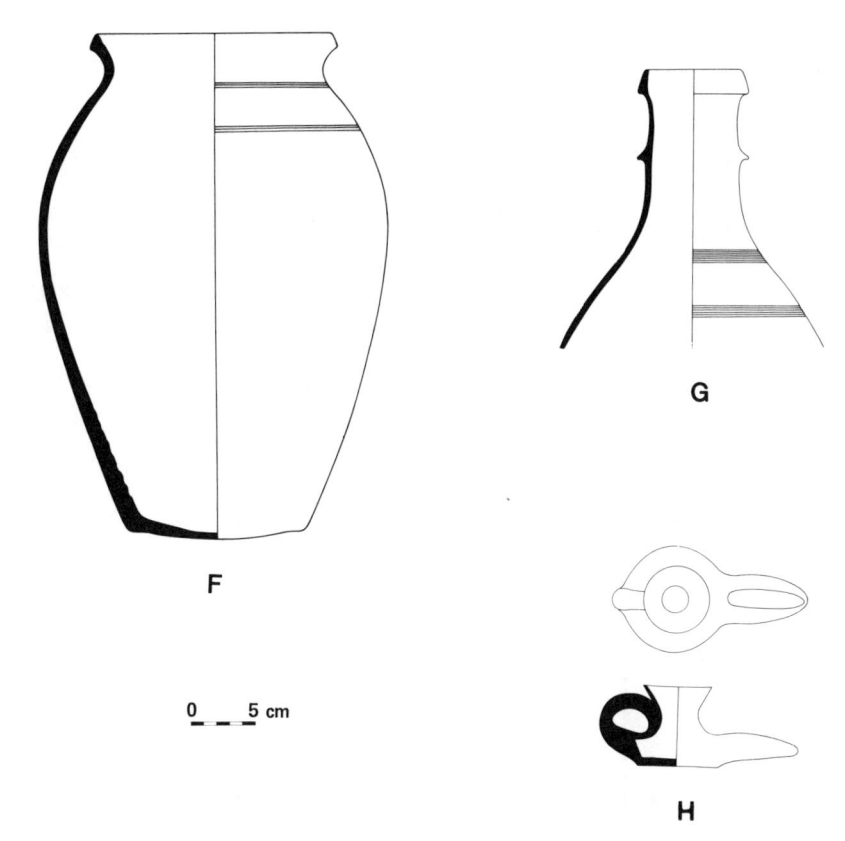

Fig. 3. Profiles of commonly produced al-Basra pottery forms: (A) Pitcher with simple lip. (B) Carinated serving jar. (C) Grooved-band rim jar. (D) Band rim jar. (E) Small jar with triangular rim. (F) Large jar with triangular rim. (G) Tall necked jar. (H) Nosed lamp.

types of items present in an assemblage (the dimension of *richness*) and to the uniformity with which items are distributed among the types (the dimension of *evenness*). This concept of diversity, which was developed in the field of mathematical ecology,[13] has been applied recently to a number of archaeological artifact studies.[14]

Functional and Technological Diversity

In order to fully understand the changes that took place in the organization of pottery production at al-Basra over a period of time, the *total* diversity of

Table 2
Counts of Rim Sherds for 21 Technological Types, by Occupation Phase

Occupation Phase	Total Sherds[1]	Carinated Jars Sandy	Carinated Jars Fine	Carinated Jars Very Fine	Sandy	Triangular Rim Jars Fine	Triangular Rim Jars Very Fine	Cream	Band Rim Jars Sandy	Band Rim Jars Fine
5 Post-urban	204	2	19	2	20	37	5	9	0	0
4 Late	819	3	42	53	13	94	74	5	2	1
3 Middle	672	14	126	11	22	112	14	3	3	3
2 Transition	710	60	107	3	32	67	3	11	11	19
1 Early	325	20	32	0	12	13	1	8	49	25

Occupation Phase	Grooved Band Rim Jars Sandy	Fine	Very Fine	Simple Rim Pitchers Fine	Very Fine	Cream	Fine	Lamps Very Fine	Cream	Tall-necked Jars Fine	Very Fine	Large Jars Fine
5 Post-urban	2	18	3	34	25	4	7	4	3	8	0	2
4 Late	7	59	34	155	99	41	30	34	16	18	25	14
3 Middle	18	68	11	95	36	40	27	10	20	17	6	16
2 Transition	49	154	9	32	2	78	14	5	23	27	1	3
1 Early	40	73	0	11	0	20	4	1	6	7	0	3

[1]The sherds used in the diversity study represent about half of the al-Basra rim collection. The sample was selected from representative provenience units at the site.

Table 3
Counts of Rim Sherds for 6 Functional Classes, by Occupation Phase

Occupation Phase	Total Sherds[1]	Small Storage Jars	Pitchers	Lamps	Carinated Serving Jars	Large Storage Jars	Water Storage Jars
5 Post-urban	204	94	63	14	23	2	8
4 Late	819	289	295	80	98	14	43
3 Middle	672	254	171	57	151	16	23
2 Transition	710	355	112	42	170	3	28
1 Early	325	221	31	11	52	3	7

[1]The sherds used in the study represent about half of the al-Basra rim collection. The sample was selected from representative provenience units at the site.

pottery assemblages is examined at two hierarchical levels. At the more general level, *functional diversity* measures the amount of heterogeneity among functional classes of pottery, such as small storage jars, pitchers, serving jars, and so forth. At the more specific level, *technological diversity* assesses the amount of heterogeneity among technological types *within* each functional class.

In a very real sense, these two components of total diversity stem from different behavioral or environmental factors. Functional diversity, on one hand, is related primarily to socio-economic, ethnic, or environmental forces. The variety of functional pottery classes, for example, may vary because of the appearance of a new ethnic group whose traditional cooking and serving customs require a new set of ceramic utensils. It may vary because of a change in socio-economic or occupational groups whose statuses or jobs require a new class of vessel, such as military cooking pots or élite ceremonial plates. Functional diversity may also vary because of shifting climatic or ecological conditions that stimulate a need for vessels of a certain class, such as water storage jars during periods of drought.

The amount of technological diversity, on the other hand, is primarily related to production factors. In a rough way, the diversity of technological types within a functional class reflects the number of artisans and/or workshops that produce that vessel class and their relative share of the market. When the number of producers increases and/or they gain a more evenly distributed share of the market, reflecting a more competitive industry, the amount of technological diversity increases. When the number of manufacturers decreases and/or a few manufacturing units expand to monopolize the production of a certain class of vessels, the amount of technological diversity drops. By measuring the diversity of technological types within functional classes of pottery and by comparing the resulting diversity values for ceramic assemblages from different time periods, it is possible to monitor changes in the number and/or scale of production units and, consequently, detect major shifts in competition within a local pottery industry.

Hierarchical Diversity Index

In order to examine these two related but separate components of ceramic diversity at al-Basra, the study employs a hierarchical diversity index.[15] The measure takes into account the hierarchical nature of certain classifications, such as that of pottery, in which the total diversity of an assemblage consists of the diversity present at both the genus, e.g., functional, and the species, e.g., technological, levels. In terms of pottery assemblages, total diversity represents the sum of functional diversity and technological diversity within functional groups. Over a period of time, total diversity may remain the same while the diversity of the other two components may vary in relation to each other. The formula used to calculate hierarchical diversity is:

$$H'(f,t,) = H'(f) + H'(t)$$

where $H'(f,t)$ is the total diversity; $H'(f)$ is the diversity of functional classes; and $H'(t)$ is the sum of the weighted mean diversity of technological types within each functional class.[16] This index takes on a value of zero when diversity is at its theoretical minimum, i.e., when all of the pottery in an assemblage belongs to a single type. As the number of types and the evenness of the distribution of items among types increase, so too does the value of the index.

Selection of Pottery Samples

The pottery used in the diversity study consists of material that was most likely produced in al-Basra's specialist pottery workshops. It includes a sample of 2,730 buff- and cream-firing rim sherds from residential and industrial areas of the site and excludes glazed and handmade sherds as well as those that occurred rarely at the site.

The sherds come from five stratigraphic levels that are associated with occupation, construction, and/or abandonment phases at al-Basra. Of the total, 325 sherds come from Phase 1 strata, which represent the earliest occupation. Another 710 sherds derive from Phase 2 strata, which represent a temporary occupation and/or abandonment and reconstruction phase. Some 672 sherds come from Phase 3 levels, which are associated with the second major occupation phase. Another 819 sherds are derived from Phase 4 strata, which represent the third and final occupation at al-Basra. Finally, 204 sherds come from

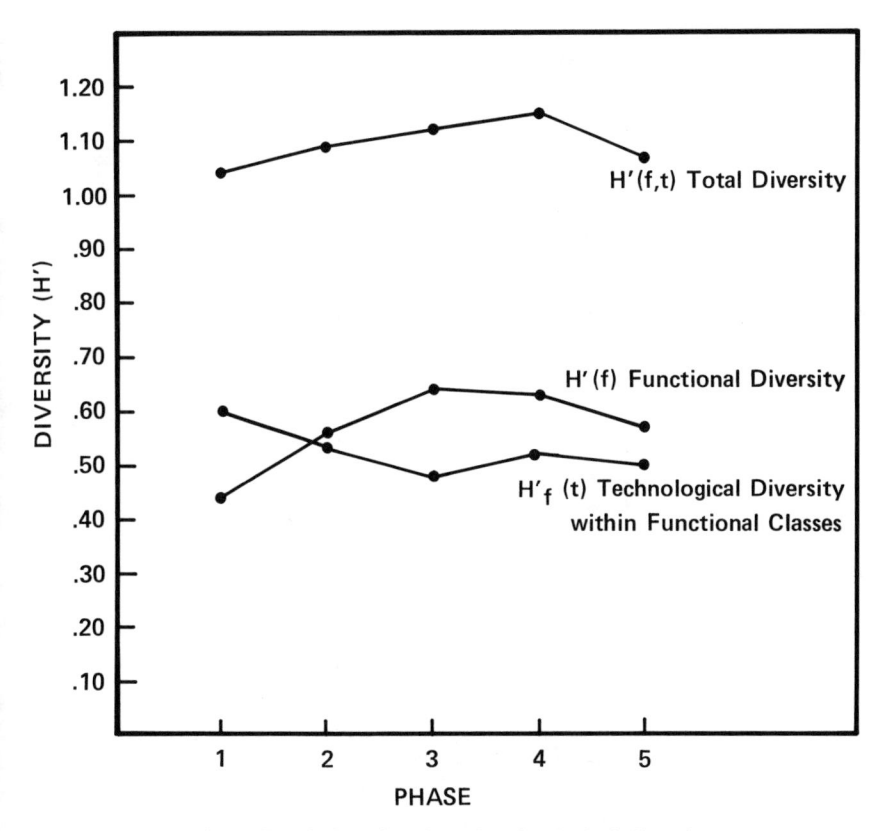

Fig. 4. Total, functional, and technological diversity within functional groups, by occupation phase.

Phase 5 levels, which are associated with the final collapse, abandonment, and erosion of the site.[17]

Analysis of Functional Diversity

As figure 4 shows, the diversity of al-Basra's six functional classes of pottery—small and large storage jars, carinated serving jars, pitchers, oil lamps, and water storage jars—changes rather dramatically. The variety increases sharply from Phase 1 to Phase 3, levels out in Phase 4, and falls a little in Phase 5. In general, the distribution of functional classes is more even in Phases 3 and 4 than it is in the earliest and last phases.

These changes in evenness are illustrated in the bar charts in figure 5, which show the relative frequency of each functional class by occupation phase. The

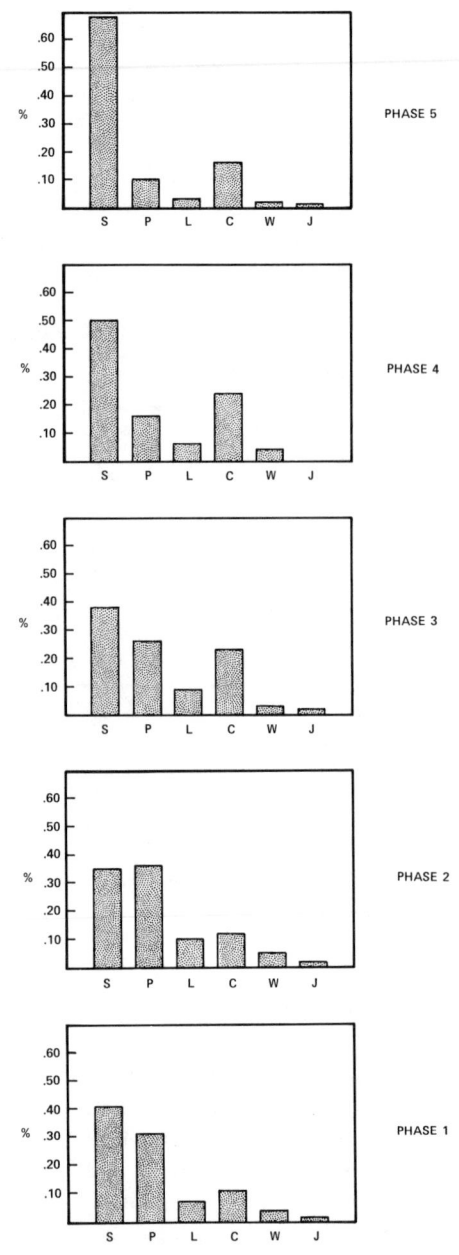

Fig. 5. Relative frequency of six functional classes, by occupation phase. Key: S, small storage jars; P, pitchers; L, lamps; C, carinated serving jars; W, water storage jars; J, large storage jars.

relative abundance of small storage jars decreases sharply from Phase 1 to Phase 4, and then rises slightly in Phase 5. By contrast, the relative frequency of pitchers, carinated bowls and, to a lesser extent, lamps increases steadily from Phase 1 to Phase 4, and drops a little in Phase 5. As the charts indicate, three classes — small storage jars, pitchers, and carinated jars — are distributed rather evenly in assemblages from Phases 2, 3, and 4, while only one class — small storage jars — dominates the earliest and latest phases.

In summary, we can say that although al-Basra's pottery workshops produced the same range of functional types over a period of 300 years, they manufactured varying proportions of these classes through time. For some yet unknown reasons, local production of several classes — pitchers, carinated bowls, and lamps — rose in relation to the manufacture of small storage jars in the middle and final occupation phases at al-Basra.

Analysis of Technological Diversity within Functional Classes

Like functional diversity, the diversity of technological types within functional classes changes through time, but in the opposite direction (fig. 4). It drops from Phase 1 to Phase 3, rises slightly in Phase 4, and falls again in Phase 5. In general, technological diversity is at its lowest point in Phase 3, the second occupation phase.

We can get a better idea of the reasons for the overall decline in diversity at this level by examining the heterogeneity *within* each functional class separately. As figure 6a shows, diversity within the largest functional group — small storage jars — decreases gradually from Phase 1 to Phase 3, rises slightly in Phase 4, and falls again in Phase 5. This general decrease in diversity occurs at the same time that the overall proportion of small storage jars as a functional group declines (fig. 6b). In terms of production factors, it appears that fewer and/or larger workshops produce small storage jars at a time when consumer demand for this kind of jar declines. As demand for small storage jars drops, competition among producers making this jar appears to decline as well.

A different pattern emerges within two other functional groups — pitchers and lamps. As figures 7a and 8a show, technological diversity within each group rises from Phase 1 to Phase 4 and drops somewhat in Phase 5. The general increase in technological diversity within these two groups takes place at the same time that the relative proportion of each class rises (figs. 7b and 8b). It appears that a larger number of small workshops produce pitchers and lamps as consumer demand for both items grows. Competition among potters making pitchers and lamps seems to grow as consumer demand increases.

By contrast, a third trend occurs within another of the major functional

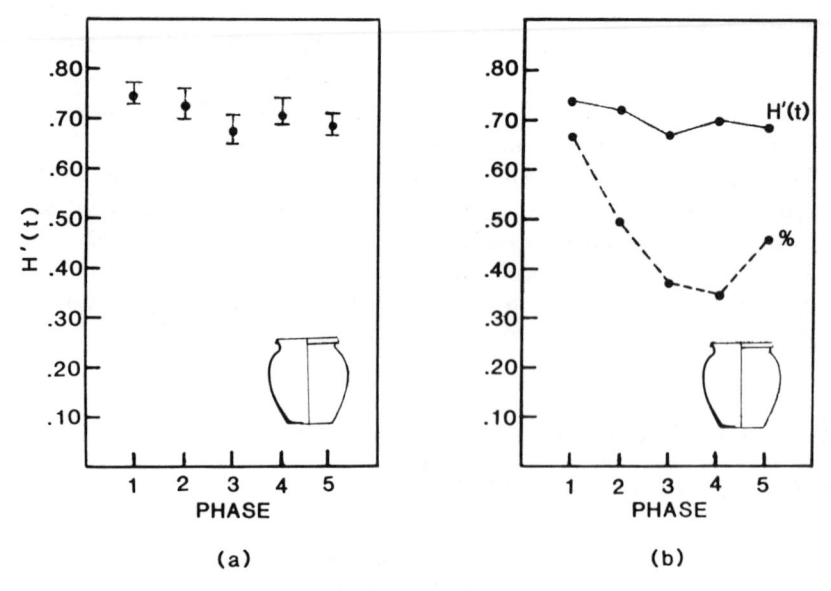

Fig. 6. (a) Technological diversity of small storage jars, by occupation phase. Diversity values are enclosed by 80% confidence intervals. (b) Technological diversity and relative frequency of small storage jars, by occupation phase.

groups—carinated jars. As figure 9a illustrates, the diversity of types within this functional group changes erratically, dropping in Phase 3, rising in Phase 4, and falling again in Phase 5. In general, diversity is higher in Phases 1, 2, and 4 and lower in Phases 3 and 5. In spite of the higher relative proportion of this functional group in Phase 3, technological diversity is at its lowest point during this time. In terms of production, the diversity of carinated serving bowls drops at a time when consumer demand for this vessel type appears to be relatively high.

Because the remaining functional classes—water storage jars and large storage jars—consist of one or two types and low relative proportions, their contribution to the technological component of diversity is relatively low and so they are not discussed in detail here.

In summary, two points regarding technological diversity within functional groups need to be emphasized. First, the overall decline in variety at this level largely reflects the drop in diversity of small storage jars, the largest functional group. It is also partly due to the decline in variety of carinated jars, which reach their lowest point in Phase 3. Second, the trends that we found within each functional group are what we would expect under normal market conditions, except for that of the carinated jar group. Instead of an increase in

Diversity in Ceramic Production / 113

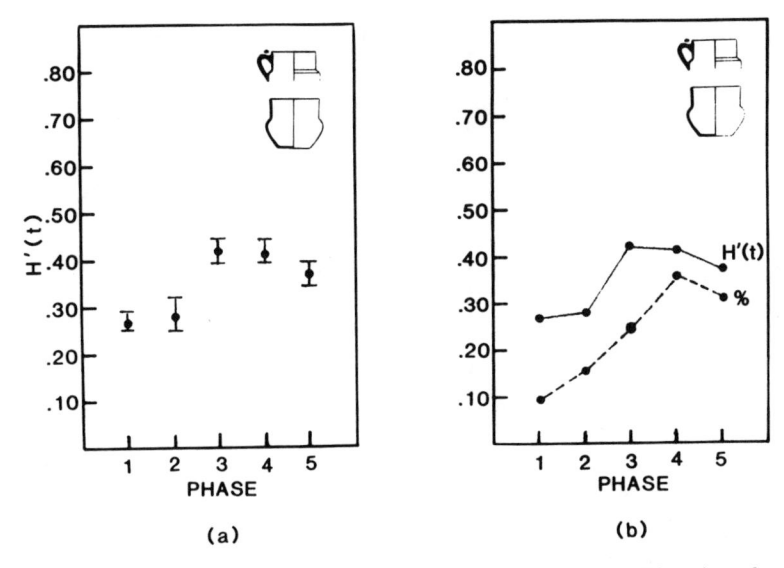

Fig. 7. (a) Technological diversity of pitchers, by occupation phase. Diversity values are enclosed by 80% confidence intervals. (b) Technological diversity and relative frequency of pitchers, by occupation phase.

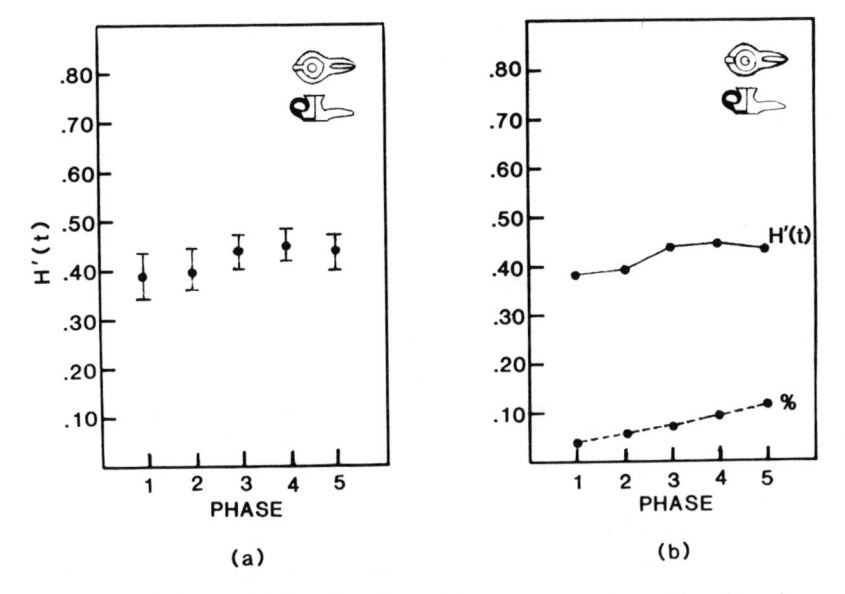

Fig. 8. (a) Technological diversity of lamps, by occupation phase. Diversity values are enclosed by 80% confidence intervals. (b) Technological diversity and relative frequency of lamps, by occupation phase.

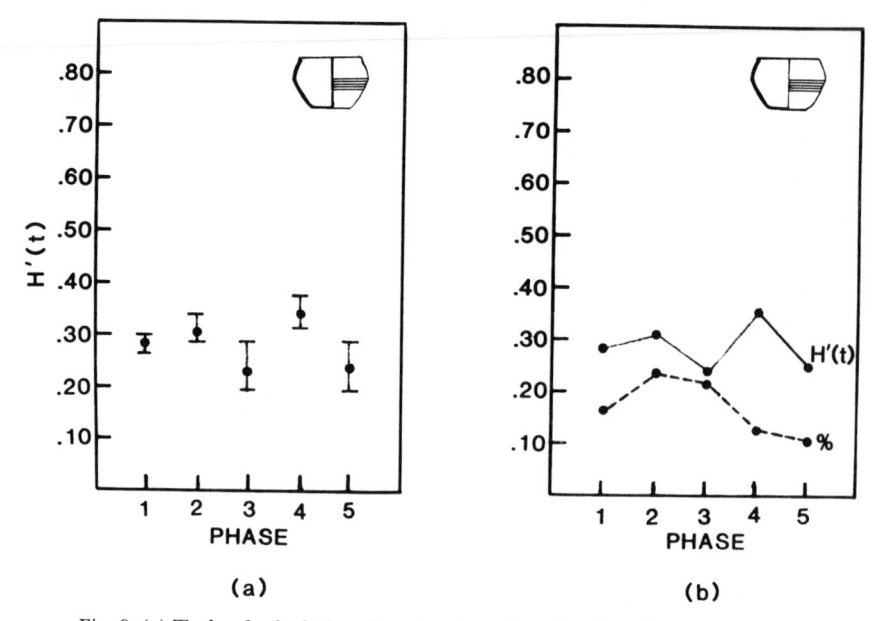

Fig. 9. (a) Technological diversity of carinated serving jars, by occupation phase. Diversity values are enclosed by 80% confidence intervals. (b) Technological diversity and relative frequency of carinated serving jars, by occupation phase.

diversity as demand stayed high, the variety within this group decreased, suggesting that fewer producers may have monopolized the production of this vessel class.

Total Diversity

Total diversity in the al-Basra pottery assemblages, as we noted above, is equal to the sum of functional and technological diversity. As figure 4 shows, total diversity changes very little through 300 years of occupation at the site. It rises slightly between Phase 1 and Phase 4 and drops somewhat in Phase 5.

This study indicates that the examination of total diversity alone, as previous studies of ceramic heterogeneity have attempted,[18] can be misleading. For example, while total diversity of the al-Basra assemblages increases slightly, the diversity of each component—functional and technological within functional groups—changes in very different ways. Functional diversity increases and technological diversity decreases from one occupation phase to the next (fig.

4). Furthermore, the shift in each component can be related to different factors. Thus, by splitting total diversity into its component parts, we are able to isolate and measure the variability due to production factors, independently of that due to environmental or socio-economic considerations.

Summary and Conclusions

The results of the diversity study are particularly interesting in light of the model we presented earlier. As the analysis shows, there is some indication of a change in the organization of ceramic production during Phase 3, the second major occupation period at al-Basra, and this change continues into Phases 4 and 5. The shift is from a more diverse and, presumably, more competitive ceramic industry in the early period to a less diverse and, by implication, a less competitive production context in the middle and late phases. In other words, relatively fewer and/or larger workshops appear to dominate the pottery industry in the middle and late phases at the early medieval site.

In part, these results conform to the expectations of the historical model (Table 1). If government interference in craft production increased during the middle Fatimid period, as we proposed it did, competition among potters/workshops would have declined, leading to a lower technological diversity of ceramic products. The diversity study indicates that this may have occurred. Furthermore, the analysis shows that the specific vessel form that did not conform to the normal supply and demand pattern was the carinated jar, a serving vessel that conceivably was used by military troops, and therefore may have been the product of administratively controlled workshops.

On the other hand, if administrative involvement in production activities decreased during the final period at al-Basra, when the Zenata Berbers and Spanish Umayyads were in power, competition among producers would have increased and technological diversity would have also increased. The diversity analysis, however, shows very little change in pottery variety between the middle and late occupation phases (fig. 4). In this case, then, the expectations of the model do not seem to hold true.

While it is tempting to attribute changes in pottery diversity to shifts in political/administrative involvement in the ceramic industry at al-Basra, particularly in the middle phase, alternative possibilities need to be considered. While the shift toward larger and/or fewer pottery workshops in the middle and late phases is relatively clear, the reasons for the change are not as straightforward. It is possible that the shift consisted of a change toward larger commercial workshops operated by private entrepreneurs, rather than toward state-controlled facilities.

It is expected that some of these issues will be clarified as further research into other aspects of the ceramic industry at al-Basra continues. Hopefully, this work will lead to an increasingly detailed reconstruction of the pottery industry in one of Morocco's earliest Islamic cities and to a clearer understanding of the relationships that existed between political and economic structures in ancient societies.

Acknowledgments. The research for this paper was supported by grants from the National Science Foundation (BNS-83-11644), Sigma Xi, and the Foundation of the State University of New York Special Projects Fund. I am grateful to Vincas Steponaitis for his help in working out the idea of hierarchical diversity and to Keith Kintigh and Prudence Rice for their valuable comments on earlier drafts of this paper. I am indebted to Charles Redman and Joudia Hassar-Benslimane, chief of the Moroccan Archaeological Service, for kindly providing me with access to the al-Basra pottery collection.

Notes

1. For example, Dean E. Arnold, "Ceramic Ecology of the Ayacucho Basin, Peru: Implications for Prehistory," *Current Anthropology* 16 (1975): 183–205; Prudence M. Rice, "Evolution of Specialized Pottery Production: A Trial Model," *Current Anthropology* 22 (1981): 219–40; and Henry T. Wright and Gregory A. Johnson, "Population, Exchange, and Early State Formation in Southwestern Iran," *American Anthropologist* 77 (1975): 267–89.

2. Gary Feinman, "The Relationship Between Administrative Organization and Ceramic Production in the Valley of Oaxaca" (Ph.D. diss., City University of New York, 1980); Craig Morris, "Reconstructing Patterns of Non-Agricultural Production in the Inca Economy: Archaeology and Documents in Institutional Analysis," in *Reconstructing Complex Societies*, ed. C. Moore, (Bulletin of American Schools of Oriental Research, 1974), 49–60; John Riley, "Industrial Standardization in Cyrenaica during the Second and Third Centuries A.D.: The Evidence from Locally-Manufactured Pottery," *Society for Libyan Studies 11th Annual Report* (1979-1980), 73–78; Michael W. Spence, "Obsidian Production and the State in Teotihuacan," *American Antiquity* 46 (1981): 769–88.

3. For example, G. William Skinner, "Mobility Strategies in Late Imperial China: A Regional Systems Analysis," in *Regional Analysis*, vol. 1: *Economic Systems*, ed. Carol A. Smith (New York: Academic Press, 1976), 353–62; idem, "Regional Urbanization in Nineteenth-Century China," in *The City in Late Imperial China*, ed. G. William Skinner (Stanford: Stanford University Press, 1977), 211–49; idem, "Cities and the Hierarchy of Local Systems," in Skinner, *The City in Late Imperial China*, pp. 275–351; Carol A. Smith, "Regional Economic Systems: Linking Geographical Models and Socioeconomic Problems," in *Regional Analysis*, vol. 1: *Economic Systems*, ed. Carol A. Smith (New York: Academic Press, 1976), 3–63; idem, "Exchange Systems and the Spatial Distribution of Elites: The Organization of Stratification in Agrarian Societies," in *Regional*

Analysis, vol. 2: *Social Systems*, ed. Carol A. Smith (New York: Academic Press, 1976), 309-70; Immanuel Wallerstein, *The Modern World-System I: Capitalist Agriculture and the Origins of the European World-Economy in the Sixteenth Century* (New York: Academic Press, 1974).

4. Skinner, "Regional Urbanization in Nineteenth-Century China," 211-49.
5. Skinner, "Cities and the Hierarchy of Local Systems," 275-351.
6. Skinner, "Mobility Strategies in Late Imperial China," 359.
7. Smith, "Regional Economic Systems: Linking Geographical Models and Socioeconomic Problems," 20.
8. Smith, ibid., 32.
9. Most of the documentary information regarding al-Basra and its region has been compiled by Daniel Eustache. It appears in Eustache, "El-Basra, Capitale Idrissite, et Son Port," *Hesperis* 42 (1955): 218-38; and *idem*, *Corpus des Dirhams Idrisites et Contemporains* (Rabat: Banque du Maroc, 1970-1971). Among the relevant Arab chroniclers he cites are al-Bakri (ca. 1068), *Description de l'Afrique Septentrionale*, ed. and trans. M. de Slane, 3rd edition (Paris: Adrien-Maisonneuve, 1965); al-Mukaddasi (ca. 985), *Description de l'Occident Musulman au IVe-Xe Siecle*, ed. and trans. Charles Pellat (Alger: Editions Carbonel, 1950); and Ibn Hawkal (ca. 977), "Description de l'Afrique," trans. M. de Slane, *Journal Asiatique*, 3rd series, vol. 13 (February 1842): 153 ff.
10. Charles L. Redman, "Comparative Urbanism in the Islamic Far West," *World Archaeology* 14 (1983): 355-77; *idem*, "Survey and Test Excavation of Six Medieval Islamic Sites in Northern Morocco," *Bulletin d'Archeologie Marocaine* 14, in press; and Nancy L. Benco, "Organization and Technology of Pottery Production in Early Medieval Morocco" (Ph.D. diss., State University of New York at Binghamton, 1986).
11. Nancy L. Benco, "Chemical and Mineralogical Analyses of Early Islamic Pottery from al-Basra," mimeographed (Department of Anthropology, State University of New York at Binghamton, n.d.).
12. Other indicators that will be used to investigate the degree of political/administrative involvement in craft production are the degree of pottery standardization, the use of simplification procedures in the manufacturing process, and the scale of production facilities.
13. E. C. Pielou, *Mathematical Ecology* (New York: John Wiley and Sons, 1977), 291-311.
14. Archaeological applications of ecological diversity measures are discussed in two recent articles by Keith Kintigh, "Measuring Archaeological Diversity by Comparison with Simulated Assemblages," *American Antiquity* 49 (1984): 44-54; and "Sample Size, Significance and Measures of Diversity" (Paper delivered at the Forty-Ninth Annual Meeting of the Society for American Archaeology, Portland, Oregon, April 1984). Other works that employ diversity indices are by Warren DeBoer and James A. Moore, "The Measurement and Meaning of Stylistic Diversity," *Nawpa Pacha* 20 (1982): 147-62; Margaret Conkey, "The Identification of Prehistoric Hunter-gatherer Sites: The Case of Altamira," *Current Anthropology* 21 (1980): 609-30; Prudence M. Rice, "Evolution of Specialized Pottery Production: A Trial Model," 219-240.
15. Pielou, *Mathematical Ecology*, 303-304.
16. As adapted from Pielou, the diversity of functional classes is calculated as

$$H'(f) = -\Sigma p_i \log p_i$$

where p_i is the proportion of the i functional class within the total assemblage. The weighted mean diversity of technological types within functional classes is calculated as

$$H'(t) = -\Sigma p_i H'_i$$

where H'i is the diversity of technological types *within* each functional class. The diversity within each functional class is computed as

$$H'_i = -\Sigma p_{ij} \log p_{ij}$$

where p_{ij} is the proportion of technological type *j* within functional class *i*.

17. Because of the possible effect of sample size on diversity indices, the al-Basra assemblages were tested with a computer simulation program developed by Keith Kintigh and discussed in "Measuring Archaeological Diversity by Comparison with Simulated Assemblages" and in "Sample Size, Significance, and Measures of Diversity." Although the sizes of the five al-Basra assemblages varied from a low of 204 sherds to a high of 819 sherds, the simulation program indicated that sample size differences had no significant impact on the diversity values that were obtained. In other words, the differences in diversities are due, not to variation in sample size, but to typological variability in the assemblages themselves.

18. Feinman, "The Relationship between Administrative Organization and Ceramic Production in the Valley of Oaxaca,"176ff.

Numismatics and Medieval Archaeology

ALAN M. STAHL

Medieval coins are the material product of a past culture and are frequently discovered in excavations. As such, they are archaeological artifacts and are subject to the same types of analysis and inference as ceramics, jewelry and weapons. Medieval European coins, however, have certain characteristics which distinguish them from other artifacts, and from other coinages, and which need to be taken into account before inferences can be made from their discovery. In this essay, I will examine some of the aspects in which coins can be treated like other artifacts and survey some of the distinctive characteristics of medieval coinage which should be understood by the archaeologist.

The production of coins in a given time and place can be of importance in investigating how the producers related to their environment. The most evident example of such a relationship is the minting in the early fourteenth century of silver coins near the rich mines of Bohemia and of gold coins in Hungary, which had become the major European source of new gold.[1] Another example of numismatic evidence for settlement and land use is the distribution of Merovingian mints along river valleys, which testifies to settlements not known from upland cemetery sites.[2]

Coins were probably the artefact produced in the greatest volume in the Middle Ages, and inferences about their manufacture can be of importance in understanding the technology and organization of medieval production. An example is the rich and varied series of coins issued by the dukes of Bohemia in the twelfth century. On each issue there is a distinct obverse and reverse image which is identical from specimen to specimen. The lettering of the legend around the edge, however, varies considerably. The reason for this must be that the minter carved the central image in relief into a punch which he then drove into a succession of dies. The letters of the legend were each carved into a separate punch and sunk individually into the die.[3] This is a sophisticated technique of die making that was apparently unknown to Greek and Roman minters and was not widely adopted in Europe until after the fifteenth century. In a study of a hoard of these coins, it was estimated that about four million coins were minted in a period of six months, requiring as many as fifteen workers in the actual striking and probably a total of three times as many for the entire mint staff.[4] Such inferences could be of importance in understanding the social and political structure of twelfth century Bohemia.

The choice of the imagery to be put on coins can be a reflection of the symbolic identifications of the issuer. An example is the coinage of the rulers of Greece in the thirteenth century. Their coins bear a stylized tower copied from the *denier tournois* of contemporary French royal coinage. This is not surprising, as many of these rulers were of French origin and had obtained their Aegean domains as a result of the Fourth Crusade. It is, however, of interest that they chose to impose a French coinage rather than imitate what was already circulating there or establish new coin types to support their independent claim of sovereignty. It is especially indicative of the impact of French culture on medieval Greece that a member of the Comnenus family, ruling in Greece as John II Angelus, Sebastocrator of Greater Valachia, copied this French coin type for his own coinage.[5]

Finds of coins of one mint in a context away from their place of manufacture can easily lead to inferences of communication, but caution must be shown in seeking to determine such contacts.[6] For practical purposes, trade usually took the form of the transport of commodities in both directions rather than the flow of goods one way and of coins the other. In fact, coins themselves often can be viewed as a commodity, a manufactured product which was imported into a region to fill the need for a circulating medium, rather than as the unintentional result of an uneven balance of trade. Nor does a coin-find necessarily demonstrate the direct contact of one culture with another; the find of a coin of eleventh-century Norway in an Indian mound in Maine is exceptional and does not imply that a European brought the coin to its deposition site.[7] Probably of much greater significance for cultural interaction is the large number of English coins of this era found in southern Scandinavia.[8]

The context of finds of medieval coins can sometimes be of value for cultural interpretation. Gold Roman coins and imitations of them are frequently encountered in inhumations of the fifth through seventh centuries, sometimes pierced or mounted as jewelry.[9] It is often inferred that these were some sort of talisman and may have played a role in burial rituals, an interpretation which is nuanced though not contradicted by the presence of such coins in regions known to have been orthodox as well as Arian and pagan.[10]

In addition to providing the basis for cultural inferences, ancient coins are of special interest to the archaeologist as they can provide a basis for the absolute dating of features and strata. This is especially the case for excavations of Roman sites, where coins are usually abundant and can often be dated within a few years. That such a situation does not often arise on medieval sites can best be understood as a factor of the nature of medieval coinage and of the medieval economy.

The most apparent characteristic of the coinage discovered at many medieval sites is its paucity. While the lack of coins from a given era can be frustrating to an excavator, it can moreover be misleading if the archaeologist interprets this lack without an understanding of the circulation of the coinage. Many sites of Gaul are lacking on coinage from the fifth through seventh centuries, and this has been interpreted to imply a discontinuity of settlement. What must be taken into account is that even in such sites as urban Trier, known to have been occupied continuously through this period, such coinage is also lacking or scarce.[11] It is most likely that the importation of coins into Gaul and Germany ceased at the end of the fourth century and that fourth century coins continued circulating through much of the fifth and even into the sixth century. Not only have villas been characterized as having been abandoned by the year 400 on the basis of the lack of finds of later coinage, but a major site of late Roman pottery manufacture was similarly given a terminus of AD 400 on the same grounds, leading to a compressed ceramic chronology which has in turn caused the misdating of further sites.[12]

The situation is different, though no better for the archaeologist, in contexts from the sixth and seventh centuries. In this period the only coins minted in much of Europe were small gold tremisses, about a gram of often base gold, but still of such value as to make their presence at many habitation sites unlikely and their loss and lack of recovery all but impossible. In fact, the few coins of this era that have been found in excavation are almost entirely from inhumations, where their value for chronology is ambiguous. The most noteworthy such case is the Sutton Hoo burial, where the date of the minting of the latest coin may be well before the actual deposition.[13]

Even after the change from gold to silver coinage, which took place in most of Europe in the seventh century, each coin was often of too great a value to allow the kind of common loss which permits secure dating of strata. The earliest silver medieval coins were irregular and crude; they might not even be recognized as coins by unprepared excavators. Such coins do not appear to have circulated widely and are not often found on habitation sites. After about AD 800, most of Europe used a broad silver penny, worth about a day's wages for a field hand. Such large, valuable coins were rarely lost without being recovered. In the later medieval period, a wider variety of denominations came into being, and daily coin use spread to the lower social ranks. Small, base coins of the fourteenth and fifteenth centuries are those most commonly found on medieval sites. Even a carefully excavated aristocratic residence might turn up only a handful of earlier pieces.

Not only are medieval coins found in relatively small numbers on many sites, but those found may be of only limited value in dating. A primary problem is the poor legibility of most legends on medieval coins. In a great number of cases, the legend on a single specimen cannot be fully read, even by an experienced numismatist. It may take the comparison of several identical specimens to reconstruct the entire text, a situation enjoyed by few excavators. Moreover, coins found singly in the earth are frequently so corroded as to render the deciphering even more difficult, especially base coins of a high copper content.

Once the legend has been read or reconstructed, it may not be a simple task to identify the coin. There has been only one comprehensive handbook of medieval coins, a turn-of-the-century work in three volumes which illustrates only a small percentage of coins with engravings.[14] For some areas, such as Anglo-Saxon England, there are well-illustrated, up-to-date catalogues in which the archaeologist can find any coin likely to be encountered on a site. For other regions, most notably Germany, there are no comprehensive works and it may be necessary to spend days in a highly specialized library to identify a given coin. The underlying causes of this situation are the great number of mints in operation, the repetition of names within families, frequency of changes of types, and the lack of basic information in many legends.[15]

Though sketchy attributions may in part be blamed on the state of research and publication of medieval coinage, much of the difficulty in chronology derives from the nature of the coins themselves. Medieval people were cautious and conservative when accepting a coin, and this led to the retention in some places of familiar coin types and to a process known as immobilization. A well-known example of an immobilized coinage is the short-cross issue of Henry II of England. His heirs Richard and John not only maintained the images of this established coinage, but even kept their father's name Henry in the legend. The coin type remained essentially unchanged through the reign of Henry III, for a total of almost seventy years. Through the careful work of generations of English numismatists, minute variations in the portrait and letter forms have permitted the construction of a chronology for short-cross pennies which allows most of them to be dated to within a decade or less.[16]

A similar situation is found in Italy. To distinguish themselves from their neighbors who were ruled by a succession of hereditary lords, most Italian communes identified on their coins only their patron saint or the emperor who first granted them minting privileges. For the denari of many communes, pieces can only be placed in a period from the earliest documented minting of coins to the end of communal government. In a study of a hoard of denari of Ancona, a distinguished medieval numismatist was able only to divide the coins into groups on epigraphic and metrological grounds and suggest a plausible relative chronology for the groups; the dating of any given specimen remains "thirteenth or fourteenth century."[17]

A further complication can be seen in the history of the sterling penny. The long-cross sterling penny of Edward I of England was so successful that, like the short-cross penny before it, it remained unchanged through succeeding reigns. On the continent, local pennies had often been minted of an alloy much baser than the English sterling, which circulated there as a multiple. In the thirteenth and fourteenth centuries, rulers from Flanders to Coblenz to Norway issued copies of the long-cross sterlings of Edward with alterations of legend that were calculated to be unnoticed by users or with no changes at all which would permit the localization of the mint. There is even a series which appears in turn to be copied after such continental imitations of English sterlings, making the time and place of minting yet more difficult to determine with precision.[18]

Even when the issue date of a coin can be accurately determined, it is not always easy to gauge the time that may have elapsed between mining and loss. A hoard of base coins recently discovered in Greece contained coins clearly minted after 1462, setting a *terminus post quem* for its deposition. The earliest coin in the hoard, however, was minted by Conrad I in Sicily between 1250 and 1254; it had circulated more than two centuries between its minting and burial. In this same hoard, eighty per cent of the coins were minted before the year 1400, six decades before its burial.[19] The explanation for this is the uneven minting rate of the principal coin in the hoard, the Venetian tornesello. This denomination was initiated in 1353, but saw its major minting in the period 1380 to 1410, after which time new coins were seldom issued and old coins made up the bulk of circulation in Greece. Without an understanding of such uneven rates of minting and long circulation, the discovery at the Athenian Agora of large quantities of coins minted from 1360 to 1425 and none from the following six decades might lead to a mistaken inference of the abandonment of diminution of activity at the site in the later fifteenth century.[20]

It is evident that there are still many questions of chronology of medieval coins that must be answered to make them more useful as a secure basis for the dating of archaeological features and associated finds. For such study, the numismatist uses a variety of techniques akin to those employed for establishing relative and absolute chronologies for any artefact type. Seriation and stylistic development allow the ordering of imitations of Byzantine coins produced in the Germanic kingdoms of the early Middle Ages.[21] Comparison of declining amounts of precious metal has allowed the ordering of other series of medieval coins.[22]

For coins, like other objects, however, the most reliable method of establishing a chronology is through the comparison with other objects found in association. As has been noted above, medieval coins tend to be scarce in excavations, and too few have been published with adequate reference to context to allow the numismatist to use such excavations as the basis for chronology. The fact that archaeological levels are often dated by coins would make much of such inference circular in most cases.

The most useful context for the numismatist is usually the hoard, the discovery of a group of coins buried together. Few medieval people of any class had access to banking services, and most wealth was secreted in or near the home. At the time of departure on a voyage or of a perceived threat of attack, an individual would usually bury such coins in a secret place; should he or she fail to retrieve the savings, it might go undiscovered until modern times. Many such treasures were buried in fields or yards rather than within the habitation area, and are discovered more often by farmers than by archaeologists. The increased use of metal detectors has recently added to the number of hoards which are found outside of controlled contexts. The antiquities laws of European countries vary considerably; in some countries even coins discovered by treasure hunters are routinely reported to the authorities and examined by qualified numismatists before being dispersed. Hoards found in other countries, however, are usually known only from the time at which they appeared in the stock of a dealer and must be reconstructed on the basis of fragmentary and often questionable information. By the time it is analyzed, such a hoard may have been adulterated by intrusions or by the removal of rarities.

In theory there exist two types of hoards: the circulation hoard and the savings hoard.[23] A circulation hoard would represent the burial of a group of coins recently received by an individual in commerce. A savings hoard would be the accrued treasury of an individual or institution, added to sporadically and diminished at any time up to its final, unretrieved, burial. A circulation hoard is of more interest to the numismatist, as it reflects the coinage in use at a given moment, allowing the determination of the circulating period of various issues. In practice, it is seldom possible to distinguish clearly between a circulation hoard and a savings hoard, as any coin in circulation might have been recently removed from savings and because medieval coins often circulated in sealed bags, thus closing various components of a hoard long before they were brought together and buried.

It is through the comparison of a series of hoards that the numismatist can reconstruct the coinage in circulation at a given time and place. Through die studies performed on coins from such hoards it is often possible to gauge the relative activity of mints and even to estimate the quantities of coins minted in various issues. The archaeologist can then use such information as the basis for interpreting the presence or absence of certain coins in excavation contexts. It is only with a sophisticated understanding of the circulation of coinage at the period of site use that the archaeologist can make valid and useful inferences from the excavation of coins in a medieval context.

Notes

1. Karel Castelin, *Grossus Pragensis: Der Prager Groschen und seine Teilstücke*, 2nd ed. (Braunschweig, 1973) 1-18; Arthur Pohl, *Ungarische Goldgulden des Mittelalters* (Graz, 1974) 7-12.
2. Alan M. Stahl, *The Merovingian Coinage of the Region of Metz*, Publications d'Histoire de l'Art et d'Archéologie de l'Université Catholique de Louvain 30 (Louvain-la-Neuve, 1982) 115-125.
3. Jarmila Haskova, "Die böhmische Münztechnik in der Zeit des Feudalismus," *Arbeits- und Forschungsberichte zur Sächischen Bodendenkmalpflege* 20-21 (1976): 559-82.
4. Ruth Mazo Karras, "Early Twelfth-century Bohemian Coinage in Light of a Hoard of Vladislav I," *American Numismatic Society Museum Notes* 30 (1985): 179-210.
5. Gustave Schlumberger, *Numismatique de l'Orient Latin* (1878; rpt. Graz, 1954) 382-83.
6. Philip Grierson, "Commerce in the Dark Ages: A Critique of the Evidence," *Transactions of the Royal Historical Society*, Ser. 5, 9 (1959): 123-40; rpt. in idem, *Dark age Numismatics* (London, 1979).
7. Kolbjørn Skaare, "En norsk penning fra 11. årh. funnet på kysten av Maine, U.S.A.," *Norsk Numismatisk Forening-Nytt* 2 (May, 1979): 4-17.
8. Nils L. Rasmusson, "An Introduction to the Viking-Age Hoards," in *Commentationes de Nummis Saeculorum IX-XI in Suecia Repertis*, Kungl. Vitterhets Historie och Antikvitets, Akademiens Handlinger, Antikvariska Serien 9 (Lund, 1961) I:3-16.
9. E.g., Joan M. Fagerlie, *Late Roman and Byzantine Solidi Found in Sweden and Denmark*, American Numismatic Society Numismatic Notes and Monographs 157 (New York, 1967) 137-44.
10. Bailey Young, "Paganisme, christianisation et rites funéraires mérovingiens," *Archéologie Médiévale* 7 (1977): 40-43.
11. *Die Fundmünzen der römischen Zeit in Deutschland*, Trier, Abt. IV, Bd. 3, ed Maria R. Alföldi (Berlin, 1970).
12. Georges Chenet, *La céramique gallo-romaine d'Argonne du IVè/s siècle* (Mâcon, 1941) 155.
13. J. P. C. Kent, "The Date of the Sutton Hoo Hoard," in *The Sutton Hoo Ship-Burial*, by Rupert Bruce-Mitford, Vol. 1 (London, 1975) 607-47.
14. Arthur Engel and Raymond Serrure, *Traité de numismatique du moyen âge*, 3 vols. (Paris, 1891-1905).
15. Basic bibliographies of works on medieval coinage are: Philip Grierson, *Bibliographie numismatique*, 2nd ed. (Brussels, 1979) 101-211; and Elvira E. Clain-Stefanelli, *Numismatic Bibliography*, (Munich, 1984) 456-690.
16. John D. Brand, "Some Short Cross Questions," *British Numismatic Journal* 33 (1964): 57-69.
17. D. M. Metcalf, "Classification of the *Denari Primitivi* of Ancona in the Light of a Recent Hoard," *Numismatic Circular* 82 (1974): 378-80.
18. Nicholas J. Mayhew, *Sterling Imitations of Edwardian Type*, Royal Numismatic Society, Special Publication 14 (London, 1983).

19. Alan M. Stahl, *The Venetian Tornesello, A Medieval Colonial Coinage,* ANSNNM 163 (New York, 1985) 71-81.

20. *The Athenian Agora.* II *Coins from the Roman through the Venetian Period,* by Margaret Thompson (Princeton, 1954) 80-82.

21. E.g., Wallace J. Tomasini, *The Barbaric Tremissis in Spain and Southern France, Anastasius to Leovigild,* ANSNNM 152 (New York, 1964) 135-72.

22. E.g., Brita Malmer, *Den senmedeltida pennigen i Sverige,* KVAAH, Antikvariska Serien 21 (Stockholm, 1980) 14-48.

23. The best introduction to numismatic methodology is Philip Grierson, *Numismatics* (London, 1975); cf. pp. 124-39 for hoard and find interpretation.

Novgorod Birchbark Documents: The Evidence for Literacy in Medieval Russia[1]

EVE LEVIN

When archaeologists excavating the old Russian trading city of Novgorod discovered private correspondence written on birchbark, they immediately recognized the inaccuracy of the previous assumption that medieval Russian lay society was illiterate. Subsequent excavations of layers dating from the late tenth century through the fifteenth have yielded over six hundred scraps of birchbark bearing inscriptions, etched into the soft surface with a stylus. The texts range in length from a few characters to many sentences, and concern primarily financial, legal, or familial matters. With only a very few exceptions the documents are written in the Novgorodian dialect of Old Russian in Cyrillic *ustav* (block-capital) script. The telegraphic style is reminiscent of the modern memo. The authors and recipients include representatives of all social classes: both men and women of the aristocracy, clergy, tradesmen, servants, and peasantry.[2]

Soviet historians eagerly concluded that the birchbark correspondence implied extensive literacy—certainly in Novgorod, and probably elsewhere in Russia as well.[3] Gone were the feeble attempts to argue for the existence merely of a literate aristocracy on the basis of scattered references in medieval manuscripts to books and schools.[4] To most Soviet scholars, the question of literacy in the medieval period had been solved, and it required no further investigation.[5] To them, it was obvious that the individuals listed as authors had written the birchbark letters personally, proving that persons of all classes were literate. Soviet studies tend to gloss over such questions as the extent of literacy in the lay population, the means of education, and whether Novgorod was unique. Instead, most discussion concerns the role of Christianity in the development of literacy and secular education, with the weight of Soviet scholarship downplaying the importance of the Church.[6] Soviet national pride was doubly enhanced by the discovery of birchbark documents. First, the Soviet academic community possessed a primary source for history, ethnography, and linguistics unequaled in Europe. Second, the Soviet Union could boast of an educated medieval citizenry as a foil to Western accusations of backwardness and barbarism. Such an attitude did not foster a truly critical and detailed examination of the problem.

Even after the discovery of the Novgorod birchbark documents, Western scholars remained skeptical about literacy in medieval Russia.[7] A thesis of widespread literacy would require a re-evaluation of established conceptions of Russian society. Medieval Russia is usually portrayed in Western studies as primitive and uncultured. In the view of many scholars, literacy in sixteenth-century Muscovy was limited to narrow circles of clerics and bureaucrats, who wrote in dialects so distant as to approach mutual incomprehensibility. It has been seriously proposed that two major leaders of the sixteenth century, Prince Andrej Kurbskij and Tsar Ivan IV (the Terrible) might themselves have been virtual illiterates.[8]

Broader literacy is just barely conceivable in eleventh to fifteenth century Novgorod, and the cultural level of the city presumably declined quickly under Muscovite rule after 1471. Most Western scholars still subscribe to the nineteenth-century romantic depiction of Novgorod as Russia's democratic alternative to Muscovite oriental despotism.[9] Supposedly Novgorod escaped the debilitating Mongol conquest, and preserved a high cultural and moral level in its society, thanks to continuing commercial and cultural contacts with Western Europe. Only Novgorod, it is argued, required literacy to maintain the written documents necessary for economic transactions. Only Novgorod enjoyed a continuous stream of traveling merchants from the Latino-Germanic West to encourage the development of a culture receptive to education. And only the Novgorodian aristocracy possessed sufficient wealth to afford the luxury of educating the young.[10] The fact that birchbark documents have not been unearthed in the excavations of other Russian cities has served as confirmation of the thesis that lay literacy was strictly a Novgorodian phenomenon.[11] But Western scholars are reluctant to accept the notion of universal literacy even for enlightened Novgorod. Usually the documents are characterized as the work of scribes, drawing on standard formulae from Church Slavonic, Hanseatic German, and medieval Latin.[12]

Thus Western scholars have regarded birchbark documents primarily from the viewpoint of linguistics, discounting significant research on the history of Novgorod and archeological evidence. Soviet scholars, for whatever reason, have failed to refute the arguments put forth by their Western colleagues. A resolution of the differences between the two interpretations of the implications of the birchbark correspondence for medieval Russian literacy requires a thorough examination of the documents in their historical and archeological context.

The historical framework espoused by most Western historians of Russia was abandoned by serious students of the Novgorodian past several decades ago. Novgorod is no longer seen as more cultured than the rest of Russia. It is now clear that Novgorod was as much under Mongol rule as other Russian principalities. The Mongols, however, cannot be blamed for a lowering of the cultural or moral level of Russia, because none took place.[13] "Democracy" in Novgorod consisted of rule by an aristocratic oligarchy, which dominated trade, land ownership, the military, and the government, including the famous veče, or city assembly.[14] In religion, social attitudes, and literary forms, Novgorod differed little from Muscovy, and neither city revealed a propensity for the adoption of Western European ideas.[15] Most of the types of transactions described in the birchbark correspondence—administration of land, loans, court cases, and the like—took place in all cities of Russia, not only in Novgorod. The aristocracy of fifteenth-century Novgorod was surely not appreciably wealthier than that of Moscow in the same period. In short, little about the society of Novgorod would lead a researcher to expect a higher level of literacy there than in other Russian cities. Thus, while the historical context neither supports nor refutes the Soviet assertion of extensive literacy, it does contradict the notion among most Western scholars that Novgorod was unique.

The archeological data support the conclusions that persons of all social classes were functionally literate in Novgorod and that they were also literate in other territories of medieval Russia. The birchbark documents themselves provide the strongest evidence for literacy. Their form and language indicate that they were not composed by professionals, but by the individuals identified in the salutation as authors. The content of the letters substantiates the prevalence of written communication in Novgorodian society.

The birchbark correspondence depicts a society in which literacy was far from unusual. Letters contain frequent references to the written word. In document no. 27, Falej wrote to Esif to remind him of a previous letter: "I sent you a birchbark, saying. . . ."[16] No. 424, dating to c. 1102 and thus one of the oldest extant documents, similarly mentions the written word in a casual way. A son urged his parents to leave famine-stricken Novgorod for the more prosperous Smolensk or Kiev, concluding, "If you don't come, send me a letter to say that you are well." The word used for "letter," *gramatica*, can mean only a written message.[17] The text of a document occasionally refers directly to the literacy of the author or recipient. In no. 271, Jakov asked his friend Maksim to purchase oats on his behalf, making sure to get a receipt. In addition he begged, "Send me some good reading!"[18] To collect accurate receipts and select suitable reading material, Maksim would have to be literate. If the author wanted books, it can reasonably be supposed that he was capable of reading. No. 53 serves as another example of literacy. A landlord, Peter, wrote to his wife Marija:

> Greetings from Peter to Marija. I mowed the meadow, and the Ozerci took my hay. Write out a copy from the purchase document and send it here. When the document explains, I'll be understood.[19]

Peter uses the imperative, *spiši*, "write out" implying that Marija would make the copy herself. Had he intended her to have a copy made, the Old Russian would have been *veli spisati*.

Document no. 53 further implies that the peasants of Ozero as well as their lord, Peter, were literate. Unless the Ozerci could read for themselves, Peter could not hope to substantiate his claim to hay by presenting them with written documentation. In no. 307, peasants recognized that certain legal documents presented to them were inaccurate, and appealed to their lords and lady to have them changed.[20] A steward in a third case complained to his lord, "The peasants won't pay me without an agreement, and you did not send a man with the document. . . ."[21] From the recalcitrant peasants' perspective, the absence of a written contract meant that no agreement had been reached. Similarly, a merchant ordered that goods remain in storage in a cellar, until someone came with written authorization to take them.[22] In short, Novgorodian society respected and relied upon the written word. Persons of all classes expected agreements and authorizations to be confirmed in writing, and were capable of verifying the written version of the contract.

The twelfth-century cleric Kirik inadvertently confirmed the extent of private correspondence in a question to Bishop Nifont. Kirik asked about the propriety of "walking on documents." He was referring to outdated birchbark letters, thrown into the street, as archaeologists have discovered. It should be noted that Bishop Nifont assured Kirik that it was no sin to step on something with writing, provided holy words were not visible.[23]

While this need for written documentation suggests literacy among all levels of the population, could it be, as many Western scholars have argued, that professional scribes wrote and read for the less educated? The peasants' desire to see something in writing might prove only that they had access to a literate person. This thesis is untenable, however, Available information on the Russian countryside in the fourteenth and fifteenth centuries precludes a thesis that literate outsiders were permanent residents of the villages. Villages frequently contained five households or fewer, which could not support the services of a resident priest or scribe.[24] The steward often lived in the village, and literacy would certainly enhance his abilities in record-keeping. Although a steward might on occasion have written letters for the peasants in his charge, he would not have taken down a note to the lord complaining of his incompetence and dishonesty. No. 370, from the mid-fourteenth century, is a case in point:

Greetings to Jurij and to Miksim from all the peasants. What sort of person did you give us as steward? He does not defend us, he sells us out, he robs us. We have suffered from him; if he doesn't leave, we will perish from him. If he remains here, we will not be forced to stay here, too. Give us a peaceful man. And we petition you about this.[25]

Crises in the countryside often could not await the arrival of a literate itinerant steward, priest, or scribe. For example, in no. 17, the peasants required immediate authorization from the lord to take the seed from his storehouse at planting time.[26] Under the constraints of the short North Russian growing season, the peasants could not have spared the time to wait for some outsider to arrive in order to dispatch a message. Had nobody in the village been able to write, the peasants doubtless would have sent word verbally instead. The existence of such a letter in itself testifies to literacy among the rural population.

Other sorts of messages would not have been entrusted to the discretion of a scribe. In a fragmentary letter, no. 24, the author asked the recipient to "send a man with a letter secretly."[27] In order to preserve the secrecy of the correspondence, the recipient would not have gone to a public scribe, although it is conceivable that he would have one in his pay. It is difficult to imagine that no. 377 passed under the stylus of any scribe whatsoever: "From Mikita to Ulijanica. Marry me. I want you and you want me. . . ."[28] The letter is not a formal marriage contract, but rather an expression of love, with blatant sexual overtones. Medieval Novgorod practiced a strict propriety in sexual matters which precluded public admission of sexual desires.[29] Any expression of love could have been made only privately.

The form of the birchbark letters reinforces the conclusion that the individuals named as authors themselves held the stylus. Most of the letters on birchbark are short — only three or four sentences. Such messages could easily have been sent orally by the courier required to carry the document, if either the author or recipient would be inconvenienced by the written form. The information conveyed was rarely so complicated that a person of average intelligence would garble it. The purpose for writing the message would lie in the preference for written authorizations. Also, a letter on birchbark could be sent with a child who might misunderstand or forget verbal instructions. For example, Smen entrusted two letters to his child. One was a reply to a flustered query from his new daughter-in-law about where the baking supplies were kept. The second was a note to a business associate, which mentions how the letters were to be conveyed. The youngster lost them while taking a short cut across a neighbor's yard. There archaeologists found the two pieces of birchbark, rolled up together, five hundred and fifty years later.[30]

The manner of writing on birchbark precludes attributing them to scribes. Etching into birchbark is a slow and cumbersome method of writing. Certainly any scribe would possess pen and ink, to be used for writing on parchment and paper in addition to birchbark. In fact, three extant birchbark documents were written in ink, including the only one with a text in Latin.[31] Probably an itinerant scribe who also carried the messages he wrote would put more than one message on a piece of birchbark, but no such document survives. Each of the over six hundred birchbark documents represents a distinct letter to a single recipient (or group of recipients) or a single author's reminders to himself. In almost every case in which more than one letter survives from a given author, the orthography matches, proving that the same person held the stylus. For example, the *posadnik* (mayor) Oncifor sent two letters to his mother and one to his grandmother, all in the same hand. Although it is possible that a man of stature would travel with a scribe, he probably wrote the letters himself.[32] A servant, Grigorij, sent two letters to a housekeeper, Domna; again the handwriting matches. As a servant himself, Grigorij would not have a scribe at his command.[33]

The language of the birchbark documents is also in accordance with non-professional authorship. Most letters reflect pure Novgorod dialect, although an occasional birchbark exhibits the phonological characteristics of other Russian vernaculars.[34] Borrowings from Church Slavonic—the written language of the educated clergy—are very rare in the birchbark correspondence. For example, the letter щ, which represents one of the major distinctions between Old Russian and Church Slavonic phonology, appears only a handful of times in the language of the birchbarks, in passages copied from ecclesiastical readings, in place and personal names, or as a means of rendering the combination of sounds *z* and *č*, as in the typically Russian word *bezčest'e*.[35] In comparison, the percentage of Church Slavonicisms is much higher in the secular land documents which were certainly produced by professional scribes.[36] Also as compared to the official parchment documents, the literary style of the birchbark correspondence is crude. Sentence fragments abound; there are numerous obvious orthographic mistakes; and poor usage obscures the meaning. The abbreviations of key words which were standard in scribal manuscripts appear only sporadically in the birchbark correspondence. Frequently the authors wrote the word out in its entirety, indicating a lack of familiarity with the abbreviations. Latin and Germanic words, like those of central Asian origin, are limited to an occasional term for an imported product.[37] It is hard to imagine that the same class of scribes could have written both the secular and ecclesiastical parchment manuscripts and the birchbark documents.

The authors of birchbark documents were not highly educated men and women. They knew the alphabet, and how to sound out words in order to read and spell them phonemically. They had learned the proper formulae for the greeting and closing, which the birchbark correspondence shares with the epistolary style of official communiques. Respectful letters begin *poklon" ot*, "greetings from" or "respects from." Notes between equals might omit the word *poklon*", and read simply "From X to Y." The closings were equally simple: *Jazo tobe klanjajusja*, "I bow to you." One need not postulate more than a very elementary education or familiarity with formal style to account for these formulae. In sum, the language of the birchbark documents suggests that the authors possessed the bare, functional literacy which might be gained in two or three years of schooling.

The significance of birchbark documents as evidence for extensive, if low-level, literacy, can be evaluated only in the context of other archeological discoveries. Archaeologists have found writing in places other than on birchbark. Numerous household items bearing etched inscriptions have been unearthed. These inscriptions establish the ownership or use of the object.[38] Other finds include several boards for holding wax tablets, used by schoolchildren to practice their lessons.[39] The walls of the archiepiscopal cathedral of St. Sophia in Novgorod have yielded hundreds of examples of graffiti written by bored church-goers over the centuries. Many of these inscriptions consist of short prayers (sometimes with pagan elements); others are purely secular.[40] In order to write on the walls of the church, the congregants must have carried styluses with them.

A phenomenal number of styluses (*pisala*) have been unearthed: more than fifty from Novgorod alone.[41] This number includes only those discovered before 1960, and excludes the smaller, needle-like *prokolki* and *ostrija*. Many of the styluses were made with a hole or a double hook at the upper end to permit attaching the tool to the belt with a thong. Iron and leather carrying cases also survive. The styluses are found at all levels of the Novgorodian excavation. The earliest examples date to the second half of the tenth century. At eleventh-century levels, styluses are common. The excavations of virtually every *usad'ba* (enclosed yard) in Novgorod have yielded at least one stylus and birchbark document.[42]

Archeology also confirms the hypothesis based on historical studies that Novgorod was not unique in having a literate population. A small number of birchbarks have been unearthed elsewhere in Russia: handfuls at Staraja Russa, Pskov, and Smolensk; single documents at Vitebsk and Mstislavl'; and three at Toržok.[43] Before 1960, sixty-six styluses were uncovered in Minsk, Kiev, Novogrudok, Galič, Vladimir, and other cities, although excavations at those sites have not been as extensive as in Novgorod.[44] The discovery of styluses points to widespread literacy in those cities even though birchbark documents have not been found.

The absence of birchbark evidence for much of medieval Russia is more readily explained by differing soil types than by great societal distinctions. The ground of Novgorod is unique in its wetness. Objects of wood and leather, including birchbark, rapidly became saturated with water and covered with mud. Deterioration was halted, and as a result these objects survive in great numbers, especially in layers from the mid-fifteenth century or earlier. The drier soil at higher levels did not preserve organic materials as well; few extant birchbark letters date to the mid- to late fifteenth century, and none to the sixteenth. In this context, however, the lack of birchbark letters cannot be taken as a sign of declining literacy. The soil of other cities was generally not as moist, and finds of wooden objects are rare. Therefore, Novgorod was not unusual in the extent of literacy in its domain, but rather in its topography and its archeological resources.

Thus archeology provides the most reliable evidence about literacy: the presence of letters and writing materials. The evidence is not sufficient, however, to prove universal literacy, although certainly in each household and each peasant village at least one person could read and write. The authors of the birchbark documents held the styluses themselves; nothing about the correspondence justifies the view that these letters were the handiwork of Church-educated scribes. Writing on birchbark was a phenomenon common to both sexes and all social classes. With the exception of a few documents which were clearly derived from ecclesiastical texts, the birchbark correspondence is written in the language of the people. The level of education implied by the birchbark documents is not high, and such basic literacy would not be difficult to attain. Furthermore, the presence of *pisala* in tenth-century layers grants credence to the Soviet theory that literacy predated the formal adoption of Christianity in 987. The weight of the historical, linguistic, and especially the archeological evidence supports the Soviet thesis of extensive literacy among the lay population of medieval Russia.

Notes

1. The author would like to express her appreciation to Professors Valentin Lavrent'evič Janin, Elena Aleksandrovna Rybina, the members of the Novgorod Seminar at Moscow State University, and the staff of the Novgorod State Museum. The research in the Soviet Union was conducted under the auspices of the International Research and Exchanges Board (IREX) and a Fulbright-Hays grant.

2. Seven volumes of birchbark documents have been published by A. V. Arcixovskij *et al.*, *Novgorodskie* gramoty na bereste (Moscow, 1953-78); another volume is in preparation. The publication includes a tracing of each document, a transcription, a description of where it was found, and a brief discussion of the content. Dating was established by dendrochronology. These volumes provide the numbering of the documents which has become standard.

3. V. L. Janin, *Ja poslal tebe berestu* (Moscow, 1975) 41-42.

4. For example, see the article in *Istorija kul'tury drevnej Rusi* (Moscow-Leningrad, 1951) 2:216-44, written by N. S. Čaev. Despite his desire to extend his estimates of literacy to the maximum, the author had to admit that he was dubious of the references to education of girls, and made no attempt to argue for literacy among the lower classes.

5. E. D. Dneprov is highly critical of this lack in his forthcoming article, " 'Relentlessly Running in Place': The Historiography of Schools and Pedagogical Thought in Medieval Russia (Some Conclusions, Problems, and Perspectives)," *History of Education Quarterly*, 26, 4 (1986): 539-51.

6. For an example of this literature at its best, and directly related to birchbark documents, see E. A. Rybina's "Berestjanaja biblioteka," *Nauka i religija* 4 (1977): 46-50.

7. Simon Franklin authored the most careful consideration of the question of literacy in the light of the birchbark discoveries, albeit only for the eleventh and twelfth centuries, cf. "Literacy and Documentation in Early Medieval Russia," *Speculum* 60 (1985): 1-38. He concedes functional literacy for the urban elite of Novgorod and other Russian cities but denies its existence among other social classes. Furthermore he argues that writing was used only casually and privately, while official transactions were made orally. The paucity of surviving official documents from the eleventh and twelfth centuries has been interpreted variously as evidence of illiteracy, as evidence of disregard for the written word, as evidence of the absence of a government bureaucracy, as evidence of the absence of private landholding, and as evidence of poor survival of documents. Such arguments from silence remain highly speculative.

8. Edward L. Keenan, *The Kurbskii-Groznyi Apocrypha*, (Cambridge, MA: Harvard Univ. Press, 1971), Chapter 3 and especially note 33 to that chapter.

9. Alexander Herzen seems to have been the first to voice this dichotomy, as part of a denunciation of nineteenth-century Russian government, but it has been extremely tenacious. For example, the emigré linguist A. V. Isačenko repeats the same stereotypes in his article "Esli by v konce XV veka Novgorod oderžal pobedu nad Moskovoj (ob odnom nesostojavsemsja variante istorii russkogo jazyka)," *Wiener Slavistisches Jahrbuch* 18 (1973): 48-55. In his recent collection of essays, Henrik Birnbaum espouses the same view: *Lord Novgorod the Great* (Columbus, Ohio: Slavica, 1981).

10. Riccardo Picchio, "The Slavonic and Latino-Germanic Background to the Novgorod Texts on Birch Bark," *Eucharisterion: Essays Presented to Omelyan Pritsak*, Harvard Ukrainian Studies, vol. 3/4, pt. 2 (1979-1980), pp. 650-51. Picchio presents these three assumptions about the nature of Novgorod as a "general consensus among scholars," but there are numerous prominent dissenters in the international academic community.

11. Isačenko, 51.

12. Picchio, 652-57.

13. Charles J. Halperin has authored the primary revision of the theory of the effects of the Mongol conquest. See his article "George Vernadsky, Eurasianism, the Mongols, and Russia," *Slavic Review* 41 (Sept. 1982): 477-93, and Chapters 9 and 10 of his monograph *Russia and the Golden Horde* (Bloomington, Ind.: Indiana Univ. Press, 1985).

14. V. L. Janin, *Novgorodskie posadniki* (Moscow, 1962), and his numerous other works.

15. On Novgorod's commercial and intellectual relations with the West, see Thomas S. Noonan's article, "Medieval Russia, the Mongols, and the West: Novgorod's Relations with the Baltic, 1100-1350," *Medieval Studies* 37 (1975): 316-39.

16. No. 27, Arcixovskij, 2:29. (dated to 1382-1392).

17. No. 424, Arcixovskij, 7:32-33.

18. No. 271, Arcixovskij, 5:96-97 (dated to 1369-1382).

19. No. 53, Arcixovskij, 2:56-57 (dated to 1313- 1340).

20. No. 307, Arcixovskij, 5:137-40 (dated to 1429-1446).

21. No. 99, Arcixovskij, 3:26-28 (dated to 1340-1369).
22. No. 40, Arcixovskij, 2:39 (dated to 1409-1422).
23. "Voprašanie Kirika," Article 64, *Russkaja istoriceskaja biblioteka*, (St. Petersburg, 1908) 6:40.
24. *Novgorodskie piscovye knigi*, vols. 1-6 (St. Petersburg, 1895-1915).
25. No. 370, Arcixovskij, 6:68-71 (dated to 1369-1382). See L. V. Čerepnin, *Novgorodskie berestjanye gramoty kak istoričeskij istocnik* (Moscow, 1960), 170 and V. L. Janin, *Ja poslal tebe berestu*, 108 for discussions of some of the obscure phrases. The overall tone of the document is beyond question. See also no. 94, Arcixovskij, (dated to 1369-1409) 3:20-22; no. 157, 4:38-41: (1409-1422); and no. 311, 5:144-45 (1396-1409).
26. No. 17, Arcixovskij, 2:16-17 (dated to 1409-1422). Other urgent messages concern providing horses for plowing and additional seed after a late frost, cf. no. 35, 6:41-43; no. 242, 5:64-65.
27. No. 24, Arcixovskij, 2:26 (dated to 1422-1429).
28. No. 377, Arcixovskij, 6:76-77 (1281-1299).
29. See my dissertation, *The Role and Status of Women in Medieval Novgorod*, Indiana University, 1983, for a discussion of attitudes toward sexuality.
30. Nos. 363, 364, Arcixovskij, 6:58-61 (dated to 1396-1409). Janin plausibly reconstructs the incident in *Ja poslal tebe berestu*, 143-45.
31. No. 496, Arcixovskij, 7:88-90, no. 13, 2:14. The Latin text is no. 488, 7:80-83 Picchio places much emphasis on this one document, using it to justify a depiction of Novgorod as a portal into Russia for Western Catholic and Latino-Germanic culture (658-60). As discussed above, specialists on the history of Novgorod no longer accept this thesis. The document was found in the Hanseatic enclave, where there was a Latin church, and thus it adds nothing to our knowledge of Western cultural influences in Novgorod. For a discussion of the archeological context of this document, see E. A. Rybina, "Raskopki gotskogo dvora v Novgorode," *Sovetskaja arxeologija*, 3 (1973): 100-07.
32. Nos. 354, 358, Arcixovskij, 6:43-47; 50-52 (dated to 1340-1369); No. 578, unpublished.
33. No. 134, Arcixovskij, 3:73-74; no. 259-265, 5:85, 91-93 (dated to the late 14th century). Janin reconstructs Grigorij's status in *Ja poslal tebe berestu*, pp. 133-42.
34. No. 246, Arcixovskij, 5:67-69 (dated to 1055-1096), is written in Smolensk dialect, according to the analysis of A. A. Zaliznjak in a lecture in the Novgorod Seminar at Moscow State University, March 16, 1982. A few documents are in a Finnish dialect, written in Cyrillic letters.
35. *bezčest'e*, spelled *b'ščesti*, appears in no. 67, Arcixovskij, 2:66-68. No. 128, 3:62-64 provides an example of the use of the letter in a text clearly of ecclesiastical origin.
36. Cf. S. N. Valk, *Gramoty velikogo Novgoroda i Pskova* (Moscow-Leningrad, 1949) for the texts of many of these documents.
37. Picchio attempts to argue that several common turns of phrase might be calques from German or Latin, but he provides inadequate evidence to trace the derivation (657-61). I am inclined to think of a more distant connection, perhaps through Greek ecclesiastical literature, known in the West in Latin and in Russia in Slavonic.
38. For examples, see the appendix to volume 1 of Arcixovskij's *Novgorodskie gramoty na bereste*.
39. A. F. Medvedev, "Drevnerusskie pisala," *Sovetskaja arxeologija* 2 (1960): 81-88.
40. A. A. Medynceva, *Drevnerusskie nadpisi novgorodskogo Sofijskogo sobora XI-XIV veka* (Moscow, 1978). Similar inscriptions adorn the walls of other Russian cathedrals, for example, St. Sophia in Kiev.

41. Medvedev, pp. 63-68. To the best of my knowledge, no scholar has updated Medvedev's study to include items discovered since 1960.

42. Medvedev, pp. 65-66.

43. L. V. Alekseev, "Berestjanaja gramota iz drevnego Mstislavlja," *Sovetskaja arxeologija* 1 (1983): 204-12, includes a total count of birchbark documents discovered through 1980. The information on the excavations at Toržok is from a lecture by P. D. Malygina in the Novgorod Seminar at Moscow State University, March 23, 1982. V. L. Janin believes that the custom of writing on birchbark was followed throughout Russia, Poland, and Scandinavia: *Ja poslal tebe berestu*, 222-24.

44. Medvedev, pp. 66-72.

Underwater Archaeology and Medieval Mediterranean Ships

GEORGE F. BASS

Until recent years we knew more about almost every aspect of antiquity than we did about the ships of antiquity. Handbooks of Greek, Roman and Medieval archaeology still describe and illustrate coins, sculpture, pottery, tools, tiles, jewelry, graves, architecture, and weapons without reference to the ships on which civilizations depended for commerce, defense, and colonization. Thanks to the invention of self-contained diving equipment, however, the new discipline of nautical archaeology is providing details of early ships that will take their rightful place in the general literature.

Even now we have learned more about merchant ships than about ferries, warships, fishing boats, and pleasure craft, because non-perishable cargoes of stone and pottery remain visible on the seabed for millennia, whereas empty wooden hulls survive destruction by shipworms only if buried in protective blankets of sand or mud. Still, through archaeological excavation of sunken merchantmen, we are beginning to trace the development of ship construction from the Bronze Age forwards.

The detailed study of early Mediterranean hull construction from shipwrecked remains is so new that our major task remains the gathering of primary data on which to base hypotheses concerning causes of evolutionary changes. Although the use of mortise-and-tenon joints in shell-first construction has been known for most of this century,[1] for example, it has been only during the past two decades that direct evidence for stages in the evolution from shell-first to skeleton-first construction has been discovered.[2]

My current excavation of a fourteenth-century BC shipwreck off Ulu Burun, Turkey, is providing the first evidence that mortise-and-tenon hull construction extends back into the Late Bronze Age,[3] but the fourth-century BC Kyrenia wreck excavated by Michael and Susan Katzev off Cyprus provides our most complete picture of a classical Greek ship.[4] After its curved, rocker-shaped keel was laid, and its stem and sternpost attached, its sides were built up one strake (or row of planking) at a time, the Aleppo pine planks tightly together with approximately four thousand hardwood tenons fit snugly into twice that number of mortises notched into opposing edges of the planks. Wooden pegs driven into holes drilled through each mortise-and-tenon joint, one on either side of the planking seam, secured the tenons. Once the hull was completed, pine frames (commonly called ribs) adzed from naturally curved timbers were inserted and fastened by foot-long copper spikes driven through the hull from outside and clenched over on the inner face of each frame. The entire hull was sheathed with thin lead plate, both as protection against marine borers and as a kind of caulking. The mast for a single squaresail was stepped a bit forward of amidships in an elaborate mast step; lead brailing rings allowed the sail to be positioned so that the ship could sail with the wind abeam. A pair of steering oars were mounted astern.

The building of the 14-meter Kyrenia ship, 4 meters abeam and of about 25 tons burden, required no knowledge of naval architecture as we think of it today. Planks of uniform thickness, like those now nailed to pre-erected skeletons of frames, were not used. Instead, according to the ship's reconstructor, J. Richard Steffy, the hull was virtually carved out of its side timbers in a process that wasted more than half of the wood of some of the planks. Such construction, with the careful cutting and fitting of thousands of mortises and tenons, clearly was highly labor intensive. Further, the hull's strength lay more in its shell than in its framing.

The Kyrenia ship, which sank with a cargo of 400 wine amphoras and 10,000 almonds at the end of the fourth century is probably typical of small freighters of the classical Greek period, but it is today a unique artifact because of its state of preservation. The Portecello wreck from the Straits of Messina, although less well preserved, shows the use of similar construction techniques about a century earlier.[5]

Ship construction during the Roman period continued the same tradition (fig. 1), as shown by many excavated hulls, some much larger, capable of carrying several hundred tons of stone or up to 10,000 amphoras.[6]

The succeeding Byzantine period, however, is critical to our understanding of the development of later Mediterranean hull design. Our basic question is how modern, frame-first or skeletal construction arrived in the Mediterranean by the end of the Byzantine era. Was it a sudden, overnight development, the brainchild of a single innovative shipwright? Or was it the result of a slow, evolutionary process down the ages? It now seems clear that it was not influenced by developments in northern Europe as once was thought.[7]

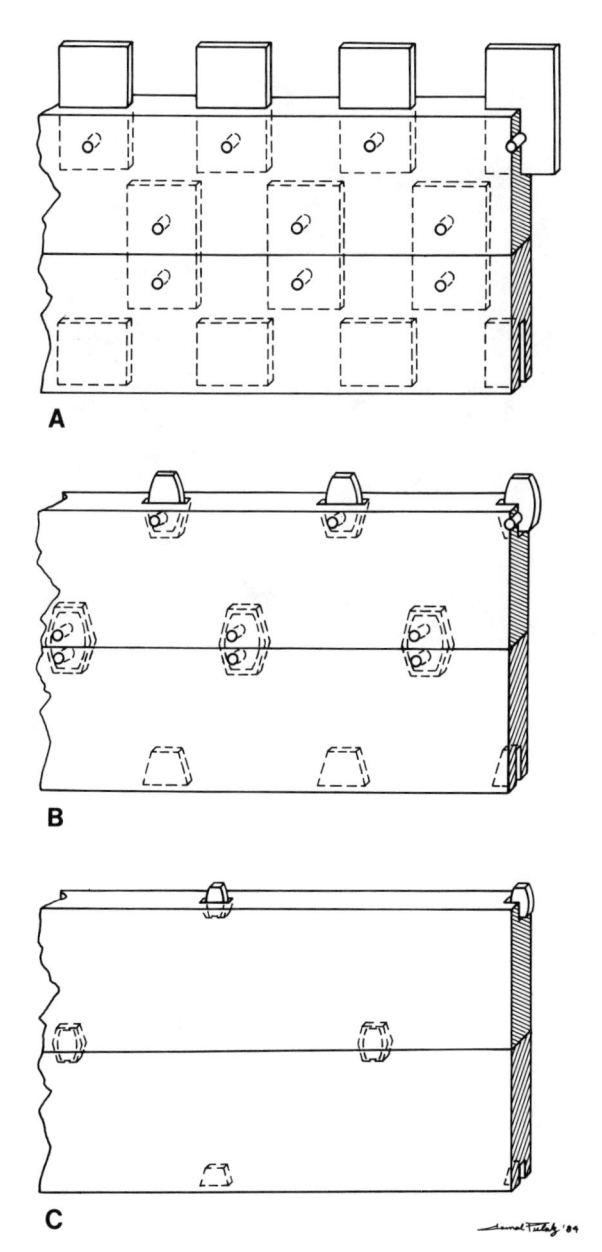

Fig. 1. Schematic drawings comparing edge-joining of shell planking in A, a typical Roman hull; B, the fourth-century Yassi Ada hull; and C, the seventh-century Yassi Ada hull (from F. H. van Doorninck, Jr., *Intern. J. Nautical Archaeology* 5 [1976]: 122).

Fig. 2. F. H. van Doorninck marks with white tacks the ends of wooden pegs holding tenons in place on the fourth-century Yassi Ada hull.

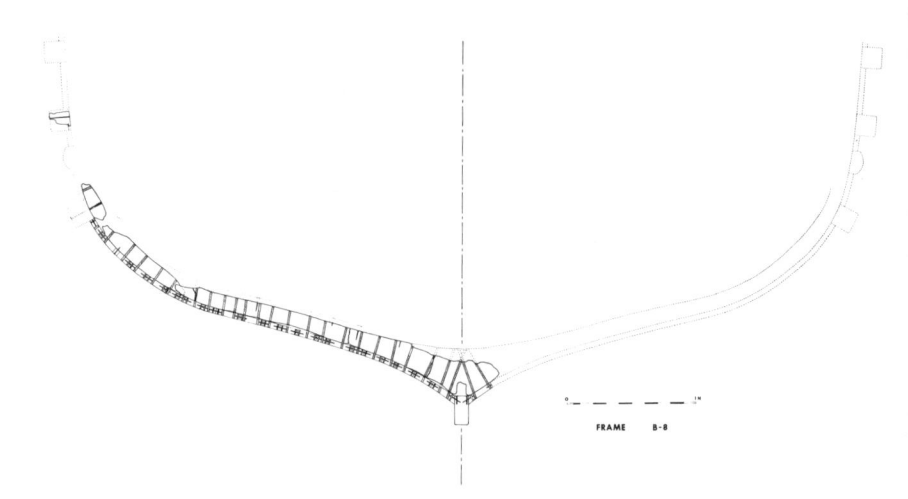

Fig. 3. Section of fourth-century Yassi Ada ship shows use of mortise-and-tenon joints to at least the height of the third wale. Each joint is pegged on either side, and the frame is attached to the planking by long wooden dowels.

The excavation of an early Byzantine shipwreck at Yassi Ada, Turkey, from the late fourth or possible early fifth century AC, points toward an answer, although in isolation the evidence of its hull might not have been fully appreciated.[8] This 20-meter vessel, with a beam of just under 8 meters, has been described by Frederick van Doorninck as having considerable overhang at bow and stern, like ships depicted in Roman art. It carried approximately 1,100 wine amphoras in a cargo hold separated from a stern galley which may well have been roofed with terra-cotta tiles. Although never completely excavated, the galley area already has yielded lamps, weighing implements, and the expected assortment of cooking and eating wares. The ship's anchors have not been found.

In the main, the hull of this early Byzantine ship was constructed like that excavated off Kyrenia. That its cypress planks were edge-joined with mortises and tenons as high as its third wale is certain, and we may speculate that the entire hull was similarly constructed, from oaken keel to gunwale, as at Kyrenia (figs. 2–3). Again as at Kyrenia, with one possible exception, the frames (fig. 4), in this case of cypress, were added to the hull afterwards; at Yassi Ada, however, the frames were attached to the hull with oak treenails (dowels) rather than with copper nails. The Yassi Ada hull was not lead-sheathed in its entirety, as was the Kyrenia ship, although lead patches were attached outside with iron tacks.

There is, however, a more significant difference between the Yassi Ada ship and earlier Mediterranean vessels, and it is one which points toward the future. The mortises are smaller than before (ca. 7 to 9 cm by 7 mm, and 5 cm deep), and the tapered oak tenons, being even smaller, fit quite loosely inside them (fig. 1). The tenons were fixed in place, once the planks were together, with wooden pegs driven through their tops and bottoms from within the hull, as in previous centuries. Until they were pegged, however, these loose mortise-and-tenon joints allowed the shipwright a great deal of play in positioning his planks. Further, the joints were more widely spaced than before, although not uniformly separated, being usually 25 to 32 centimeters apart instead of the 10 centimeters normally found in Greco-Roman hulls.

"It seems to me," van Doorninck writes, "that the considerable variance in joint spacing, the generally larger intervals involved, and the loose-fitting tenons in the hull represent an early and cautious phase toward reducing both the number of hull joints and the time and effort involved in fashioning them, thereby cutting construction costs. We find this trend will advanced in the Pantano Longarini and 7th century Yassi Ada Ships. By late Byzantine times, shipwrights had learned to dispense with joints entirely."[9]

The later Byzantine ship excavated at Yassi Ada is noteworthy to Byzantinists because of its firmly dated collections of ceramics, weights, tools, and other artifacts, which, together with coins from AD 625 and before, provide

Fig. 4. Frame from fourth-century Yassi Ada ship being recorded by F. H. van Doorninck, Jr., and P. Fries.

a strikingly complete picture of an early seventh-century commercial voyage.[10] The 20-meter merchantman (fig. 5), with a 12-meter cypress keel, and with a beam of only 5.2 meters, cost approximately 460 solidi to build. She carried more than 850 amphoras, many filled with spiced wine, perhaps worth an additional 70 solidi, and cash worth another 7 solidi, sufficient to feed fifteen peo-

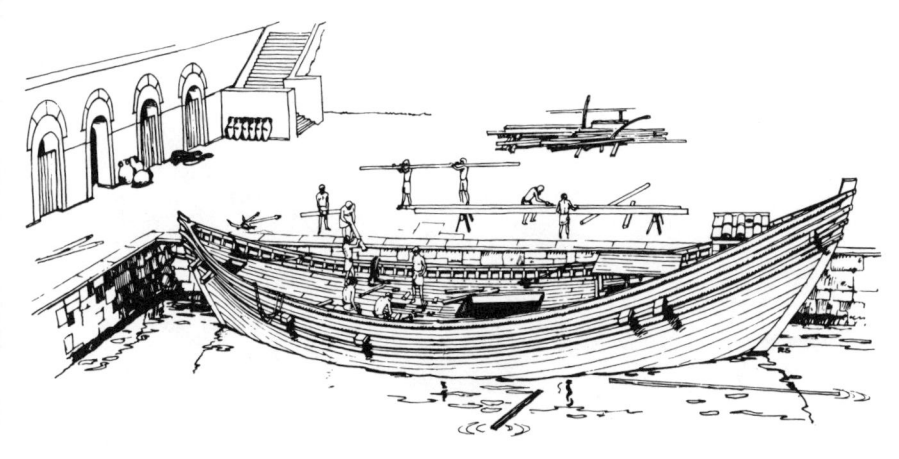

Fig. 5. Reconstruction drawing of seventh-century Yassi Ada ship by Richard Schlect.

ple for a month, even if we ignore the evidence of fishing *en route*. From careful excavation, we know where the helmsman manned his giant steering oars, where the carpenter kept his tools, where the boatswain stored his boat's anchor and tools for landing parties, and where the cook prepared meals over a low firebox on the port side of a crowded, tile-roofed galley. We suspect, from van Doorninck's calculations, that the uniformity of the weights of eleven iron anchors on board, based on a Roman pound of 315 grams, foretells later medieval statutes which specified numbers and weights of anchors on different classes of ships.

It is the hull of this ship, however, that interests us here, for it differs appreciably from earlier Mediterranean hulls. It is built in the shell-first manner only below the waterline (fig. 6), but even there its oak tenons not only are loose-fitting within their mortises, as on the entire fourth-century Yassi Ada hull, but they are smaller, spaced even farther apart (up to 90 centimeters), and they are not secured with pegs (fig. 1). In other words, the mortise-and-tenon joinery adds little to the structural integrity of the hull, but serves mainly to hold the pine planks in place until they are nailed to the frames. And here, too, we have a difference, for it seems that framing was erected almost simultaneously with the erection of the planking, several rows of pine planking followed by various parts of the elm framing, followed by several more rows of planking, and so on. Above the waterline, the frames were installed completely before the planking which, without any edge-to-edge joinery, simply was nailed to them with iron nails. Heavier strakes called wales were attached to the frames with iron bolts. There is no evidence of lead sheathing or patches on the hull.

SECTION 3
(FRAME 27)

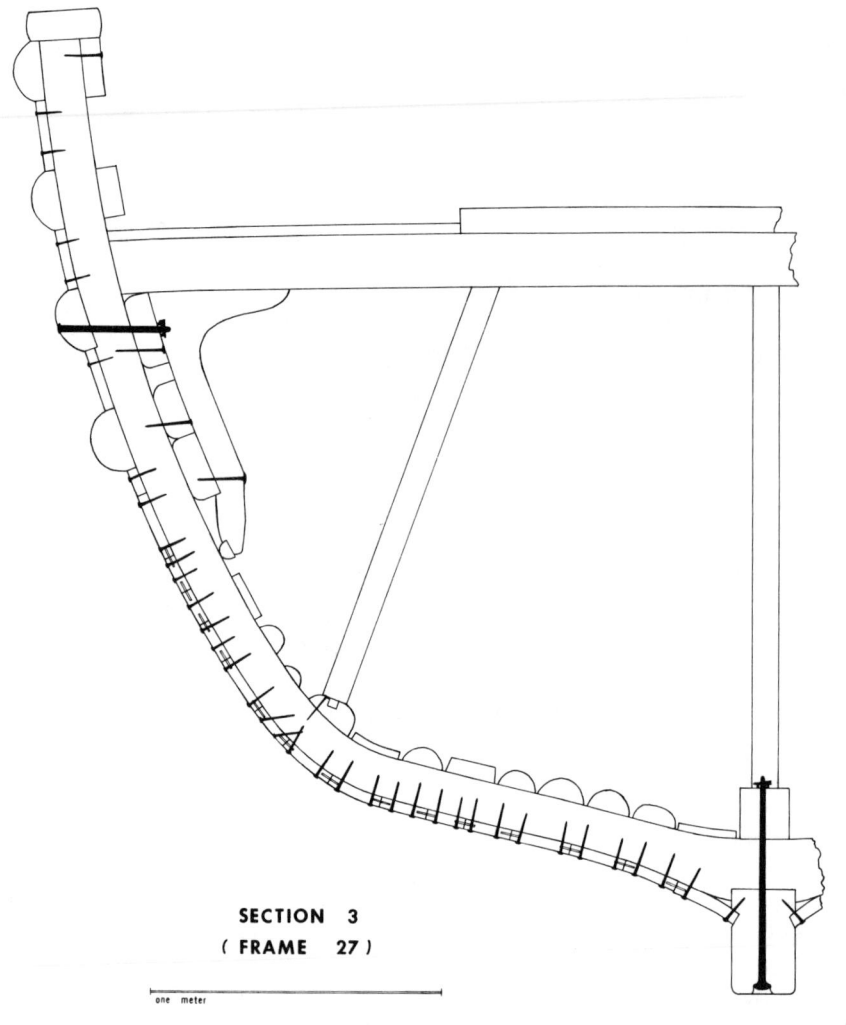

one meter

Fig. 6. Section of seventh-century Yassi Ada ship shows use of mortise-and-tenon joints only to level of waterline.

The seventh-century Yassi Ada ship is even more economical of labor and wood than the fourth-century Yassi Ada ship. I have in the past attributed this economy to the rise of modest, independent shipowners in the seventh century, just as I attributed the ship's sleek design to increasing numbers of hostile ships on the sea.[11] I now question the validity of these conjectures for the early seventh century when the ship sailed, before Arab expansion, especially as the economies seem simply to follow trends begun centuries earlier.

There are contemporaneous shipwrecks in the Mediterranean, at least one with part of its hull well preserved in a swampy part of southernmost Sicily known as Pantano Longarini.[12] Dated approximately to the seventh century, this ship of about 30 meters' length also shows a transitional type of construction, being built shell-first only up to the waterline. The pistachio tenons are set loosely in large mortises cut about a meter apart into the edges of cypress planks; as on the seventh-century Yassi Ada ship, the mortise-and-tenon joints are not pegged. "This must be," Throckmorton suggests, "because they functioned only as a convenience to the carpenter in setting up the immersed part of the hull by the 'shell first' method."[13] The hull was fastened with iron nails and bolts throughout.

The next steps between these "transitional" hulls and "modern" hulls in the Mediterranean remain unknown; evidence for this period lies buried beneath the seabed not far from Bozburun, Turkey, on a wreck we date tentatively to the ninth or tenth century on the basis of its amphoras; a brief inspection dive revealed solid timbers just below the surface of the sand.[14]

We know, however, that the transition from Greco-Roman shell-first hull construction to frame-first construction was more or less complete in the Mediterranean by the eleventh century.

Around AD 1025, as known from dated Islamic glass weights and Byzantine coins carried on board, a 15-meter merchantman with a beam of just over 5 meters sank inside Serçe Limanı, locally called simply Serçe Liman, a natural harbor on Turkey's southern coast just opposite Rhodes.[15] Probably lateen-rigged, and still using steering oars rather than a stern-mounted rudder, the ship represents the earliest known skeletal-built seagoing vessel in the Mediterranean. It was excavated by the Institute of Nautical Archaeology under the direction of the author and van Doorninck, during the summers of 1977 through 1979 (fig. 7).

Wooden hull remains were labeled and mapped on the seabed (fig. 8), then raised in hundreds of fragments (fig. 9) which were then kept wet to prevent their shrinking and warping beyond recognition (fig. 10). Each fragment, however, was removed from its fresh-water bath long enough to be traced at full scale on sheets of clear plastic. Then, while the wood underwent a two-year conservation treatment in polyethylene gylcol, the tracings were used by Steffy to reconstruct the hull through a series of tenth-scale research models which will lead to full-scale restoration.[16]

Steffy determined that ten frames adzed from naturally curved softwood timbers were nailed to the rocker-shaped keel, near the middle of the ship, in order to determine the hull's shape before the shipwright began planking. After erecting these frames, the shipwright fastened belts of bottom and side planking to them with iron nails and a lesser number of treenails. He then installed the other frames, which in turn allowed him to go back and plank the bilge area

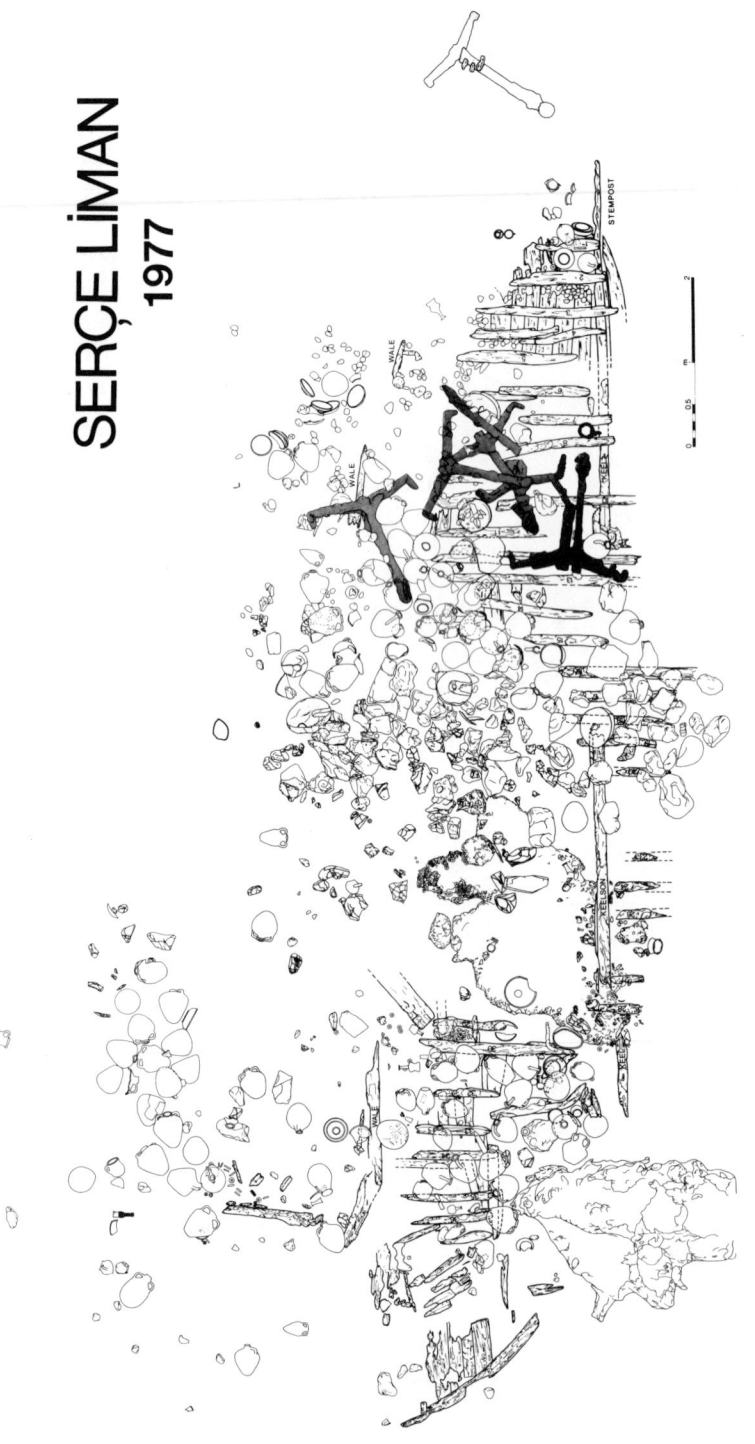

Fig. 7. Plan of the eleventh-century Serçe Limani shipwreck during course of excavation.

Fig. 8. Hull remains of the eleventh-century Serçe Limani ship are labeled and mapped on the seabed.

Fig. 9. Wooden hull fragments are transported from the seabed to the surface in custom-made boxes.

Fig. 10. Wood from the Serçe Limani shipwreck is kept wet until chemically conserved.

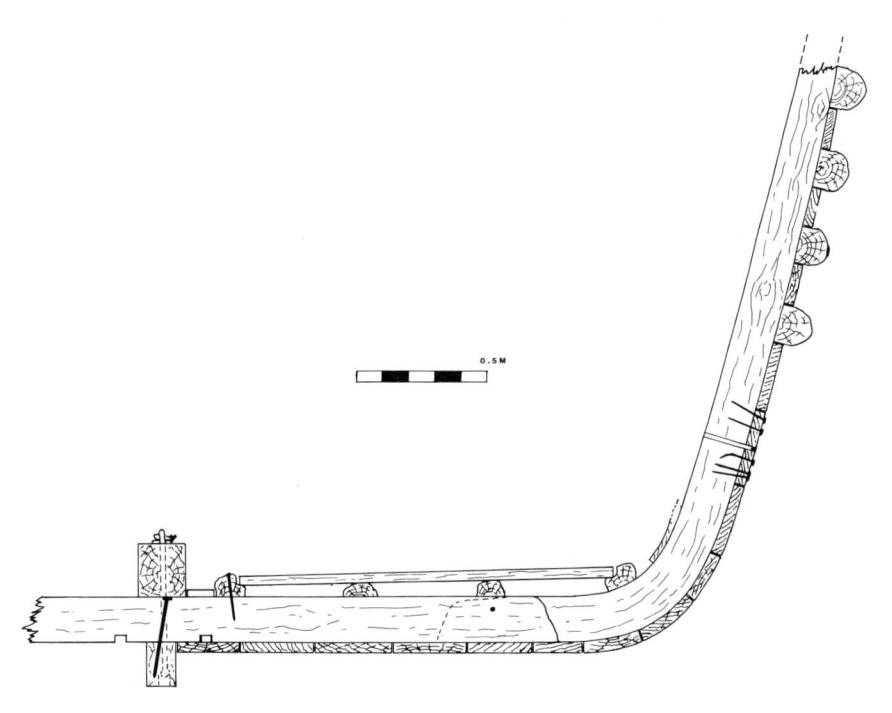

Underwater Archaeology and Mediterranean Ships / 151

Fig. 11. Section of eleventh-century Serçe Limani ship shows no use of mortise-and-tenon joints.

Fig. 12. Reconstruction drawing of eleventh-century Serçe Limani ship by J. Richard Steffy.

between the bottom and side planking, as well as to continue on up the ship's sides. None of the planks were edge-joined with mortises and tenons.

This prototype skeleton-first construction allowed a "boxier" hull shape (figs. 11–12), with a sharper turn of the bilge, than was possible in shell-first construction. This, in turn, provided greater cargo space; the Serçe Limani ship could carry, according to Steffy, 30 to 40 tons of cargo.

Frame-first construction, according to Steffy, freed shipwrights from the limitations of size and shape imposed by shell-first construction. But the construction of the Serçe Limani ship, he writes, "was no more a pure skeletal process than that of the 7th century Yassi Ada ship was a pure shell process. Our shipwright was still essentially using planks to determine hull shapes in all but the middle of the ship. . . . It seems obvious that not too many generations would evolve before shipwrights learned to pre-determine a few more shapes fore and aft, to soften the bilges, and to add complexity to frame curvatures, all of which would lead to carracks and beyond."[17]

It is clear, in addition, that the Serçe Limani ship represents one more step in the trend we have followed toward greater economy of labor and wood. How much this trend was due to socio-economic conditions, deforestation, technical advances, or, at the end, new traditions introduced by Arab seafarers—or, indeed, various combinations of all these factors—is a question faced by archaeologists and historians alike.[18] Thus, a determination of the nationality of the Serçe Limani ship is of historical interest. That determination, however, will not be as simple as I had at first anticipated. During the course of excavation, most of the noteworthy finds seemed clearly Islamic in origin, leading me to title a talk given shortly after my return from Turkey "A Medieval Islamic Merchant Venture."[19]

Sixteen glass weights, used for weighing flakes of gold and other precious items on balance scales, are impressed with the names and years of caliphs in Egypt. One of several copper or bronze buckets bears an Arabic inscription. The ship's ceramics—a single terra-cotta lamp, glazed bowls, and gargoulettes—all seemed at first to be Islamic. Gold coins (and cuttings from others) were Islamic. A preliminary study of metal balance-pan weights suggested them to be Islamic. But mainly it was the cargo of three and a half tons of glass, including 80 intact vessels whose closest parallels were Islamic, which led to my preliminary conclusion; I considered dozens of amphoras with Greek graffiti as simple a secondary cargo on an Islamic ship.

Diving and excavation, however, take but a small part of a nautical archaeologist's time. It was during the following years of conservation that a more complex picture of the nationality of the ship came to light.

Although we knew during the excavation that we had Byzantine as well as Islamic coins, it was not until later, while cleaning four "silver coin remnants," that we realized we had four Byzantine lead seals, one bearing the Virgin and the Christ child, one bearing the ecstatic meeting of Peter and Paul, and one still unused. It was also later, during conservation, that Greek graffiti were noticed on some of the cooking wares used on board; still later, through a study of their distribution on the wreck, van Doorninck determined that the Islamic glazed bowls were probably cargo rather than for shipboard use. Only after identification of the 150 bones found on the site did we know we had pig bones, remains of a pork meal. The cleaning and drawing designs on 900 lead fishing-net weights revealed that many bear Christian symbols, including crosses and the name Jesus. A steelyard recently removed from seabed concretion bears a boar's head at either end, reminding us of the boar's head at one end of the large Byzantine steelyard from the seventh-century Yassi Ada wreck; we have not yet studied the Serçe Limani steelyard, however, to be sure of its origin.

Much of the new evidence, but not all, suggests the presence of Christian crewmen; van Doorninck has discovered an Arabic inscription stamped on one of the ship's eight anchors (as he discovered recently a Greek letter stamped on one of the seventh-century Yassi Ada ship's anchors). Many other artifacts and remains, however, must be considered: wooden chessmen, gold and silver jewelry, millstones, copper and bronze vessels, iron locks, bone spindle whorls, wooden combs, seeds and pollen, all currently being studied. An identification of the wood has revealed that the ship's keel was possibly of elm, its frames, planks, and wales were probably pine, and its treenails were of a species of the heguminosae family; future wood studies, including those of the timber trade, may suggest probably places where the ship was built, and current lead-isotope analyses of cargo glass, glazes from ceramics, a metal sword hilt, and fishing weights may provide vital information concerning the route of the ship. A determination of the origins of dozens of iron weapons may reveal at least who controlled the ship during her final moments, but nearly contemporaneous accounts of piracy along the same coast suggest that even that would not necessarily tell us who built and originally manned the ship.

Notes

1. Peter Marsden, "The County Hall Ship," *Transactions of the London and Middlesex Archaeological Society* 21, part 2 (1965): 118-31, and "The County Hall Ship, London," *International Journal of Nautical Archaeology* 3 (1974): 55-65; Peter Throckmorton, "The Ship," in G. D. Weinberg, "The Antikythera Shipwreck Reconsidered," *Transactions of the American Philosophical Society* 55, pt. 3 (1965): 40-47; Guido Ucelli, *Le navi di Nemi* (Rome, 1950).

2. Frederick H. van Doorninck, "Byzantium, Mistress of the Sea: 330-641," in *A*

History of Seafaring Based on Underwater Archaeology, ed. G. F. Bass (London and New York, 1972) 134-58.

3. G. F. Bass, D. A. Frey, and C. Pulak, "A Late Bronze Age Shipwreck at Kaş, Turkey," *International Journal of Nautical Archaeology* 13 (1984): 271-79; G. F. Bass, "A Bronze Age Shipwreck at Ulu Burun (Kaş): 1984 Campaign," *American Journal of Archaeology* 90 (1986): 269-96.

4. J. Richard Steffy, "The Kyrenia Ship: An Interim Report on its Hull Construction," *American Journal of Archaeology* 89 (1985): 71-101; Michael L. Katzev, "Assessing a Chance Find Near Kyrenia," "A Cargo from the Age of Alexander the Great," and "The Study and Conservation of an Ancient Hull," in Keith Muckelroy, ed., *Archaeology Under Water, An Atlas of the World's Submerged Sites* (New York and London, 1980) 40-45.

5. Cynthia Jones Eiseman, *The Porticello Shipwreck: A Mediterranean Merchant Vessel of 415 to 385 B.C.* (Texas A&M University Press) in press.

6. Peter Throckmorton, "Romans on the Sea," in *A History of Seafaring Based on Underwater Archaeology*, ed. G. F. Bass (London and New York, 1972) 72-76.

7. A. E. Christensen, "Lucien Basch: Ancient Wrecks and the Archaeology of Ships — A Comment," *International Journal of Nautical Archaeology* 2 (1973): 143.

8. G. F. Bass and F. H. van Doorninck, Jr., "A Fourth-Century Shipwreck at Yassi Ada," *American Journal of Archaeology* 75 (1971): 27-37; F. H. van Doorninck, Jr., "The 4th Century Wreck at Yassi Ada: An Interim Report on the Hull," *International Journal of Nautical Archaeology* 5 (1976): 115-31.

9. van Doorninck (see above, n. 8), 123.

10. G. F. Bass and F. H. van Doorninck, Jr., *Yassi Ada I: A Seventh-Century Byzantine Shipwreck* (Texas A&M University Press, 1982).

11. G. F. Bass, "A Byzantine Trading Venture," *Scientific American* 225, no. 2 (August 1971): 24.

12. Peter and Joan Throckmorton, "The Roman Wreck at Pantano Longarini," *International Journal of Nautical Archaeology* 2 (1973): 243-66.

13. Ibid., 263.

14. G. F. Bass, "Turkey: Survey for Shipwrecks, 1973," *International Journal of Nautical Archaeology* 3 (1974): 335-38 (337, no. 6, with fig. 4 on p. 338).

15. G. F. Bass and F. H. van Doorninck, "An 11th Century Shipwreck at Serçe Liman, Turkey," *International Journal of Nautical Archaeology* 7 (1978): 119-32; G. F. Bass, "The Shipwreck at Serçe Liman, Turkey, *Archaeology* 33 (1979): 36-43; G. F. Bass, "Glass Treasure from the Aegean," *National Geographic* 153 (June 1978): 768-93; F. H. van Doorninck, Jr., "An 11th Century Shipwreck at Serçe Liman, Turkey: 1978-81," *International Journal of Nautical Archaeology* 11 (1982): 7-11; G. F. Bass, J. R. Steffy and F. H. van Doorninck, Jr., "Excavation of an 11th-Century Shipwreck at Serçe Liman, Turkey," *National Geographic Society Research Reports* 17 (1984): 161-82; G. F. Bass, "The Nature of the Serçe Limani Glass," *Journal of Glass Studies* 26 (1984): 64-69.

16. J. Richard Steffy, "The Reconstruction of the 11th Century Serçe Liman Vessel: A Preliminary Report," *International Journal of Nautical Archaeology* 11 (1982): 13-34.

17. Barbara Kreutz, "Ships, Shipping, and the Implications of Change in the Early Medieval Mediterranean," *Viator* 7 (1976): 79-109.

18. G. F. Bass, "A Medieval Islamic Merchant Venture," *Archaeological News* 8, 2/3 (Summer/Fall 1979): 94-94.

19. J. R. Steffy (see above, n. 16), 32.

Beowulf and the Language of Hoarding

ROBERT PAYSON CREED

Janet E. Levy begins a recent article titled "The Bronze Age Hoards of Denmark" with the following passage:

> The study of prehistoric religion is one of an archaeologist's most fascinating, yet elusive tasks. How, after all, can prayers, beliefs, values, and symbols—the basic stuff of religion—be dug up?[1]

I came across Professor Levy's article at the very time when I was beginning to explore the possibility that the Old English poem *Beowulf* might have much to say about the beliefs and values of the Anglo-Saxon settlers of Britannia who migrated across the North Sea from their continental homeland in the fifth and sixth centuries. The last third of the poem deals with a hoard and the dire consequences of stealing from it. Levy's article suggested to me, then, the possibility of trying to use *Beowulf* to help interpret hoards, in turn, trying to use hoard to help interpret the poem.

Such reciprocal support can occur only under certain conditions. In the best possible circumstances both artifact and text will have been constructed by the same society during the same period. But those circumstances are probably rare. In the present case we have to settle for trying to interpret Danish hoards with the help of a poem preserved in Anglo-Saxon England. I shall try to show that that is not so far-fetched as it might at first appear.

Although Levy's question about beliefs associated with hoarding was inspired by Danish Bronze Age hoards, it can also be asked about Iron Age hoards of other prehistoric societies. Since the hoard the *Beowulf* poet deals with contains iron weapons, the poet clearly tells of an Iron Age deposit. Further, the poet locates the hoard not in Denmark but in southern Sweden. It is not, however, the hoard itself that the poet is concerned with, although he does characterize its contents on a number of occasions. What most interests the poet is the behavior of both the consigners and the discoverer of the hoard. As he tells about that behavior, he dramatizes actions that are appropriate and inappropriate, particularly when a hoard accidentally comes to light.

Before I begin to sketch a reading of *Beowulf* in the light of contemporary studies of hoarding behavior, it is necessary to say something about the nature of this unique poem. Although the poem was composed in the Old English language and probably in Anglo-Saxon England, it is not about either early English people or English places. The first two-thirds of the poem takes place in eastern Denmark and the last third in what is now southern Sweden. The poem tells about a Geatish[2] hero who comes across the water to the aid of a Danish king and, after his return home, becomes king of his people. He is supposed to have succeeded his cousin, Heardred, who ruled for a short time after Hygelac, his father and Beowulf's uncle, was killed in the mouth of the Rhine at the end of a raiding expedition against the Franks. Since that raid is mentioned by Gregory of Tours, and dated on that basis to the beginning of the third decade of the sixth century, the references to the raid in the poem have often been used to date the reign of King Beowulf to the middle of the sixth century.[3] But the existence of a "real" Beowulf is problematic. He seems to have been introduced into a possibly genuine sixth-century Geatish royal family which was later submerged when the Swedes extended their power southwards. But his superhuman strength and even, perhaps, his willingness to use it for the good of the Danes as well as his own people, suggest a mythological rather than historical figure.

The question of the composition of the poem has recently become, I think, less problematic. The best hypothesis to account for the fact that the prosody of the poem consists of an isorhythmic grid built around capsules of information consisting of two or three sound-linked syllables is this: the poem is a performance of the Memorable Speech of the western branch of the Germanic peoples.[4] Memorable Speech exploits what later generations will call "poetic devices"—alliteration, assonance, consonance, rhyme, rhythm, and meter—in order to preserve important information by making it memorable to the ear. In traditional—preliterate—societies these devices did not serve simply as ornamentation as they usually do for us. The harnessing of mnemonic devices in *Beowulf* makes it clear that the poet did not need to compose his poem with the aid of writing, and might, indeed, have found it inhibiting to try to do so. I take *Beowulf*, then, to be a traditional oral poem composed while the tradition that had been handed from generation to generation, first in the continental homeland of the Anglo-Saxons and then in Britannia, was still very much alive.

We cannot be sure exactly when the performance we know as the poem was first taken down in writing. That could have happened, of course, only after Christian missionaries had brought writing to the Anglo-Saxons, in 597. More important, the writing down of *Beowulf* had to wait until the missionaries, or literate Anglo-Saxons, had worked out a way of reducing the spoken language to letters. The only surviving manuscript containing the text of the poem was made late in the Anglo-Saxon period, between about 975 and 1025. But at least one poem composed during this period, "The Battle of Maldon," differs in style from *Beowulf*.[5] I think the evidence — the prosody, geography, and subject of the poem — indicates that the poem was composed while being taken down in writing early in the Anglo-Saxon period, perhaps as early as the second quarter of the seventh century.

I have recently suggested that the *Beowulf* poet is a better source than Tacitus for the beliefs and customs of pre-historic Germanic peoples.[6] In the following account of the last third of the poem I shall try to flesh out this idea.

The account of the accidental discovery of a valuable hoard occurs in the last thousand lines of *Beowulf*. The hoard is cached in a stone structure that the poem calls a *beorh* (2241b; elsewhere *beorʒ*),[7] the source of Modern English BARROW.[8] The stone barrow lies NEAR the WATER, [*þe*]*teryðū* neah (2242b); in fact, the poet says at one point, a STREAM BREAKS OUT of the BARROW: *streā ut bonan. / brecan [o]f beorʒe* (2545b-2546a). The barrow is NEW(ly-built) on a headland: *niþe be næsse* (2243a), and made FAST — difficult to enter — by special CRAFT: *nearo[cræ]ftū fæst* (2243b). The ceiling of the chamber of the barrow STANDs on STONE BOWS — probably arches formed by corbelling — [*st*]*odan stanboʒan* (2545a). This structure, and the hoard it contains, stand center stage during the last third of the poem.

We hear of this structure for the first time at line 2213, just fourteen lines into the final section of the poem. A dragon has been living in the barrow for a long time watching over the HOARD (*hord beþeo[tode]*, 2212b) that it contains. Then "some man or other" (*nið[a] nath[þylc]*, 2215a) finds this HEATHEN HOARD (*hæðnðū* h[*orde*], 2216a) and steals from it. Because the manuscript is in very bad shape at this point, it is only later that we learn that the thief has taken from the hoard a *fæted [þ]æʒe* (2282a), an ornamented, possibly gold-plated, vessel. The thief carries the vessel to his lord. Apparently the treasure is enough to cause the lord to make peace with the thief and then to have the latter lead him back to explore (*rasian: rasod*, 2283b) the hoard.

The discovery of the hoard and the theft of the vessel may be fine for the relationship between the thief and his lord, but it doesn't suit the dragon at all. He retaliates that night. He flies to King Beowulf's — fortunately empty — hall and burns it down. By choosing the king's hall, the dragon intends, it seems, to make the entire folk pay for his loss.

Now it is Beowulf's turn. After only a moment's hesitation, he orders an iron shield to be made, chooses eleven companions, and sets out with the thief as a reluctant guide to the dragon's barrow. With the help of only his kinsman, Wiglaf — the other companions flee at the sight of the monster — Beowulf manages to kill the dragon but, in doing so, is mortally wounded himself. He dies rejoicing that he has won the hoard for his people.

But his people are not to benefit from the hoard. Wiglaf, as his successor, decrees — apparently with the consent of the folk — that the hoard is to be placed in Beowulf's barrow after his cremation. It is, and the great poem ends.

Wiglaf overrules Beowulf's wishes because, as he says, his ten companions have behaved in a cowardly way in not helping their lord in his battle with the dragon. For their cowardice the whole people will forego the treasure and face attacks from their enemies, attacks that will lead to death for the warriors and slavery for the women.

The modern reader may wonder why Wiglaf doesn't use the wealth of the hoard to buy off his people's enemies with tribute. The poet supplies an answer: the hoard has been cursed:

þōn þæs þ yrfe	eacencræftiȝ
iumonna ȝold	ȝaldre beþunden
þ ðam hrinȝsele	hrinan ne moste
ȝumena æniȝ	nefne ȝod sylfa
siȝora soðcyninȝ	sealde þā ðe he þolde
he is manna [ȝe]hyld	hord openian
efne sþa hþylcū manna	sþa hī ȝemet ðuhte:- (3051-57)

Then WAS THAT heritage of great power [powerfully protected?], GOLD of MEN of old WOUND about with a spell [an incantation], so THAT Not ANY of men was able to touch [or reach] THat RING-hall, unless GOD himSELF, true KING of triumphs — HE IS MEN'S protector — gave to whomever HE WOULD [permission] to OPEN the HOARD, EVEN to SUCH of MEN, as to HIM it seemed MEET.

A little later the poet says that the well-known princes (*þeodnas mære*, 3070a) who put (*dydon*) the treasure there (3070b) "NAMED about it" DEEPly (*diope benemdon*, 3069b; declared a curse around and below it?) that would be effective till DOOMSDAY (*oð domes dæȝ*, 3069a). The poet then paraphrases the curse:

þ se secȝ þære	synnū scildiȝ
herȝū ȝeheaðerod	hellbendū fæst
þōmū ȝeþitnad	se ðone þonȝ str(u)de (3071-73)

THAT that man would be guilty of SINS [confirmed in wrong doing], confined in heathen temples, FAST in HELL-BoNDS, terribly tormented, who plundered THat place.

This is strong stuff. The poet seems to indicate that both heathen and Christian torments will be the fate of anyone who plunders the hoard. But what is most interesting—and most curious—is that the poet at *this* point in the poem indicates that not one "Last Survivor" but more than one well-known prince pronounced this powerful curse. I shall return to this point toward the end of this paper.

The poet never makes clear Beowulf's relationship to the curse. But, even if the king didn't know about it or was in some way immune to the curse, Wiglaf knows about it and knows that the folk at least are not exempt from its effects.

It is the curse that suggests to me the possibility of a relationship between the *Beowulf* poet's account of the dragon's hoard and the hoards unearthed in northwestern Europe by archaeologists. That relationship can be characterized by the term *hoarding behavior*.[9]

The economic aspects of hoarding behavior appear to be relatively simple: a society will take certain goods out of circulation in order to ensure the value of similar goods left in use. Hoards that contain objects made of precious metal or exotic objects obtained from far away by exchange (or warfare) may well have been deposited because of their value. Levy treats the economics of hoarding behavior in the context of what she calls the "offering ritual," which she associates with "fertility religion":

> It would have been very useful to the elite if they could have maintained their control over fertility religion. A population is not likely to rebel against those who control access to a spiritual world which influences health and prosperity. Yet, where differences in wealth and authority exist, resentment and rebellion may grow in spite of fears of spiritual retribution. The offering ritual, as reflected in the hoards, also helped to ameliorate these tensions. It consisted, after all, of burying wealth and status symbols. The ritual thus allowed high-status individuals to demonstrate their power by making the appropriate gifts to the gods. At the same time, it served to remove wealth and sumptuary goods from the elite's control. When the offering ritual was over, the elite were reduced in wealth and lost control of the very sumptuary goods which had set them apart from the general population. Tensions would be eased, yet the hierarchical ranking would remain clear.[10]

Levy's account of the economic reasons for hoarding behavior is woven into her discussion of the cult practices and the beliefs and values of the people who deposited some of the hoards surviving from Bronze Age Denmark. In the following pages I use the poem as commentary on the archaeological reconstruction of hoarding behavior.

The hoard for which Beowulf fought and died did not always belong to the dragon. It was once, the poet tells us, *eorl[ʒest]reona* (2244b), "the treasure of important men." It was the great legacy of a noble KIN (*eormenlaf . . . [æþe]lan cynnes*, 2234), all but one of whom had perished before the hiding of the treasure. That one, the so-called "Last Survivor," consigns the hoard to the earth in one of the most moving speeches in the entire poem. I discuss that speech later. First I want to stress that at both the beginning and the end of the final third of the poem the poet makes it clear that the hoard belonged to men. Less than twenty lines from the end of the poem, the poet refers to the hoard as *eorla ʒstreon* (3166a). In the longest passage in which he characterizes the hoard,[11] the poet refers to part of the hoard as *fyrnmanna fatu* (2761a), "the vessels of MEN of the past."

Beowulf's defeat of the dragon puts the treasure back into men's hands. But his people refuse to keep it. Instead, they return it to the earth along with the ashes of their great king:

```
hi on boerʒ dydon        beʒ 7 siʒlu
eall sþlyce hyrsta       sþlyce on horde ær
niðhediʒe m̄             ʒnum hæfdon
forleton eorla ʒstreon   [eo]rðan healdan
ʒold on ʒreote           þær hit nu ʒen lifað
[  ]dū sþa unnyt         sþa h[         ] þæs    (3163-67)
```

They into [the] BARROW put ring and brooches, ALL SUCH accoutrements as in [the] HOARD earlier wrong-thinking MEN HAD taken; they let the EARTH HOLD great men's treasure, GOLD IN dust, where IT NOW yet LIVES . . . as useless as . . . WAS . . .

Perhaps the most important word in this passage is *unnyt*, "useless," in the final line. The poet concludes his account of the reburial of the hoard by proclaiming its uselessness.

The contents of the hoard were anything but useless. The armor and weapons were rusty and some of the vessels needed polishing. But the hoard contained gold and exotic objects. We know about the gold from the fact that the poet uses *ʒold* more than any other word whenever he is characterizing the hoard.[12] In such passages he uses *ʒold* or *ʒylden*, "GILDED," sixteen times. We know about the *exotic* origin of objects in the hoard from the fact that the poet characterizes them as *maðm* twelve times. The Indo-European root of *maðm* is *mei-*, "to change, go, move; with derivatives referring to the exchange of goods and services within a society as regulated by custom or law" — to quote the etymologists of the *American Heritage Dictionary*.[13] A *maǫm*, which our textbooks rather colorlessly translate "treasure," is, etymologically, and *exotic* treasure, something obtained by trade or raid, as lines 36b–37 of the poem remind us:

> þær þæs madma fela
> of feorþeʒum frætþa ʒelæded.
>
> THERE WAS much exotic-treasure, valuable
> things, brought from FAR-WAYS.

Both gold and foreign objects generally cost the ancient inhabitants of the geographical world of the poem — southern Sweden and eastern Denmark — much effort to produce or obtain. Yet the poet has Wiglaf and Beowulf's people consign these treasures to the earth as useless.

I think the poet has Wiglaf act in response to his determination that *this* gold and *these* exotic treasures had been obtained illegally. Wiglaf seems to be concerned with more than the fact that the thief had stolen treasure from the dragon. The thief certainly began the series of illegal acts. But his lord may have compounded the crime, as I shall show. In any case, Beowulf has to fight the dragon, the current guardian of the hoard. And Wiglaf, his successor, seems to know that the only proper course is to consign the hoard to the earth again.

It is true that both Wiglaf and the messenger who informs the folk of Beowulf's death foretell terrible calamities that will come about *not* because the hoard has been rifled but rather because of past feuds between Beowulf's people and their neighbors. Yet it is the tale of the accidental discovery of a hoard, the foolish attempt to use one small part of it, and its final return to the earth that encloses the accounts of dynastic feuds. Indeed, the accounts of the origins and the predictions of the results of the feud are introduced — despite their apparent importance — almost casually into the main tale, that of the dire consequences of stealing from a hoard.

The feuds may have come into the tale in an attempt to explain older practices the memory of which was beginning to fade because these practices were less useful in Anglo-Saxon England. But, however dim the memory of those practices had become, it is their traditionally kept memory as it appears in the poet's account that offers, I think, some confirmation of the economics of archaeologically reconstructed hoarding behavior.

The dragon plays a crucial role in the economics of hoarding. The function of this creature from folk belief is to ensure that hidden treasure will not be used even if it is rediscovered. In traditions recorded in Old English poetry, the dragon seeks out "heathen gold" and guards it. The *Beowulf* poet refers to this tradition: *he ʒesecean sceall . . . þær he hæðen ʒold / þarað . . .* (2275b–77a), "HE SHALL (= has to) SEEK . . . THERE [where] HE guards HEATHEN GOLD." From another Old English poem, the so-called "Maxims II," we learn that a "dragon has to [be] in a mound (Scots. "LAW"), old, proud of his precious objects": *Draca sceal on hlæwe, / frod, frætwum wlanc.*[14] Beowulf learned too well what a dragon's pride in his treasure could drive him to.

The society that is so vividly recreated in the poem believed that it was dangerous to steal from a hoard. Further, that society had worked out ways to deal with the accidental discovery of a hoard and with those who foolishly stole from it. Such protocol governs much of the action of the final third of *Beowulf*.

When the thief, at the beginning of this part of the poem, takes the *fæted þæʒe* to his once angry lord he receives a "compact of peace" from his lord. But the latter is curious about the source of the gift. He forces the thief to return with him to the hoard:

> [ ] þæs hord rasod
> onboren beaʒa [h]ord   bene ʒetiðad
> feasceaftū men   [f]rea sceaþode.
> fira fyrnʒeþeorc   [fo]rman siðe.   (2283b-86)

Then WAS [the] HOARD explored, [the] HOARD of rings BORNE off, the petition granted to the wretched MAN; the lord looked at men's ancient WORK for the first time.

It is possible that the thief's lord merely looked at the hoard. It is possible that 2284a, "the HOARD of rings BORNE off," simply refers to the earlier theft of the vessel. The second possibility is strengthened by the occurrence of *sceaþode* in 2285b. In *Beowulf*, forms of *sceaþian* are always used with "wonders" such as the footprints of a monster or the casting of lots. In fact, *þundor*, "WONDER," collocates with *sceaþian* twice in the poem. It is possible that prosody controls the choice of *sceaþian* rather than the more frequent *seon* in such lines as 2285.[15] But it is more likely that something else is at work. In his last speech in the poem Wiglaf says that Beowulf

> heold on heahʒesceap   hord ys ʒsceaþod
> ʒrīme ʒeʒonʒen . . .   (3084-85a)

HELD ON [his] HIGH-destiny; [the] HOARD IS *ʒesceaþod*, GRIMly won . . .

Sceawian, the infinitive of *ʒesceaþod*, is usually translated "look at, view." Frederick Klaeber, probably the most careful modern editor of *Beowulf*, glosses *ʒesceaþod* in this passage as "perh[haps] 'shown,' 'presented' . . ."[16] Klaeber's choices are apt: Wiglaf's words suggest an *epiphany*, a *showing forth*: *this* is the hoard that cost us our leader!

Wiglaf's actions in dealing with the hoard have a ceremonial ring. Towards the end of this same speech he will say:

Uton nu efstan   oðre . . .
seon 7 secean   searo ʒeþræc
þundor under [þ]ealle   ic eoþ þisiʒe
þ ʒe ʒenoʒe   neon sceaþiað
beaʒas 7 brad ʒold . . .   (3101–3105a)

Let us hasten anOTHER [time?] to SEE AND SEEK [the] cunning heap, WONDERs UNDER (the) WALL. I shall guide YOU, [so] that YE shall *sceapiað* [behold] NEar eNOUGH rings AND BROAD GOLD

Then Wiglaf chooses seven of the best thanes of the king and goes with them under the hostile roof to carry forth the "DEAR" (= precious, 3131a) *maðmas* to place in the barrow being built for Beowulf.

The halfline *seon 7 secean* may not be a demonstrable poetic formula—it occurs only once in *Beowulf*—but it sounds like a legal one. And the poet has Wiglaf include *sceapiað* as well in this speech. Earlier in this speech Wiglaf has given a detailed account of his actions after the slaying of the dragon. He went into the dragon's barrow, he says, and looked all around it. Then he carried outside for Beowulf to see a huge burden of the hoarded treasure. Since the poet has already shown Wiglaf doing these things, this repetition is, strictly speaking, unnecessary—unnecessary, that is, unless, perhaps, the protocol of hoarding behavior demanded such strict accounting.

Almost from its first mention until the account of its final return to the earth, the hoard is spoken of in formal language and—nearly always—dealt with by formal acts. The informal act causes the trouble. An outcast seeking shelter stumbles on a way to regain the favor of his lord. Apparently the lord accepts the cup taken from the hoard but insists on examining the hoard. But, before any further action can be taken, the dragon responds to the theft and forces the king to respond to the attack on his folk. The folk can only try to set matters right after Beowulf has slain the dragon. They must, first, reexamine the hoard more formally than the thief and his lord did. The folk do so as a whole people, carefully guided by their young leader. They have to "see and seek" the hoard. Wiglaf will direct them so that they will "behold near enough" the rings and broad gold. As their leader, Wiglaf himself descends with seven of the best men into the barrow for the last time, so that the folk will see the treasure as it lies in its building before they carry it forth to Beowulf's grave. In this fashion the hoard is shown—*hord ys ʒesceapod* (3084b).

In summary, I argue that the last third of *Beowulf* can be read as a traditionally preserved account of the appropriate behavior to be followed when a valuable hoard is accidentally discovered. The discoverer should either leave the hoard intact or rebury it. But it should be reburied only after it has been seen and examined by the folk acting in concert and only after it has been formally declared useless. If the discoverers behave in this way, they will keep the curse from the people and leave undisturbed the dragon that always finds such treasure and enforces the cause. From the point of view of the archaeologist, the curse and the dragon can be seen as folk-beliefs that ensure that the goods taken out of circulation will remain unused. The goods must be formally declared *unnyt* (3168a) "useless" because the folk will recognize their true value. The goods are indeed precious (2236a, 3131a) in themselves.

It is with what Levy calls "the offering ritual" that archaeology and the poem seem to come closest together. Early in the final third of the poem the *Beowulf* poet powerfully evokes the image of a lonely Last Survivor addressing the earth by a name that links her to humankind and offering to her what men had once taken from her.[17] Late in the poem, as we have seen, the poet will appear to contradict himself on the question of the number of those who consigned the treasure to the barrow (*þeodnas mære*, 3070a, "famous princes"). In the earlier passage the poet permits no plural to mar the splendid isolation of the figure who speaks these powerful words over the great treasure he has just placed in the barrow:

heald [þu] nu hruse   nu hæleð ne mæstan
eorla [æ]hte   hþæt hyt ær on ðe
ʒode beʒeaton . . .   (2247–49a)

HOLD THOU NOW, earth, (what) NOW men MUST not, the possessions of EARLS (= great men). Indeed, GOOD ones GoT IT (possessions) before IN THEE . . .

These words are among the most beautiful in the great poem. They begin with what can be best characterized as an apostrophe, perhaps even an incantation—an address to *hruse*, the earth. The Last Survivor commands her (like the more familiar *eorðe*, "EARTH," *hruse* is feminine) to hold what men can hold no longer. This, the song implies, is only right, since men took the treasure from the earth long ago.

A sense of ritual thus seems to mark the opening lines of the Last Survivor's speech. These lines suggest a *circle*: *hold now what long ago you held*. We are familiar with such ritual circles in the burial formula "ashes to ashes, dust to dust." The entire final third of *Beowulf* can be characterized as circling back to the ritual performed near its beginning by the Last Survivor. Here is, again, one line from a very late passage in the poem:

forleton eorla ʒstreon   [eo]rðan healdan   (3166)

they LET EARTH HOLD EARLS' treasures

This line, though it recalls 2247–48a, is not only nearly so powerful as the Last Survivor's incantation; if it were, it might detract from the focus on Beowulf's funeral. But both words and effect are similar: long ago the Last Survivor had consigned to the earth what had been taken from her; now the survivor's of Beowulf's battle with the dragon consign the same hoard back to her. The folk repeat the Last Survivor's ritual as the poem draws to its close.

The poet does not tell us that the Last Survivor was a priest who worshipped Mother Earth. He cannot. He was, after all, a Christian for whom the worship of any god other than the eternal lord (*ece drihten*, 108, etc.) was anathema. Yet, because he is a careful keeper of the tradition, he is able to tell the tale of the pagan folk of Denmark and Sweden with remarkable tolerance. It seems to me that he is even able to conjure for us a priest who presided over the "offering ritual," though, of course, without naming him as such.

It may be only a pious hope, but I would like to think that the opening lines of the Last Survivor's great consigning speech—lines that are echoed in one of the last passages in the poem—recreate an ancient prayer to the Earth as a producer and ultimate keeper of men's possessions. It is possible, then, that we may actually be able to *hear* in *Beowulf* a reflex of one of the prayers spoken over the artifacts that Levy and other archaeologists have dug from the silent earth.[18]

Notes

1. Janet E. Levy, "The Bronze Age Hoards of Denmark," *Archaeology*, 35, no. 1 (January/February 1982) 37-45. The quotation is on p. 37.

2. The name of a modern city and the names of two provinces in south central Sweden preserve reflexes of this tribal name as *göt-*. Perhaps this is the place to note that scholars have long assumed that the *Beowulf* poet had access by some means more or less reliable to information about his people's past. What is perhaps the best-known account of such a view, H. Munro Chadwick's *The Heroic Age* (Cambridge: Cambridge Univ. Press, 1912, reissued 1926), despite its age, remains a classic of the historical approach. Chadwick puts the issue clearly in his Preface: ". . . the resemblances in the poems [*Beowulf* along with other Germanic heroic poems and the Homeric poems] are due primarily to resemblances in the ages to which they relate and to which they ultimately owe their origin. The comparative study of heroic poetry therefore involves the comparative study of 'Heroic Ages'; and the problems which it presents are essentially problems of anthropology" (p. viii). Neither Chadwick nor the author of a recent account of treasure in the poem, Michael D. Cherniss, in a chapter titled "Treasure: the Material Symbol of Human Worth" in his *Ingeld and Christ: Heroic Concepts and Values in Old English Poetry* (The Hague: Mouton, 1972) 79-101, specifically discusses hoarding behavior, nor does either approach a discussion of the last part of the poem from the point of view of the present study.

The present study represents an extension of Chadwick's approach in the light of recent thinking to the effect that every composition in language, whether oral of written, contains indications of the social structure of the society that has produced it. L. L. Cavalli-Sforza and M. W. Feldman, in *Cultural Transmission and Evolution: A Quantitative Approach* (Princeton, 1981) seem to me to support the case for such an approach.

3. For a useful summary of the so-called "Historical Elements" in the poem as well as a carefully edited text of the poem, see *Beowulf and the Fight at Finnsburg*, 3rd. ed. with Supplements, ed. Fr[ederick] Klaeber (Lexington, Mass.: D. C. Heath, 1950 f.). The summary of Geatish and Swedish history is on pp. xxxviii–xlviii.

4. For a fuller account of Memorable Speech and a fuller treatment of some of the evidence for the claim that *Beowulf* represents a performance in an oral tradition that was flourishing at the time the poem was taken down in writing, see my "*Beowulf* on the Brink: Information Theory as Key to the Origins of the Poem," forthcoming in John Miles Foley's memorial volume dedicated to Milman Parry.

5. The "battle" that the poem recounts in a beautiful attempt to keep alive the old poetic tradition was fought early in the last decade of the tenth century. For an attempt to date the composition of *Beowulf* to the time of the making of the surviving manuscript, see Kevin S. Kiernan, *Beowulf and the Beowulf Manuscript* (New Brunswick, NJ: Rutgers Univ. Press, 1981). Kiernan's attempt to redate *Beowulf* is considered by various scholars in *The Dating of Beowulf*, ed. Colin Chase (Toronto, 1981). In the latter volume, see, in particular, Leonard E. Boyle, "The Nowell Codex and the Poem of *Beowulf*," 23–32.

6. See my "The Remaking of *Beowulf*," in *Oral Tradition in Literature: Interpretation in Context*, ed. John Miles Foley (Columbia, Mo: Univ. of Missouri Press, 1986) 136–46.

7. All quotations from Beowulf are taken from a combination of only two sources: (1) facsimiles of the folios of the MS, British Library Manuscript Cotton Vitellius A. xv, and (2) facsimiles of "Thorkelin A," the late 18th century transcript of the MS made by an unidentified amanuensis working for G. J. Thorkelin. I have mainly used the facsimiles of the MS in Julius Zupitza, ed., *Beowulf* . . . second edition, Early English Text Society (London: Oxford University Press, 1959), but I have also used the excellent photographs illustrating K. S. Kiernan's *Beowulf and the Beowulf Manuscript* (New Brunswick, 1981). My second source is Kemp Malone, ed., *The Thorkelin Transcripts* . . . (Copenhagen, 1951), 1–90. I fall back on Thorkelin A's readings *only* when I cannot make something out in or something seems to be missing from the facsimiles. Material from Thorkelin A appears here in square brackets. Line numbers follow Klaeber's; see above, note 3. The punctuation and capitalization of my translations usually follow Klaeber's punctuation of the Old English text.

8. I follow the convention of printing in capitals modern descendants (reflexes) of Old English words.

9. Timothy Champion, Clive Gamble, Stephen Shennan, and Alasdair Whittle, in a recent textbook, *Prehistoric Europe* (London, etc: Academic Press, 1984) usefully summarize the economic aspect of hoarding behavior without using that phrase. I quote from p. 294: "The value of the status conferred by such objects [prestige objects obtained by exchange], however, depended on control over their supply and on limitation of the quantity available; the more bronze there was in a society, for instance, the harder it would be to restrict access to it, with the consequent risk of diminution in the status to be derived from its manipulation. One solution to this problem was to take prestige items out of circulation by depositing them where they would not be recovered; it would then be possible to continue to acquire them by exchange without the risk of lowering their value. The deposition of wealthy grave goods was, therefore, not just a means of demonstrating the status of the deceased, but also a way to keep

up the value of the items still in circulation . . . the large numbers and the exotic nature of these objects [in rivers and bogs . . . (or) from eroded riverside settlements] suggest a widespread practice of ritual deposition in watery places."

10. Levy, p. 45.

11. The passage runs, with two brief interruptions, from line 2756 to line 2777a.

12. I summarize here the results of a computer program that analyzes each of the passages in *Beowulf* that characterizes the hoard. Wade Tarzia, in a similar but unpublished study, comes to a similar conclusion.

13. See *mei-*[1] in the Appendix titled "Indo-European Roots," pp. 1505-50 in *The American Heritage Dictionary of the English Language*, ed. William Morris (Boston: American Heritage Publishing Co., 1969). The quotation is from p. 1528.

14. "Maxims II," lines 26b-27a, in *The Anglo-Saxon Minor Poems*, ed. Elliott van Kirk Dobbie (New York: Columbia Univ. Press, 1942), 56.

15. Many inflected forms of *seon* are monosyllabic; *all* forms of *sceawian* contain a long syllable followed by at least one short syllable. These differences are significant in the prosody of the poem.

16. Klaeber (see above, note 3), 391.

17. Julius Pokorny, in *Indogermanisches Etymologisches Wörterbuch* (Bern: Band I, 1959; Band II, 1969), under "*1. kreu-, kreu -: krū-* 1." (pp. 621-22) connects Old English *hrūse* with "dickes, stockendes Blut, blutiges, rohes Fleisch," and also with "Eis" and "Kruste."

18. It is a pleasure to acknowledge the encouragement and help of Catherine Hilton and Wade Tarzia. Both have read and offered advice on early and late drafts of this paper, a version of which I read at the Binghamton conference with the title "*Beowulf* as a Resource for the Archaeologist: Hoarding Behavior and the Language of Hoarding." It is to Tarzia that I owe my introduction to the concept of hoarding behavior.

SECTION III
Rural Community Studies

The Role of Cemeteries in the Formation of Medieval Settlement Patterns in Western France*

ELIZABETH ZADORA-RIO

Archaeological interest in the cemeteries of the Early and Later Middle Ages has focused mainly on grave goods, human bones, and funeral rites. The topographical relationships between the necropolis and inhabited areas have attracted little attention, despite the fact that their evolution in the course of the Middle Ages might reveal a great deal about territorial organization, inter-relationships between lay and ecclesiastical powers, and the respective positions accorded the living and the dead in medieval society.

The aim of this article is twofold: firstly, to study the graveyard as a dwelling place, namely the different types of inhabited cemeteries, their chronology and their areas of diffusion, and secondly, to study the location of cemeteries within a given territory and its influence on territorial boundaries.

The study is concerned with western France, specifically the ecclesiastical province of Tours, which includes Brittany, Anjou, Maine and Touraine.[1]

Cemeteries as Settlements
Classification of inhabited cemeteries (fig. 1)

Inhabited cemeteries can be divided into two main groups depending on the temporary (type A) or permanent (type B) nature of the settlement. Type B can be subdivided according to the chronological relationship between the cemetery and the settlement into B1 (cemetery created prior to the habitat within its boundaries) and B2 (cemetery created simultaneously with the habitat). Fi-

```
                    Inhabited cemeteries
                   /                    \
     Type A:                              Type B:
   Temporary settle-                    Permanent settle-
   ment (asylum)                             ment
                                        /              \
                                   B.1:                 B.2
                             Cemeteries created    Cemeteries created
                               prior to the       simultaneously with
                                settlements         the settlements
                              /          \
                         B.1.1:            B.1.2:
                    Progressive allotment   Borough foundation
```

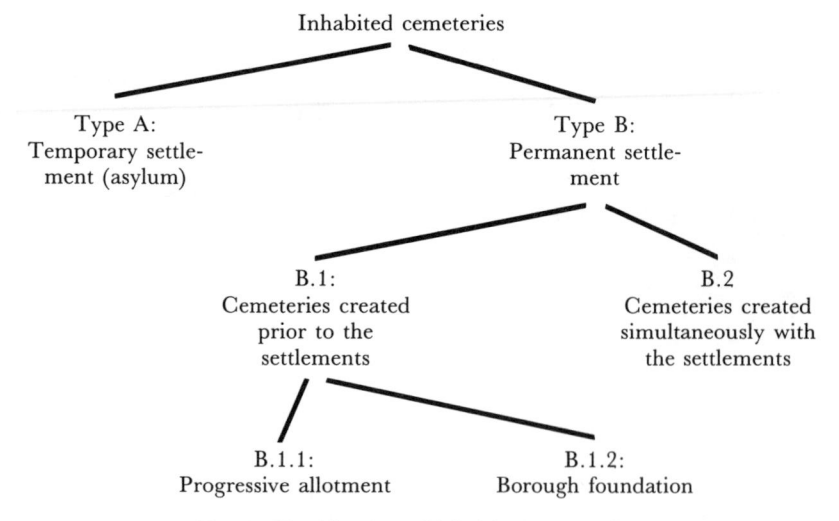

Fig. 1. Classification of inhabited cemeteries.

nally, type B1 can be divided further according to the way in which the settlement developed: by progressive allotment of the ground of the churchyards (B.1.1) or by the foundation of boroughs within the cemeteries (B.1.2).

Temporary settlement (Type A)

Almost everywhere, cemeteries were occupied temporarily in time of war. Both cemeteries and churches bore immunity from danger of attack. Territorial asylum existed as of the 5th century, and extended beyond the walls of the church. Its range was sometimes defined by a measured distance. The law of November 21st, 419, which recognized and outlined the institution of asylum, widened the area of protection to 50 steps surrounding the sanctuary.[2] However, the limits of the asylum were also frequently defined purely by the area covered by the church's annexes and, more particularly, by the *atrium*, or cemetery. In the 6th century, a decree issued by Clotaire II stipulated that when the *atria* of the churches were not enclosed, asylum was to extend one arpent of land on each side of the church.[3]

By virtue of this immunity, churchyards offered some security to those seeking protection within their boundaries. Respect for the rights of asylum was favored by the development of the worship of saints, and areas neighboring famous relics were especially sought: St. Martin at Tours and St. Hilaire at Poitiers gave refuge to many people fleeing the authorities. The accounts of different chroniclers give evidence of the frequent recourse of fugitives to the protection provided by cemeteries during the Early Middle Ages.[4] At the start of the 11th century, the movement for the Truce of God further strengthened the asylum as an institution.

Violation of cemeteries was punishable: at the beginning of the 12th century, the seigneur of Laval, in Maine, was excommunicated for a period of three years for having set fire to the cemetery and church of Gennes, belonging to the abbey of St. Nicolas d'Angers.[5] The spiritual protection offered by the cemetery was sometimes reinforced by material fortifications. In 1036, the Count of Anjou built a fortified enclosure around the churchyard of the St. Florent le Vieil monastery. In the mid-11th century, at St. Vincent du Lorouer, in Maine, a *vallum* was built around the church. At the beginning of the 12th century, there is a reference to a ditch around the cemetery at Combourg, in Brittany. Judging from the papal prescription at the Council of Clermont in 1095, which forbade the erection of new fortifications in churchyards,[6] we may conclude that these constructions were commonplace.

The manner of applying the right of asylum varied greatly from one place to another. Three 11th century cemeteries in Brittany, lying merely fifteen to twenty kilometers apart and all belonging to the same monastery, offer evidence of such differences. At Tremaheuc, people who moved to the churchyard in time of war were exempt from taxes. At Romazy the same was true, but here, in addition, people were also permitted to dismantle their homes and reestablish themselves with their possessions. At Saint-Germain-sur-Ille, on the other hand, refugees continued to pay taxes to their lord even while staying in the churchyard; afterwards, the houses they had built remained the property of the monastery.[7] This last example clearly indicates how a temporary occupation could change into a permanent settlement: once the refugees departed, the monks were free to rent the dwellings to other occupants.

Permanent settlement (Type B)

B.1: *Cemeteries created prior to the habitations*

B.1.1: Progressive allotment of cemeteries. The existence of permanent habitations within cemetery boundaries is commonplace from the middle of the 11th century onwards. This phenomenon is certainly related to the usurpation of churches and their dependent patrimonies by powerful laymen who took advantage of their newly acquired ownership to give, sell or rent a single plot, a few houses, half or even the entire cemetery, to their vassals or a monastery. At times, the contract could apply to a group of allotments: in the second half of the 11th century, the Canons of St. Jean Baptiste d'Angers made an agreement with an important lay lord regarding the allotment of all their cemeteries and the sharing of the expected income.[8] This type of churchyard settlement seems to have been quite widespread in France, existing not only in the west of the country but also in Burgundy, Savoie, even Alsace and Lorraine.[9] It is very difficult to ascertain how many churchyards were involved in this kind of progressive allotment. Many such minor transactions must have taken place without any written records. Within the ecclesiastical province of Tours, the concentrations of such cemeteries varied greatly from one diocese to another: in the dioceses of Angers, Le Mans and Rennes, there were many of them, whereas elsewhere there were very few or none at all. The chronology is more or less identical in the different bishoprics, with the greatest number of references to the progressive allotment of churchyards dating from the period between 1050 and 1100.

B.1.2: The foundation of boroughs in churchyards. In other instances, the colonization of the cemetery did not take the form of a progressive housing allotment but rather of the foundation of boroughs.[10] This type of churchyard settlement seems to have been restricted to western France. It is found mainly in Anjou and Maine, although it existed also in Normandy, Poitou and Brittany.[11] Sometimes the area designated for the borough had exactly the same surface as the churchyard itself; such is the case of Saint-Georges-du-Puy-de-la-Garde, in Anjou; often, though, the borough could be larger or smaller than the cemetery.

Like the progressive allotment of cemeteries, borough foundations seem to have been at their height in the second half of the 11th century.

B.2: The foundation of new inhabited cemeteries

There is yet another type of churchyard settlement in which the cemetery and the settlement within its boundaries were created together *ex nihilo*. It is stated explicitly in the foundation charters that the cemetery was created for both the burial of the dead and the dwelling of the living: *ad corpora defunctorum sepelienda et ad homines recipiendos ad habitationem*.[12] Whereas in the first three types of inhabited cemeteries, the settlement always followed the foundation of the churchyard and the church, and had no influence on the parish network, type B2 demonstrates the simultaneous creation of the churchyard, the settlement within its boundaries and a new parish. The regions in which this type of cemetery is found (Anjou and Maine) are far more restricted geographically than those of the previously mentioned cemetery types. Not appearing before the 12th century, type 2 cemeteries are later than others. Most were founded between 1125 and 1160.[13]

Topography

It is not known if inhabited cemeteries as a whole had special characteristics when compared to other settlements. Despite the fact that some of these sites are nearly deserted and are easily accessible, none has been excavated. Historical sources give some idea of their topography. It is known that the boundaries were marked by crosses, walls or ditches, but there is only scanty information about the dimensions of these cemeteries. From the few indications available, it would appear that some were less than one hectare. This was more or less equivalent to the area of territorial asylum. Others were certainly much larger.[14] The buildings and structures inside these cemeteries were not different from those found in any other village: in addition to the church and the monastic buildings, there were fountains, wells, barns, ovens. In some cases, the landlord or some of his knights had their own residences in the cemetery, most frequently near the church.[15] Gardens, courtyards and pasture areas within the cemetery are also mentioned. One might well ask where the dead were buried in these inhabited cemeteries. Although some of the charters give fairly detailed information, there is never any mention of an area specifically allocated for burials. Since all of the ground was consecrated, one wonders whether people did not simply bury their relatives around their homes. Because there has been so few extensive excavations, very little is known about medieval graveyards from the 8th century onwards. As the density of the settlement increased with more and more allotments, the houses most certainly encroached upon the graves. A text from the second half of the 12th century reports that many corpses were removed when a house was built in the cemetery of St. Germain-la-Blanche-Herbe in Normandy.[16] It seems that people did not always take the trouble to move the dead. The excavation of the village of Mondeville, near Caen, illustrates how houses were built on top of graves.[17] Considering the shallowness of medieval burials, this must have been rather unpleasant. In historical sources one often reads of corpses being exhumed in churchyards by heavy rains or by animals, mainly pigs or dogs.[18]

The inhabited cemeteries and the Church

The Gregorian reform brought about a thorough change in the relations between ecclesiastical and civil powers in the 11th–12th centuries, insisting on the emancipation of the clergy from secular control and the restitution of parish churches, tithes, interment taxes and other ecclesiastical incomes retained by laymen; strangely enough, however, it does not seem to have opposed the creation of settlements in churchyards.

In certain bishoprics of western France, the attitude of the bishops may have hindered the multiplication of inhabited cemeteries. As early as 1080, the Norman bishops who gathered in council at Lillebonne tried to limit the occupation of cemeteries to periods of war and to prevent the settlement from becoming permanent.[19] There was nothing comparable, it appears, in the ecclesiastical province of Tours in the 11th and 12th centuries. The bishops of the dioceses in which inhabited cemeteries were the most numerous often encouraged their creation. It is interesting to note that bishop Ulger, one of the most zealous propagators of the Gregorian reform in the diocese of Angers in the second quarter of the 12th century, personally entered into several contracts with lay lords to create inhabited cemeteries. The bishops of Le Mans were equally tolerant. In 1217, a court action was brought against the abbey of St. Vincent du Mans by a priest from Saint Longis, in Maine, who claimed immunity from taxes for the village because it was situated inside a cemetery. The representative of the bishop sided with the abbey and maintained that the Custom of Maine authorized lords, whether lay or ecclesiastical, to collect taxes from villages built in cemeteries.[20] It is only with the synodal statutes of Angers, written about 1219-1220 and soon after adopted in all the bishoprics of western France that a more restrictive attitude appears. The statutes forbade new constructions in churchyards, and the rebuilding of any house left in ruins for one year.[21] Their obvious aim was to gradually eliminate permanent settlements within cemeteries.

Spatial distribution of the inhabited cemeteries (fig. 2)

Originally, the right of asylum certainly played an important role in the establishment of inhabited cemeteries, but it does not account for the permanent nature of the settlements. The reasons for that, as they appear in written sources, seem to be mainly economic: the lords rented out the churchyard's ground, controlled the ovens and mills, collected market tolls within the cemetery; with the help of monks and the secular clergy, they recruited a labor force to work the land and at times to serve as guards in their castles. Yet, how is it possible to explain that these cemeteries were so numerous in some bishoprics, such as Angers, Le Mans, Rennes, and rare or entirely absent from others in the same ecclesiastical province? The contrast might be due to gaps in the extant documentation for different regions. This would account for the rarity of inhabited churchyards in certain bishoprics in Brittany—Quimper, Saint-Pol-de-Léon or Tréguier, for example, where documents are scarce. However, it would not explain the case of the diocese of Tours, where ample documentation does exist.

It appears that the uneven distribution of inhabited cemeteries might be related to patterns of rural settlement. In particular, the contrast between Touraine, on the one hand, Anjou and Maine, on the other, is to be linked to other differences which exist between these regions. In Touraine, where the permanent occupation of cemeteries was much less developed, rural settlement had been organized hierarchically from Carolingian times,[22] the parish network was old, and there are many references to fortified settlements (*castra*)

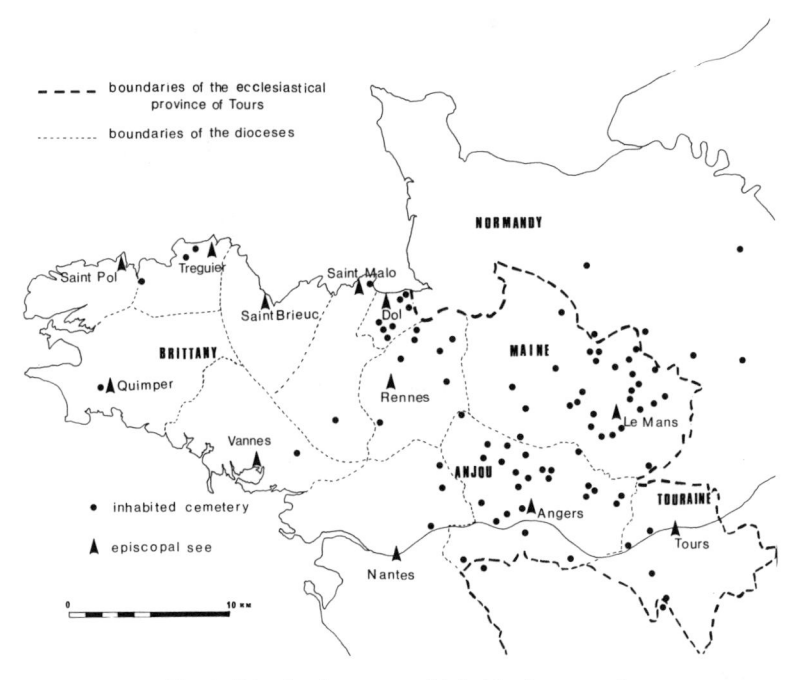

Fig. 2. Distribution map of inhabited cemeteries.

prior to the 11th century. In Anjou and Maine, on the contrary, the Carolingian administrative framework is not well documented, the parish network was not completed before 1150, and there seem to have been very few fortified clustered settlements before the 11th century. Inhabited cemeteries of type B.1.1 (progressive allotment of the churchyard) and B.1.2 (borough foundation) appear to have created embyronic nuclear settlements in areas which were already partially developed. Cemeteries of type B.2, created simultaneously with the village within their boundaries and a new parish, seem to have been a factor in the clearing of land for cultivation (figs. 3a, 3b and 4). The multiplication of inhabited cemeteries during the 11th and 12th centuries is to be linked to the general move toward the nucleation of settlements under the joint influence of lay lords and the Church.[23] The unequal distribution of inhabited cemeteries within the ecclesiastical province of Tours might reflect the opposition between areas where some forms of clustered settlements had already existed in Carolingian times, and those where a dispersed pattern prevailed.

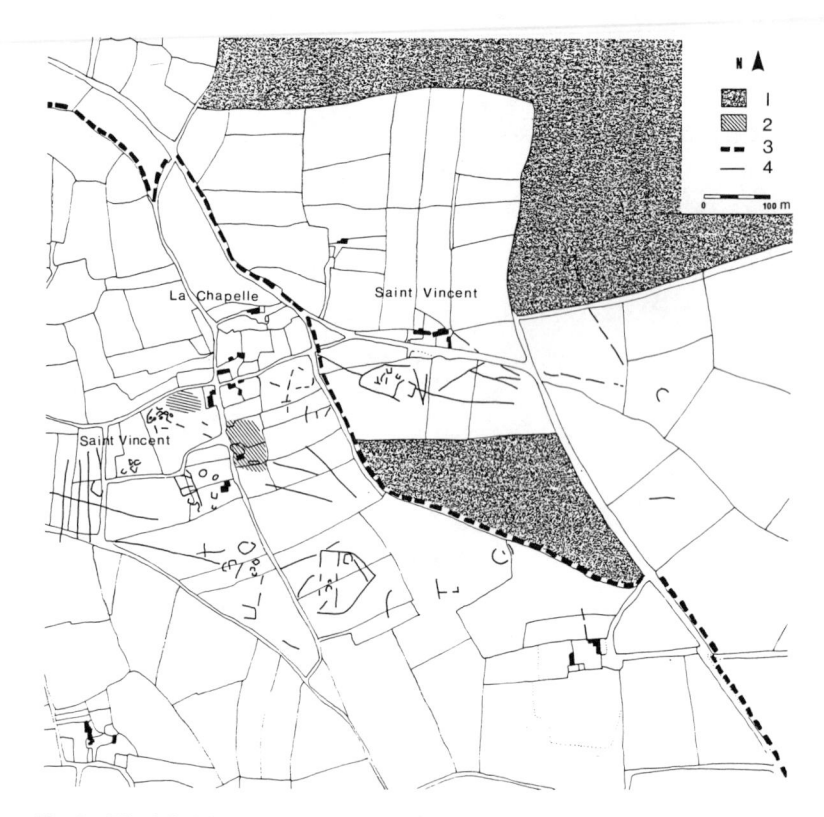

Fig. 3a. The inhabited cemetery of Saint-Vincent-des-Bois (Maine-et-Loire) from the cadastral plan of 1826 and the results of a thermographic aerial survey. 1 = woods; 2 = concentration of medieval pottery; 3 = communal boundary; 4 = thermic anomalies.

The creation of the inhabited cemetery of Saint Vincent des Bois (type B2) results from a contract associating the Bishop of Angers and a lay lord between 1125 and 1138. Each cofounder was to possess a house within the cemetery.

The parish was suppressed before the end of the medieval period. On the cadastral map of 1826, its territory is divided between two communes, and two groups of dwellings, on each side of the border, retained the name of Saint-Vincent. A chapel still remained on the edge of the road from Craon to Segré, on the site of the church mentioned in the 12th-century charter. The small fields south of the chapel seem to have preserved the plan of the medieval street-village. An aerial thermographic survey realized by Alain Tabbagh (Centre de Recherches Géophysiques du CNRS in Garchy) revealed many anomalies on the site of the former village. Fieldwalking gave only limited results because only a small part of the ground is now under cultivation.

Cemeteries and Medieval Settlement Patterns / 179

Fig. 3b. Aerial thermic survey of Saint-Vincent des Bois (Maine-et-Loire).

Fig. 4. Aerial photograph of the site of the inhabited cemetery of Belle Noue (Maine-et-Loire), created at the beginning of the 12th century in a former comtal forest (type B2). The foundation act provides for the construction, within the boundaries of the new cemetery, of a church, dwellings, and an oven. A single farm now remains on the site; the motte of the seignorial castle of Belle Noue can still be seen nearby (marked by an arrow on the photograph).

Cemeteries and Territorial Boundaries

The influence of cemeteries did not confine itself to the nucleation of settlement. It was equally apparent in the parochial network.

There is much written evidence from the 11th and 12th centuries to indicate that place of burial served as the criterion for being considered a resident of a particular parish. For instance, a judgement in 1125 by the papal legate in Anjou dealt with a conflict between the nuns of Fontevraud and a monastery regarding the tithe of a territory of the border of the three bishoprics of Angers, Tours and Poitiers. After an enquiry, the decisive factor was held to be the burial place of people dwelling in the area: land formerly occupied by the deceased[24] belonged to the parish in whose churchyard they were buried. It was the cemetery which ensured the boundaries of the land. This accounts for the violent disputes which sometimes occurred over burials, occasionally even those of very poor people. Historical documents of the 11th and 12th centuries tell of monks and nuns kidnapping dying people, disinterring and stealing corpses at night and fighting each other with candlesticks. What was really at stake was not the small amount of money paid for the burial but rather the relation of the deceased's dwelling place to the parish: where he was buried was taken as evidence of what parish he belonged to, and hence to what parish were owed the taxes incumbent on his dwelling place.[25]

This close link between the churchyard and the parochial territory is evident in the creation of the last type of inhabited cemeteries, type B.2, where the foundation of a cemetery was the preliminary act for the creation of a new parish and settlement within the churchyard. When consecrating in the middle of a forest a new churchyard belonging to the abbey of La Roe, the Bishop of Angers gathered together the priests of the neighboring parishes and the local lords, and asked them "who would be the parishioners of this cemetery?" The owner of the land then showed the boundaries of the property he was willing to give and, as the priests and the other lords did not raise any objections, a new parish was created.[26] Many of these cemeteries were founded on marginal lands which remained outside the parochial network, so that generally there was no conflict regarding parish boundaries. It was different when the ground already belonged to a parish. Disputes usually ended with some kind of agreement among the conflicting parties. On occasion, however, they resulted in the suppression of a new cemetery. There are two remarkable examples of this, both dating from the middle of the 12th century. In one case, the Bishop of Rennes acknowledged that a cemetery he had recently consecrated was founded on ground already belonging to a parish, and he stipulated that the new cemetery should be used only for asylum, and not for burials (*cimiterium ad refugium tantum vivorum, non ad sepulturam mortuorum*).[27] In the second case, the Bishop of Angers acknowledged that he had been in the wrong when he consecrated a new cemetery in a parish belonging to the abbey of Marmoutiers, and he anathematized anybody who would either live or be buried in this churchyard.[28] The motive behind these suppressions was the fact that it was impossible to found a cemetery without automatically creating a new parochial territory.

The centripetal function of the cemetery in the 11th and 12th centuries is in contrast to what has generally been considered the clear separation between necropolis and habitation area, deduced from archaeological excavations of Early Medieval sites. Certain texts from the 11th to the 13th century show that this dissimilarity between medieval and earlier burial places was very evident at the time.[29] One may ask whether Early Medieval cemeteries situated at some distance from the settlement had a specific place within the land unit or whether their locations had no special meaning. Certain archaeologists, particularly in Great Britain, have emphasized the topographical coincidence between the necropolis and territorial limits. The distribution of graves in relation to boundaries has been especially investigated by D. Bonney. He observed that a considerable proportion of pagan Saxon burial sites in the south of England, both in flat graves and in barrows, are found on or very near the boundaries of ancient ecclesiastical parishes. These findings have been taken to suggest earlier origins for the boundaries and units of land which they enclose.[30] The hypothesis is all the more attractive in light of written sources indicating that parishes frequently coincided with former estates whose boundaries they fossilized. Unfortunately, it is hardly possible through archaeology alone to prove an intentional association between burial places and parish boundaries. In order to obtain convincing results, it would be necessary to quantify these observations by defining precisely what is meant by "near the boundary." Are the land strips considered to be 50, 100, or 200 meters wide? The results can vary completely depending on the choice. Insofar as boundaries in the Early Middle Ages were rarely linear, it would be reasonable to favor the idea of a wide strip. If this were the case, however, the strips would take up proportionally so much of the parochial territory, that the significance of a statistical test would be negligible.[31]

In some cases, the intentional association between burial places and territorial boundaries is confirmed by written sources. T. M. Charles-Edwards has offered historical evidence on the use of burial sites as boundary marks for late pagan Ireland. Burial upon the boundary was intended to defend inherited land from the claim of outsiders: a person who claimed a particular piece of land by virtue of hereditary rights, had to take his horse over a grave-mound. This act was considered safe only if the person really had hereditary rights to the land; the buried man was thought to reject outsiders, but not kinsmen.[32]

In France, as in England, we lack the written evidence necessary to confirm the existence of an intended link between the localization of the necropolis and territorial boundaries during the Early Middle Ages. Roman legislation forbidding the burial of the dead in inhabited places only applied to the area inside the town. Cemeteries were located on the outskirts of cities and, thus, marked the boundary of urban territory. There were no legal constraints of this type in the countryside. No penalty was imposed on those who buried their dead in the *vici* and in the *oppida*.[33] Many tombs, of both the rich and poor alike, were isolated in fields. Collective necropolises seem also to have been situated a certain distance away from inhabited areas, but it was not a general rule.[34] Moreover, Germanic laws did not issue directives regarding burial locations in rural areas, and the Church itself seems to have been uninterested in the matter for a long time.[35] It does not appear that regulations were imposed concerning the siting of necropolises on marginal lands near the outer limits of territorial units, and nothing indicates that their localization was significant.

The grouping of graveyards around churches was linked to the development of the veneration of saints and to the fashion of *ad sanctos* interment, which is apparent from written sources dating from the 6th century, and perhaps even earlier.[36] The phenomenon appeared first in towns. The prohibition of burial within the city walls was lifted in the case of saints, and later, for other Christians; eventually it was abandoned altogether. In 563, the first council of Braga permitted that the dead be buried around the walls of churches. The grouping of burials around rural parish churches occurred later. Archaeological evidence shows it took place progressively during the 7th and 8th centuries. The capitulary of 775-790, which prescribed the carrying of the remains of Christian Saxons to churchyards (*ad cemeteria ecclesiae et non ad tumulos paganorum*), is the first text that defines the localization of sepultures in rural areas.[37] By the 9th century, inhumation was still not exclusively restricted to consecrated places. Jonas, the Bishop of Orléans, condemned those who, through greed, demanded a fee for allowing the dead to be buried in their fields (*in agris suis*).[38]

The grouping of burials around parish churches certainly favored the emergence of the concept of a church community that included both the living and the dead. This idea had been first expressed in Carolingian times. In his treatise *De ecclesiis et capellis* (857-858), Bishop Hincmar opposed the division of rural parishes and the displacement of churches. He purported that a church was a spiritual entity that encompassed both its living parishioners and the deceased who are buried around the church. He attacked the division of church patrimony as a serious threat to the continuation of liturgy on behalf of the dead and hence to the unity of the church community itself.[39] It is, no doubt, this notion of church community, uniting both the living and the dead, which accounts for the relationship between the location of sepultures and parochial boundaries that is so clearly formulated in the 11th- and 12th-century texts.

This same notion was at the origin of the emergence of village communities whose institutions developed at a later date.

Many aspects of this evolution still elude us. What happened from the time when isolated cemeteries were abandoned (around the 7th and 8th centuries) until the 11th century, when inhabited cemeteries appear in historical documents as an already commonplace phenomenon? We have seen that settlements within the churchyards implied a profound transformation in the attitude towards death. Over how long a period of time did this change take place? One can ask if the settlements were created immediately after burials were grouped around parish churches, or if some time elapsed before this major move.

It is worth noting that archaeologists generally make two assumptions, both or either of which may be wrong: (1) when they find Early Medieval graves in a churchyard, they usually assume the existence of a contemporary village; (2) when they find medieval houses covering former graves, they usually assume that the funeral function had disappeared by the time the houses were built. Historical evidence proves that both residential and funeral functions could have co-existed on the same piece of land. These two assumptions, together with the fact that very little interest has been shown in later medieval churchyards, account for the poor archaeological documentation of inhabited cemeteries.

It is obvious, however, that cemeteries played a dynamic role in settlement history, particularly between the 8th and the 11th centuries. This was precisely the period in which the present patterns of rural settlement were coming into existence. The grouping of burials around the church, which often preceded the clustering of dwellings, played an essential role in the genesis of the medieval village.[40] The inhabited cemetery is the concrete expression of that solidarity between the living and the dead which gave the medieval parish its cohesive unity. In regions of late colonization and dispersed habitation, it played a determining role in fixing settlement choice and territorial limits. It seems that it was in Anjou and Maine that this institution saw both its greatest development and greatest diversity.

Notes

[*]I wish to thank M. Jablkowska, Margery Safin and Bailey Young for their help with the translation of this text.

1. Brittany was divided into nine dioceses: Rennes, Nantes, Quimper, Saint-Pol-de-Léon, Tréguier, Saint-Brieuc, Saint-Malo, Dol and Vannes. The bishopric of Ang-

ers corresponded, more or less, with Anjou, the bishopric of Le Mans with Maine, and the bishopric of Tours with Touraine.

References to inhabited churchyards in Touraine can be found in: *Cartulaire de Noyers*, ed. Chevalier (Tours 1872) 10, 36, 42, 68, 111, 292; *Chartes de St. Julien de Tours*, ed. Abbé Denis (1913) 33 and 80; *Cartulaire de l'archevêché de Tours*, Mémoires de la Société Archéologique de Touraine, vol. 37, 33; vol. 38, 180 and 312.

For references concerning cemeteries in Anjou, see E. Zadora-Rio, "Les cimetières habités en Anjou aux XIe–XIIe siècles," *Actes du 105e Congrès National des Sociétés Savantes* (Caen, 1980) archéologie, 319–29.

There is no study concerning cemeteries in Maine, and the source-documents are too numerous to be listed within the framework of this article. They come mainly from: *Cartulaire de l'abbaye Saint Vincent du Mans*, éd. R. Charles et Menjot d'Elbenne (Mamers, 1886–1913); *Liber controversiarum Sancti Vincentii Cenomanensis*, ed. A. Chédeville (Paris, 1968); *Cartulaire manceau de Marmoutiers*, ed. Laurain (1911–1940); *Cartulaire St. Pierre de la Couture*, ed. Bénédictins de Solesmes (Le Mans, 1881).

Where Brittany is concerned, references can be found in: H. Guillotel, "Du rôle des cimetières en Bretagne dans le renouveau du XIe et de la première moitié du XIIe siècle," *Mémoires de la Société d'Histoire et d'Archéologie de Bretagne*, (1972–1974) 52:5–26.

2. Timbal Duclaux de Martin, *Le Droit d'Asile* (Paris, 1939) 77.

3. Ibid. 135.

4. G. Le Bras, article "Asile" in the *Dictionnaire d'Histoire et de Géographie Ecclésiastiques* (Paris, 1930) 4:1040.

5. Bertrand de Broussillon, *La Maison de Laval*, vol. 1 (Paris, 1895) p. 74 no. 91 and p. 103, no. 128.

6. Mansi, *Sacrorum cocniliorum nova et amplissima collectio* (Paris, 1903–1927), vol. 20, col. 914.

7. Livre Blanc de Saint-Florent de Saumur, Archives Départementales de Maine-et-Loire, H3713, fol. 63v, 64r; Livre Noir de Saint-Florent de Saumur, Bibliothèque Nationale, n. a. lat. no. 1930 fols. 64v, 65r, 66v, and 67r.

8. Archives Départmentales de Maine-et-Loire, G 677 (1083–1086).

9. Cf. Pierre Duparc, "Le cimetière, séjour des vivants (XIe–XIIe siècles)," *Bulletin philologique et historique du Comité des Travaux Historiques* (1967) 489–90.

10. The word "borough" is used for the French *bourg* which refers to villages created deliberately by seigneurial will in the 11th–12th centuries.

11. L. Musset, *"Cimiterium ad refugium tantum vivorum, non ad sepulturam mortuorum,"* Revue du Moyen Age Latin 4:1 (1948); P. Duparc, 487.

12. Bertrand de Broussillon, ed., *Cartulaire Saint Aubin d'Angers* (Angers, 1896) no. 710.

13. To the Angevin cemeteries documented in the above-mentioned article (note 1), cemeteries of the same type should be added: Guécélard, Brigne, Ruperford, Champfleur in Maine (*Cartulaire St. Pierre de la Couture*, no. 31 and 49; *Cartulaire Manceau de Marmoutiers*, 2:365; *Cartulaire St. Aubin d'Angers*, no. 716), and Oudon in the diocese of Nantes (*Cartulaire St. Aubin d'Angers*, no. 869).

14. P. Duparc, 469.

15. In 1096 in Dangeul, Maine, Guillaume de Braiteau donated the entire cemetery and church, with the exception of a knight's house; at Beaufay, in Maine, Raoul de Tercé gave the church and the whole cemetery, apart from a house which he kept for his own residence (*Cartulaire St. Vincent du Mans*, nos. 738 and 779). At Broc, in the diocese of Angers, Hamelin donated half of the income from the houses within the cemetery together with his own residence including the oven, the well, the garden, the

courtyard and the barn (*Cartulaire de la Trinité de Vendôme*, [Paris, 1893–1897] vol. 1, no. 265.

16. L. Musset, "Le Cimetière dans la vie paroissiale en Basse-Normandie (XIe–XIIe siècles)," *Cahiers Léopold Delisle* 12 (1963) 25.

17. C. Lorren, "L'église Saint-Martin de Mondeville (Calvados): Quelques questions," in *Mélanges d'Archéologie et d'histoire médiévales en l'honneur du Doyen Michel de Boüard*, (Genève-Paris, 1982) 267–68.

18. P. Aries, *L'Homme devant la Mort* (Paris, 1977).

19. L. Musset, "Le Cimetière dans la vie," 16.

20. "... *generalis consuetudo antiqua et approbate in tota Cenomannia obtinet que domini villarum, sive sint clerici sive sint laici, quamvis etiam ville in cimiteriis sint site, habent in eis census, custumas et alia servitia sua . . .*" (*Liber controversiarum Sancti Vincentii Cenomanensis*, 153).

21. O. Pontal, *Las Statuts Synodaux francais au XIIIe siècle* vol. 1, *Les Statuts de Paris et le Synodal de l'Ouest*, (Paris, 1971) 158, no. 30.

22. In written sources concerning Touraine, place-names are usually located within the Carolingian administrative framework (*villa-vicaria-pagus*), whereas in Anjou they are very often situated only in relation to topographical features.

23. R. Fossier, *Enfance de l'Europe, Xe–XIIe s. Aspects économiques et sociaux* (Paris, 1982) vol. 1, chap. 2.

24. Ramackers, *Papsturkunden in Frankreich*, (Göttingen, 1956) vol. 5, no. 43.

25. J. M. Bienvenu, "Les conflicts de sépulture en Anjou aux XIe et XIIe siècles," *Bulletin philologique et historique de Comité des Travaux Historiques* (1966) 673–85.

26. Ibid. 685.

27. Cf. note 11.

28. Archives Départmentales de Maine-et-Loire, Prieuré de Daumeray, 40 H 1 no. 43.

29. E. Salin, *La Civilisation mérovingienne, 2e Partie, Les Sépultures* (Paris, 1952) 13.

30. D. Bonney, "Early boundaries in Wessex," in *Archaeology and the Landscape: Essays for L. V. Grinsell*, ed. P. J. Fowler (London, 1972): 168–86; "Early boundaries and Estates in Southern England," *Medieval Settlement, Continuity and Change*, ed. P. H. Sawyer (London, 1976) 72–82.

31. Subsequent to the writing of this paper (end of 1983), such a quantification has been carried out by Ann Goodier in an article published in *Medieval Archaeology* 1984 ("The formation of boundaries in Anglo-Saxon England: a statistical study"). The paper deals with a sample of 754 burials, 135, or 17.9 percent of which occur on civil parish boundaries. In the first stage of the statistical study, the author establishes the non-randomness of the distribution, comparing the density of cemeteries situated on boundaries with that of cemeteries situated elsewhere; to this end, the author allocates a theoretical 100-meter width (50 meters on each side) for the parish boundaries. In the second part of the paper, the author tries to demonstrate that the association between burials and boundaries is deliberate, and not produced by a third factor which independently influenced the siting of both burials and boundaries (the same type of topographical feature, for example a watershed, river, or marginal land that might have been attractive at different times for both boundary demarcation and burials). To test this hypothesis, the author attempts to check whether the association between burials and boundaries changes over time, which would not be the case if it were produced by a geographical factor. For this test, burials datable within a century, amounting to only 168 of the original sample, were examined, and the result was found significant.

Although Ann Goodier's demonstration is very interesting and clearly argued, it fails to convince, mainly because of the poor quality of the archaeological data. The burials in the sample cannot be located more precisely than within a hundred meters; many of them are known only through ancient excavations, and their dating is not accurate. It seems rather obvious that the archaeological data are not adequate to support the far-reaching interpretations of the author: one can hardly give credit, for instance, to the diagram which is supposed to demonstrate that the proportion of burials on boundaries reaches its highest point in the 8th century with 33.3 percent when one notices that this remarkable proportion represents only one site, and there are only three burials ascribed to this period within the sample!

32. T. M. Charles-Edwards, "Boundaries in Irish Law," *Medieval Settlement, Continuity and Change*, ed. P. H. Sawyer (London, 1976) 83-87.

33. *Digeste* 47 (12).

34. J. Toynbee, *Death and Burial in the Roman World* (London, 1971) 48 and 73-93.

35. B. Young, "Paganisme, christianisation et rites funéraires mérovingiens," *Archéologie médiévale* 12(1977): 10.

36. E. Salin, 34 and 361; P. A. Fevrier, "La Tombe chrétienne et l'au delà," *Le temps chrétien de la fin de l'Antiquité au Moyen Age, IIIe-XIIIe s.*, Colloques internationaux du CNRS no. 604, 9-12 mars 1981 (Paris, 1984): 163-83.

P. Brown, *The Cult of the Saints: Its Rise and Function in Latin Christianity*, The Haskell Lectures on History of Religions, N.S.2 (Chicago: University of Chicago Press, 1981).

37. E. Salin, 34 and 12.

38. E. Lesne, *Histoire de la Propriété Ecclésiastique* (Paris, 1943) 3:123. In Brittany, vestiges of practice can still be found in the 12th century. In 1129, the bishop of Saint-Brieuc forbade the inhabitants from the *castrum* of Jugon to be buried by the crucifix at the crossroads or in unconsecrated ground (H. Guillotel, op. cit. in note 1, pp. 12-14). At this time, interments outside the cemeteries must have been a rarity.

39. J. Devisse, *Hincmar, Archevêque de Reims, 845-882*, vol. 2 (Genève, 1976) 2:831-33.

40. J. Chapelot and R. Fossier, *Le Village et la Maison au moyen âge* (Paris, 1980) 143-44.

Hillfort Reuse in Gloucestershire, AD 1–700*

JANICE B. KLEIN

The phenomenon of post-Iron Age use of Iron Age hillforts in Britain has been recognized for over half a century. It is only recently, however, that it has become the subject of systematic study. Most recent research has concentrated on hillfort reoccupation during the fourth through sixth centuries AD, the transitional period between Roman Britain and Anglo-Saxon England, variously called the post-Roman, sub-Roman and "Dark Age" period. This emphasis is due, in part, to the discoveries at the Somerset hillforts of South Cadbury (Alcock 1972) and Cadbury-Congresbury (Fowler et al., 1970) of substantial reuse in the fifth and sixth centuries AD Hillfort reuse is, of course, by no means restricted to the fifth and sixth centuries, but is well known from Roman, Anglo-Saxon and Norman periods. A change in the frequency or kind of hillfort reuse during this transitional period, however, might be a reflection of the changes in the contemporary social, political and economic conditions. By studying the evidence for fifth and sixth century hillfort reuse, in the context of the preceding centuries, it may be possible to identify and understand some of the factors which affected the settlement pattern, and thus society as a whole, during this time.

The work presented here looks in detail at hillfort reuse in a single county in Britain: Gloucestershire. It is in many ways an extension and complement to work recently carried out by Ian Burrow in the adjoining county of Somerset (Burrow 1979).

While Gloucestershire is, today, an artificial administrative region, for most of the time under consideration it was a coherent cultural unit and formed at least part of the nucleus of historically identifiable territories during the late Iron Age, Roman and Anglo-Saxon periods. The county of Gloucestershire lies in the west of Britain, at the edge of the Lowland Zone. It consists of three major geological areas: to the east, the oolitic limestone Cotswolds, to the south and along the Severn River valley, the clay Vale, and to the west, the Forest of Dean.

Numismatic evidence indicates that during the first century BC Gloucestershire was part of the territory of the Dobunni, which also included parts of Oxfordshire and northern Somerset (Allen 1961). In the Roman period this territory was incorporated into the *civitas Dobunnorum*, with its capital at Cirencester (*Corinium Dobunnorum*). The area was heavily Romanized, with a large number of urban and rural sites. Several of the rural villa sites show evidence of occupation through the fourth century and into the fifth, while at others the villa estate itself appears to have continued intact into the Anglo-Saxon period (Finberg 1959; Smith and Ralph 1972). Germanic settlement in Gloucestershire appears to have preceded political domination by at least half a century. West Saxon immigrants from the upper Thames settled in the south-eastern part of the county in the early sixth century, and Mercian occupation developed in the north (Meaney 1964). It was not until 577, however, that the *Anglo-Saxon Chronicle* records the defeat of the regional British kings at Deorham. By the early seventh century Gloucestershire was in Mercian hands, and the sub-kingdom of the Hwicce established, with a territory encompassing most of Gloucestershire, Worcestershire and west Warwickshire (Wilson 1968).

The term "hillfort," with its implicit meaning of hilltop location and military function, has often been criticized (e.g., May 1976). The variety of sizes and shapes included in this category have also made the use of a single term questionable. It is, however, the common and most convenient way to identify these sites. In general, a hillfort may be defined as an enclosed area which exploits the natural terrain, and has artificial defenses raised to protect it. These sites are primarily of Iron Age date, although the origin of many lies in the Bronze Age. The diversity of hillfort morphology is reflected in the variety of functions attributed to these sites. Their suggested use as settlement sites, religious foci, areas of specialized industrial activity, agricultural or pastoral enclosures, and defended refuges (Forde-Johnston 1976) are relevant not only to the Iron Age, but to the post-Iron Age periods considered here as well.

Methodologically, this study deals with three different types of evidence for hillfort reuse: the surface morphology, consisting of the unexcavated hillfort earthworks themselves; the documentary material, consisting primarily of place-name and charter analyses; and the archaeological remains, consisting both of excavated material and surface finds. These categories of evidence are presented independently, before a synthesis is attempted. The value of analyzing the different forms of evidence separately is clear. Documentary sources often focus on different aspects of society than those illuminated by the analysis of material remains, resulting in the development of seemingly incompatible, but equally valid frameworks. It is important that the archaeological evidence not be placed on a framework based on historical evidence, but evaluated independently, using the methodology of prehistoric archaeology.

Surface Morphology

Any consideration of the evidence for hillfort reuse should begin with the study of the sites' surface morphologies. As an independent source of evidence, it enables the identification of atypical sites whose anomalous appearance may have been caused by post-Iron Age modification. It also allows comparison with hillfort earthworks known to have been refortified during the Roman and post-Roman periods. In addition, it provides a foundation on which to place the other types of evidence.

There are two main difficulties in the use of morphological evidence. First, reuse of a hillfort does not necessarily involve modification of its earthworks. A site may have been reused without any corresponding refortification. Secondly, different cultural periods need not produce morphologically different earthwork configurations. Similar function, location and materials might well produce a similar form, regardless of period of construction.

One hundred and twenty-one sites in Gloucestershire have, over the last one hundred years, been identified as hillforts. Detailed investigation suggests that, of these, fifty-five are earthworks of actual Iron Age date (Table 1). The fifty-five sites have been divided into four types, based on size, topographical siting, complexity of earthworks (number and spacing of the banks and ditches) and arrangement of earthworks (type of enclosures). While this typology is tailored to the hillforts of Gloucestershire, and may have little applicability to the classification of sites in other areas, it does agree to some extent with other recent typologies for the region, in particular with Burrow's typology of Somerset hillforts.

The four types are:

Type I: These sites are less than 25 acres in area and include promontory, cliff and plateau-edge sitings, all of which use the natural terrain for only part of the site's boundary. This type includes univallate and multivallate sites, and is sub-divided by complexity of the earthworks (31 sites).

Type II: These sites are less than 30 acres in area and are all contour sites, using the natural terrain for the entire site's boundary. All but one site in this type are univallate (8 sites).

Type III: These sites are less than 15 acres in area and make little or no use of the natural terrain. This includes hillslope, low-lying and plateau sites. All are univallate (7 sites).

Table 1: Gloucestershire Hillforts

Hillfort	Ordnance	Survey	Reference
Abbey	ST	650	888
Bagendon	SP	017	062
Beckbury	SP	064	299
Bibury	SP	105	073
Blaise Castle	ST	558	783
Bloody Acre	ST	689	915
Brackenbury Ditches	ST	744	948
Burhill	SP	084	363
Bury Hill	ST	652	791
Camp Hill	ST	658	927
Churchdown	SO	882	190
Cleeve Cloud	SO	985	255
Clifton	ST	566	733
Combe Hill	ST	561	782
Combesbury	ST	553	954
Crickley	SO	927	161
Dean	SP	165	087
Dowdeswell I	SO	999	191
Dyrham	ST	741	767
Freezing Hill	ST	723	713
Haresfield II	SO	829	091
High Brotheridge III	SO	890	137
Horton	ST	764	844
Icomb	SP	205	230
Kimsbury	SO	869	121
Kings Weston	ST	555	780
Knole Park	ST	596	833
Leckhampton	SO	948	183
Little Sodbury	ST	760	826
Lydney	SO	616	027
Minchinhampton	SO	860	010
Norbury Colesbourne	SO	990	150
Norbury Northleach	SP	127	155
Nottingham	SO	984	284
Oldbury	ST	568	976
Oldbury-on-Severn II	ST	611	927
Oxenton	SO	973	313
Pinbury	SO	958	052
Ranbury Ring	SP	090	009

Table 1: Gloucestershire Hillforts *(Continued)*

Hillfort	Ordnance	Survey	Reference
Roel	SP	047	243
Salmonsbury	SP	173	208
Shenberrow	SP	080	334
Spital Meend	ST	540	967
Symonds Yat	SO	564	158
Tallards Marsh	ST	540	934
Toddington	SP	024	317
Towbury	SO	880	370
Trewsbury	ST	981	998
Tytherington	ST	664	883
Uley Bury	ST	784	989
Vineyards Brake	ST	608	884
Welshbury	SO	678	156
Willersey	SP	117	384
Windrush	SP	181	123
Woodmancote	SO	996	095

Type IV: These sites are all over 30 acres in area. This type includes all types of topographical siting and is subdivided on this basis (7 sites).

Within this typology several sites stand out as unusual. Within the group of sites larger than 30 acres (Type IV) one site [Nottingham], at 120 acres, is one half again as big as the next largest hillfort. At the other end of the scale, one site [Combesbury] contains only one acre. Although generally considered to be of Iron Age date, it has similarities in both size and shape to sites identified as Norman earthworks (Hogg and King 1963). The only other site of this size [Tallards Marsh] is thought to have been an integral part of Offa's Dyke, and possible constructed in the eighth century AD (Fox 1955).

Six sites have secondary enclosures. Annexed enclosures, apparently integral parts of the original design, are found at two sites [Trewsbury and Welshbury]. A crossbank at one hillfort [Kings Weston] has been suggested to be of similar construction, and therefore date, as the main Iron Age earthwork. Three sites [Abbey, Little Sodbury and Salmonsbury] have projecting earthworks which define an additional area. Only at one site [Little Sodbury], however, has it been suggested that the extension is of a later date than the main area of the hillfort.

Over fifty Iron Age hillforts throughout Britain are suggested to have been reused during the first seven centuries AD (Fowler 1971). Only a small number of these have been shown to have had their earthworks modified during this period. While there may be too few sites to actually build a typology, some common features emerge from an examination of known post-Iron Age earthworks. These include simple heightening of the defenses [Castle Dore, Cissbury and Lydney]; construction of new banks or ditches [Cissbury and Lydney]; addition of low internal and perimeter banks [Cadbury-Congresbury]; and the elaboration of entranceways [Cadbury-Congresbury, Castle Dore, Chun Castle, Maiden Castle, South Cadbury, and possibly Brent Knoll]. Several Gloucestershire hillforts exhibit some of these apparently characteristic features. While they may not all be the result of post-Iron Age modification, they are worth noting for comparison with the other forms of evidence. Internal divisions are found at three sites [Bury Hill, Clifton and Spital Meend], all of which have been suggested, either through excavation or survey, to be later than the main boundary defenses. Elaborated looped entrances may be present at two sites [Knole Park and Welshbury]. Finally, at one site, [Bury Hill], the only non-univallate Type II or III site, the defenses are separated (more than fifty feet apart) and some of the excavated earthworks appear to be of Roman date, suggesting parallels with the northern defenses of Lydney.

Documentary Evidence

There are two major types of documentary evidence which are of value in the analysis of hillfort reoccupation. The first is the study of place-names: both those of the hillforts themselves, and the distribution of the place-name element *burh*, meaning "a defended place." The other main source of evidence is the perambulations or boundaries attached to the Anglo-Saxon manor charters of the seventh to eleventh centuries. In addition, there are also a few possible references to hillfort sites in the *Anglo-Saxon Chronicle*.

The study of the association of place-names and archaeological sites serves a number of purposes for both the archaeologist and the philologist. First, and most importantly, certain place-names may be used to identify the sites of archaeological remains. Hillfort place-names may show which sites were identified in the Anglo-Saxon period as "defended places," as well as how or by whom they were used. Secondly, the association of certain types of sites with specific place-name elements or compounds may be used by the philologist to identify "site specific" names, providing additional or more exact meanings for the place-name elements. Finally, place-names may be used to suggest areas of early Germanic settlement, as well as those of continued British occupation. The use of British or Latin place-names for hillfort sites may show continued or renewed use of those sites by the Romano-British.

The most common Old English place-name element which refers to hillfort sites is *burh* (dative *byrig*), the modern "borough" or "bury." Although this term *can* refer to a hillfort, it may also be interpreted as meaning "a defended manor house" and, in late Old English, "town." *Burh* also refers to Roman forts, although this occurs more frequently in the north of England than the south. A further complication in the analysis of "borough" and "bury" place-names is the possibility of confusion with the Old English *beorg* or "barrow." *Beorg* and *burh* became confused in Middle English, and while they often result in similar modern spellings (including "borough," "bury," "berrow" and "barrow"), they have totally different origins and meanings. In addition to referring to a barrow or tumulus, *beorg* may also refer to a natural hill. Other place-name elements which may become confused with *burh* include *būr* (bower or cottage), *burg or *borow* (burrow) and *bearu* (grove) (Gelling 1978).

A survey of place-names in *burh* in Gloucestershire indicates that twenty refer to actual hillfort sites, while an additional seventeen are found in the immediate vicinity of hillforts and possibly refer to them (Table 2). A survey of the hillfort place-names indicates that, in addition to the names in *burh*, two are Celtic-English hybrids of the tautological type, in which a Celtic topographical term is linked with the same term in Old English. In this case, the Celtic word for "hill" (*crūc*) is linked with two different Old English words for "hill" (*dun* [in Churchdown] and *hyll* [in Crickley]). This type of place-name is thought to have been coined by non-Celtic speaking Anglo-Saxons in an area in which Celtic speakers lived, and, in general, suggests continuity of British settlement near these sites. The name of one site [Welshbury: "the fortified place of the Welshman"] also suggests possible use of the site by the British during the early Anglo-Saxon Period, while another [Freezing Hill: possibly "Frisian's Hill"] may indicate a place of early Germanic settlement. Unfortunately, the earliest reference to the first place-name is thirteenth century, while the second is more likely a reference to cows than people.

The estate boundaries or perambulations attached to many of the Anglo-Saxon royal and ecclesiastical charters of the seventh to eleventh centuries often contain valuable information about the early medieval landscape and settlement patterns, as well as references in individual hillfort sites. The earliest of the charter boundaries were brief and in Latin, but by the ninth century they were set out in detail in English. For the charters to be useful in archaeological studies, diplomatic, paleographic, geographic and linguistic analyses must have first been undertaken. The most important of these is the clear topographical identification of both the estate and boundaries being described. Without these studies, further archaeological analysis is extremely limited.

The terms which are used to describe the individual sites may give an indication of the hillforts' functions either at the time the boundaries were written or when they first acquired Anglo-Saxon names. Hillfort sites are referred to in charter boundaries as both *burhs* and *dīcs*. While *dīc* (ditch) is a word commonly used for linear earthworks, it most often refers not to prehistoric or de-

Table 2: Significant Place-Names in "Burh"

Place-Name	Significance
Almondsbury	parish containing Knole Park hillfort
Beckbury	hillfort
Besbury Farm	near Minchinhampton hillfort
Bibury	hillfort
Brackenbury	hillfort
Burhill	hillfort
Burleigh	near Minchinhampton hillfort
Bury Bower	near Bury Hill hillfort
Bury Fields	near Salmonsbury hillfort
Bury Hill	hillfort
Bury Moor	near Minchinhampton hillfort
Buryhill Farm	near Bury Hill hillfort
Bury's Barn	near Salmonsbury hillfort
Cockbury Butts	near Nottingham hillfort
Cockbury Court	near Nottingham hillfort
Combesbury	hillfort
Henbury	parish containing Blaise Castle hillfort
Highbury	near Lydney hillfort
Kimsbury	hillfort
Little Sodbury	hillfort
Milbury Heath	near Camp Hill hillfort
Norbury Colesbourne	hillfort
Norbury Northleach	hillfort
Oldbury	hillfort
Oldbury-on-Severn	hillfort
Pinbury	hillfort
Ranbury Ring	hillfort
Rushy Cockbury	near Nottingham hillfort
Salmonsbury	hillfort
Shenberrow	hillfort
Southbury	near Norbury Colesbourne hillfort
Stony Cockbury	near Nottingham hillfort
Thornbury	parish containing Camp Hill hillfort
Towbury	hillfort
Trewsbury	hillfort
Uley Bury	hillfort
Welshbury	hillfort

fensive earthworks, but to drainage and boundary ditches. Thus the hillforts referred to as *dīcs* are less likely to have been reused than those referred to as *burhs*. Several hillfort sites are identified in charter boundaries by a reference to Wodin or *Grīm* (a common nickname for Wodin). While these may be interpreted as showing that the earthworks were believed to have been the work of Wodin, or a vague expression of religious awe, the use of these terms may also indicate that the site was sacred or dedicated to Wodin.

The geographical relationship between hillfort sites and the land grants outlined in the charters is also a source of information about the hillforts' status. If a hillfort lies on the boundary of a charter grant, and is mentioned in the perambulation, it is likely that the site was not reused, and served only as an identifiable border marker, similar to the Saxon burial mounds identified this way to Wessex (Bonney 1966). The siting of a hillfort in a "central place" within the land grant set out in the charter may be indicative of an economic, social or political relationship between the hillfort site and the land area, suggesting a continued importance of the hillfort down to the time of the charter. The large number of problems, both practical and theoretical, in identifying the hillfort territories and linking them through time to the charter land grants, place this type of analysis beyond the scope of this study.

Nine charters of the Anglo-Saxon period make reference to Gloucestershire hillfort sites. All except one [Salmonsbury], which is mentioned as adjoining the area of a land grant, are identified as boundary points. One site [Freezing Hill] is identified as an *ealden dīc,* while another [Roel] is called *grymes hylle.* The others [Nottingham, Salmonsbury and Willersey] are identified as *burhs.*

Two entries in the *Anglo-Saxon Chronicle* may refer to Gloucestershire hillforts. In 577 "Cuthwine and Ceawlin fought against the Britons and killed three kings, Conmail, Condidan and Farinmail, at the place which is called Deorham; and they captured three of their cities Gleawcestre (Gloucester), Cirenceaster and Bapanceaster (Bath)." Deorham is generally identified as Dyrham, the site of a hillfort. The hillfort itself was not, however, referred to as Dyrham Camp until the end of the nineteenth century, but was called "Burrill" or "Barhill."

In 893 the English army besieged the Danes at "Buttingtune on the banks of the Severn," camping "on the two sides of the river." A number of places have been suggested for these sites, one of which is the hillfort at Oldbury-on-Severn. The hillfort is now mostly destroyed, but may have been similar to the D-shaped earthworks suggested as one class of fortification typical of the Danelaw frontier (Dyer 1972).

196 / JANICE B. KLEIN

Archaeological Remains

The archaeological evidence found on the sites of Iron Age hillforts, either through excavation or as casual finds, offers an obvious, but often ambiguous source of information about the reuse of the sites.

While material of the Roman period has been well studied, and in general provides clear dating evidence, the absence of Roman coins as a dating guide from about AD 400 places a greater reliance on the identification of diagnostic or type artifacts. At present the main artifacts diagnostic of the post-Roman period are certain classes of metalwork and pottery. The occurrence of some types of late Roman material in conjunction with the diagnostic post-Roman finds suggests that when these fourth century artifacts are found on their own, they may be indicative not only of Roman period activity, but of fifth and sixth century occupation as well. The late Roman artifacts may be residual, present at the site in pre-existing Roman deposits, and disturbed by post-Roman activity. They may be recycled from other Roman sites, either through the artifacts' presence in material brought to the site, such as dumped soil, or intentionally, so that the artifacts may be used as raw materials. The Roman artifacts may also be curios or heirloom, preserved out of context for idiosyncratic reasons, or they may be present because of continued use or manufacture.

There are seven main types of archaeological material found on hillfort sites. These can be divided into artifacts, including coins, pottery and metalwork, and features, including stone foundations, post-holes, ditches, burials and stone and earthwork defenses. While the artifacts, or portable remains, may occur in secondary, or non-use-related contexts, resulting from disturbance and displacement during subsequent site activity, or from casual site use, the features, or non-portable remains, are direct evidence of past behavior, and therefore more reliable indicators of actual site occupation.

Archaeological evidence from the first seven centuries AD has been found on thirty-two of the fifty-five hillfort sites in Gloucestershire. Forty-eight percent come from excavations, while fifty-two percent are casual finds. Eighteen sites have had excavation of some type, ranging from rescue work in advance of pipe-line trenching to research programs of several seasons' length. Of the excavated sites, fifteen yielded post-Iron Age material.

Coins were found on seventeen sites, ten of which had coins dating to the fourth century. At two sites [Lydney and Salmonsbury] coins of some of the latest issues to reach Britain were found.

Eighteen sites had Roman pottery. Six of these had fourth century material. None of the post-Roman imported wares were found, although a small amount of the calcite-gritted [Lydney] and grass-tempered [Crickley] wares, typical of the early Anglo-Saxon period, did occur. Much of the pottery from the substantial excavations of three sites [Leckhampton, Lydney and Salmonsbury] is as yet unstudied.

Metalwork was found on fourteen sites, with material at six identified as fourth century Roman. This includes late Roman cruciform [Lydney] and penannular fibulae [Haresfield and Lydney (Fowler B3, D2, E and G)], a late fourth century belt buckle [Lydney (Hawkes IIa)], part of a zoomorphic buckle [Haresfield], and a plate brooch of unusual form, possibly of post-Roman date [Lydney]. Four sites yielded metalwork thought to be Anglo-Saxon, including strap ends [Blaise Castle, Crickley and Kings Weston] and weapons [Salmonsbury]. Evidence of post-Iron Age metalworking was found at three sites [Bury Hill, Crickley and Lydney].

Human remains were found at eight hillforts. Four were individual burials in or just outside the hillforts [Nottingham and Tytherington (unassociated human bone) and Kimsbury and Norbury Northleach (with Roman material)]. Multiple burials in the defenses themselves were found at two sites [Bagendon and Salmonsbury], one of which [Salmonsbury] contained separate Romano-British and Anglo-Saxon cemeteries. In addition, cemeteries of late or "sub-Roman" date have been suggested at two sites [Blaise Castle and Kings Weston].

Occupation debris and structural remains were found at ten sites in a variety of forms. Individual structures were identified at six sites, including two villas [Haresfield and Norbury Northleach], and two less permanent "hut-like" structures [Crickley and Shenberrow], as well as other less identifiable building remains [Bury Hill ("barracks"), Crickley and Lydney].

Evidence indicative of more extensive settlement occurred at six sites, of which two [Salmonsbury and Woodmancote] suggested occupation lasting into the fourth century.

Evidence of religious or ritual activity was identified at seven sites, including a major fourth century temple complex [Lydney] and two "Roman" wells [Bury Hill and Salmonsbury], of which one [Salmonsbury] contained probable votive deposits of Roman date. In addition an altar was found in association with remains tentatively identified as a Roman temple, although a medieval chapel is also thought to have existed on the site [Blaise Castle].

Finally, seven sites have evidence of modification or reuse of the defenses. At four [Clifton, Little Sodbury, Lydney and Kings Weston] this is thought to be new construction, although none is closely dated. Three others [Crickley, Leckhampton and Salmonsbury] demonstrate some modification of the existing earthworks.

Analysis and Conclusions

Not all of the forms of evidence carry equal weight in the determination of site reuse. While the potential of the non-archaeological evidence is apparent, the clearest and most conclusive evidence for the reuse of hillforts comes from the study of the archaeological remains, and it is primarily on this basis that the determination of site reuse has been made.

The hillfort sites with the most positive evidence of post-Iron Age utilization are distributed fairly evenly throughout the three main regions of the county. There appear to be two slight biases. First, larger sites seem to be favored, although the largest hillforts do not appear to have been reused. Secondly, there is a bias towards sites which utilize the topography (both contour and promontory forts), and towards sites with bivallate defenses, although may be partially the result of reuse (i.e., post-Iron Age fortification), rather than a reason for it.

There is some correlation between the non-archaeological and archaeological evidence. Over half the sites with the clearest archaeological evidence for reuse also have significant place-names. One third of the sites with each of the other classes of evidence also yielded positive archaeological evidence. Of the fourteen sites with substantial excavation, twelve showed positive evidence of reuse.

Five models may be suggested for non-casual hillfort reuse: settlement or habitation; military or defence; industrial activity; religious activity; and burial. Variants of all these occur on the Gloucestershire hillforts. Although presented here separately, it is clear that a number of sites fit more than one model. In some cases the various activities occurred concurrently, while in others the function of the site changed over time.

Nine hillforts were used as settlement sites. The level of utilization ranged from temporary structures within the shelter of the earthworks [Crickley and Shenberrow], to individual buildings, including villas [Haresfield and Norbury Northleach], to extensive settlements, both Romanized [Norbury Northleach, Salmonsbury and Woodmancote] and native [Lydney], and varying in length of occupation and percentage of the hillfort interior used.

Military or defensive functions may be suggested for six sites. At three of these [Bury Hill, Clifton and Little Sodbury], the shape of the internal enclosures and structural remains tentatively suggest that the sites were Roman in design. Three hillforts [Spital Meend, Symonds Yat and Tallards Marsh] lie along the line of Offa's Dyke and have been identified as integral parts of the eighth century boundary. There is, however, no archaeological evidence that any of them was actually constructed or modified as part of the Dyke.

Industrial activity was identified on three sites, and ranges from intensive iron-mining with trade relations on a regional scale [Lydney] to limited work by small groups of individual craftsmen [Bury Hill, Crickley and Lydney], either in iron or bronze-working.

Three sites show evidence of religious or ritual activity. This includes a large scale Roman temple complex of major regional importance [Lydney], as well as two smaller local shrines [Blaise Castle and Salmonsbury].

Finally, identifiable burial were found on six sites, in both cemeteries [Blaise Castle, Kings Weston and Salmonsbury] and individual graves [Bagendon, Kimsbury and Norbury Northleach], and are of both Roman and Saxon date.

Roman material was found on over fifty-five percent of the hillfort sites in Gloucestershire, compared to only twenty-eight percent in Somerset. Clear evidence of permanent occupation, including scatters of pottery, tiles and building material, as well as actual structural remains, occurred on nineteen percent of Gloucestershire sites, compared to thirteen percent in Somerset. These figures suggest that permanent occupation, although slightly higher in Gloucestershire, was on approximately the same scale in both areas, while there was greater casual use of hillforts in Gloucestershire. The stray finds of Roman coins and pottery, here interpreted as evidence of casual frequentation or agricultural activity, may, however, actually represent more intensive use of the sites.

Not all of the post-Iron Age activity identified on Gloucestershire hillforts need be related to the presence of the hillfort itself, but may be interpreted as the result of geographical coincidence. In most of the cases discussed here, however, the reuse of the hillfort site appears to have been motivated by the existence of the earthworks and enclosed area, or by the high status or superstition attached to them. At some sites the importance of the hillfort can be clearly identified. Activity may be totally confined to the area within the earthworks [e.g., Bury Hill or Lydney], or specific areas within the hillfort may be defined and utilized [e.g., the entranceway at Leckhampton]. In other cases, the relationship between the Iron Age earthworks and subsequent activity at the sites is more difficult to establish. At Salmonsbury, for example, occupation involved not only part of the interior of the hillfort, but the surrounding area as well, and thus it is possible that this settlement was not related to the presence of the hillfort. The unusual elongated shape of the Bourton-on-the-Water *vicus* away from the Fosse Way, and towards Salmonsbury (Todd 1976), however, suggests that a deliberate attempt was made to utilize the hillfort enclosure. Prestige or religious association, rather than the actual physical remains themselves, may explain the reuse of a hillfort, not only for ritual activity, but also as a burial place [e.g., Bagendon and Kimsbury].

While there was substantial use of the hillfort sites in Gloucestershire during the Roman period, there appears to be very little activity at the sites in the later, post-Roman centuries. Only at a few sites [Bury Hill, Crickley, Haresfield and Lydney] is there any indication of fifth century occupation. Nowhere in Glouchestershire is there evidence of post-Roman site use as intensive as that in Somerset at South Cadbury or Cadbury-Congresbury. While this may be a function of excavation size or strategy, it may also be indicative of a real difference in settlement patterns between the two areas during the post-

Roman period. Level of romanization or proximity to the "Celtic West" may be partial explanations for this apparent difference, but future analyses are essential.

It will be necessary to place the hillfort sites within the context of the total settlement pattern of the Roman and post-Roman periods, and study the relationship of the reused hillforts to the rest of the landscape. In this way the reuse of not only individual sites, but of hillforts as a class, may be further understood, and a more complete picture of society during the first seven centuries AD developed.

Note

*This paper is based on my M.A. Thesis (University of Birmingham [U.K.] 1981) and carries with it the debt I owe to those who aided my research, particularly Dr. I. C. G. Burrow, Mrs. Margaret Gelling and my supervisor, Professor P. A. Rahtz.

References

Alcock, L. 1972	*Was This Camelot? Excavations at Cadbury Castle, 1966-70.* New York.
Allen, D. F. 1961	A Study of Dobunnic Coinage. IN E. M. Clifford *Bagendon: A Belgic Oppidum.* Cambridge. 75-149.
Bonney, D. J. 1966	Pagan Saxon Burials and Boundaries in Wiltshire. *Wiltshire Archaeological and Natural History Magazine* 61:25-30.
Burrow, I. C. G. 1979	Aspects of Hillfort and Hill-top Settlement in Somerset in the First to Eighth Centuries AD. Ph.D. Dissertation, School of History, University of Birmingham (U.K.).
Dyer, J. 1972	Earthworks of the Danelaw Frontier. IN P. J. Fowler *Archaeology and the Landscape.* London. 222-36.
Finberg, H. P. R. 1959	Roman and Saxon Withington: a Study in Continuity. *Occasional Paper of the Department of Local History,* no. 8. Leicester.
Forde-Johnston, J. 1976	*Hillforts of the Iron Age in England and Wales.* Liverpool.
Fowler, P. J. 1971	Hillforts, AD 400-700. IN D. Hill and M. Jesson *The Iron Age and Its Hillforts.* Southampton. 203-313.
Fowler, P. J. et al. 1970	*Cadbury-Congresbury, Somerset 1968. An Introductory Report.* Bristol.

Fox, C. 1955	*Offa's Dyke.* London.
Gelling, M. 1978	*Signposts to the Past.* London
Hogg, A. H. A., & D. J. C. King 1963	Early Castles in Wales and the Marches. *Archaeologia Cambrensis* 112:77-127.
May, J. 1976	British Antiquity 1975-76. The Iron Age. *Archaeological Journal* 133:265-75.
Meaney, A. 1964	*A Gazetteer of Anglo-Saxon Burial Sites.* London.
Smith, B. S. & Ralph, E. 1972	*A History of Bristol and Gloucestershire.* Beaconsfield.
Todd, M. 1976	The *Vici* of Western England. IN K. Branigan and P. J. Fowler *The Roman West Country.* London. 99-119.
Wilson, M. 1968	The Hwicce. *Worcester Archaeological Society Transactions* 2:21-25.

Zooarchaeology at Early Anglo-Saxon West Stow

PAM JEAN CRABTREE

The contributions of faunal analysis to prehistoric archaeology are well known. Zooarchaeology has played an important role in our understanding of hominid origins, of the evolution of hunting technology, and of the origins and development of animal husbandry in the Old and New Worlds. Animal bone studies have an equally important role to play in medieval archaeology. For the early Anglo-Saxon period in Britain faunal remains can (i) inform us about the nature of animal husbandry and rural economy and (ii) contribute to our understanding of the economic changes which accompanied the *Adventus Saxonum,* or the arrival of the Anglo-Saxons in Britain.

Early Anglo-Saxon Animal Husbandry

Recent archeological excavations at the emporia of Hamwih[1] and Ipswich have shown that the Middle Saxon period in England witnessed the beginnings of urbanism and the development of a market system. These changes surely affected systems of rural production. Before we can understand the effects of these developments on rural production, however, we need to document the nature of faunal exploitation in the period immediately preceding the development of these emporia, i.e., the fifth to seventh centuries AD. Unfortunately, the traditional documentary sources—Bede, Gildas, Nennius, and the Anglo-Saxon Chronicle—provide no evidence for Early Anglo-Saxon animal husbandry and hunting practices. Thus zooarchaeology must play a major role in the reconstruction of Early Anglo-Saxon subsistence economy. The West

Stow site is a unique source for paleoeconomic data. It is the only fully excavated Anglo-Saxon site in England, and particular emphasis was placed on the recovery of faunal remains during excavation.

West Stow[2] is located on the River Lark in East Anglia in eastern England. The site was completely excavated by Dr. Stanley West between 1965 and 1972, and excavation revealed approximately 70 *grubenhäuser* or sunken featured buildings clustered around half a dozen small rectangular halls. The Anglo-Saxon occupation of West Stow lasted about 250 years from the early fifth to mid-seventh century AD. Although the site was continuously occupied, the occupation has been divided into three successive chronological phases corresponding roughly to the fifth, sixth, and earlier seventh centuries, respectively. In addition to the extensive Anglo-Saxon settlement evidence, the West Stow excavations also revealed a complete Iron Age farmstead and a small number of late first- to early second-century pottery kilns and associated features.

The impressive Iron Age and Anglo-Saxon settlement archaeology at West Stow is complemented by an exceptionally well-preserved faunal assemblage including nearly 200,000 animal bones and fragments. Analysis of the West Stow faunal remains focused on variables which provide evidence for the types of animals herded and the uses to which they were put. Inferences about Early Anglo-Saxon animal husbandry were drawn from analyses of the animal species present and their relative importance, bone measurements, ages at death and kill-patterns for the domestic mammal species, and butchery practices.

The faunal evidence from West Stow indicates that a wide range of domestic and wild mammal species was exploited, at least occasionally, at the site. Nevertheless, the vast majority — over 99% — of the West Stow mammal bones are those of the domestic species: cattle (*Bos taurus*), sheep (*Ovis aries*), goat (*Capra hircus*), horse (*Equus caballus*), pig (*Sus scrofa*), dog (*Canis familiaris*), and cat (*Felis catus*). Throughout the Anglo-Saxon period sheep and goats are the predominant food mammals, representing just under 50% of the domestic food mammal bones (fig. 1). Although both identifiable sheep and goat bones were recovered from almost all Anglo-Saxon feature types, sheep fragments outnumber goat remains by a factor of more than 40:1. Thus most of the indeterminate sheep/goat fragments are probably sheep rather than goats. As small numbers of goat remains were present in all three Anglo-Saxon phases, it is possible that goats were kept for a specialized purpose such as dairying. Sheep and goats are followed by cattle which make up about 35% of the domestic food mammal bones; pigs, about 15%; and horses, only about 1%. Cattle, however, would have produced the majority of meat by weight (fig. 2), followed by sheep, pigs, and horses, respectively. In contrast, cattle are the numerically predominant species in the West Stow Iron Age. Approximately 50% of the identifiable bones are cattle remains, while sheep and goats make up only about 30% of the Iron Age faunal assemblage. Horse remains are con-

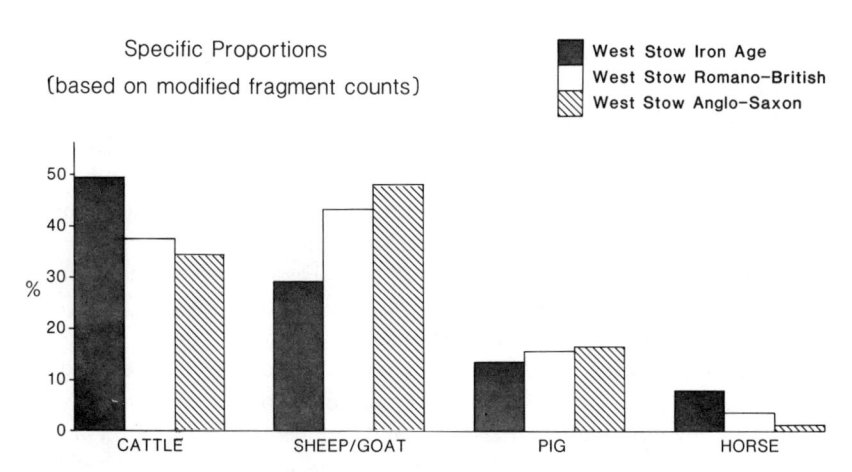

Fig. 1. Species ratios for main domestic mammals from the Iron Age, Romano-British, and Anglo-Saxon features at West Stow. These estimates are based on modified fragment counts or total numbers of maxillae, mandibles, scapulas, humeruses, radiuses, ulnas, pelves, femurs, and tibias. Calculations based on minimum numbers of individuals, relative frequencies, and total fragment counts (numbers of identified specimens per taxon) produce similar results.

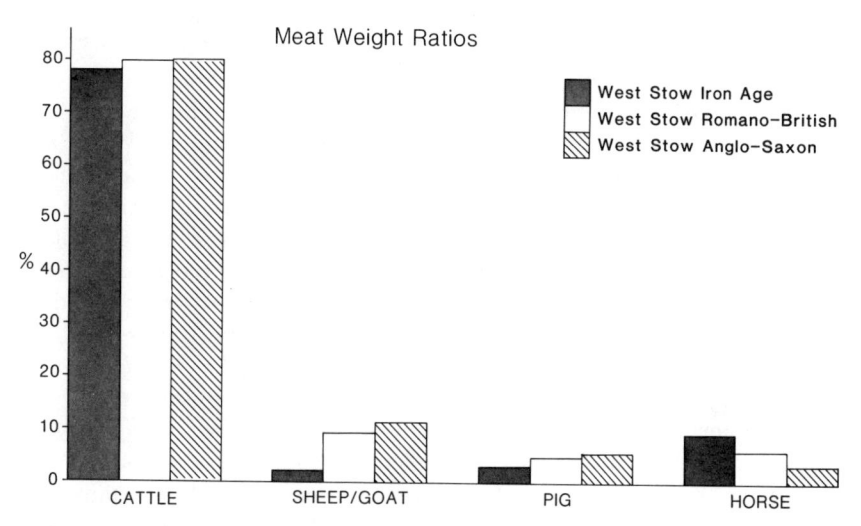

Fig. 2. Relative meat contributions for the domestic mammals. These estimates are based on the assumption that a horse can produce 12 times, a cow 10 times, and a pig 1.5 times as much meat as a sheep or goat.

siderably more common than they are in the Anglo-Saxon period, while pigs are less numerous in the Iron Age features. During the Iron Age cattle also provided the majority of the meat, but horses rather than sheep were the second most important meat source. The West Stow Romano-British specific proportions and meat weight ratios are intermediate between the Iron Age and the Anglo-Saxon, but the Romano-British faunal sample is small, and any conclusions drawn from it should be treated with some caution. The overall trend, however, seems to indicate that sheep and pigs were becoming more numerous through time, while horses were declining in frequency.

Wild mammals present in the West Stow faunal assemblage include red deer (*Cervus elaphus*), roe deer (*Capreolus capreolus*), badger (*Meles meles*), hare (*Lepus* sp.), fox (*Vulpes vulpes*), beaver (*Castor fiber*), and the European brown bear (*Ursus arctos*). There is no clear evidence for boar hunting during the Early Anglo-Saxon period at West Stow. Of the wild mammals present at West Stow, the most commonly represented are red deer and roe deer which are found in small numbers throughout the Early Anglo-Saxon period. Although both species are represented by some post-cranial elements, a significant number of shed antlers of red and roe deer were recovered. Since artifactual evidence indicates that antler-working was an important craft activity at West Stow, it is likely that shed deer antlers were collected as raw material for the production of antler objects.

Despite the interesting range of wild mammals present at West Stow, their contribution to the diet would have been small indeed. At Anglo-Saxon West Stow wild mammals always represent less than 1% of the identifiable faunal sample, a pattern also seen in the West Stow Iron Age and Romano-British faunal assemblages. This evidence indicates that the West Stow animal economy was based overwhelmingly on husbandry rather than hunting.

Although most of the bones from the Anglo-Saxon features at West Stow were mammal remains, fish and fowl also played a role in the domestic economy at this site. The vast majority of the bird remains are those of the domestic species: fowl (*Gallus* sp.), goose (*Anser* sp.), and domestic duck or mallard (*Anas platyrhynchos*). Although a range of wild bird species is represented in the Anglo-Saxon features, most of these are large water birds or waders including teal (*Anas creca*), white-fronted goose (*Anser albifrons*), swan (*Cygnus olor*), and crane (*Grus grus*). The fish remains include freshwater pike (*Esox lucius*) and perch (*Perca fluviatilis*). A single fragment of a flatfish was also present.

Measurement studies[3] were carried out to determine the size of the West Stow stock, to build up a relatively complete measurement series for an Early Anglo-Saxon site, and to allow for intersite comparisons. Measurements on cattle limb bones show that the West Stow Early Anglo-Saxon cattle were slightly larger, on the average, than British Iron Age cattle. Shoulder height estimates[4] for the West Stow Early Anglo-Saxon cattle range from 104.6 to

121.4 cms. The largest of these are larger than any British Iron Age cattle including those from Iron Age West Stow. The West Stow Early Anglo-Saxon cattle are very comparable in size to Roman cattle from sites such as Portchester Castle[5] and Alcester.[6] This would suggest that the Early Anglo-Saxon cattle from West Stow continue to show the size improvement that has been traditionally attributed to the Romans.[7] Further size increase, however, may have taken place later during the Middle Saxon period, as the largest cattle from sites such as Hamwih, Saxon Southampton,[8] are larger than any known from West Stow.

The West Stow Anglo-Saxon sheep are large (average estimated withers' height = 64.1 cms.) and significantly more robust than the small, slender sheep known from Iron Age sites such as Croft Ambrey[9] in southern Britain. They are most comparable in size to later Saxon sheep from East Anglia.[10] This large size, however, may be attributable to regional variation rather than Anglo-Saxon size improvement, as the West Stow Iron Age sheep are not significantly smaller than their Anglo-Saxon counterparts.

The West Stow pigs are large sized, comparable in robusticity to the middle Saxon pigs from Hamwih.[11] Measurements of the distal humeral breadth, which correlates with the animals overall body weight, indicate that the West Stow Anglo-Saxon pigs are more robust than the swine from the Iron Age settlement of Gussage All Saints in southern England.[12]

Estimates of ages at death can be used to make inferences about the uses, such as meat, milk, wool, and hides, to which the domestic animals were put. They can also be used to document changes in animal husbandry techniques through time. Estimates of ages at death for the domestic mammals at West Stow are based on dental eruption and wear, following Grant.[13]

At Anglo-Saxon West Stow only 45% of the cattle survived to maturity as indicated by a fully erupted permanent dentition. There is high mortality in the first two years of life, and most of the adult cattle are females. This evidence suggests that milk, in addition to meat production, may have been an important element in West Stow cattle husbandry. The Anglo-Saxon cattle from West Stow were killed at significantly younger ages than were the cattle from later Saxon sites including Middle Saxon Hamwih.[14] It is possible that Hamwih—an urban center—was provisioned with cattle of selected older age groups. The faunal remains from rural West Stow probably included a high proportion of immature cattle selected for slaughter because they were not required for breeding or working purposes. The kill-pattern for cattle seen at West Stow is most closely paralleled by the patterns seen at small, self-sufficient Iron Age sites in southern Britain, including Gussage All Saints Phase I[15] and Ashville.[16]

About two-thirds of the West Stow sheep were killed during the first two years of life suggesting that these animals were kept for meat, and possibly milk, production. The small numbers of mature sheep provide no evidence for large-scale wool production. The West Stowe sheep are significantly younger than the sheep from later Saxon sites including Hamwih[17] and Portchester Castle.[18] Once again, the West Stow ageing evidence is most closely paralleled by the kill-patterns seen at later Iron Age sites such as Ashville in Oxfordshire[19] and Barley in Hertfordshire.[20]

The faunal assemblage from West Stow also includes a substantial number of pigs which were killed during the first year of life, a pattern which is paralleled at Romano-British sites such as Exeter[21] and Fishbourne.[22] A substantially smaller number of adult pigs is seen at West Stow than at Middle Saxon Hamwih.[23] One reason for the large number of immature pigs seen at West Stow is that the area around the site is not ideal pig country. Trees are scarce today, and documentary evidence suggests that they would have been so in the Anglo-Saxon period. As pannage for pigs was not readily available, the inhabitants of West Stow may have had to provide substantial amounts of feed for their pigs. If sty husbandry was practiced, there would have been a strong economic motive to eliminate excess young animals.

Butchery practices at West Stow involved two distinct techniques: heavy chopping with a cleaverlike instrument and fine knife cuts. Sawing seems to be restricted to boneworking, a pattern which was also seen at Hanwih.[24] Some West Stow butchery practices, such as the use of fine knife cuts to disarticulate the hock joint, parallel those seen at a number of other Iron Age, Romano-British, and Anglo-Saxon sites in Britain. On the other hand, the rarity of longitudinal splitting of the long bones at West Stow is in sharp contrast to the patterns seen at later Anglo-Saxon sites such as Hamwih[25] and Portchester Castle.[26]

The zooarchaeological evidence for Early Anglo-Saxon West Stow indicates that this village was a small, self-sufficient farming settlement. Although a wide range of bird, fish and wild mammal species was occasionally exploited, the animal economy was based on cattle, sheep, and pig raising. The animals served primarily to provide meat and milk for domestic consumption. Was this pattern established by the Early Anglo-Saxon settlers, or can we see the roots of this economic strategy in the rural economies of the preceding Iron Age and Roman periods in Britain?

Faunal Analysis and the Adventus Saxonum

When the West Stow data on Anglo-Saxon animal sizes, specific ratios, butchery, and ages at death are considered as a whole, the overall impression is one of continuity from the preceding periods. Although the West Stow cattle remains are larger in size than Iron Age cattle, they are comparable in size to cattle from Romano-British sites. Evidence for Saxon size increase is more convincing for the Middle Saxon period, as the largest cattle from sites such as Hamwih,[27] Ramsbury[28] and North Elmham[29] are bigger than the largest Early Anglo-Saxon cattle from West Stow. While the Anglo-Saxon sheep from West Stow are large, the large size of the Iron Age and Romano-British sheep from the site suggests that this robusticity may be the result of regional variation rather than size improvement during the Early Anglo-Saxon period. This would suggest that the Saxon settlers did not bring new cattle or sheep breeds or radically new husbandry techniques with them when they came to Britain. Alternatively, if the Anglo-Saxons did introduce new breeds or types into Britain, they were so similar to the indigenous Romano-British stock that they are indistinguishable archaeologically. On the other hand, the large size of the West Stow pigs is comparable to the evidence from later Saxon sites such as Hamwih. However, the paucity of large measured pig bone samples from Romano-British sites makes comparisons of West Stow pigs and Roman swine difficult. It is possible that the Early Anglo-Saxons may have been responsible for some improvements in pig husbandry.

The evidence for specific ratios shows a higher proportion of sheep and pigs and fewer horses in the Anglo-Saxon features than in the Iron Age deposits. This change, however, should be seen as part of a long-term trend toward increased pork and decreased horse-flesh in the diet. The West Stow Romano-British features show intermediate proportions, and the trend toward increased pigs and fewer horses through time had been seen at other sites in Britain. The evidence from Roman Iron Age sites on the continent indicates that these changing species ratios are probably not the result of Saxon influence on animal husbandry. At Feddersen Wierde, a site in northwest Germany occupied between the first century BC and the fifth century AD, cattle make up just over 65% of the animal bone remains identified, while less than 15% of the bone fragments are sheep. Horses also make up about 15% of the identified fragments, while pigs comprise only about 5% of the identified animal bones.[30] Thus, the specific ratios seen at Feddersen Wierde are in fact closer to the proportions seen at Iron Age West Stow than they are to the Early Anglo-Saxon specific proportions.

The absence of quantitative data on butchery from other sites makes inter-site comparisons of butchery practice difficult. However, certain well-documented Anglo-Saxon butchery patterns seen at West Stow, such as the treatment of the hock joint, have parallels at other Iron Age and Romano-British sites, suggesting at least some measure of continuity in butchery practice.

The ageing evidence, in particular, points to continuity in economic pattern. The ageing distributions for Anglo-Saxon cattle and sheep from West Stow are most closely paralleled by those from pre-Roman Iron Age sites, while the West Stow Saxon pig kill-patterns have their closest counterparts at a number of Romano-British sites. The zoological evidence for West Stow sheep and goats, in particular, does not support an interpretation of large-scale wool production. The high proportions of older sheep at later Saxon sites such as North Elmham would indicate that the wool trade was well developed by later Saxon times.[31] However, the roots of this development are clearly not Early Anglo-Saxon, at least as far as the evidence from West Stow is concerned. It might more reasonably be suggested that the development of wool production on a large scale was related to the increasingly well-documented later Saxon advances in urbanism and the development of a market system.

The kill-patterns for the West Stow domestic mammals are also very different from those seen at continental Saxon sites such as Feddersen Wierde.[32] At Feddersen over 60% of the sheep survived to more than two years of age, while at West Stow nearly two-thirds were killed in the first two years. Over 60% of the Feddersen Wierde cattle survived to more than three years of age, and only a small proportion were killed during the second year. At West Stow, in contrast, we see a high slaughter rate during the second year of life and a smaller proportion of cattle surviving to adulthood. Similarly, at Feddersen Wierde over one quarter of the pigs survive to more than three years of age, while at West Stow less than 10% of the swine do so. It is therefore clear that the kill patterns seen at Anglo-Saxon West Stow are not the result of continental influence, but rather represent continuity in animal husbandry practice from the Iron Age and Romano-British periods.

The fundamentally conservative nature of the West Stow Anglo-Saxon animal economy has important implications for our understanding of the *Adventus Saxonum*. The fifth and sixth centuries in Britain were marked by changes in political organization, settlement pattern, and language. These changes included the withdrawal of Roman military power from Britain, the abandonment or reduction in size of the urban centers, and the replacement of British language by Anglo-Saxon. The Anglo-Saxons in the countryside, however, continued to practice patterns of animal husbandry that were not unlike those of previous centuries. In short, the zooarchaeological evidence from West Stow indicates that animal husbandry practices showed remarkable continuity in the face of large-scale changes in other aspects of culture.

It has traditionally been assumed that linguistic change, accompanied by migration, should be reflected in substantial and easily recognizable changes in artifact types and settlement patterns. However, there may be distinct advantages in preserving the ongoing pattern of rural economy. Even major population replacements do not result in a *tabula rasa*, in which the previous population has disappeared, and in which the previous landscape has been miraculously returned to its natural state. On the contrary, where really thorough and detailed research has been carried out, it has been found that many features of local and regional landscapes are retained through phase after phase of political and economic change.[33] In addition, documentary, linguistic, and place-name evidence argues against the complete replacement of Romanized-Britons by Anglo-Saxons. The place-name evidence, in particular, provides some evidence for British survival. Although Celtic names survive more frequently as names of the larger rivers, forests, and hills, a variety of other British place-names survive as well. These names increase in frequency as one moves from east to west; there are, however, a number of notable exceptions, including a concentration of Celtic place-names near Penge in Surrey.[34] Moreover, even in areas where Celtic names are rare, such as Berkshire, Oxfordshire, and Warsickshire, those that do survive tend to occur in clusters, suggesting small groups of Celtic speakers in an Anglo-Saxon context. In addition, English place-names containing the Old English place-name elements of *walh* and *Cumbre* seem to refer to people of either whole or partial British descent.[35] Documentary evidence would also support some British survival. For example, St. Guthlac encountered Celtic-speaking Britons in the Fenland as late as AD 700, i.e., after West Stow was abandoned.[36] Viewed from this perspective, the Anglo-Saxons, whether we see them as a warrior elite or a larger group of settlers, would have had little to gain and much to lose by the disruption or profound alteration of the indigenous food- production system.

Thus, while there is no denying the linguistic change and the large number of artifact types that can plausibly be attributed to the Anglo-Saxon settlers, we do not have quantitative knowledge of the extent to which the native population survived in areas of Anglo-Saxon settlement, let alone the regional variation in that probable survival. Every additional indication for native survival would—theoretically at least—provide more reason to expect continuity in rural settlement patterns, land use, and rural economy.

Notes

1. P. Holdsworth, *Excavations at Melbourne Street, Southampton, 1971-76*, C.B.A. Research Report no. 33 (London: C.B.A., 1980).

2. For a complete report on the West Stow excavations, see Stanley West, *West Stow: The Anglo-Saxon Village*, East Anglian Archaeology Report no. 24 (Ipswich: Suffolk County Planning Department, 1985).

3. Following Angela von den Driesch, *A Guide to the Measurement of Animal Bones from Archaeological Sites*, Peabody Museum Bulletin, no. 1 (Cambridge: Harvard University Press, 1976).

4. Following Angela von den Driesch and J. Boessneck, "Kritische Anmerkungen zur Widerristhöhenberechnung aus Längenmassen vor- und frühgeschichtlicher Tierknocken," *Säugetierkundliche Mitteilungen* 22 (1974): 325-48.

5. Annie Grant, "The Animal Bones," in *Excavations at Portchester Castle, Vol. I: Roman*, ed. B. Cunliffe (London: Society of Antiquaries, 1976) 401.

6. Mark Maltby, "Iron Age, Romano-British and Anglo-Saxon Animal Husbandry—A Review," in *The Environment of Man: The Iron Age to the Anglo-Saxon Period*, ed. M. Jones and G. Dimbleby, B.A.R. British Series, Report no. 87 (Oxford: B.A.R., 1981) 187.

7. See, for example, Grant, 402.

8. J. Bourdillon and J. Coy, "Statistical Appendix to Accompany to Animal Bone Report on Material from Melbourne Street (Sites I, IV, V, VI, and XX) Excavated by the Southampton Archaeological Research Committee between 1971 and 1976," TS available from the Faunal Remains Unit, Department of Archaeology, University of Southampton, p. 23.

9. R. Whitehouse and D. Whitehouse, "The Fauna," in *Croft Ambrey*, ed. S. C. Stanford (Hereford: Privately published, 1974) 238.

10. J. Clutton-Brock, "The Animal Resources," in *The Archaeology of Anglo-Saxon England*, ed. D. M. Wilson (London: Methuen, 1976) 381.

11. Bourdillon and Coy, "Statistical Appendix," 13–16.

12. R. Harcourt, "The Animal Bones," in *Gussage All Saints: An Iron Age Settlement in Dorset*, ed. G. J. Wainwright, D.o.E. Archaeological Report no. 10 (London: HMSO, 1979) 152.

13. Annie Grant, "Appendix B: The Use of Tooth-Wear as a Guide to Ageing the Domestic Animals—a Brief Explanation," in *Excavations at Portchester Castle, Vol. I: Roman*, ed. B. Cunliffe (London: Society of Antiquaries, 1975) 437–50.

14. Bourdillon and Coy, "Statistical Appendix," 25.

15. Harcourt, 151.

16. J. Hamilton, "A Comparison of the Age Structure at Mortality of Some Iron Age and Romano-British Sheep and Cattle Populations," in *The Excavation of an Iron Age Settlement, Bronze Age Ring-ditches and Roman Features at Ashville Trading Estate, Abingdon (Oxfordshire) 1974–76*, ed. M. Parrington, C.B.A. Research Report no. 28 (London: C.B.A., 1978) 133.

17. Bourdillon and Coy, "Statistical Appendix," 25.

18. Annie Grant, "The Animal Bones," in *Excavations at Portchester Castle, Vol. II: Saxon*, ed. B. Cunliffe (London: Society of Antiquaries, 1976) 278.

19. Hamilton, 126–31.

20. J. M. Ewbank, D. W. Philipson, R. D. Whitehouse, and E. S. Higgs, "Sheep in the Iron Age: A Method of Study," *Proceedings of the Prehistoric Society* 30 (1964): 423–26.

21. Mark Maltby, *Faunal Studies on Urban Sites: The Animal Bones from Exeter 1971–1975*, Exeter Archaeological Reports no. 2 (Sheffield: Department of Prehistory and Archaeology, 1979) 57.

22. Annie Grant, "The Animal Bones," in *Excavations at Fishbourne 1961–1969*, ed. B. Cunliffe (London: Society of Antiquaries, 1971) 2:383.

23. Bourdillon and Coy, "Statistical Appendix," 25.

24. J. Bourdillon and J. Coy, "The Animal Bones," in *Excavations at Melbourne Street, Southampton, 1971–76*, ed. P. Holdsworth, C.B.A. Research Report no. 33 (London: C.B.A., 1980) 97.

25. Bourdillon and Coy, "The Animal Bones," in *Melbourne Street*, 97.

26. Grant, "The Animal Bones," in *Portchester: Saxon*, 273.

27. Bourdillon and Coy, "Statistical Appendix," 23.

28. J. Coy, "The Animal Bones," in "A Middle Saxon Iron Smelting Site at Ramsbury, Wiltshire," ed. J. Haslam, *Medieval Archaeology* 24 (1980): 47.

29. B. Noddle, "The Animal Bones," in "Excavations at North Elmham Park, 1967–1972," ed. P. Wade-Martins, *East Anglian Archaeology* 9 (1980): 387–88.

30. H. Reichstein, "Einige Bemerkungen zu den Häustierfunden auf der Feddersen Wierde und vergleichbarer Siedlungen in Nordwestdeutschland," *Die Kunde* 23 (1972): 144.
31. Noddle, 396.
32. Reichstein, 152-54.
33. See, for example, Christopher Taylor, *Village and Farmstead: A History of Rural Settlement in England* (London: George Philip, 1983).
34. M. Gelling, *Signposts to the Past: Place-Names and the History of England* (London: J. M. Dent, 1978) 90.
35. Gelling, 93. For an extensive, recent discussion of the *walh* element in place-names, see Kenneth Cameron, "The Meaning and Significance of old English *walh* in English Place-Names" (with appendices: Malcolm Todd, "The Archaeological Significance of Place-Names in *walh*," and John Insley, "The Continental Evidence: OHG *wal(a)h*, OSx *walh*"), *Journal of the English Place-Name Society* 12 (1979-80): 1-53.
36. S. Frere, *Britannia: A History of Roman Britain* (London: Cardinal, 1974) 419.

Acknowledgment

The research on which this article is based was funded by the National Science Foundation (Grant no. BNS 77-08141), by the Wenner Gren Foundation for Anthropological Research (Grant no. 3267), and by a Fulbright-Hays Full Grant and Renewal. Special thanks are due to Jennie Coy, Faunal Remains Unit, Department of Archaeology, University of Southampton, who identified the bird and fish remains from West Stow, and to Helen Schenck, MASCA, The University Museum, University of Pennsylvania, who produced the figures which accompany the text.

Bibliography

Bourdillon, J.; Coy, J.
1977	Statistical Appendix to Accompany the Animal Bone Report on Material from Melbourne Street (Sites I, IV, V, VI and XX). Manuscript available from the Faunal Remains Unit. Department of Archaeology. University of Southampton (England).
1980	The Animal Bones. In *Excavations at Melbourne Street, Southampton, 1971-76*. R. Holdsworth, ed. C.B.A. Research Report No. 33. Pp. 79-121. London: C.B.A.

Cameron, Kenneth
1979-80	"The Meaning and Significance of Old English *walh* in English Place-Names" (with appendices: Malcolm Todd, "The Archaeological Significance of Place Names in *walh*," and John Insley, "The Continental Evidence: OHG *wal(a)h*, OSx *walh*"). *Journal of the English Place-Name Society* 12: 1-53.

Clutton-Brock, J.
1976	The Animal Resources. In *The Archaeology of Anglo-Saxon England*. D. M. Wilson, ed. Pp. 373-92. London: Methuen.

Coy, J. The Animal Bones. In J. Haslam, A Middle Saxon Iron Smelt-
1980 ing Site at Ramsbury, Wiltshire. *Medieval Archaeology* 24: 41-51.

Ewbank, J. M.; Philipson, D. W.; Whitehouse, R. D.; Higgs, E. S.
1964 Sheep in the Iron Age: A Method of Study. *Proceedings of the Prehistoric Society* 30: 423-26.

Frere, S. *Britannia: A History of Roman Britain.* London: Cardinal.
1974

Gelling, M. *Signposts to the Past: Place-Names and the History of England.* London: J. M. Dent.
1978

Grant, A. The Animal Bones. In *Excavations at Fishbourne 1961-1969*, vol.
1971 II. B. Cunliffe, ed. Pp. 377-88. London: Society of Antiquaries.

1975a The Animal Bones. In *Excavations at Portchester Castle, Vol. I: Roman.* B. Cunliffe, ed. Pp. 378-408. London: Society of Antiquaries.

1975b Appendix B: The Use of Tooth-Wear as a Guide to Ageing and the Domestic Animals — A Brief Explanation. In *Excavations at Portchester Castle, Vol. I: Roman.* B. Cunliffe, ed. Pp. 437-50. London: Society of Antiquaries.

1976 The Animal Bones. In *Excavations at Portchester Castle, Vol. II: Saxon.* B. Cunliffe, ed. Pp. 262-87. London: Society of Antiquaries.

Hamilton, J. A Comparison of the Age Structure at Mortalityof Some Iron
1978 Age and Romano-British Sheep and Cattle Populations. In *The Excavations of the Iron Age Settlement, Bronze Age Ring-ditches and Roman Features at Ashville Trading Estate, Abingdon (Oxfordshire) 1974-76.* M. Parrington, ed. Pp. 125-33. C.B.A. Research Report No. 28. London: C.B.A.

Harcourt, R. The Animal Bones. In *Gussage All Saints: An Iron Age Settlement in*
1979 *Dorset.* G. J. Wainwright, ed. Pp. 150- 60. D.o.E. Archaeological Report No. 10. London: HMSO.

Holdsworth, P. *Excavations at Melbourne Street, Southampton, 1971-76.* C.B.A. Research Report No. 33. London: C.B.A.
1980

Maltby, M. *Faunal Studies on Urban Sites: The Animal Bones from Exeter 1971-1975.*
1979 Exeter Archaeological Reports, Volume 2. Sheffield: Department of Prehistory and Archaeology.

1981 Iron Age, Romano- British and Anglo-Saxon Animal Husbandry — A Review. In *The Environment of Man: The Iron Age to the Anglo-Saxon Period.* M. Jones and G. Dimbleby, eds. Pp. 155-203. B.A.R. British Series, Report No. 87.

Noddle, B. The Animal Bones. In P. Wade Martins, *Excavations at North Elham*
1980 *Park, 1967-1972.* Pp. 375-409. *East Anglican Archaeology*, Report No. 9.

Reichstein, H. Einige Bemerkungen zu den Häustierfunden auf der Feddersen
1972 Wierde und verglieichbarer Siedlungen in Nordwestdeutschland. *Die Kunde* 23: 142-56.

Taylor, C.
1983 *Village and Farmstead: A History of Rural Settlement in England.* London: George Philip.

von den Driesch, A.
1976 *A Guide to the Measurement of Animal Bones from Archaeological Sites.* Harvard University, Peabody Museum Bulletin No. 1.

von den Driesch, A.; Boessneck, J.
1974 Kritsche Anmerkungen zur Widerristhöhenberechnung aus Längenmassen vor- und frühgeschichtlicher Tierknocken. *Säugetierkundliche Mitteilungen* 22: 325–48.

West, S.
1985 *West Stow: The Anglo-Saxon Village.* East Anglian Archaeology Report No. 24. Ipswich: Suffolk County Planning Department.

Whitehouse, R.; Whitehouse, D.
1974 The Fauna, In *Croft Ambrey.* S. C. Stanford, ed. Pp. 215–21, 238–42. Hereford: Privately published.

Historical Archaeology of Medieval Muslim Communities in the Sierra of Eastern Spain

KARL W. BUTZER and ELISABETH K. BUTZER

Perspectives

Archaeologists today strive to go beyond the elucidation of material culture by attempting to identify social aggregates and to generate evidence of and explanations for change. The degree to which such goals can be realistically achieved in prehistoric archaeology is open to debate. In historical archaeology, the possibilities are substantially better, particularly if the approach is interdisciplinary and adequate research is directed towards archival documentation. But there is no unanimity as to the goals and methodology of historical archaeology, a feature that becomes obvious when comparing substantive work in Medieval archaeology in Europe or North Africa with its much younger counterpart in Colonial and nineteenth century North America. For the present, therefore, projects in historical archaeology tend to reflect regional paradigms, and both the opportunities and constraints of available written records particular to an area and time range.

In the Mediterranean world, historical archaeology has the potential of elucidating a number of processes that are critical not only to a more comprehensive understanding of Medieval history but also to basic concerns in cultural ecology. These include continuity and change in settlement patterns (as a tangible reflection of social populations), demographic shifts and cycles, the interaction between people and their environment, technological diffusion and socioeconomic transformation, and acculturation or cultural change in a broader sociopolitical context.

In the case of the Iberian Peninsula, the big issues center on the Arab conquest and the Christian *Reconquista:* how fundamental were religious conversion and arabization after AD 711? how significant was the Islamic heritage

218 / KARL W. BUTZER AND ELISABETH K. BUTZER

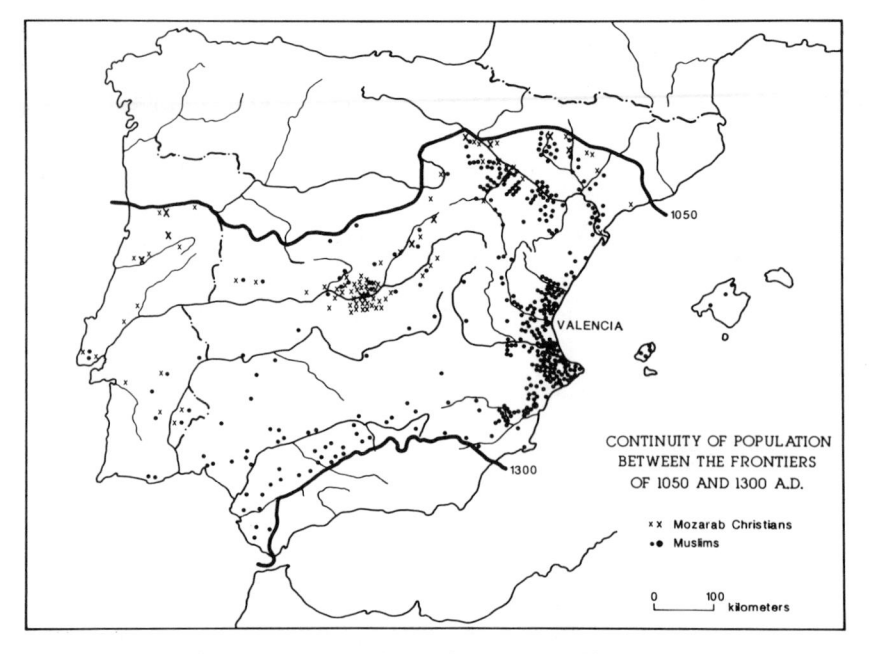

Fig. 1. Continuity of population between the Christian-Muslim frontiers of AD 1050 and 1300.

in post-*Reconquista* Spain? was the discontinuity of the conquest more incisive than that of the reconquest, or vice versa?

For over a century, macro-historical research has argued for a monolithic interpretation of Islamic Spain, with essentially complete cultural assimilation of its earlier Hispano-Roman population. More recent works, such as those of Lapeyre[1] and Ladero Quesada,[2] further suggest that emigration and expulsion of the post-*Reconquista* Muslim populations were more or less total, which would imply that the Islamic legacy to modern Spain was limited to material features of the cultural landscape and indirect, partial acculturation. Both positions appear to be oversimplified (see fig. 1).

In the heart of tenth century Andalusia, the language of communication remained the Romance vernacular, not Arabic;[3] therefore when Guichard[4] concludes that the social structure of Islamic Spain was basically "eastern," he probably describes the customs of the ruling elite. Islamic agriculture and irrigation technology, long assumed to be a hallmark of the Islamic contribution to Spain, has been shown to be more deeply anchored in the Roman Mediterranean world than in the Middle East.[5] Archival study of the Toledo area, following its reconquest in 1085, documents countless villages with a substantial core of older Christian inhabitants, while the Mozarab Christian liturgy remained vital in urban Toledo well into the late Middle Ages.[6] The surviving *aljamiado* literature of the fifteenth and sixteenth century Muslim minority in Aragón is written in Romance dialects, but with Arabic script:[7] this has been interpreted as a matter of post-*Reconquista* assimilation, but in a region where the Islamic elite of the ninth and tenth centuries intermarried with the Christian aristocracy of Navarre and León,[8] it could equally well reflect a bilingual society antedating the reconquest. In the Valencia region, where Arabic evidently was the sole language of rural Muslims[9] during some 375 years of bicultural ambience,[10] the names of many topographic features and land parcels used in Arabic had remained almost unchanged from their earlier Romance forms.[11]

These points do not minimize the cultural contrasts between Christian and Islamic Spain, accentuated as they were by the much older dichotomy between the intensified agrosystems of the urbanized south and east, on the one hand, and the extensive and more pastoral economies of the interior and northwest, on the other. Rather, they suggest that the degree of islamization and arabization was variable in both time and place, and that we need to distinguish between the elite and the remaining populace, and between countryside and city. The literature is unduly biased in favor of urban elites, political events, religious conflicts, and artistic concerns. The social processes of Medieval Spain have been delineated with too broad a brush, and popular assumptions require careful reevaluation. This can only be done at the micro-scale, and with the benefit of an interdisciplinary, social science perspective. Preferably, such efforts should concentrate on rural social units, for which strong archaeological and ecological components are essential.

The present paper provides a synopsis of such a research project, to study a small, rural area exhaustively.

The Espadán Project

The Sierra de Espadán is a cluster of mountains and deep valleys, situated just above the Mediterranean coastal plain, some 50 km north of Valencia (fig. 2). Sixteen Muslim communities persisted here, as a minority enclave, from the *Reconquista* in AD 1238 to the Expulsion of 1609. The resilience of these communities, surrounded by Christian or mixed villages, and their clear ecological circumscription, suggested an historical, social unit amenable to systematic study. A long-term research strategy was developed in 1979–1980, in conjunction with Juan Mateu and Ismael Miralles of the University of Valencia.

The exploratory season of 1980 focused on the "traditional" cultural landscape of the Espadán, with mapping of settlement morphology and land use in eight villages. Despite inherited, irregular street layouts in some of the vil-

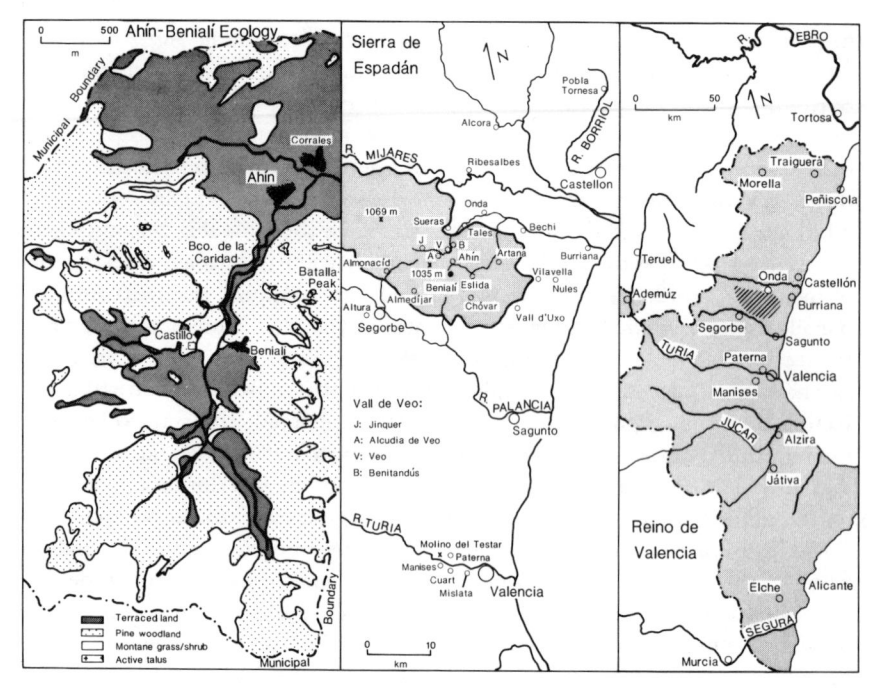

Fig. 2. Situation of the Sierra de Espadán in eastern Spain.

lage nuclei, standing houses all postdated Christian resettlement after 1610; the oldest architectural elements were Renaissance-style arcade windows under the eaves, a feature popular ca. 1600; ground floors commonly incorporated sets of rounded arches, identical to those of traditional sheep corrals, and were generally built on bedrock. This limited their archaeological potential, although seventeenth century potsherds are occasionally found in wall mortars. However, an abandoned Medieval hamlet, still known as Benialí, was discovered on the basis of wall foundations and fourteenth to fifteenth century pottery; it was selected for subsequent excavation (fig. 2). A search was begun in the rich, Valencian archival repositories for references to Benialí and its larger, corporate community, Ahín. Evidence for ecological change was also identified during this first season. Medieval and "traditional" sherds were recovered from old stream deposits—that accumulated as a result of upslope soil erosion, as well as in the mortar of an abandoned "sweep" or *shaduf,* the well of which is now high above the stream floor, because of changing stream-flow patterns.

Excavations were carried out in Benialí during 1981–1982, concurrently with archival research and ethnoarchaeological study in Ahín. It was possible to identify soil erosion contemporary with the occupation at Benialí—now archivally dated between AD 1342 and 1526—and to link it with the absence of artificial terracing of the cultivated slope as well to the mass of goat bone recovered from the excavations. Botanical remains analyzed by specialists allowed reconstruction of the agricultural economy, while the excavations located cisterns and the irrigation arrangement at Benialí. In 1983 archival research was expanded to other Espadán communities, parish registers were discovered for three villages (beginning after 1610), pottery studies were carried out at traditional and Medieval centers, and the work on ethnoarchaeology, traditional irrigation, and historical village growth was essentially completed.

After a break for analytical research during 1984, the Valencian archival sources for the Espadán were essentially exhausted in 1985, and 15 abandoned, "lost" villages identified from the archives were located in the field and recorded. Excavation was also carried out in the castle of Ahín, directly across the valley from Benialí. Contrary to general belief, the castle proved to be Islamic rather than Christian, occupied for at least two generations prior to 1238; it contained highly informative domestic structures and occupation residues, and was reoccupied by local villagers in 1276, during a Muslim uprising, and subsequently assaulted and destroyed. Thus the settlement history of the area was extended back to the mid-twelfth century.

For 1986 another excavation had been planned in the castle at Xinquer, which has much thicker deposits (7 m), as well as in adjacent Islamic settlement residues; on the basis of the thirteenth century spelling, *S(h)entqueir,* the toponym derives from either Saint Quirico or Quirino, Paleochristian names that hint at a possible Visigothic church or monastic site. It had therefore been hoped to extend the settlement record through the Islamic period, into the seventh century; at the same time archival research in Barcelona was planned to amplify the fourteenth century documentation for the Espadán. But the funding proposal was rejected by the National Science Foundation, so that the early Medieval period, critical to understanding Islamic acculturation of the Hispanic population, remains obscure.

In sum, the Espadán Project represents a complex, interdisciplinary project that combines an archaeological and "landscape" approach with thorough archival research. Study alternatingly proceeded at two different scales, intensive investigation of Benialí and Ahín, coupled with more extensive attention to the other communities of the Espadán, to encompass the effective social unit of the Muslim population in the sierra, across the period of the *Reconquista* to the eve of the Expulsion.

Basic Archaeological Contributions

The results of the excavations in the castle of Ahín and the hamlet of Benialí can be outlined as follows, with further details and documentation presented elsewhere.[12]

(a) The oldest part of the castle is the round, central tower or "keep" and the attached, triangular precinct formed by massive walls that enclose a large cistern; both the Islamic pottery and the architectural elements indicate a (?mid-)twelfth century date.

(b) Subsequently, a more elaborate castle was built, beginning with a trapezoidal platform of 650 m², upon which walls of poured concrete were raised, including two, double-storied corner bastions. Low external ramparts were constructed around the perimeter and a separate, square watchtower erected at the other end of the ridge, 80 m away. Small living quarters with tiled roofs were attached to the base of the older, now interior wall. Table wares argue for a small but permanent garrison, but the absence of luxury pottery precludes a resident officer of any status. Although the architecture is more modern than that of the original castle, it suggests a date before AD 1200, while the pottery indicates a distinct stylistic shift. Judging by the network of other late twelfth or early thirteenth century castles in the Espadán, the expanded fortress of Ahín appears to represent a low-order link in a larger Islamic plan of defense for the mountains along the Aragónese frontier.

(c) The castle was subsequently vacated, without destruction, and remained unoccupied sufficiently long to allow weak calcification of the sediments.

(d) The next level in the castle consists of a minimally compacted, destruction rubble, initially intermixed with occupation residues. The pottery is stylistically the same as that of the previous occupation, but there are more water containers and fewer glazed plates or cooking vessels; this suggests lower economic status and temporary occupation, probably by local villagers, prior to an assault that destroyed the two long walls.

(e) Some 1813 pottery fragments were recovered from the three Islamic levels; the fabrics suggest several pottery centers, as yet unidentified. Functional comparison with pottery from the later hamlet of Bernialí indicates similar proportions of water containers and fire-resistant kitchen/cooking vessels, but fewer storage wares and more table dishes, in the Islamic castle.

(f) The animal bone is dominated by goat, together with sheep, cow, chicken, and another, unidentified bird. Metal finds include a gilded brass tunic clasp, a barbed crossbow bolt, a slender brass point for a longbow arrow, and parts of two muleshoes; pieces of 16 large or small nails and chunks of iron slag, in six excavation units, indicate metallurgy on the site. Pine logs with diameters of 15 to 25cm were used as beams, and the many cork slabs suggest use between the roof beams and tiles, as was the custom in nineteenth century Ahín. This castle inventory provides a surrogate record of material culture shared by the twelfth and thirteenth century villagers of Ahín.

(g) The ruined castle was abandoned so long that a reddish weathering horizon developed. Then the keep was rebuilt, and the inner precinct subdivided into three animal pens. Minimal evidence for occupation includes diagnostic, mid-fifteenth century pottery. A Christian watchpost is suggested, contemporary with the adjacent settlement at Bcnialí. At a later point, the tower and inner wall were again partly demolished.

(h) Benialí was initially constructed on an unterraced virgin hillside, no earlier than the fourteenth century, judging by the absence of characteristic pottery types and styles recorded in the castle.

(i) A first settlement phase allows identification of several generations of houses, none of which preserve rich occupation residues.

(j) A long settlement break followed, during which thick soil wash accumulated, and the sierra woodland regenerated to some measure.

(k) A second occupation focused on the eastern half of the site, was laid out with no relation to the previous house foundations or walls, and expanded to a new area on the higher slope. Occupation was more intensive and continuous, and included more houses, as well as an elaborate slope irrigation network, with at least one large storage tank. Houses were small and consisted of a single room, with average interior dimensions of 11.2 m^2. Animals were sometimes stalled in separate structures, at other times probably kept directly inside the home. There is evidence of low rock-and-fill ramparts in front of some houses, or of higher retaining walls, serving as foundations; but there is no indication that the hillside was systematically terraced. Houses were built of mortared, trimmed local rock, the insides of which were often plastered; doors and windows consisted of wood, fastened to door-posts, or with iron hinges, to a wooden frame. Roofs were flat or tilted, constructed of primary and cross-beams, and mainly thatched. House floors were coated with mortar and kept clean during occupation; the garbage was thrown out next to the door.

(l) The settlement arrangement was loose and irregular (fig. 3), with houses placed roughly parallel to the contours, and often clustered in groups with attached walls but separate doors. This suggests autonomous households within extended families. Some 25 house sites can now be directly or indirectly verified, but at least 5 of these were exclusively used during the first occupation; some 15 to 20 houses were certainly in use during the second.

(m) Two coins and most of the 8600 potsherds from Benialí are associated with the second settlement, dating it to the fifteenth and early sixteenth centuries.

(n) Domestic kitchen, table, and storage pottery was obtained from proximal production centers such as Vall d'Uxó, possibly by direct market exchange. Luxury pottery made in distant ceramic centers such as Teruel, Paterna, and Manises implies sophistication and possibly a measure of wealth; these wares were probably obtained through middlemen, perhaps in the markets of Eslida and Segorbe. There is no evidence for a concentration of luxury wares, found in 14 of the 22 excavated structures, in any one house or group of houses (fig. 4).

(o) Both summer and winter crops were cultivated on irrigated and dry-

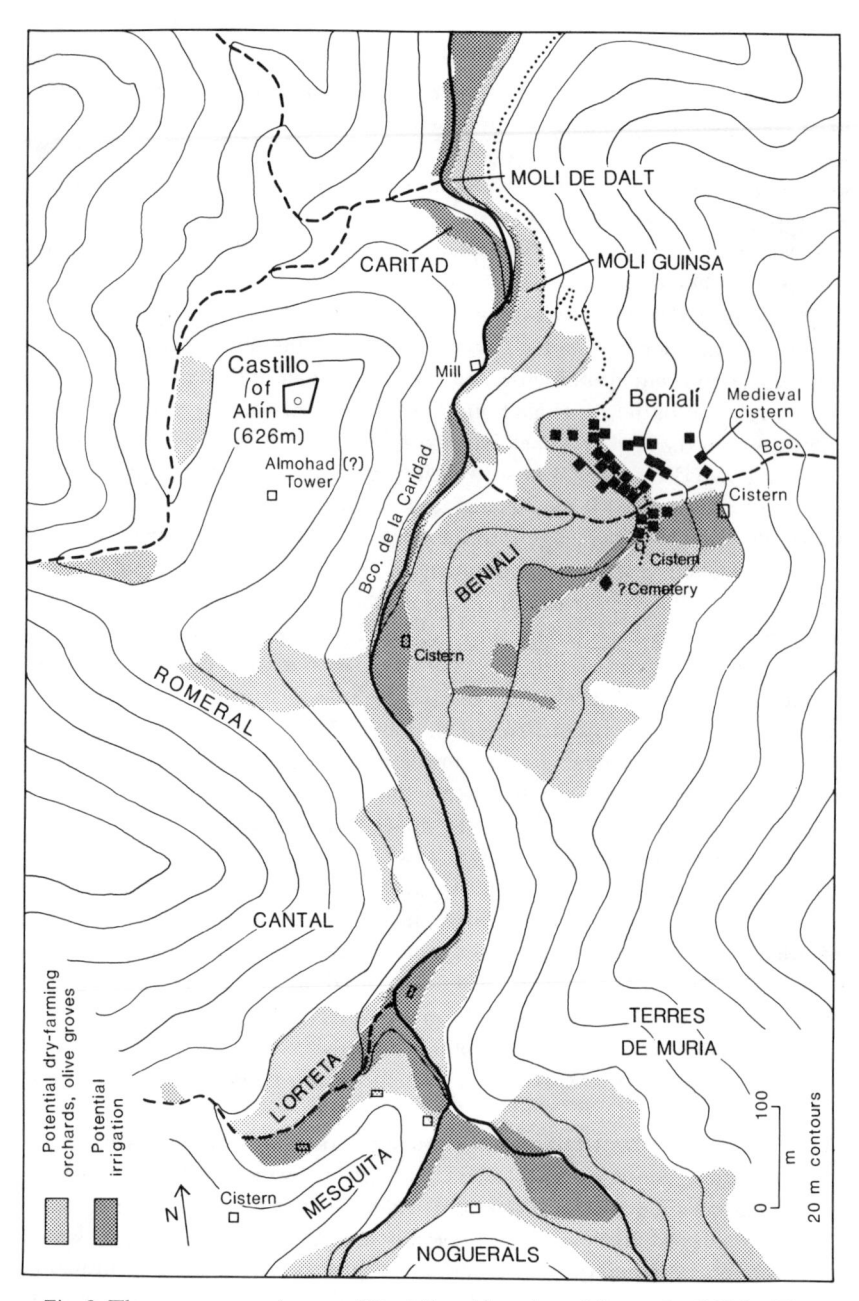

Fig. 3. The resource catchment of Bení alí and location of the castle of Ahín. The fourteenth- to early sixteenth-century houses are shown schematically. Base map by Pavel Kraus.

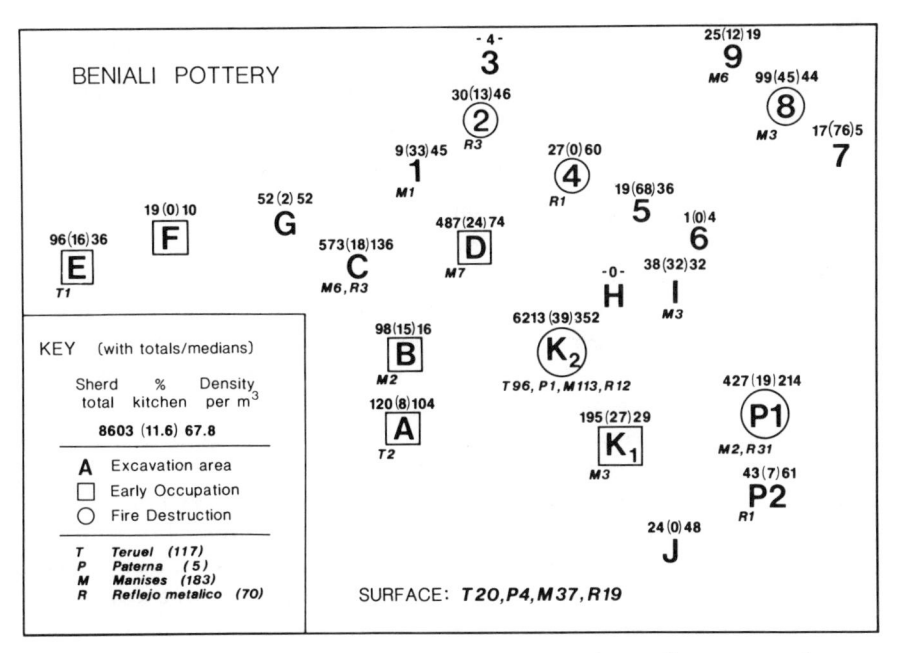

Fig. 4. Summary pottery inventory of Benialí, arranged according to excavation areas that approximate their spatial distribution. Teruel, Paterna, Manises and *reflejo metálico* (lusterware) represent luxury pottery.

farming plots. The major verified crops are hard wheat and breadwheat, sorghum, oil seeds, green beans, olives, almonds, and various orchard fruits. The principal source of meat was from goats herded on the higher slopes; they represent 95% of the 2250 identified pieces of animal bone. Some chickens and cows were also kept; both horses and mules, verified by horseshoes and muleshoes, were used as work animals. Pine wood and cork oak were exploited, although the sierra was largely deforested during the second occupation phase, judging by the impoverishment of tree species in the charcoal record, and the use of dead olive branches or woody shrubs for fuel.

(p) Copper ornaments were worn, in part of fine quality, including a decorated and gilded tunic clasp. Belt buckles and a wide range of household goods were made of iron, smelted and forged on the spot. However, most of the copper items, as well as the delicate blown glass vessels, would have been obtained via local market centers from Valencia or more distant, Islamic manufacturing centers.

(q) The wide range of goods imported from beyond the confines of the sierra, the disposal of the entire flax crop (indicated by the exclusive presence of its symbiotic plant, *Camelina sativa*), and the presence of coins all indicate some degree of participation in a cash economy.

(r) Early in the sixteenth century, Bcnialí was abruptly destroyed by fire, and many walls collapsed or were overthrown. Completely abandoned, the ruins were filled with soil wash, and the slope was no longer cultivated.

(s) Many of the deteriorating walls of Benialí still stood during the early eighteenth century, when the Christian farmers of Ahín began to construct the elaborate terrace system still in evidence. During the course of grading and wall construction, the remaining ruins of Benialí were leveled and their foundations covered with soil.

Compared with the tiled roofs of the Islamic era, the thatched roofs of fifteenth century Benialí suggest a poorer population. A living area of 11 m^2, barely larger than the houses of the castle garrison, is very small even for a nuclear family, and compares with 20 m^2 of living space in "basic," Christian houses of the seventeenth and eighteenth centuries. The Muslim hearth was on the floor, in the center of the room, and there was no chimney; early Christian houses we studied in the Espadán had a stone fireplace and chimney. Despite the limited nucleation of Benialí, many of the Muslim houses were attached in a row, and were never enlarged; Christian houses initially stood free, but were steadily expanded by the addition of rooms and, eventually, a second floor.

Different forms of social organization are implied: the Muslims appear to have built separate quarters for the younger generation of adults next to the existing house, whereas Christians expanded their houses to incorporate their sons' families under one roof. The investment in house construction also differed between Muslims and Christians: in addition to being poorer, the Muslims were apparently willing to accept much lower levels of comfort and possibly spent more of their time outdoors. Muslim houses show no differentiation of wealth, whereas the first houses built in Ahín after 1610 vary considerably in the elaboration of their facades. In combination with the lack of status differences in pottery finds, the Muslim villagers appear to have been more egalitarian. Finally, the quality of the pottery in Benialí suggests that fine wares were more highly prized than personal adornments.

One reason for the poverty of the Benialí inhabitants is the limited area of cultivable land within the valley catchment of the site: 24 ha, of which less than 10% was irrigable, for at least 20 families. By comparison, during the late nineteenth century, when population pressure forced demographic curtailment, the farmers of Ahín each cultivated an average of 2.4 ha, of which 5% were irrigated. Another difference is that the Christian farmers enhanced productivity and expanded agriculture by constructing terrace systems; the Muslim farmers did not and, in combination with uncontrolled goat grazing, their soils were rapidly degraded by erosion. Also, Christian farmers in Ahín traditionally kept pigs, that thrived on the acorns of the widespread cork oaks; their Muslim counterparts were interdicted from using pigs. The basic economy of both groups was a Mediterranean-style agriculture, with similar crops, but the Muslim variant was less progressive and inefficient by comparison.

Complementary Archival Data

Assembling the documentary evidence directly applicable to the castle of Ahín and Bienalí,[13] considerable information can be added to the archaeological framework already outlined above.

(a') The castle of Ahín is repeatedly mentioned between 1242 and 1272, but not thereafter. The second construction phase of the castle may have been triggered by the Aragónese cross-border campaigns that began in 1179, which would be consistent with other lines of evidence. Abandonment of the castle probably coincided with the capitulation of the Espadán in 1238. The Espadán Muslims revolted in 1276 and endured a long siege in Eslida, although the villagers of Ahín did not participate in that rebellion. The castle was probably destroyed at this time, although its defenders did not come from Ahín, as might have been expected.

(b') Bienalí was founded in 1342 as a satellite village of Ahín, but apparently with settlers from Eslida. Colonization was part of a royally sponsored expansion of settlement, and seven other new villages or hamlets were begun during the 1330s and 1340s.

(c') Benialí is not cited again until 1417, in a document that refers to privileges given to Benialí and another village by King Martin I (1396-1410). This seems to imply a second founding of the hamlet, which may have been abandoned as a result of the destructive war with Castile 1363-1365.

(d') Benialí is repeatedly mentioned in documents dating between 1418 and 1475 that deal with tax exemptions for commercial or craft activities; debts or unpaid inheritance taxes; property disputes adjacent to the mill below the site (with a citizen of Ahín); chickens in Benialí stolen by a man from Veo and on another occasion by two inhabitants of Benialí itself; and unfulfilled job obligations of a man from Benialí in Valencia. A total of 13 exemptions (*franquicias*) were granted over the years to six families probably engaged in some form of commerce, i.e. part-time merchants.[14]

(e') Some 19 citizens of Benialí are documented by name between 1418 and 1500. The largest families were the Khalils and Mansurs (6 individuals each), followed by the Masuds (3 individuals), the Quraysh and Salih (2 each). Seven of the eight recorded surnames were not found in Ahín, but are known from other neighboring villages; this suggests that the second group of colonists ca. 1400 was drawn from all over the sierra. The surnames used in Benialí and

Ahín remained discrete, indicating little or no intermarriage between the neighboring places, either because of older external roots or intercommunity rivalry. Four of the Beniali families—the Quraysh, Khalil, Mansur, and Riyal—suggest Arab lineages, and one documented individual, Jusuf Bar-robi, was a Jew, surprising in such a small settlement. New villages were frequently named after their founders, and the name Beniali (from *Banu Khalil,* judging by the fifteenth century orthography, Benihelil) suggests that the site was originally named after the Khalils. In Ahín, where the documentation of *nomina* is more extensive, the mayors (*alamís*) and village elders (*jurats*) can be identified from 1380 to 1563; significantly, these positions of authority were not inherited from father to son, were not monopolized by certain families, but were sometimes conferred on individuals resident in the community for as little as a single generation. This suggests that wealth and prestige were not synonymous and again argues for an egalitarian society. In 1500, Beniali had a *jurat* but no *alamí*.

(f') The population of Beniali consisted of 23 families in 1415, 20 in 1427, and 27 in 1451. Two or three of these families were at various times unable to pay the head tax, and presumably were indigent. Between 1451 and ca. 1524 the combined population of Ahín and Beniali declined from 71 to only 47 families. This was part of a general trend in the area, related to growing insecurity and increasing tax demands, with the result that economic productivity was reduced. Several sierra hamlets were abandoned at this time and Beniali probably declined as well.

(g') There are no direct records for Beniali in regard to crops or animals, but those of other Espadán villages are compatible with the archaeobotanical remains. Such records also indicate that villagers frequently purchased large quantities of grain (sorghum, barley, millet) on credit at the regional market in Onda, and sometimes even oil or beans. This startling fact indicates the sierra was not self-sufficient in staples, and allows the assumption that the almonds, olive oil, and flax of Beniali were traded for grain. Annual data for the income from the flour mills and the butchery in Eslida show that more animals were slaughtered in years when less grain was ground, implying that goats were primarily eaten during poor harvest years. The faunal data from Beniali elucidate this point: female goats were slaughtered somewhat earlier than would be ideal for maximum herd reproduction, a trait symptomatic of people living near the hunger mark. This supports the other archaeological indicators for a community with marginal resource access.

(h') During the great Muslim revolt of 1526, the retreating sierra rebels fortified themselves in seven different positions around Beniali, where they were besieged and routed on July 26th. The hamlet was then sacked, the soldiers finding hoarded wheat and other foods, as well as a fortune in clothes that the Muslims had looted in Christian settlements earlier in the year. This is compatible with the archaeological evidence for destruction by fire, and probably also explains the further damage to the castle.

(i') Bénialí is not mentioned again and was evidently abandoned. However, in 1530 and 1563 the characteristic Beniali surnames Khalil, Mansur, and Masud reappear, in Ahín, indicating that five specific Beniali families had relocated to Ahín. None can be traced in other, surrounding settlements, implying that the Quraysh, the Salih, and at least two other extended families had perished in 1526.

These interdigitating archaeological and archival records for Beniali (and the castle of Ahín) provide a concrete example of the micro-level data generated in the Espadán Project. The two records are complementary and almost never overlapping, and the absence of one or the other would have severely limited our understanding of the whole. The archaeology illuminates the material culture, the way of life, the social structure, and the relative values placed on material goods. The archival documents inform us about the people as individuals, and about the dynamics of regional and local processes or events. The archival sources indicate *direct* contacts with the world outside of the sierra, a conclusion that could not be drawn from the archaeology alone. The excavations detail living arrangements and subsistence patterns only vaguely hinted at in the written documents.

The composite picture is one of an impoverished community, living in a seemingly inaccessible valley, yet participating actively in a market economy as well as in the broader cultural world of the substantial Muslim minority. Despite the commonality of their basic Mediterranean-style economy with that of the new Christian settlers after 1610, the inefficient land use, the settlement pattern, and the social organization of Beniali appear to have more in common with Berber communities in the northwestern Rif Mountains of Morocco.

General Discussion

The archival records, primarily in the form of missives, legal summonses, and individual or communal privileges and tax demands from the royal administration in Valencia, are complemented by long lists of signatures to deeds and by inventories of persons.[15] When these documents were studied it became apparent that the social dynamics of the sierra communities could be elucidated to some degree. Many hundreds of individuals were identified in the 14 villages between 1380 and 1563, names that proved to be patronymic and that allowed the tracing of family lines in both Beniali and Ahín. Of the 142 individuals identified over this 183 year period in Ahín,[16] 105 belong to 23 families present in that village before 1500 and verified at least twice. Similar lists compiled for the other Espadán communities showed that surnames were clustered in one or two places, suggesting that such names provided a powerful tool to establish intermarriage spheres between villages.

An important inference that emerged was a considerable movement of families between certain communities, or exogamy, or both. Of the seven oldest and largest families of Ahín, all shared surnames with families in Eslida and with at least one other, neighboring village. Of the remaining 16 names, only three were unique to Ahín and two of these were toponymic, suggesting immigration from villages located elsewhere in Valencia. The most common affinities of Ahín surnames were with 5 communities located an average of 8.9 km away, most probably representing the mean marriage radius. However, the local parish registers after 1624 show that the Christian inhabitants of Ahín regularly intermarried into only two other villages, with a marriage radius of just 2.7 km. This implies that Muslim family networks were much larger, encompassing more villages and significantly greater distances. The Muslim sierra was a far more tightly knit community than its later Christian counterparts, and traditional Muslim blood relationships appear to have provided strong integrative forces that facilitated family relocation and intercommunity cooperation.

These ties probably played a fundamental role in the changing interrelationships between the Muslim minority in the Espadán and the dominant Christian society within which it was embedded.[16] From the first military contacts of 1237 to the suppression of the 1276 revolt, the sierra was repeatedly in turmoil, as the Muslims sought vainly to shake off foreign control at a high cost in lives and property destruction. But in 1277 their leaders evidently saw fit to accept the renewed offer of a concordat, first signed in 1242, that granted them full cultural autonomy. Peaceful participation within the larger framework of Valencian society was temporarily interrupted in 1363, when a Castilian army invaded the sierra, apparently finding local support; in 1365 the king of Aragón preceded his successful counteroffensive by renewing the concordat, on condition that the Muslims provide troops to assist his forces. In 1429–1430 the threat of another war with Castile saw a new demand for Muslim conscripts, but the sierra communities only complied reluctantly, after dire threats from the authorities in Valencia. In 1455 when word of the Christian pogrom against the Muslims of Valencia reached the Espadán, orders to repair the local castles were met by passive resistance. But in 1525 the Hapsburg monarch of Spain signed the edict for forcible conversion; the mosques were closed and arrogant preachers, ignorant of Arabic, entered the villages. It was the king who had broken his own concordat, and in 1526 the Espadán erupted in a popular revolt that stunned Spain with its ferocity.

Socioeconomic trends oscillated between 1277 and 1526. Until the Black Death (1348) and the war with Castile (1363–1365), population increased steadily, with the result that new floodplain tracts were brought into irrigation and new villages founded. After 1365 there was rapid demographic recovery, and the population level reached in 1418 was the highest until the late eighteenth century. Many new satellite villages appeared for the first time, and Bonialí was rebuilt. Eslida was a thriving market center, with a koranic school. The rich legal documentation of the early fifteenth century includes a wide range of court cases that illuminate Muslim society in the sierra: the usual range of offenses such as unpaid debts, petty thievery, robbery and murder. But there also are more informative transgressions such as adultery, unlicensed prostitution, the rape of a Christian woman, the killing of a sister as a matter of family honor, the brutal slaying of a wife's lover, justifiable blood revenge, and an attempt to knife a castle commander.

Extraordinary fiscal demands on the sierra communities after 1400 gradually crippled them economically, and a steady population decline began with the plague of 1427. By the 1450s highway robbery and other crimes took on a more ominous note, and smaller villages began to be deserted. Indebted families abandoned their land. Eslida lost its mercantile functions and was reduced to an unimportant village. Productivity in the sierra had shifted to a lower equilibrium level.

The revolt of 1526 required 7000 soldiers to suppress, although the Espadán Muslim population totaled only 7500. Forced to live off the land, the Christian forces that besieged some 4000 Muslims holed up in the mountains for two months were also starving. As many as half of the rebels were killed after the final assault, including women who had joined their men. Eight further villages were deserted in the aftermath and the composition of families in the remaining communities changed sharply: 39% of the population of Ahín in 1563 were new residents, many of them probably refugees from destroyed Muslim quarters in the coastal cities. The centuries-old social fabric of the sierra appears to have been shattered, and the once cosmopolitan villages were reduced to a rural proletariat. The last decades of the Espadán minority were years of humiliating forced conversion, ecclesiastical oppression, and regimentation. Finally, in 1609, the brutally efficient expulsion removed whole communities and scattered families up and down the North African coast, to face a dubious welcome.

The Espadán Project represents a historical case study in interethnic relations, elucidating the interplay of culture-ecological variables in the social maintenance of these resilient communities. The divergences in lifeways and lifestyles evident between Muslims and Christians in the sixteenth century were probably much greater than they had been in 1238. Minority groups frequently remain resistant to change, and the sociocultural and economic distance between Christian Spain and Islamic North Africa has steadily increased since the twelfth century. Consequently to measure that initial distance would require comparative study of a rural social unit in Medieval Christian Aragón. Yet the changing tastes in pottery suggest that the Espadán Muslims were not as conservative as their tenacious adherence to Islam might imply. And their effective compromises with the instruments, demands, and restrictions of Aragónese government demonstrate a measure of acculturation to the dominant society in which they were irremediably intermeshed.

Whatever its shortcomings, we feel that the Espadán Project demonstrates how a judicious interpretation of archaeological data can fill in the lacunae of archival documentation, and how the archaeological materials, in turn, can be used to formulate valid archaeological hypotheses and flesh out archaeological deductions. Historical archaeology can and should combine the archival and archaeological records, if it is to successfully identify social units and explain change.[17]

Notes

1. Lapeyre, H., *Géographie de l'Espagne morisque* (Paris: Sevpen, 1959).
2. Ladero Quesada, M.A., "Los Mudejares de Castilla en la baja Edad Media" in *Actas del 1. Simposio Internacional de Mudejarismo* (Madrid: Consejo Superior de Investigaciones Cientificas, 1981), 349-90.
3. García Gómez, E., "Una extraordinaria página de Tifasi y una hipótesis sobre el inventor del zéjel," in *Etudes d'Orientalisme dediées a la mémoire de Lévi-Procençal* (Paris: Maisonneuve, 1962), vol. 2, 517-23; Lévi-Provençal, E., *Histoire de l'Espagne musulmane* (Paris: Maisonneuve, 1950), vol. 1, 76 f.
4. Guichard, P., *Structures sociales "orientales" et "occidentales" dans l'Espagne musulmane* (Paris: CNRS, 1977).
5. Butzer, K. W., Mateu, J. F., Butzer, E. K., and Kraus, P., "Irrigation agrosystems in eastern Spain: Roman or Islamic origins?" *Annals, Association of American Geographers* 75 (1985): 479-509.
6. Pastor de Togneri, R., "Problèmes d'assimilation d'une minorité: les mozarabes de Tolède (de 1085 à la fin du XIIIe siècle)," *Annales des Economies, Sociétés, Civilisations* 25 (1970): 351-90.
7. Chejne, A. G., *Islam and the West: the Moriscos* (Albany: State University of New York Press, 1983); Hoehnerbach, W., *Spanish-islamische Urkunden aus der Zeit der Nasriden und Moriscos* (Berkeley: University of California Press, 1965).
8. Granja, F. de la, "La Marca Superior en la obra de al-Udri," *Estudios de Edad Media de la Corona de Aragón* 8 (1967): 447-545.
9. Barceló Torres, M.C., *Minorías islámicas en el país valenciano: Historia y dialectos* (Valencia: Instituto Hispano-Arabe de Cultura, Universidad de Valencia, 1984) 143 ff.
10. Burns, R. I., *Muslims, Christians and Jews in the Crusader Kingdom of Valencia* (New York: Cambridge University Press, 1984).
11. Peñarroja Torrejon, L., *Moriscos y repobladores en el Reino de Valencia: La Vall d'Uxó (1525-1625)* (Valencia: Del Cenia al Segura, 1984) vol. 1, 207 ff.

12. Butzer, K. W., Butzer, E. K., Miralles, I., and Mateu, J. F., "Una alquería islámica medieval de la sierra de Espadán," *Boletín, Sociedad Castellonense de Cultura* 61 (1985): 306-65; Butzer, K. W., Butzer, E. K., and Mateu, J. F., "Medieval Muslim Communities of the Sierra de Espadán," *Viator: Medieval and Renaissance Studies* 17 (1986): 339-413.

13. See Butzer et al. (1986), note 12.

14. In 1451 a Muslim of Ahín, who held a *franquicia*, posted bail for another Muslim of the pottery center Paterna, through the intermediary of a Christian merchant.

15. See Butzer et al. (1986), note 12.

16. Eight romanized names in 1563 could not be linked to traditional Arabic family names and have been excluded.

17. This study would not have been possible without the active collaboration of Juan F. Mateu, V.M. Rosselló Verger and Carmen Barceló Torres (Valencia), Ismael Miralles (Vilareal), Agustín Ferrer and Lola Llavador (Alcira), Pavel Kraus (Zürich), Richard G. Klein (Chicago), Jack R. Harlan and Dorothea Bedigian (Urbana), Robert Stuckenrath (Washington, D.C.), Robert H. Brill (Corning, N.Y.), and Pedro Saborít Badenes (Castellon), who freely gave of their time and expertise. The staff and director of the Archivo del Reino (Valencia) were consistently helpful in many essential ways. Modest but adequate financial support was provided by the Dickson Professorship and the University Research Institite of the University of Texas, the University of Chicago, the Swiss Federal Institute of Technology (Zürich), the National Science Foundation, and the Diputación Provincial de Castellón.

SECTION IV
URBAN COMMUNITY STUDIES

Urban Archaeology in Douai (Nord, France)

PIERRE DEMOLON

In 1980 a conference about urban archaeology was held in Tours, sponsored by the National Excavation Service (*Service National des Fouilles*). It provided a good opportunity to analyze the progress of archeological research in French towns. The results have been published and are significant because of their heterogeneous content. Such an analysis is useful, even necessary; it reveals not only that many new research trends have been considered and developed at the same time, but above all how much our documentation is inadequate, scattered, and hard to use. It also shows how each town is a particular case: some started as Gallo-Roman towns succeeding tribal capitals of the *La Tene* period, others developed from mere villages of the Merovingien period.

Collecting scattered documents of a miscellaneous nature cannot provide a reliable archaeological basis for a general survey. That is why even the most notable publication (like the series called *Histoire de la France Urbaine* edited by Georges Duby which tried to assess the situation and the collected papers from the conference at Tours) are compelled to limit their synthetic interpretations to particular aspects of their problems.

The only remedy is to undertake a series of precise studies and analyses of carefully chosen towns which would, if possible, be representative of the region. In this article one of these examples is developed.

Setting Up an Archaeological Service

An archaeological service can be taken as an important example in the evolution of a town's cultural awareness. The town of Douai, 30 km south of

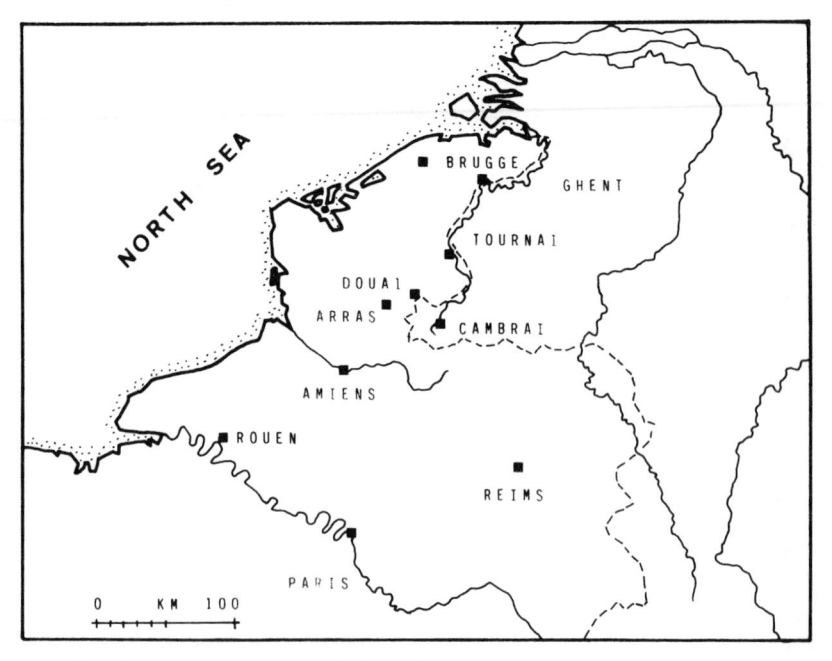

Fig. 1. Douai, a town in the French part of Flanders (Dept. Nord).

Lille, is today a small *sous-prefecture* of 45,000 inhabitants and for a long time its citizens have been interested in the story of its past (fig. 1). During the nineteenth century the municipal archives were organized with appropriate funding.

In 1800, a museum was founded. But not until 1970 and the beginning of urban archaeological research in France did public awareness result in the creation of a municipal archaeological bureau. Two full-time and three temporary employees make up the service. This is still small, but is deserves notice because it is the first such service to have been created in the Nord of France, north of Paris. Today it remains the best equipped service in personnel, surpassing bigger, neighboring cities like Amiens and Lille.

Archaeological research in Douai began with the exploration of a zone in the town's historical center at the site of the old cannon foundry which was scheduled to be torn down to make way for an underground parking lot. This research focused the interest of the towns people and their elected officials, and provided the needed awareness.

But a dig, however important, is of course only one aspect of a town whose sequence is eminently complex. In order to understand it and to integrate the archaeological notion in the town, the investigation must be globalized; in particular, inventory must be taken of all factors allowing evaluation of the potential and the quality of the available historical and archaeological heritage.

With Douai as an example, some possible methods and results of this evaluation will be shown.

Historiography

Among the elements used in the history there are, of course, written documents. Numerous historians before us have used them. They give a good idea of the evolution of the town.

Felix Brassard in an important book, *Histoire du Château et de la châtellenie de Douai*, which discusses fiefs and nobles under the town sovereign from the tenth century to 1789 offers us a scholarly analysis of the origin of the different powers established in Douai: lords, counts, provosts, and provides a volume of edited texts to support his thesis.

Jules Lepreux established and published an analytical inventory of Douai's archives and from his notes put together a precious collection entitled "Les Rues de Douai d'apres les titres de cette ville." In the text, he indicates for each street the old names designated and the date these names appeared.

In the beginning of the twentieth century, Georges Espinas in *La Vie Urbaine à Douai au Moyen-Age* gave this town an historical framework which is still used today. Although topography was not his principal interest, he had some intuitions in this regard that now seem well-founded concerning the location of the *castrum*, the bourgeois districts, and successive city walls as well as the digging of a channel to control the Scarpe River.

Since then, topographical research has been the principal objective of a series of articles which appeared in the *Amis of Douai* under the title "En flânant dans les rues de Douai" and written by Monique Mestayer.

The Archives

For the whole thirteenth century the municipal sources are very rich. Among the recorded entries in registers magistrates' proclamations (Bans echevinaux), those concerning the markets, the merchant's streets and the town's gates can be considered as topographical data.

We must emphasize the accounts which are kept for the end of the thirteenth century and for the fourteenth century. During this period some sealed acts concern the purchase or transfer of property. They contain a lot of various and often complementary topographical information.

As the world of public business grew in Douai, so did the world of private business. Thousands of acts in the form of unsealed chirographs are the written expression of business transactions by the inhabitants of Douai. The content of these documents is varied, but purchases and transfers of developed or undeveloped properties prevail over the other kinds of acts. During the fourteenth century 30% to 40% of these acts are the sale of lots, houses, gardens or land rentals, sales or transfers of life or perpetual annuities . . . and the list is not exhaustive. These acts hold information on property up to a certain degree.

Wills and marriage contracts also provide other indications even though the information is less complete.

Last, we must take into account the archives of ecclesiastic origin. They are important for the knowledge of the town because numerous buildings, and perpetual annuities based on them, were the property of religious establishments.

Use of these particular archives yields numerous topographical indications of generally precise nature. Most often texts can give a house's location or the address of an inhabitant. Then it is necessary to regroup them street by street in order to reconstruct the neighborhoods. In order to arrive at such a regrouping, it is useful to classify the data in a topographic index by street name. This index obviously gives an overall idea of each street in different periods. However, many texts cannot be integrated into it because the comments are incomplete. In effect, in the Middle Ages when houses were not numbered, an individual's address was given in three parts: his name, those of his neighbors and the name of the street. One of these indications is frequently omitted. To solve this problem, an index by inhabitant's name must be compiled to complete the topographic file of street names.

The next problem is to situate the property on the street and to relate the group of three houses—the one sold and its tenant houses—to the other properties on the street. Without detailing all the technical questions posed by the preparation of a schematic street map, two essential methodological points must be considered.

First of all, one must locate each corner house (*le Touquet*) in regard both to the street on which it is listed, and to the adjacent street at the corner of which it lies. This provides the surest reference point to use in identifying other tenants and property-holders of different houses in the quarter.

Next, and this point is also fundamental, the names of the owners involve numerous questions: Have the patronymics varied? Are there mistakes in transcription or arbitrary simplifications? Furthermore, as the reconstruction of a street is a logical juxtaposition of people, a key role is played by chronological continuity. If a transfer deed has been lost, doubt arises about the adjacent houses, especially if their owners have changed without keeping the deeds. If too many documents have disappeared, uncertainty quickly becomes total and we come to the point where the houses "accumulate" without our being able to situate them. Moreover a name change of owners is not always the result of a sale or of some kind of transfer deed but can also be due to a bequest, a legacy or a dowry.

Thus, the attempt to reconstruct a street map leads one to draw up, as best one can, the chart of inter-et-intra-familial ties. The setting up of an onomastic index and of genealogies can be, paradoxically, an effective way to reconstruct a street. Such an index is being prepared.

Historical Topography

The quantities of documents kept in the archives can be used in a great number of ways. One can, for example, use them individually in order to extract one simple fact: for example, the date of the first mention of the name of a street. From this information one can build up a picture of the town's growth that differs somewhat from the one suggested by the notices which relate to the ramparts and the town gates. The established maps are, of course, only a reflection of the current state of research.

It must first be pointed out that the earliest mention of a street does not necessarily correspond with the date of its creation, since there are often gaps between the two. Taking these reservations into account, we have constructed an hypothetical model for the urban development of Douai between the twelfth and the fifteenth centuries (figs. 2-5).

Archives and Archaeological Excavations

The interpretation of written documents, archival or otherwise, requires, above all else, critical method and strict controls. The dig of "Rue des Malvaux" is a good example of this work. Several buildings on this street were destroyed in 1982 to make room for new construction. The door lintels of the destroyed houses date to 1740 and lead one logically to think that these dwellings date to the middle of the eighteenth century. The municipal archives offer other precious information about the beginning of urbanization in these neighborhoods.

The streets which define the block under consideration are all attested since the thirteenth century:

rue des Ecoles:	rue des Bouilloires (jeux de boules) thirteenth century
	rue des Ecoles seventeenth century
rue Fortier:	rue de Corbie fifteenth century
	rue des Conins (lapins) sixteenth century

The "rue Fortier" is in fact the extremity of the "rue des Malvaux" attested under this name since the thirteenth century and linking the latter with Saint Jacques Chapel (place Carnot), a parish church since 1225.

242 / PIERRE DEMOLON

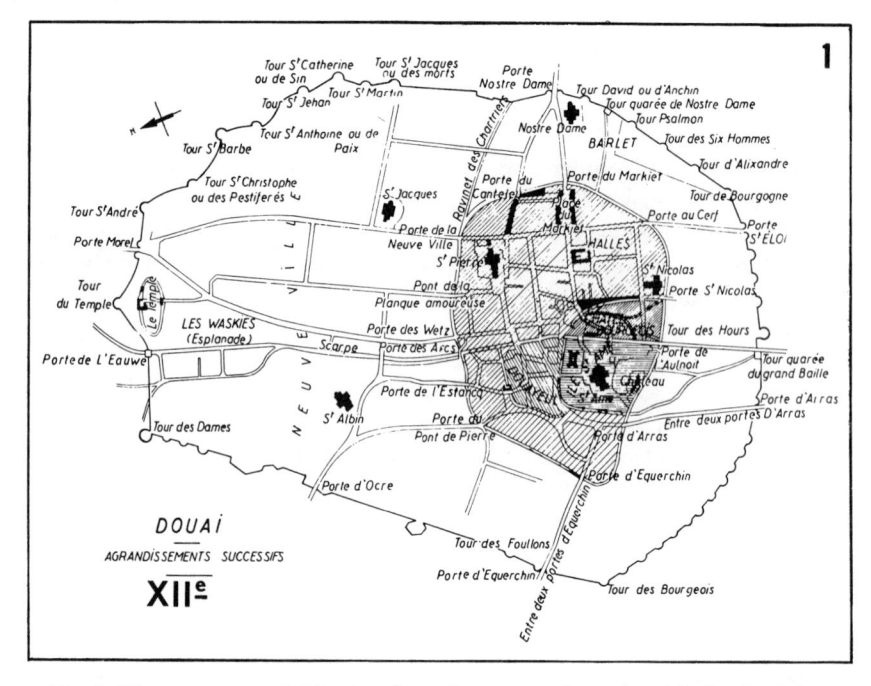

[map of Douai showing successive enlargements in the 12th century, with labeled towers, gates, and features including Tour S'Catherine ou de Sin, Tour S'Jacques ou des morts, Porte Nostre Dame, Tour David ou d'Anchin, Tour S' Martin, Tour quarée de Nostre Dame, Tour S' Jehan, Tour Psalmon, Tour S' Anthoine ou de Paix, Nostre Dame, BARLET, Tour des Six Hommes, Tour S' Barbe, Porte du Canteleu, Porte du Markiet, Tour d'Alixandre, Tour S' Christophe ou des Pestiférés, S' Jacques, Place, Tour de Bourgogne, Tour S'André, Porte de la Neuve Ville, HALLES, Porte au Cerf, Porte S' ELOI, Porte Morel, S' Pierre, S' Nicolas, Tour, Pont de la Planque amoureuse, Porte S' Nicolas, Tour du Temple, LES WASKIES (Esplanade), Porte des Wetz, Porte des Arcs, Tour des Hours, Porte de L'Eauwe, Porte de l'Aulnoit, Tour quarée du grand Baille, Porte de l'Estanca, Château, Porte d'Arras, Tour des Dames, S' Albin, Porte du Pont de Pierre, Porte d'Arras, Entre deux portes D'Arras, Porte d'Ocre, Porte d'Equerchin, Tour des Foullons, Porte d'Equerchin, Tour des Bourgeois, Scarpe, Le Temple, DOUAI AGRANDISSEMENTS SUCCESSIFS XIIe]

Fig. 2. The town extended in the eleventh century along the right bank of the Scarpe River toward an important crossroad: that of the roads of Cambrai-Lille and Valenciennes-Lens. This crossing created a new center of mercantile activity with the establishment of a great wheat market on the "Place d'Armes" (downtown square) and of a merchant's hall not far from there. For this period, documentary sources provide only two street names: "Foulons Street" (1198) and a part of "Canteleu Street." At the same time we know the limits of the town and the urban enclosure at the end of the eleventh century. This enclosure brought together two parishes "Saint-Pierre" on the right bank. Outside of the enclosure, the "Saint-Albin" parish possessed a certain independence. On the right bank, on the other hand, the chapels already on the periphery of the town still depended on the "Saint-Pierre" parish. These include "Saint-Nicolas" to the south, "Notre-Dame" on the road to Valenciennes to the west and "Saint-Jacques" to the north.

rue Berthoud: rue Fait-en-paille ou Paillery thirteenth century
                rue des Vitelots eighteenth century

The neighborhood seems to have been established in the thirteenth century.

The dig which preceded the reconstruction revealed a much different situation. Its conclusions follow:

"La Neuville" the roads of which were created in the second half of the thirteenth century was only really occupied at the end of the fourteenth century. At that period its structure resembled that of a veritable estate. In the beginning of the seventeenth century under the impulse of a certain economic comeback, Malvaux Street was once again divided up as an estate. It appears thus on a map of 1709.

The dig reveals that in the middle of the eighteenth century, a number of modifications occurred and a new building was erected in the back of the garden.

The facades on street were also modified which explains why the door lintels were engraved with the date 1740. During the excavations, we compared our discoveries with an identical neighboring house, still standing. An attentive examination of the cellar shows objects (pottery, money) sealed in the mortar dating to 1610-1620. In that condition, we can confirm that urban buildings in Douai attributed to the eighteenth century because of dates on the doors are in reality foundations from the seventeenth century, rebuilt in the mid-eighteenth century, in conformity with the "urban codes" imposed by the Flanders parliament which met in Douai (fig. 6).

It is clear from this example that, if it is easy to show how written documents are sources of historical knowledge, archaeology brings invaluable new resources to the assessment of historical materials. Today, it is more and more accepted that our buried heritage is as indispensable to history as the written documents themselves. Let us examine more closely what archaeology can offer. But, first, let us attempt to evaluate the potential value of the materials.

The Overall Archaeological Stratum

When construction is planned, the nature of the geological subsoil must be taken into consideration in order to found the buildings. The reports of these probes by different companies (Meurise, Sale, Intrafor) are filed with the Office of Geological and Mining Research in Lezennes or with the inspection of Underground Quarries in Douai.

Analysis of the upper part of these core samples allows the evaluation of thickness of the archaeological levels encountered and planning of curves of equal thickness or "isopacks." Thus an overall map of the thickness of these levels is built. This map gives a good idea of the natural site, before human settlement. It shows the lower parts of the town, where the ancient river was, hand made canals and marshes. It is a guide to evaluate quickly the historical potential of a site, and the time of rescue excavations according to the depth of the layers (fig. 7).

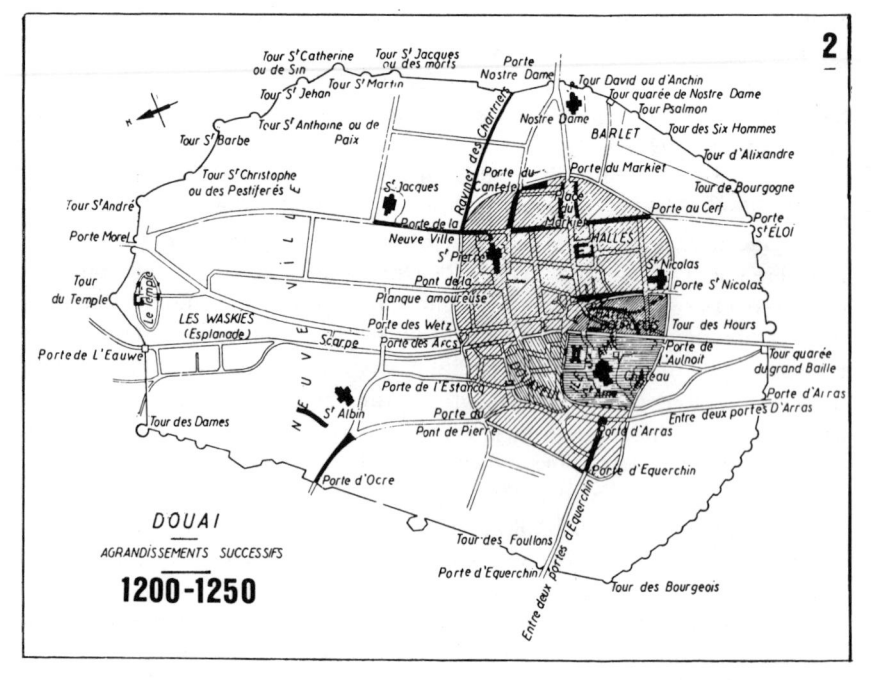

Figs. 3 and 4. "La Neuville." In the twelfth century, the town extended beyond its walls with a rapid expansion. In effect, in 1225–1228–1257, the three chapels depending on "St. Pierre" were set up as parishes, a sure sign of growth which had absorbed the small villages situated near the ramparts.

It also included "St. Alban's Church" on the left bank. In "La Neuville," on what is now "Place Carnot," "St. Jacques Church" was built. Toward the esplanade, "La Place des Moies" served as a market and a woodport, thus pushing the unloading wharves down river as far as the "Douai Marshes" which still limit the present city to the north. "Notre Dame" parish, outside the walls, was absorbed into the second enclosure, outside the "Market Gate." A reorganization

Previous Discoveries

There are also other ways of analyzing archaeological potential, notably the study of previous discoveries recorded in the town.

But Douai's medieval origins are themselves responsible for serious gaps in the record of historical discoveries which were noted in the past. In previous centuries people were interested chiefly in the remains of Roman antiquity: pieces of sculpture, imposing monuments, temples, mosaics from the forum and so forth.

No one notices the insignificant wooden vestiges, often rotting, which re-

Urban Archaeology in Douai / 245

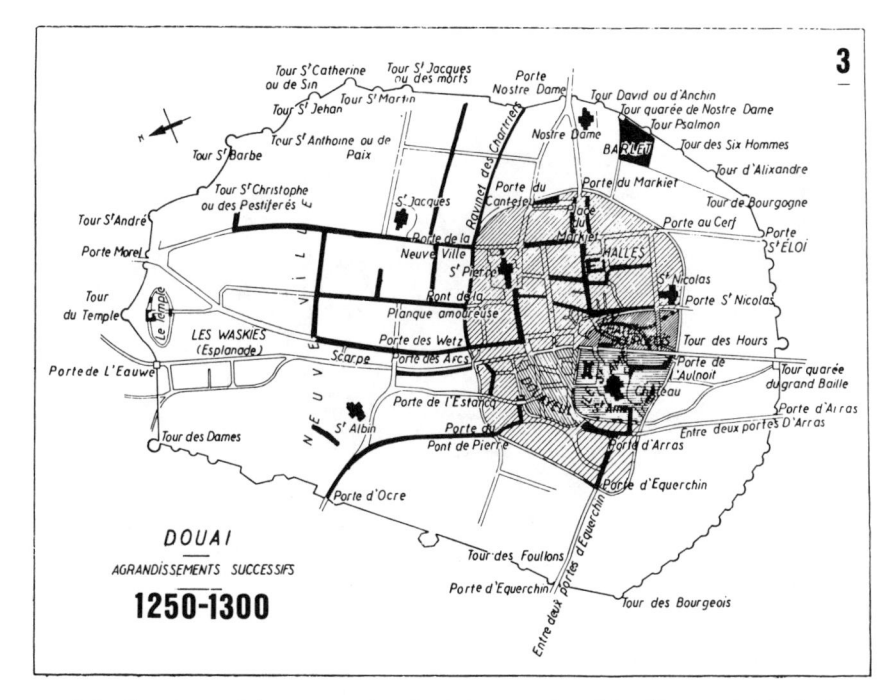

[Map: DOUAI — AGRANDISSEMENTS SUCCESSIFS 1250-1300]

of the functions of the squares involved the transfer of the "live-stock Market" to the "Place du barlet." The dominant commercial axis was then established along the Scarpe River and the road to Lille and Flanders. This axis determined the extension of the length of the town in the thirteenth century: "La Neuville." The town grew mostly along the right bank while the left bank remained agricultural. The streets were laid out straighter and more regularly than in the older "Douayeul" center. They determine regular blocks to allow a methodical siting of new residences.

lated to the origins and growth of the medieval town. The chief exceptions were stone funerary slabs from destroyed churches, and an occasional curious discovery like the following. It concerns the digging up in 1927 of a mummified body found in a lead sarcophagus where the old "Great English" college once stood. The cadaver was completely wrapped up in strips of thick cloth covered with wax, making it almost hermetically sealed. The body had been well preserved.

The top of the cranium was missing, the brain had been taken out and replaced by stuffing and the ears, severed, had disappeared. The head was sewn to the neck by a thread of flax. The spinal cord had been vertically slit. The hands, feet and genital organs had been severed and taken out. The skin was

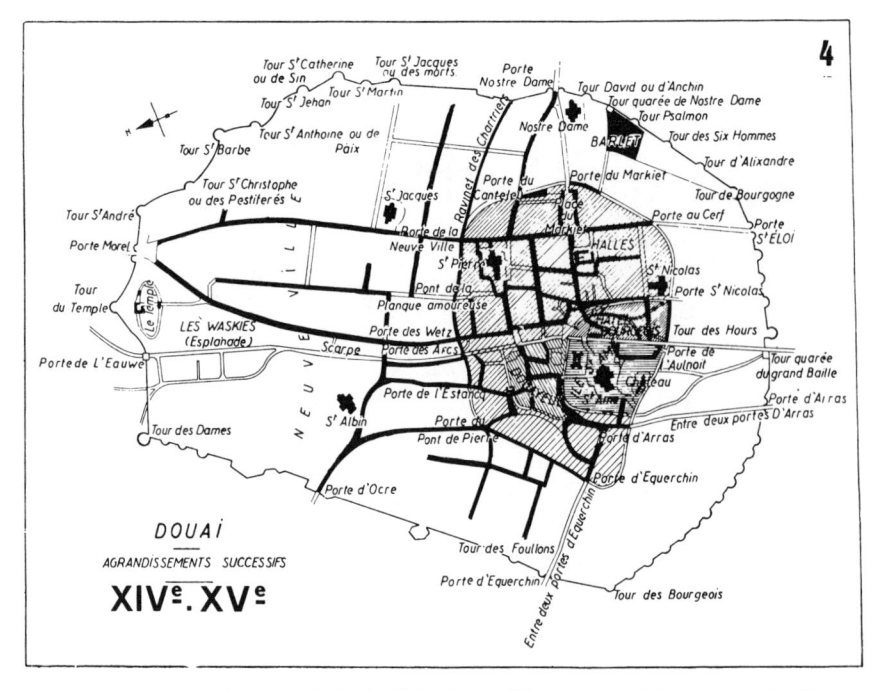

Fig. 5. Douai at the end of the Middle Ages. The names which appear in the fourteenth century show that few new streets were created on the right bank already fully developed in the thirteenth century. The left bank, however, experienced a housing densification which developed in the "Esquerchin neighborhood" around the Arras and Bethune roads and also in the direction of the rural parish of "St. Albin" which was then linked more closely to the town.

From the thirteenth century onwards, a second line of fortifications was begun in order to protect the new "neighborhoods of La Neuville." For nearly two centuries, two ramparts coexisted: the "Vies Murs" of the first enclosure and the "Darraines Fortereces" of new enclosure. We show them here as they looked at the end of this evolution, when the second enclosure surrounded the town. Built in the fourteenth century, the earlier walls were totally dismantled to make room for new paths, as the most recent mentions of streets seem to indicate.

then resewn to close the wounds. The pelvis had been sawed and the intestines replaced by aromatic substances. After an examination conducted by Medical-Legal Institute of Lille, it appeared that these substances and the treatment of the body corresponded to methods described in 1629 by Guybert. An historical inquiry then allowed surgeons, helped by Monsieur Leger, to conclude

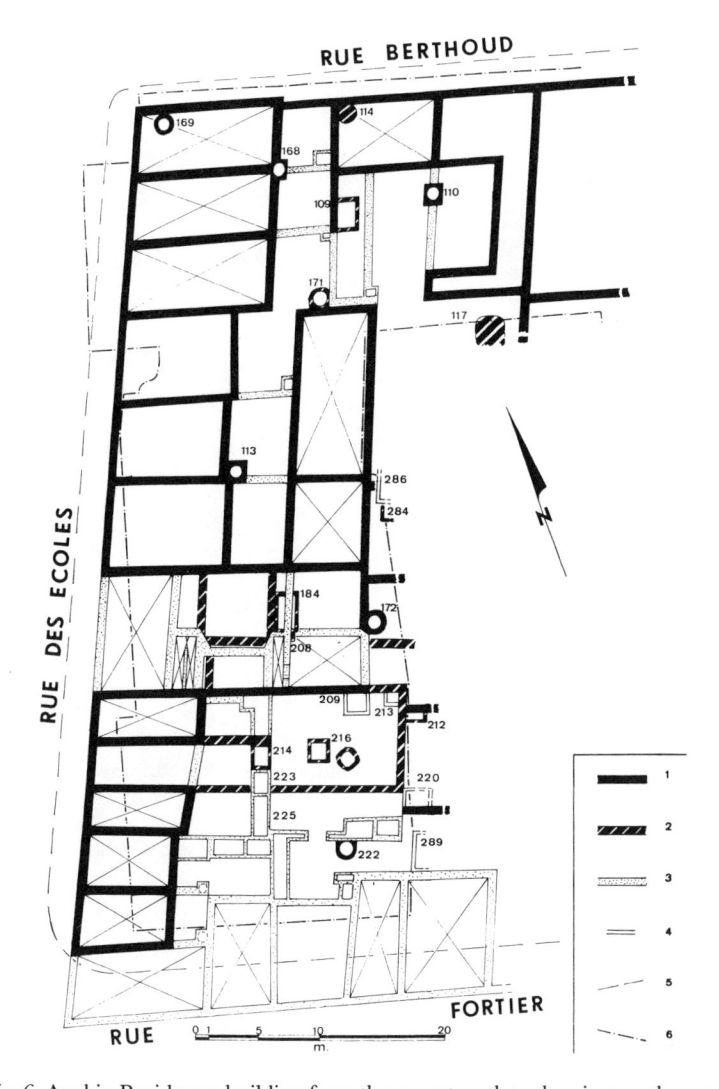

Fig. 6. Anchin Residence: building from the seventeenth to the nineteenth century.
  1. Walls of the mid-seventeenth century, still in use today
  2. Walls of the mid-seventeenth century, demolished in the eighteenth or nineteenth century
  3. Walls of the end of the eighteenth or beginning of the nineteenth century
  4. Walls after 1824
  5. Today's border of the road system
  6. Limits of the embankments

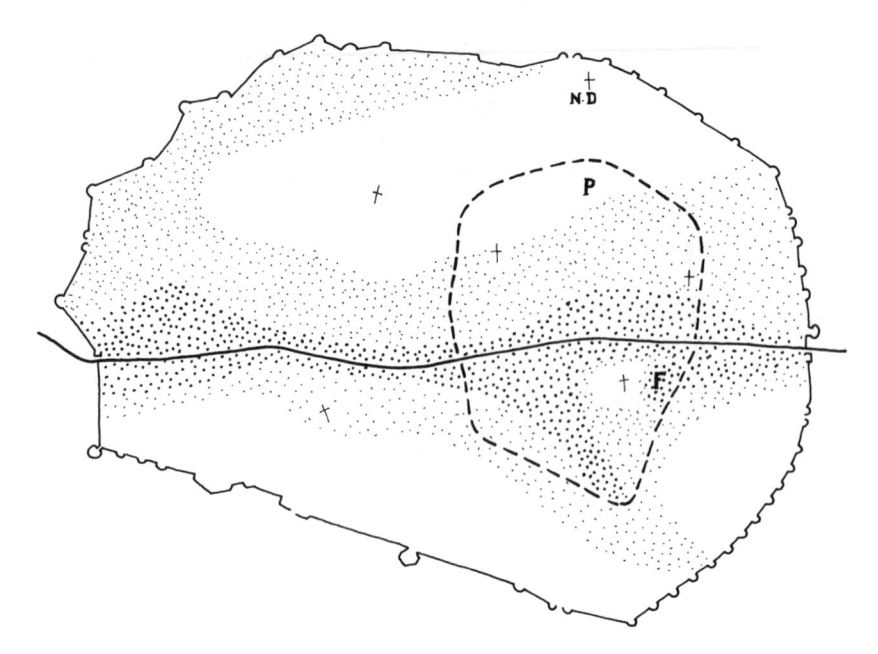

Fig. 7. Density of archaeological deposits in Douai:
   a) In white: the zones where the archaeological levels are less than 2 meters
   b) Plotted in small dots: levels at 2 to 4 meters
   c) Plotted in large dots: deeper than 4 meters
   Notice the "Foundry" zone with the staggerings of the mound and the deep marshy zones along the Scarpe River which indicate some modifications in the layout of the river and confirm the dominance of the river axis. Notice particularly that the Eastern parts of the town ("Grande-Place," "Notre-Dame" neighborhood), even though they have been there since the twelfth century, do not have an especially thick archaeological cover.

that the subject was a priest or a Catholic friar of the English Pontifical College of Douai. The College, founded in 1558, stayed open until 1792 in spite of the persecutions of Queen Elizabeth of England. Many of the religious men of this college were martyred while missionaries in England. Having been condemned to death, hung, then mutilated; head and hands were cut off to expose them to the public; the heart and entrails were taken out and burned; finally the cadaver was cut up in quarters and dispersed.

Sometimes friends reassembled the pieces and restored the body by sewing it together. Many of the bodies were brought back to Douai in the eighteenth century to be buried in their college of origin. The 1927 discovery serves as dramatic proof of this.

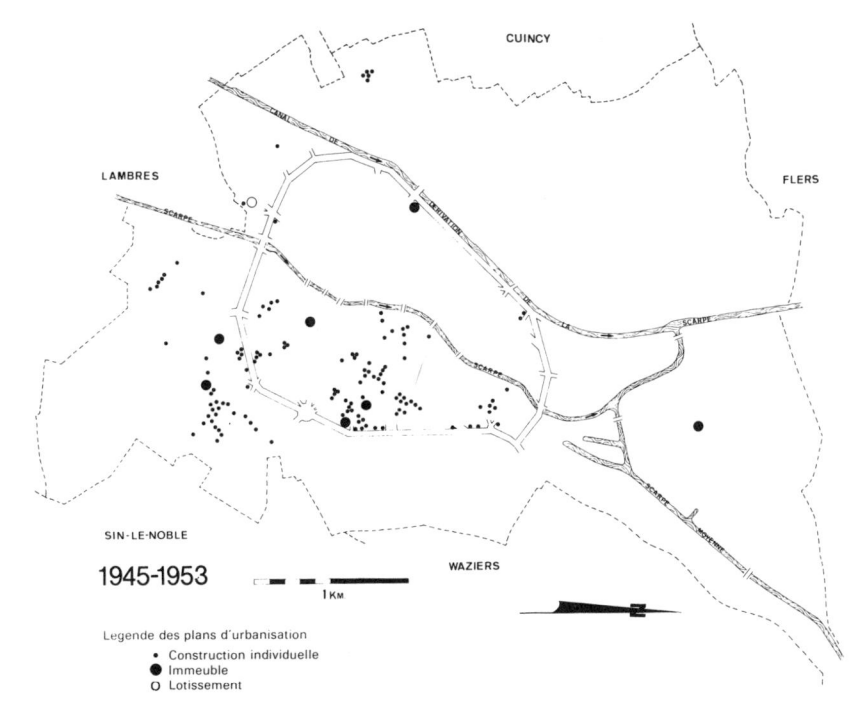

Fig. 8. Postwar Construction. Essential activity during this period is the reconstruction of war damages. The areas hardest hit were: the downtown section, the railway station and the "Place du Barlet." There are few changes in the urban patterns inherited from the past. On the other hand, on the southern border and north and northwest of the town, some new neighborhoods appear, new streets are created — these are only private constructions.

Urbanism Since 1945

After conducting an inventory of possible archaeological sources, one must try to evaluate what has been irrevocably lost, by analyzing known destructions. Consultation of building permits issued since World War II gives a precise idea of the damage: that is to say the buildings whose cellars and foundations destroyed the archaeological layers. Maps which were drawn up on the basis of these studies show several district periods in the politics of town reconstruction and development. It is especially notable that urban growth in Douai, as everywhere in France, has declined since the 1975-1978 period. Today's trend to "tighten up" the town and densify the residential sections is a

250 / PIERRE DEMOLON

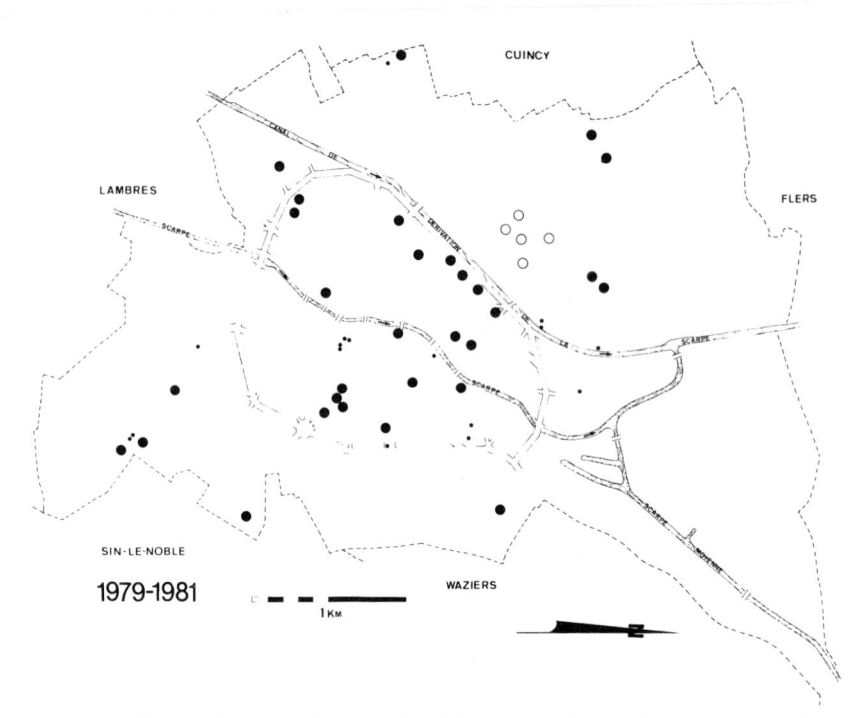

Fig. 9. Recent Construction. During this period, changes in the town's urban policies accentuate the role of "basement archaeology." In the downtown area new buildings of small or moderate dimensions, destined for collective occupancy, were built in established neighborhoods on a piece-meal basis, replacing older structures.

The result is the multiplications of deep excavations in the old town center, bringing to light various pits and pieces of the archaeological puzzle. The recent trend toward restoring the residential character of the town center must be accompanied by increased archaeological vigilance.

direct threat for the archaeological heritage which has so far been preserved there (figs. 8 and 9).

The Conservatory Excavation

The National Conservatory for the Region of Douai was built in 1856 on a foundation of several small sunken pilings which avoided disturbing the existing archaeological layers. A new project in 1980, was to build underground classrooms between the sunken pilings. This, therefore entailed the destruction of about 2.5 m of subsoil, down to below the cellar level. Archaeological excavations were carried out with the goal of examining the earth brought out by this project and making deep sounding in the earliest levels before the construction rendered all observations impossible.

The proximity of the river and of the Count's castle had a decisive influence on the occupation of the conservatory site. The land was used during the tenth or eleventh century, when the soil was dug to almost 1 m below the water level; the base of the excavation was levelled and regulated by a chalkbed in order to install large pools, fishponds or watercress beds. It is known, moreover, from more recent texts that the Count of Flanders maintained fisheries around his residence. Pontoons permitted access to the center of the pool. The land was abandoned in the twelfth century and transformed into wet meadows, proof of a regularly flowing creek.

During the sixteenth century, the demolition or transformation of buildings close by (perhaps the Bassecourt castle) brought up large quantities of bricks, mortar and tiles which add the level of about 1.5 m. In the same century, a King's college was built in the neighborhood. This college was transformed in the eighteenth century into an annex of the Royal Cannon Foundry which ceased activity only at the end of the nineteenth century.

This preventive excavation is the typical example of the possible relationship between property developers and archaeologists. With well-defined goals and time enough (before the beginning of the construction), the relationship becomes a give-and-take: the archaeologists require time to do their historical research and preserve the necessary town history materials and, in return, they provide information useful to the construction work. Here, the dig under the conservatory allowed us to specify the nature and the thickness of the different layers and to notice the presence of water. This information helped the builders to decide what machine tools were needed and to plan how the work should be carried out.

Observations Concerning the Medieval Fishmarket

Thanks to a government award intended to aid middle-sized towns, Douai redeveloped one part of the river bank. This project involved laying pipes in a trench extending from 80 cm below the street level to 220 cm. In July 1978, part of this trench on the Fishmarket Square and on the adjoining Dominican Street brought to light remarkably well preserved wooden vestiges dating to the tenth and eleventh centuries. At this point a rescue dig preceding the next phase of pipe laying on Dominican Street was considered. It would involve removing the first meter rapidly to permit detailed excavations and thus preventing traffic from passing in a busy street for three weeks. This rescue dig did not take place.

Archaeological observations were made by following the progress of the excavation cranes. Several wooden structures in an excellent state of preservation were uncovered and their interpretation allows us to reconstitute, to some extent, the history of the street. The square was built upon marshy soil thicker than 2.75 m. Successive refills have raised the ground surface steadily since the eleventh century. In the lateral passage ways, beds of wattle were laid directly on the ground. At one place, on the south side, six successive layers of wattle were found, piled one on top of another. Close to the center of the square, where the merchants set up their stalls, this system of wattle gridding was soon abandoned and replaced in the fifteenth century by a fill consisting of clay, chalk and bits of broken-up sandstone on the larger Wheatmarket Square.

In another sector, below the entrance to the square and the street which ends there, numerous wooden posts attest to the presence of tenth and eleventh century buildings. Their functions could not be ascertained.

A series of cellars, some 2 m deep, running along the axis of Dominican Street provides a link between this eleventh century street plan and the thirteenth century, when town records make reference to cellars there.

Later on, at the end of the thirteenth century, Dominican Street was rebuilt. A street surface was created by laying jointed planks upon logs cut longitudinally and covered by a thin bed of chalk. The present day street is 1 m higher.

This example demonstrates that precious information can be recovered even from a "rescue observation" of a trench. These observations of July 1978, taught us a sequential history of the fish market and the adjacent quarter (*Castel Bourgeois*) can be dated to the same period that the building of the Count of Flanders' Fortress, providing a considerable density of population for the eleventh century.

On another hand, this question raises other questions. The evaluation of archaeological potential has led to rescue work at the expense of a coordinated research program. Terms like "method," "research program," and "goal orientations" give the impression that archaeology is based on conscious choice. In fact, we must recognize that it is most often a matter of luck, a kind of game of chance in which the excavator's skill consists of making the most opportunistic situations and, after, integrating his discoveries in a large problematic system!

This system may give the reader a pessimistic idea of the archaeological evaluation of a town, but in fact, step by step, after several years' work it happens that "luck" has led us to intervene all over the town and to confront a wide variety of its historical problems.

The Foundry Excavations

There are also major excavations planned and carried out over a period of several years, yielding results of great interest.

Construction projects in the center of the original medieval *castrum* led in 1976 to four exploratory trial trenches which succeeded in locating the *donjon* of the Count of Flanders, the first city walls and the earlier merovingian occupation of the site. These promising results led to a full-scale excavation of some 1000 sq. m. The stratigraphic complexity of the site and the presence of many wooden structures necessitated a very long and painstaking dig. The work began in 1976 and was carried out with the help of many student volunteers during every school holiday (including every weekend) ending in 1981. No useful result could have been obtained by more limited digging.

The original trial trenching led us to adopt the Wheeler system of a grid composed on arbitrary 4 m squares separated by a baulk which preserved the stratigraphic record. Experience proved that this system was the best adapted to undertaking so complex a site. Each square was first excavated down to the natural soil, and interpretation kept pace with the digging. The interpretations included extrapolations defining the nature of the structure which ought to be left in the baulk. For the later stages, these were excavated, which allowed us to verify or correct the guesses we had made during the earliest phases of the dig. The inconveniences of this method is, of course, that it does not allow an overall vision of any one stratigraphic level, but it is the only method which allows us to call our original hypothesis into question and by verification obtain a higher degree of certitude.

Site history, Period I: sixth–seventh centuries

The oldest structures on the site were four sunken huts (Grubenhaus) with six posts, measuring 3.5 m long by 2 to 3 m wide. Made of wood and earth, these structures may not have had any one specific function: they could have served as granaries, barns workshops, or even, occasionally as dwellings. Other groups of multiple post-holes were also found, but in the current stage of research, no other structure can be reconstructed for this period. A silo-pit was probably used to store grains or roots.

In itself such a group of huts is not unknown in the region. Excavations at Brebieres and at Proville have uncovered more complete settlements, but this is the first time they have been shown to be the ancestors of a medieval town. The pottery proves that the village was settled by the end of the sixth century, whereas the oldest written sources which mention Douai are tenth century.

Period II: eighth century

Immediately above the merovingian structures a very densely packed level of stones defines an occupation area where it was possible to recognize a larger type of sunken-hut with 6 posts: 6 m long by 4 to 5 m wide. Three clusters of post-holes surrounding it have been identified as belonging to three other buildings, through disturbance caused by later embarkments makes it hard to be sure. A ditch and several grain storage pits complete this settlement phase. If our interpretation is right, Douai was becoming more densely settled in the eighth century. The whole group of structures is embedded in 20 cm of dark clay-like soil, fairly homogeneous and hydromorphic in character, suggesting a soil deposit that accumulated slowly.

Period III: ninth century

Around the end of the eighth or the beginning of the ninth century, settlement becomes dense enough to justify using the term pre-urban (or proto-urban) agglomeration instead of a mere village. A complex set of stratigraphic levels, pebbled occupation surfaces, dwellings with postholes and pits can be organized into three or four different phases. The dwellings had wooden frames based on posts. They were 6 m wide and their length (i.e., the axis of the roof) varied from 4 to 6 m. Pegged panels set on transversal beams which were placed directly on the ground made up the floor, which was covered with a pile of litter. A system of narrow ditches (40 to 50 cm wide) defined a network of mutual isolated dwelling units consisting of a house, sunken huts, and pits. The sunken huts were sometimes dug 1.2 m into the earth. They served as barns, granaries, and workshops built over cellars accessible by stairs. The floor level was some 1.7 m above the excavated bottom and therefore was slightly raised above the contemporary ground level. There were pits of 1 to 1.5 m in diameter and others 1 m deep. These were root or grain storage silos. They were sealed with wooden covers. Other pits of similar dimensions but cylindrical in form, held liquid manure; still others oblong in shape and shallower, were latrines with their characteristic fill. At the edge of the excavated area, vestiges were found which we interpret as proof that an earthen rampart already enclosed this "pre-urban" settlement.

The dwellings, barns and related structures of each unit were destroyed by fire, probably accidental in origin. They were quickly rebuilt using the same elements which had survived the fire. The occupation level associated with the ensuing phase is thicker than that of the preceding. Therefore, we assume a longer period of use for the rebuilt settlement. it was in turn destroyed by a generalized fire; a burnt coin of the frankish King Charles the Bald suggests that the Norman raiders, around 880, were responsible for the fire. We think that about this time the Scarpe River was modified by digging a channel in Vitry (9 km to the south) between the Scarpe and Sensee rivers which drained Douai marshes and supplied the emerging town with a means of communication and exchange.

Period IV: tenth-eleventh centuries

During this period, fundamental changes in the organization of the foundry site occurred, undoubtedly reflecting important changes in the political structures of the town. The existing building were all methodically torn down to make room for new constructions. They included a large dwelling, huge storage pits, silos and various wells. The house was more than 8 m long and 7 m wide; it was built over a large cellar more than 1.6 m deep, accessed by a wide stairway. The worn pilings had dimensions which suggest they supported numerous floors.

A six-posted barn built over a cellar measured 6.5 m by 4.5 m, and resembled the smaller raised barns of the ninth century village. Near the house entrance was a grain storage pit, a manure pit and latrines completed the group. No trace of a defensive arrangement was noted at this stratigraphic level, neither a moat nor an earth embankment.

Apart from these structures, other discoveries which included (for the first time) gold ornaments and some spurs, suggesting someone important lived there, probably the Count of Flanders named Arnould the First.

When the King of France Lothaire took the town, he fortified the residence. The first building was dismantled, and a new, more solid structure was built. Its base, at about ground level, was protected on three sides by a platform almost 2 m high. Strong wooden posts must have supported several upper stories. A pathway covered with wattle to keep off the humidity gave access to the lower story, where the livestock must have been kept. The residence, which was modified several times, was surrounded by a dry moat more than 10 m wide, the bottom of which — 3.5 m below ground surface — was perfectly flat.

In 962 the Count of Flanders, Arnould IInd, captured the town. The wooden building was partly demolished and a wooden *donjon*, 4.5 m on each side, was built. The platform, reinforced by wooden fences and vertical pilings, occupied all the central space. A small wooden tower protected the access to the moat.

Period V: eleventh-twelfth centuries

A document of 1187 refers to a *Nova turris* in Douai, the first mention of the stone *donjon* built by the Count of Flanders. This *donjon* had a square plan, 18 m on a side. It was built of sandstone from Pévèle, and held together by a grey mortar. A well, set into the northwest wall, descended to 11 m below the ground of the *donjon*. To the south, where the guard tower inside the walls had previously stood, a building slightly trapezoidal in shape — 14 m long and 7 m wide — where the Count dispensed justice and received his guests, was erected on a cellar.

The stone rampart which formed the border of the Count's castle does not seem to have changed from the earlier period. The moat, on the other hand, was enlarged and now boasted a total diameter of over 70 m (and was 5 or 6 m deep).

The plan of the *donjon* of the Count of Flanders which still stands in Ghent (Belgium), which was built at about this time, is closely comparable to the one we have described. By examining its superstructures we can get a good idea of what the "Nova Turris" or New Tower of Douai must have looked like.

Period VI: thirteenth–seventeenth centuries

From the thirteenth century onwards, written documents provide more information which can be used to interpret the archaeological findings. We can undoubtedly relate the abandonment and subsequent destruction of the *donjon* annex, which was used as a dump in the thirteenth century, to the French occupation of the town under Philippe Auguste (between 1213 and 1226).

The demolition of the Count's Justice Hall at this time was clearly a symbolic result of the victory of his French enemies.

It was probably soon after the departure of his French garrison, which was maintained until 1242, that the Count transferred his Douai residence to the other side of the brook, near what is now the Municipal Library. This residence was called the "Castle of Bassecourt." The New Tower had lost its defensive functions by this time, for in 1268 the land between the *donjon* and the rampart was ceded by the Countess Marguerite to a private person. The *donjon* remained usable, however; it was probably there that the *Chastel du Roy* prison, cited in a 1337 document during the domination of the French King Philip the Fair, was located. At this time the *donjon* well filled up with refuse and the tower was torn down. The stones were probably used to reinforce and extend the city walls.

On the ruins of the Count's reception hall a new building 6 m wide, which leaned on what was left of the earlier rampart, was put up, doubtless in the fourteenth century. This was to remain standing until the seventeenth century, as is indicated by various town maps including that of Martin le Bourgeois, which calls it "the castle."

Until the end of the sixteenth century the *donjon* served as a quarry and its stones were robbed outright down to foundation level. The plundered foundation trench was used as a domestic rubbish dump which can be dated by a series of coins; the latest is a French *double tournois* of Louis the XIIIth of 1612.

Period VII: seventeenth-nineteenth centuries

In 1667 Douai became a French frontier town whose military character was quickly affirmed by the construction of barracks and an arsenal. In 1669, a cannon foundry was built on the old castle site. A huge enclosure was built and corresponded exactly with the edge of the moats. The foundry buildings were rebuilt several times, no doubt in order to keep up with technical progress in cannon manufacture. The foundry functioned until around 1880. Numerous vestiges of this powerful industry were visible in the basement: the foundations of various workshops, the casting oven dug into the old moat, underground galleries and various waste products such as fragments of cannon and bronze objects for recasting.

Conclusions

The results achieved at Douai over the past few years show that there are ways of reaching successfully into the urban historical environment threatened with destruction. Concerted research of increasing efficiency and systematic monitoring of construction projects have led us to acquire, in a few years, the basis of an overall archaeological approach to our town and to measure the value of various types of interventions. Large scale excavations like those of the foundry raised numerous interesting questions about the town origins and the development of the Count's residences. Their scientific impact goes far beyond the city limits, even though they concerned only a tiny area in the town center and offered only a partial view of that! Excavations on a more limited scale, like those of the Anchin Residence, are easier to carry out and doubtless of more strictly local interest, but each adds its share of information about the everyday life of the people of Douai and their town environment to the general picture (fig. 10).

Naturally these operations, though carefully performed, are piecemeal and site choice depends on the hazards of urban development rather than a preconceived plan of archaeological research.

Nonetheless their frequency has lead us, in the long run, to explore the various parts of town rather completely and thus to gain a knowledge of it. To realize a program of this type one needs time, of course, and also the realization that science in general and history in particular, resemble the slow and minute reconstruction of a puzzle in which some pieces are imprecise or hard to make fit and others have disappeared forever.

What is needed is to define a true policy to adopt in regard to our heritage from the past. The first requirement would be to perfect the different approaches sketched out in this paper: to ascertain more precisely the town's archaeological potential, to refine our understanding of the urban phenomenon in order

258 / PIERRE DEMOLON

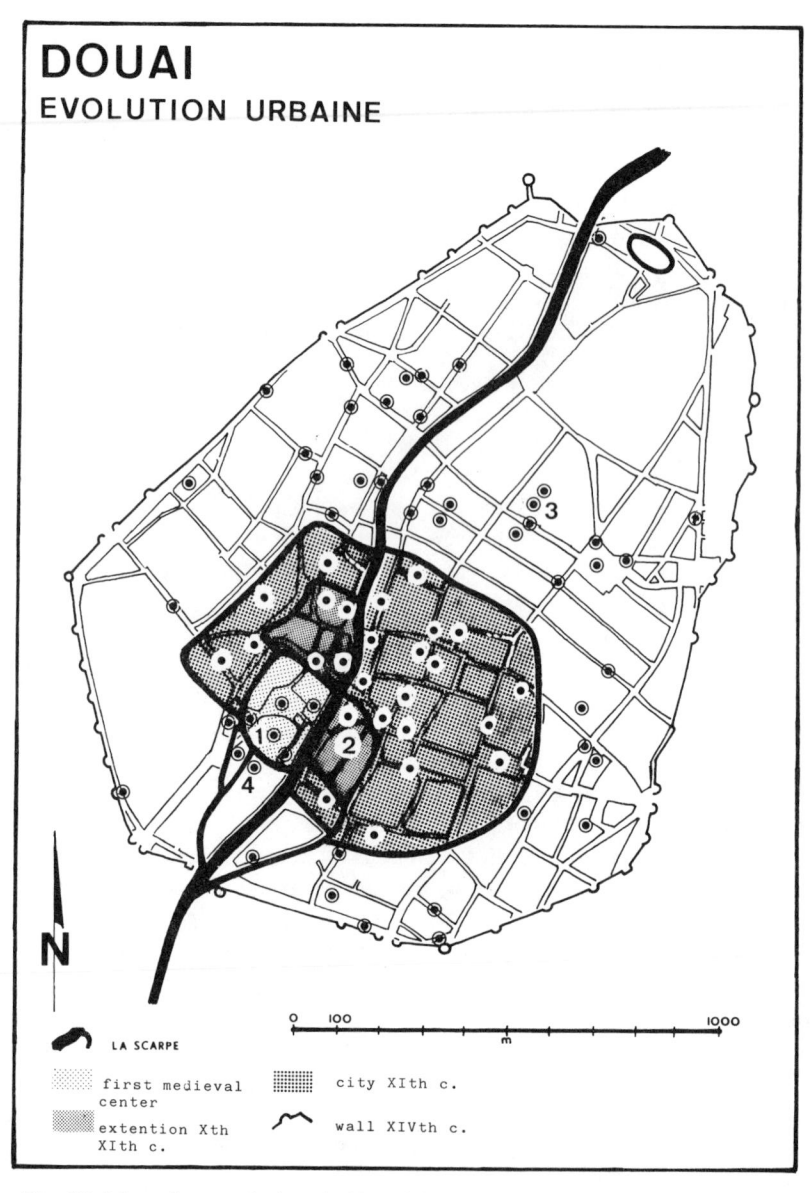

Fig. 10. Map of research done in Douai between 1976 and 1983. The sites are marked by numbers:
1. The Foundry
2. The Fishmarket
3. Anchin Residence
4. The Conservatory

to make more accurate predictions, and, finally, to integrate all the information that already exists in historical and archaeological sources, with the goal of successfully managing our underground heritage.

Of course these questions and the answers to them are similar on the local, regional and national scales. Meeting them would require a clear determination and a global grasp of the urban phenomenon. It presupposes the creation of municipal archaeological services adequately staffed and funded. In Douai such a service has been created, based at the municipal *Musee de la Chartreuse*; it is the first functioning service in the *Nord Pas de Calais* region. Its first efforts, guided by a sensitivity to the character of the town, have already given appreciable results. Thus the all important first step has been taken. No doubt the "future of the past" is on the right track in Douai.

Early Medieval Florence Between History and Archaeology[1]

FRANKLIN K. TOKER

Medieval archaeology is distinguished from prehistoric archaeology and some subfields of classical archaeology by the key distinction that it operates in a historically documented period. Somewhat illogically, medieval archaeologists pursue their excavations even though there exist documents for their contexts, which would seem to make the exploration of physical remains unnecessary and even pointless. This anomaly is nowhere more glaring than in the excavations that have been conducted in Florence, a city that was probably more intensively documented than any other in Europe from about 1200 to 1800. The Florentines have long been noted for their attachment to possessions, and documents of their past are among the most treasured possessions they have. The libraries of Rome and Paris, London and Washington are more important than those of Florence for their holdings of world-wide culture. Florentines, however, are interested primarily in local documentation, which they store up in ten major libraries, a dozen first-rank museums, and a chain of important archives. The holdings of the government archives, or *Archivio di Stato,* are calculated not in numbers of individual documents but by kilometers on the racks.

The detail that a historian can squeeze out of these records is mind-boggling. At the *Opera del Duomo,* for example, the private corporation that since 1331 has been in charge of constructing and maintaining Florence Cathedral, one finds on folio 16 of the second minute-book for March 20 of that year, 25 *soldi* were paid to the trumpeters who were hired to sound triumphal blasts when the keystone was set in place to complete construction of the second bay of the nave. But this richness of documentation constitutes as much of a problem as an advantage. Documentation can be spotty or destroyed;

or perhaps an event was never recorded in the first place. At Florence Cathedral we know all the trivia concerning the financial transactions, for these had to be recorded, but we are almost totally in the dark about artistic transactions, which for the most part were not. What Gothic architect derived the celebrated plan and the original model for Filippo Brunelleschi's later Renaissance cupola? What does the *Duomo* of S. Maria del Fiore mean in formal terms? In spiritual terms? The records say nothing at all about this. Perhaps because the fiscal documentation is so copious, art historians for the last 200 years have been asking trivial questions when they should have been asking significant questions about the structure. Hence it may be that intellectual atrophy sets in when documentation is profuse. Stylistic analysis, archaeological exploration, cultural analysis all go by the wayside in favor of the stodgiest sort of history, which is a mere compilation of documents.

This intellectual atrophy affects not only the Cathedral but the whole history of the city of Florence itself. The histories of Florence, whether medieval chronologies, Renaissance essays or nineteenth-century triumphs of positivism, show a near-total lack of interest in those periods that are less well documented. The least well documented of all periods is early medieval Florence, which tends to be glossed over in the histories as though the six centuries from AD 400 to 1000 had never taken place.

An analysis of Robert Davidsohn's definitive *Geschichte von Florenz*, written from 1896 to 1927, makes these failing clear. In its Italian edition Davidsohn's work filled seven thick volumes, plus an index and four volumes of documents in the German supplement.[2] Four of the seven text volumes constituted a political history of Florence to the cut-off year 1330; the three remaining volumes gave a social and cultural history of the city through the fourteenth century. Davidsohn treated Roman Florence, from ca. 50 BC to the year 400, in sixty-nine pages, or at a rate of one-seventh of a page per year. He then discussed the interlude of the Germanic migration period from 410 to 775, roughly 350 years, in forty pages: a treatment of one-ninth of a page per year. Carolingian-Ottonian Florence from 775 to 1000 was discussed at the rate of half a page per year. Quite different was the fate of late medieval Florence, from the eleventh to the fourteenth centuries, which Davidsohn discussed in over six thousand pages, roughly nineteen pages per year. The historian was thus 170 times more intensive in his treatment of late medieval over early medieval Florence.

This quantification of years per page is offered here as a rhetorical device rather than as a serious methodological tool, but it is of more than passing significance that the proportional distribution found in Davidsohn is not much different from that found in Renaissance histories, above all Machiavelli and Guicciardini, and in such fourteenth-century chronicles as those of Dino Compagni and Giovanni Villani two centuries before. The discrimination against the first thousand years of Florentine history results, however, from more than a simple bias: it is an accurate reflection of the paucity of documents on Florence before the Carolingian period. The origin of Roman Florence is nowhere recorded, and all references to the Roman period in general are extremely scanty. The unique substantial reference to *Florentia* in Roman literature is found in Tacitus, who reported that around AD 15 the Senate thought so little of the place that it proposed to allow the destruction of Florence by flooding the Arno in order to divert waters from the dangerously swollen Tiber. The only administrative position Florence held was the office of *corrector Italiae* for Tuscany, which we know it held in 287 and 366, but so did even smaller settlements such as Pistoia.

Of the ecclesiastical history of Florence we know just as little: there are preserved contemporary records of only three bishops in a period of 400 years. These were Felix (a presumed bishop), who was listed in attendance at a council in Rome in the year 313; Bishop Zenobius around the year 400; and Bishop Reparatus, ca. 690. There are no recorded bishops at all during the 300 years that separate Zenobius from Reparatus. One church only is recorded in documents: the basilica of S. Lorenzo, consecrated by St. Ambrose of Milan in 393 and cited a generation later in the hagiography of St. Ambrose written by his disciple Paulinus the Deacon. To judge from it geographical position, it appears almost inevitable that Florence was in the front ranks of cities vulnerable to incursions of the Germanic tribes on their way to Rome, but there are two records only that document the Goths, Ostrogoths or Lombards in or near Florence. The first of these occasions was the defeat of a great army of Ostrogoths and Vandals outside Florence around 406 by Roman troops under the leadership of the Vandal Stilicho. This narrow escape for Florence was recorded, among other places, in a passage in St. Augustine's *City of God*. The second was a note on another unsuccessful siege against Florence by Totila in 541/542, inserted by Procopius in his volumes of *The Gothic Wars*. The documentary history of Florence is otherwise nearly blank from the mid-fourth until the mid-eighth century, a space of 400 years. This historic blank led Giovanni Villani and his fourteenth-century contemporaries to suppose that Florence had been totally devastated by the barbarians and lay dormant until founded a second time by Charlemagne.

One of the most striking aspects of the historiography of Florence is how little the later Middle Ages knew about the early medieval period. The Church venerated and still venerates Bishop Zenobius as first bishop of Florence, oblivious to the existence of the still earlier bishop Felix, who was remembered in Rome as a signatory to the acts of the anti-Donatist council of 313, but of whom all written records and oral traditions had been forgotten in Florence itself. Florentines have long been proud transmitters of their historical tradition, so that Dante could write in the *Paradiso* of the women of Florence spinning tales of the Trojans and Romans as they spun out their wool. But they had few facts

Fig. 1. Growth of Florence in the Middle Ages. The three circuits of walls in progressive expansion are Roman, Romanesque, and Gothic. (Author's reconstruction drawn by Marlene Boyle; base map of Florence published by F. Fantozzi, Florence, 1843; simplified in G. Fanelli, *Firenze: Architettura e Città*, Florence, 1973.)

to work with. How did late medieval, Renaissance and modern historians react to this lack of facts? To medieval chroniclers such as Villani the historical vacuum of the early Middle Ages had to be patched up with the fabled protection of Florence by Julius Caesar and Charlemagne, all showing that the greatness of late medieval Florence was clearly pointed out from the start. Renaissance and modern historians were instead almost pleased that Florence had nothing to show for its first thousand years, because that made Renaissance Florence all the more surprising and glorious. Both approaches are equally fallacious and equally out of date, because the picture of Florence that is now

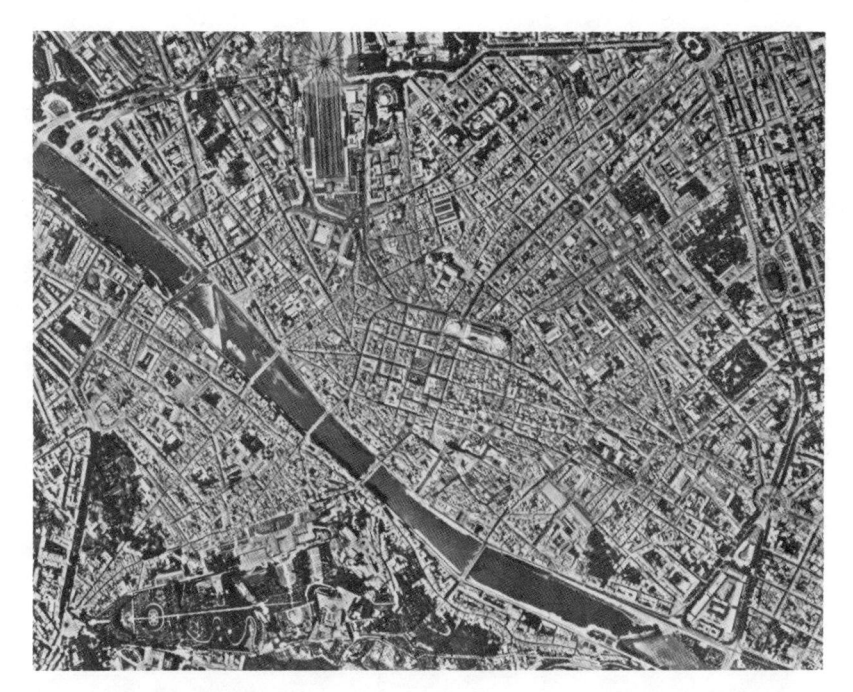

Fig. 2. Aerial view of Florence: the lines of the three major walls shown in fig. 1 are fully evident in the street system today. (Photo: Istituto Geografico Militare, Florence.)

beginning to emerge is of an early medieval city considerably less glamorous than the one Villani and Dante invented, but significantly more important than the settlement dismissed as insignificant by Machiavelli and Davidsohn.

The source of this new information is not history but archaeology, even though the archaeological investigation of Florence lags far behind that of other cities of comparable age and importance. If we begin with the simplest sort of archaeological investigation, which is merely observation of the surviving material, we can see almost at once the pattern of the three main walls that left their imprint on contemporary Florence (figs. 1 and 2). The last of these walls was built at the close of the Middle Ages, from 1284 to about 1350, and stood until the 1860s, when Florence was briefly the capital of Italy. They were then for the most part demolished, and a series of boulevards took their place. A smaller system of walls dates from Romanesque times, around 1175, and it too has left its mark as a trapezoid around the downtown area.

Also evident, though rather reworked in nineteenth-century restoration, is the mark of the gridiron plan of Roman Florence (fig. 3). The present-day

Fig. 3. Aerial view of the Roman/early medieval zone of Florence. Numbers indicate excavation sites of the principal monuments known to us from the first century BC through the sixth century AD: 1) amphitheater; 2) temple of Isis; 3) theater; 4) bath(?) complex still under excavation; 5) south Roman city gate; 6) south baths; 7) Forum; 8) Capitoline temple complex; 9) Forum baths; 10) north Roman city gate; 11) Roman-period house below Baptistery; 12) Roman-period house replaced by church of S. Reparata ca. 500; 13) cemetery basilica of S. Felicita, datable from 405; 14) cathedral of S. Lorenzo, dedicated 393.

Cathedral sits just inside the north wall of the Roman city, which formed a basic rectangle in the manner of a Roman army camp. Outside the old city walls and still visible from the air today, was the Roman amphitheater (fig. 3, number 1) that was converted a millennium later into palaces for medieval nobles. The first puzzle unlocked by archaeology concerns the original date and placement of the city, which is curious in having been founded only a few kilometers away from the much older colony of Fiesole. Various inadequate answers to these questions had been proposed until 1965, when Colin Hardie combined historical and archaeological evidence on the point.[3] Hardie deduced the presence of not one but two Roman grids for Florence: the first for the city, and a second grid for the Arno valley. Like the plan of a military *castrum*, the design of *Florentia* was set in perfect cardinal orientation. The second plan, turned at 31 degrees, was created for the centuriation of the lands on the north bank of the Arno from Florence to Pistoia, on a grid that used the river as its main spine. This Hardie established both on the basis of toponomy, with the survival of the milestone names Quarto, Quinto, Sesto and Settimo as small villages, and also through remnants of Roman land divisions that survived at least to the eighteenth century. The common point of intersection of both grids is the modern corner of via Strozzi and via de' Tornabuoni. Hardie demonstrated that the founding of the city and the centuriation of its surrounding lands were contemporary events, and through a review of other examples of this city-country relationship, he proposed the founding of Florence for agricultural motives about 41 BC under Octavian.

No Roman monument survives above ground in Florence today: the site of lost houses and baths, of the Capitol and Forum, the theater and amphitheater has been demonstrated by archaeology alone. One supposes that a close philological study of significant terms that survived in medieval Latin could buttress these physical finds, but that has still to be done. The late medieval churches of S. Maria in Campidoglio and S. Andrea all'Arco were, we know, on the site of the Roman Forum, and must have been erected when one could still see, or oral tradition recorded, the presence of the Capitoline Temple and some sort of triumphal arch.

A Roman aqueduct system is undocumented in Florence, yet fragments of one were recorded by amateur archaeologists of the eighteenth century, and the "Street of the Baths"—via delle Terme—retained its name past all human recollection that there had ever been a bath there. After the German destruction of much of central Florence in 1944 an excavation did in fact reveal a totally forgotten Roman bath immediately contiguous to via delle Terme.[4] What appears to have been another bath was revealed in excavations begun under piazza della Signoria in 1974 and still intermittently in progress. Whatever its exact character, the position of this monumental complex testifies to an expansion of Roman Florence to the south, possibly in the third century. Excavation below the Baptistery in the period 1895–1912 documented the remains of a large house of the second century, in part ornamented with rich mosaic floors.[5]

All reconstructions of the Roman city show its walls, whose lines were still in evidence in the eleventh century and which were perpetuated in legal fiction as late as the thirteenth century, much as "The City" is still referred to in London. Dante spoke of these walls as the "Prima Cerchia." The Roman wall is of undetermined date, but its foundation stones have been photographed at several points, and its north and south gates were revealed by excavation about ninety and thirty years ago, respectively. The location of certain late monuments and richly decorated houses north and south of the original walls indicates that by AD 400 the north and south walls had either been rebuilt far out from their original lines, or had been allowed to decay and not rebuilt. The latter is the more likely possibility.

Early Christian Florence

By 400 the city had at least two churches (figs. 3 and 4). We know from documentary evidence of the existence of S. Lorenzo as the cathedral, dedicated in 393 in what was evidently a rather crowded district north of the core city. Some scattered archaeological finds confirm the antiquity though not the form of this structure, which was rebuilt in the eleventh century and again in its present form in the Renaissance. But our fundamental document on the beginnings of Christianity in Florence comes from the excavation in the seventeenth century and again in 1948 of the cemetery basilica of Sta. Felicita on the south bank of the Arno. These two excavations produced nearly a hundred tomb inscriptions, some datable in a period from 405 to 547.[6] They demonstrate the considerable and possibly dominant role of Greeks and Syrians in the Christian community, as can be intuited also in the name of the celebrated bishop Zenobius, probably a Syrian, and the chief supposed early martyr, Minias or Miniatus, conceivably Egyptian.

All Florentine chronicles since the thirteenth century and all but one or two Italian art history surveys of the early Middle Ages add to these scant remains of Early Christian Florence one standing monument, the imposing Baptistery of S. Giovanni opposite the present Cathedral (fig. 5). The formal vocabulary of the Baptistery had undeniable affinities with Early Christian work, particularly the Lateran baptistery in Rome, as renovated in the mid-fifth century. To the excavators of 1912 the finding of a large baptismal font below the Baptistery and right at the center of the building made its Early Christian dating clear.

There are numerous problems with this interpretation, especially the lack

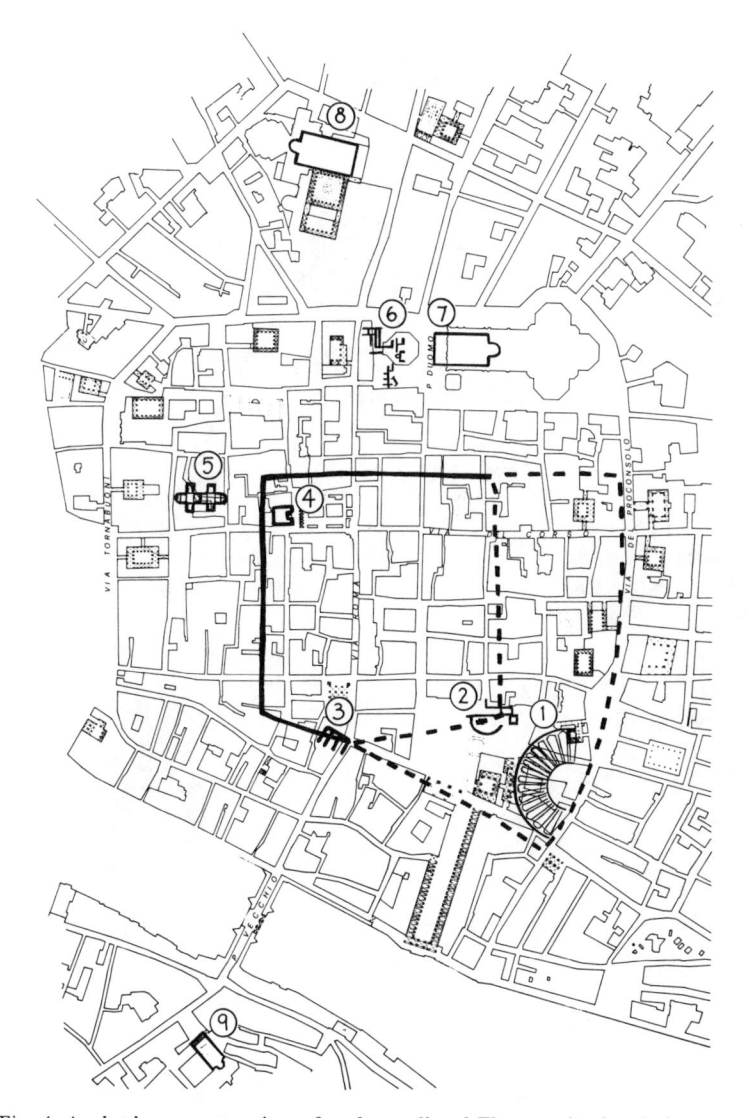

Fig. 4. Author's reconstruction of early medieval Florence in the sixth century, with the hypothetical inner wall (in two variants) proposed by Guglielmo Maetzke. Not shown is the presumed rebuilding of the Roman wall ca. 500 as rendered in fig. 1. Base map represents Florence in the mid-nineteenth century: 1) theater; 2) bath(?) complex; 3) south baths; 4) Capitoline temple complex; 5) Forum baths; 6) house below Baptistery; 7) S. Reparata; 8) S. Lorenzo; 9) S. Felicita.

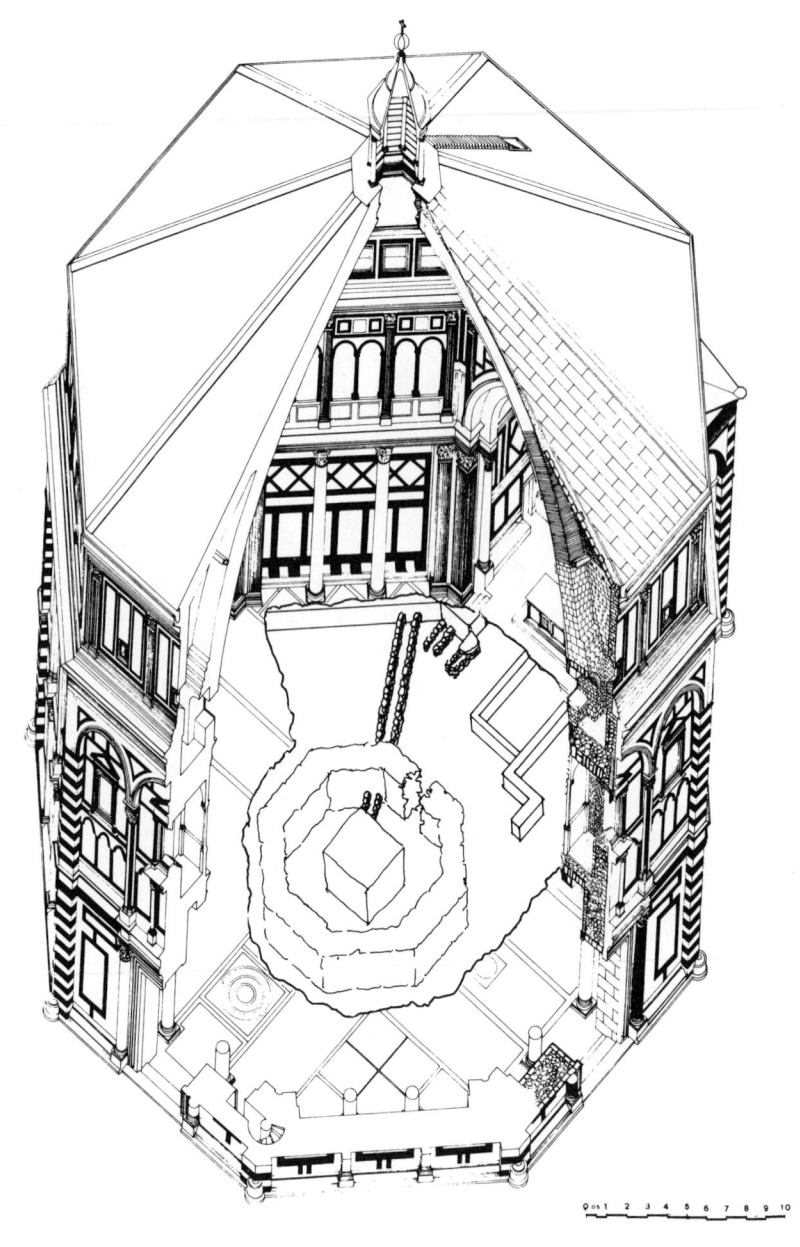

Fig. 5. Axonometric cutaway of the Baptistery of S. Giovanni in Florence, showing extant eleventh- to twelfth-century structure with excavated remains of an early medieval predecessor baptistery and a Roman-period house. (Drawing: Opera del Duomo, Florence; author's additions.)

of a floor to this "font" and its inordinately large size compared to the modest extent of the Early Christian community of Florence. In a counter-thesis I have proposed that the octagon found in 1912 was the remains of a small but self-standing baptismal building for which we have clear documentation in the ninth century, and which might have been Carolingian or Lombard in origin.[7] The present Baptistery would then have been constructed around the old one in the mid-eleventh century. When the old baptistery was demolished a screen around the new font recalled its shape, until it too was removed in the Renaissance.

Though flawed in its interpretations, the 1912 excavation under the Baptistery was meticulously executed and published. Unfortunately there were few excavations to follow it until the post-World War II campaigns of Guglielmo Maetzke on via delle Terme and at the site of the cemetery basilica of Sta. Felicita. This situation reversed itself in 1965, when the Soprintendenza ai Monumenti of Florence initiated the campaign that has totally changed our knowledge about the early medieval city. This was the excavation in the first three bays of the Cathedral of the church of S. Reparata. It was known that S. Reparata had been torn down in the fourteenth century when the Duomo of S. Maria del Fiore was built around and over it (figs. 6 and 7). Written records of this earlier church had been preserved only from 987, but particularly intriguing was its dedication to Reparata, a saint so obscure — but evidently also eastern, putatively Palestinian — that by the fourteenth century the Florentines lost interest in her and consecrated their new cathedral to the Virgin instead.

The main legend about the church was that it commemorated the victory over the Ostrogoths and Vandals outside Florence in ca. 406. The main body of the church of S. Reparata was uncovered between 1965 and 1974. In all a distance of forty-nine meters from the facade of S. Maria del Fiore to the apse of S. Reparata was revealed. In its last stage before demolition commenced in 1296, the old church had two apsidioles flanking the apse and two side chapels. Its south chapel fitted exactly within the south wall of the Cathedral, while the north chapel probably extended about a meter beyond the Cathedral north wall, which sliced through it. The first, or westernmost bay of the Duomo roughly corresponded to the nave of S. Reparata. The second Duomo bay corresponded to the old transept and chancel, while the third bay covered the old apse and apsidioles.

Five floor levels were evident in the stratigraphy (fig. 8). The top and most recent level ("A" in fig. 8) was the Cathedral pavement itself, of the fifteenth and sixteenth centuries. A few centimeters below that lay floor B, a temporary floor level of brick installed during construction of the Cathedral around the year 1300. Two meters below that, a marble and stone floor C related to a rebuilding of the ancient church in its Romanesque phase in the mid-eleventh

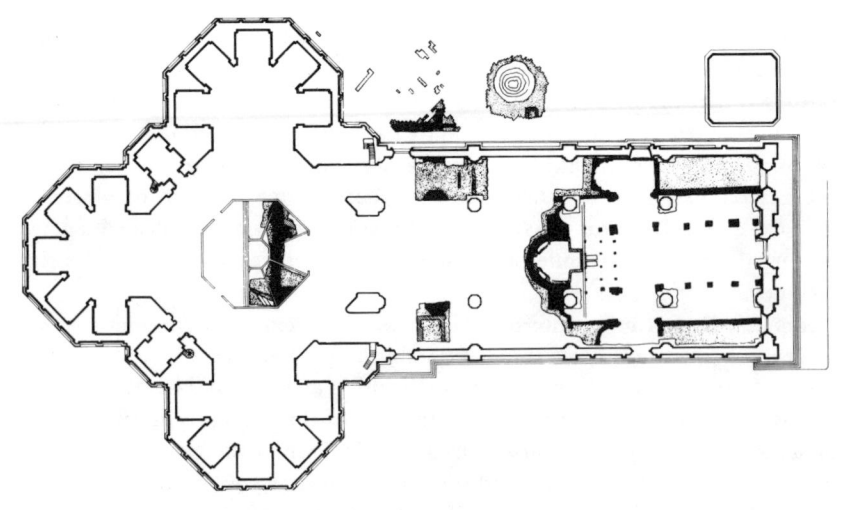

Fig. 6. Cathedral of S. Maria del Fiore, Florence (fourteenth to fifteenth centuries), with plans of predecessor structures excavated from 1965 to 1980. Scale of 1:1500. (Drawing: author and Richard Hook, Jr.)

century. About 20 centimeters lower was the mosaic floor D, of the earliest stage of the church. Below that (not present in the zone recorded in fig. 8) was a level of debris and a fifth floor made of crushed bricks cemented together, which belonged to a structure still earlier than the church.

Investigation revealed the age and function of that structure to be a Roman house that stood from the last quarter of the first century BC to the early fifth century (fig. 9). This was deduced not from the structure itself, which was only approximately datable in its masonry technique and decoration, but from ceramic fragments, the dating of coins retrieved from the foundations, and from radiocarbon dating. This house, which was constructed just after Florence was founded and which stood about four and a half centuries, has now become our major scientifically valid document on Roman Florence. It appears to have been destroyed during the first half of the fifth century and only paltry efforts were made to rebuild it. The feebleness of the walls of the rebuilding is remarkable compared to the robustness of the original structure. The building stood directly inside the north wall of Florence. While its first destruction may have resulted from an ordinary incident such as a domestic fire, it might also have been the effect of one of the Germanic migration sieges to the city. This was almost certainly the case of the second destruction of the building later in the fifth century, after which the site was strewn with ten primitive graves.

The levels and construction technique of these graves indicate a high probability that they belong to the same series as those found ninety years ago behind the Baptistery, directly over the main north-south street, or *Cardo,* of

Fig. 7. Interior view of S. Maria del Fiore with excavations in progress, 1971. (Photo: Soprintendenza de' Beni Architettonici ed Ambientali, Florence.)

Roman Florence. Whether the graves below the Cathedral and Baptistery belong to the invaders of Florence or to its defenders is impossible to tell. In either case, the double destruction of this house and its transformation into an impromptu graveyard set among the ruins clearly indicate widespread devastation in the city in the fifth century.

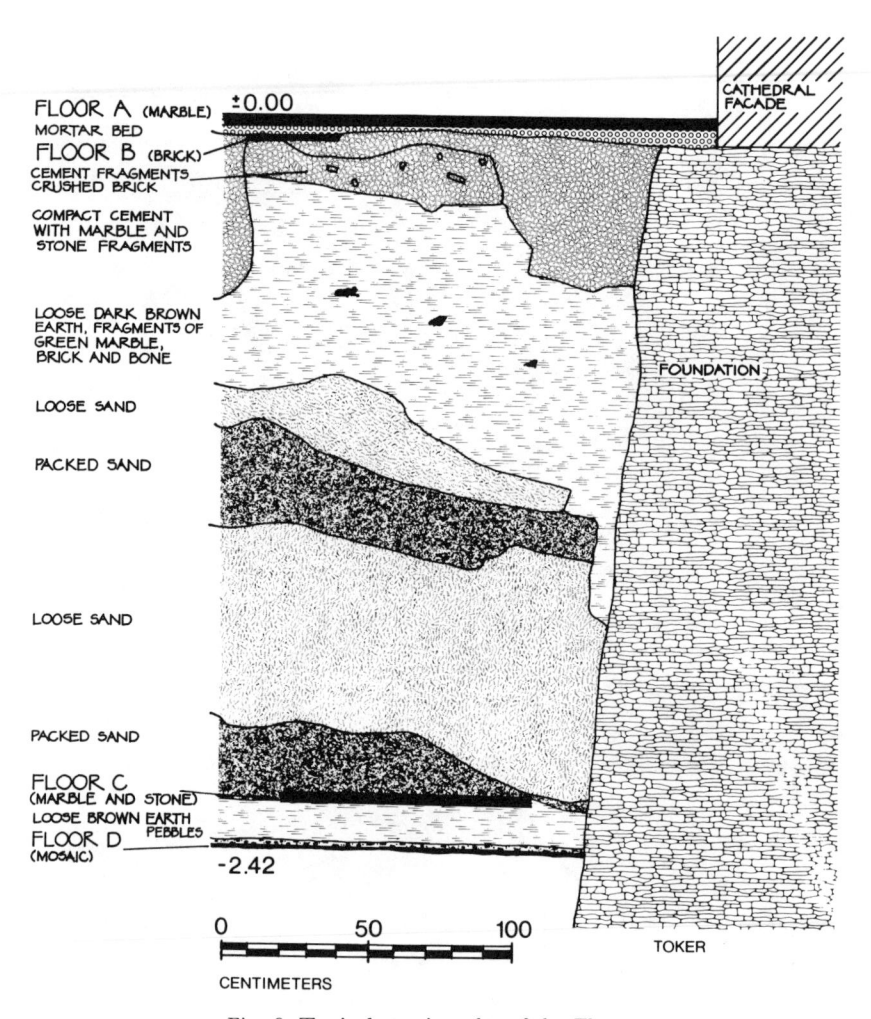

Fig. 8. Typical stratigraphy of the Florence Cathedral excavation. (Drawing: author.)

The critical transformation of Florence from a late-Roman to a medieval city can thus be fixed in the fifth and sixth centuries by the archaeological evidence, even though the documentary evidence consists of no more than the few lines in Procopius's *Gothic Wars* of skirmishes between the Goths and Byzantine troops outside Florence in the mid-sixth century. The physical extent of Florence during this transformation is unclear. Working from the text of the late-medieval Malaspini chronicle, which suggests that there had once ex-

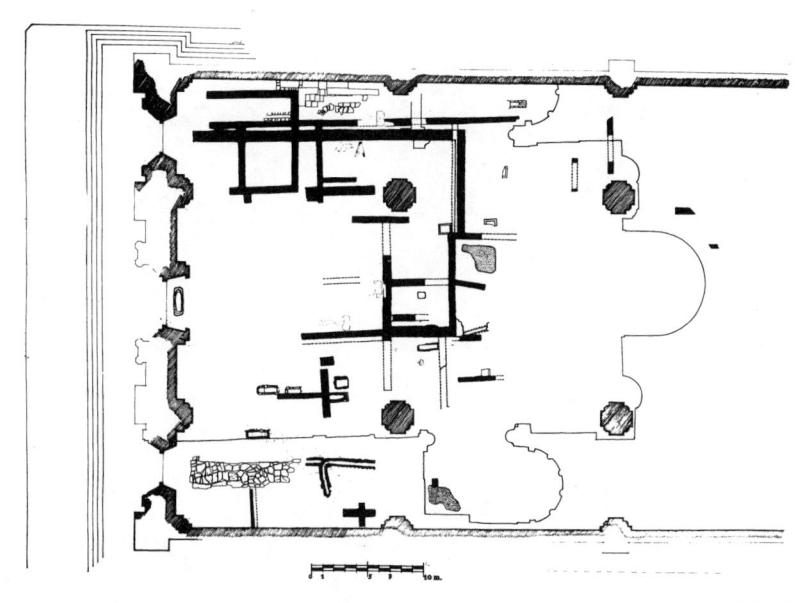

Fig. 9. Florence Cathedral excavation: plan of Roman house remains. S. Maria del Fiore foundation walls indicated in hatched lines; foundation walls of S. Reparata in its thirteenth-century state shown in outline. (Drawing: Soprintendenza, Florence, and author.)

isted an inner wall around the nucleus of central Florence, and from remains of a rubble-formed wall that were found in the nineteenth century at some of the same points referred to by Malaspini, Guglielmo Maetzke hypothesized that the Byzantine defenders of Florence had thrown up an emergency defense wall in the mid-sixth century (fig. 4).[8]

The Maetzke hypothesis is logical but not compelling, particularly now that it appears that the new church of S. Reparata (undated, but certainly standing by the mid-sixth century) would have been left out of this emergency defense circuit. An alternate date for the inner wall would be the late fifth century, which would coincide with the construction of S. Reparata just inside the north Roman wall around AD 500. At that same time we can postulate a rebuilding of the decayed Roman wall, since it was assuredly the basic city wall from Carolingian through early Romanesque times. The construction of S. Reparata and rebuilding of the old Roman city wall would have demonstrated that the city had resumed some of its earlier monumentality. The construction of a large new church so close to the extra-urban cathedral of S. Lorenzo is difficult to comprehend unless placed in the wider context of the devastated late antique city. S. Reparata stood protected within the city wall, while S. Lorenzo lay

Fig. 10. View of the mosaic floor of S. Reparata in its Early Christian state, ca. 500. (Photo: Soprintendenza.)

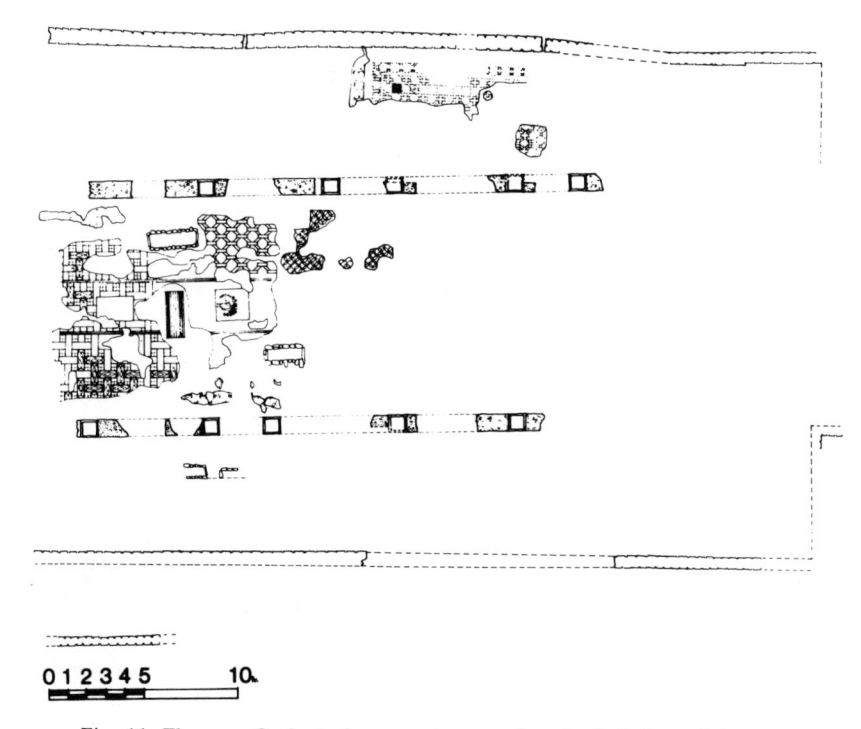

Fig. 11. Florence Cathedral excavations: archaeological plan of the remains of S. Reparata in the sixth century. (Author.)

defenseless outside it. The discovery of S. Reparata in 1965 thus places Maetzke's hypothetical inner wall in a new light. It confirms a state of devastation of Florence in late antiquity, but suggests a redating of the worst period to the mid- and late-fifth century. By the sixth century, to judge from the richness of the new church of S. Reparata, *Florentia* was well on the way to rehabilitation.

The mosaic floor of the church of S. Reparata emerged almost literally as well as figuratively from the graves and debris of the Roman stratum (figs. 10 and 11). The ruins of the Roman house offered little to the church construction crew except rubble: one wall only was solid enough to serve as the north aisle wall of the new sanctuary. The mosaics covered over the stumps of the other walls together with the graves strewn about the ruins. The church was large. Its nave and aisles were twenty-six meters wide and about fifty-two meters long. The clerestory wall was carried on fourteen pairs of columns, spaced every 3.19 meters, or eleven Roman feet. The details of this church show signs of ambition rather than of prosperity: its columns were not mono-

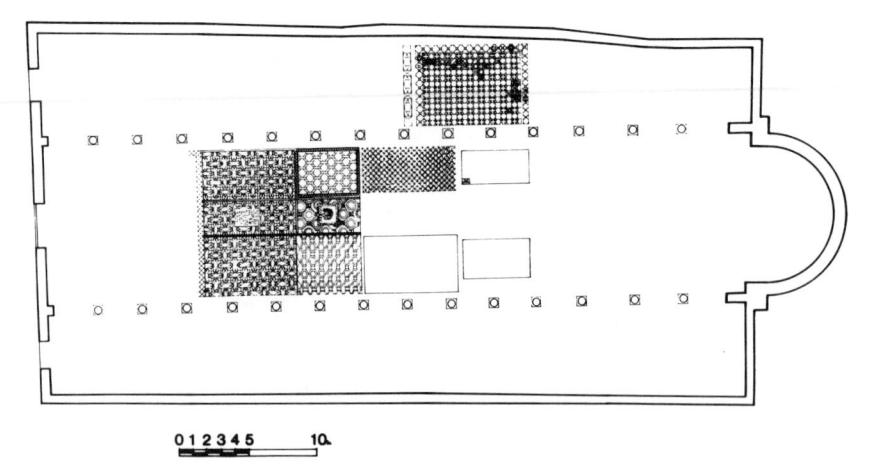

Fig. 12. Reconstruction plan of S. Reparata in the sixth century. (Author.)

liths nor even composed of stone drums, but were formed instead of hundreds of pie-shaped stone wedges mortared together to form columns that would then have been plastered over and frescoed in imitation of marble. The mosaic floor was similarly ambitious. It is the largest of its genre to have been found in Italy between Ravenna in the north and Otranto in the south, but it was poorly cut and sloppily laid. These detractions notwithstanding, the resulting church is richer than any known to us from early medieval Tuscany.

Historical records provide no clue to the date of the church of S. Reparata. The late medieval legend that dated it around 406 cannot be correct. Radiocarbon samples date the debris below the new mosaic floor to at least the mid-fifth century. The mosaic bears two inscriptions: a list of fourteen donors who paid for the central portion of the mosaic, and the name of a fifteenth donor, Obsequentius, who gave the central panel containing a peacock. None of these names have been retained in historical record, nor are they more than approximately datable through prosopography. Rather than using documents to understand the archaeological finds, the finds themselves constitute a prime new document for Florentine history.

It is at this point that the contribution of archaeology, art history, and history begin to reinforce each other. The first step is a hypothetical reconstruction of the church on art historical grounds (figs. 12 and 13). The specific features of the church, such as the width and length of the nave and side aisles, the intercolumniation and general proportions, together with the design of the mosaic floor, are all indications of a close association between this church and churches on the Adriatic coast in the hundred years from the mid-fifth to the mid-sixth centuries. More particularly, the features both of the architecture

Fig. 13. Reconstructed interior view of S. Reparata in the sixth century. (Author and Ken Diebert.)

and of the mosaic point to a date late in the fifth or early in the sixth century, around or just after the year 500. To this preliminary attribution on the basis of style may then be added arguments from context: the dates achieved from the coins, radiocarbon samples and fragments of ceramic and glass that were covered over by the mosaic. The arguments of physical context then point to considerations of a broader historical context. The building of this church must have corresponded to a period of at least minimal security and prosperity. There was one extraordinary oasis of calm in central Italy between the mid-fifth and mid-sixth centuries, in the thirty-year reign of the Ostrogoth king Theodoric, form 493 to 526. Theodoric established his capital at Ravenna, a city already celebrated for its mosaics and Early Christian churches. One of these, San Salvatore, the Arian cathedral of the city, corresponds particularly well in size to S. Reparata. It seems logical to expect that in this period, as in almost every other, the lines of art would have corresponded to the lines of power. Theodoric saw himself as the restorer of peace and of art in a devastated Italy, as indeed

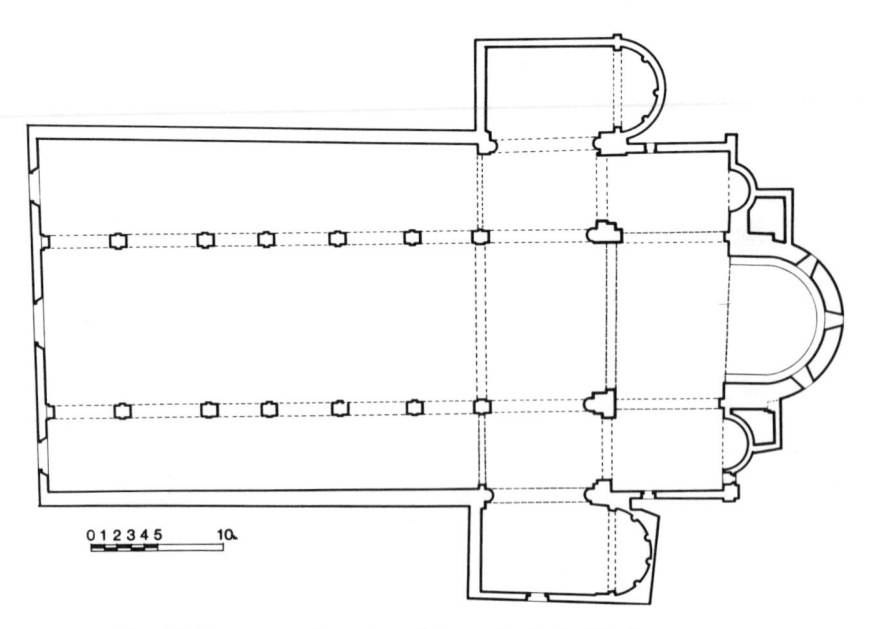

Fig. 14. Reconstruction plan of the cathedral of S. Reparata as rebuilt in the eleventh century. (Author.)

he was. There is no reason to think that he himself was connected with the building of S. Reparata, but his politics made it possible for the Florentines to recover from the destruction inflicted in the fifth century quickly enough to be able to build so fine a church. The cult of Saint Reparata appears to provide yet another link between Florence and Ravenna, because it seems to have been the Byzantine cult of Saint Pelagia under a Latin equivalent that was propagated from Ravenna.

It is curious to observe that in some garbled way the medieval tradition linking Reparata and salvation from the barbarians holds true, even though the church dates a century later than the legend supposed. In a more basic sense, Villani, Dante, and the medieval chroniclers were totally wrong in their perception of early medieval Florence. It did not languish in the ashes 400 years until revived by Charlemagne: it revived almost instantly with a major assist from an Ostrogoth king whose name and glory almost never appear in medieval or modern histories of Florence.

Since the object of this paper is a methodological consideration rather than a factual account of the Florence Cathedral excavations, it is unnecessary to cite in detail all that has been learned about Florentine history during the remainder of the chronological period covered by the excavation from the sixth through the fourteenth centuries. Having examined the plan of S. Reparata

Fig. 15. Reconstructed interior view of S. Reparata prior to its demolition in the late thirteenth century. (Author and Ken Diebert.)

at its moment of origin, it may, however, prove useful also to look at the final appearance of the church before its demolition began at the end of the thirteenth century (figs. 14 and 15). By the thirteenth century the S. Reparata complex was an accretion of four major periods: a new apse and crypt of the Carolingian period, around 870; two square towers set flanking the apse, from the Ottonian period, toward the end of the tenth century; a completely new nave and transept in Romanesque style, probably of ca. 1050; and an enlarged crypt and presbytery of the early thirteenth century. The last of these changes was minor, and concerns only art and liturgical historians. The other three are, on the contrary, significant documents for Florentine political history. The first, the Carolingian apse, is significant because it was built to hold the body of St. Zenobius when it had to be moved from the suburban cathedral of S. Lorenzo because the latter church was vulnerable to the Viking raids of the ninth century outside the city walls. With the transfer of the body of Zenobius, S. Reparata became *de facto* and later *de jure* the cathedral of Florence. The bishop of Florence also set up his episcopal palace directly opposite the church at this time, and became in effect governor of the city.

The square towers of about a century later are similarly indicative of important political changes. Their purpose was probably defensive, as they became adjunct towers to the north city wall. But they assumed an important stylistic configuration also. Square towers flanking as apse were common items in Lotharingia, and occasionally appeared in France and Germany as well. But they are in all periods extremely rare in Italy, where only five known examples survive. The location of these five examples is anything but fortuitous. Each stands in a town or at an abbey specially favored by the feudatories of the Holy Roman Empire. The Margrave Hugo of Tuscany, who we know constructed a chain of abbeys in his territory with an explicit political intent, built one such monastery with this rare feature of square flanking towers near Arezzo. The towers of S. Reparata may or may not represent the involvement of the Margrave, but more than likely they do symbolize the solidification of German hegemony over north-central Italy in the tenth and eleventh centuries.

The final instructive aspect of S. Reparata is its eleventh-century plan, which is almost certainly to be associated with the tenure in office of bishop Gerhard of Burgundy, later Pope Nicholas II. Nicholas was decisively oriented toward the reform forces within the church, particularly that of the monastery of Cluny in his native Burgundy. So too was the Margravine Matilda of Tuscany, who fixed Florence as her principal residence around 1055, probably to ally herself with the reform cause that was evidently strong there. A second reform movement that would have left its imprint on Florence was that of Lotharingia, since members of the Margrave's circle had significant Lotharingian connections. The Romanesque plan of S. Reparata, with two apsidioles and two transeptual chapels was pronouncedly Cluniac, and must have been transmitted directly from Burgundy or through a Lotharingian intermediary. Thus the city committed itself to the reform of the church not only politically, as we know from historical records, but through the symbolic language of its cathedral architecture, as the excavation now informs us.

The relationship between history and archaeology is symbiotic. Archaeology infuses history with its richness, and history guides archaeology from making mistakes. This pattern particularly applies to the archaeology of the Middle Ages. In Florence at this moment, the conjunction of the two disciplines entails more questions than answers; but it is certain that when the two are properly meshed a new and incomparably richer portrait of early medieval Florence is sure to emerge.

Notes

1. The author directed excavations below Florence Cathedral from 1969 to 1974, and a separate campaign south of S. Maria del Fiore in 1980. The complete excavation results will be included in his forthcoming volume, *Cathedral and City in Medieval Flor-*

ence: The Archaeological History of a Thousand Years (383-1375), anticipated in 1989. Reports on specific aspects of the problem have been published in F. Toker (with G. Morozzi, J. Herrmann), *S. Reparata: L'Antica Cattedrale Fiorentina* (Florence, 1974); *idem.,* "Excavations below the Cathedral of Florence, 1965-1974," *Gesta* 14/2 (1975): 17-36; *idem.,* "An Early Christian Church below the Cathedral of Florence," *Atti del IX Congresso Internazionale di Archeologia Cristiana* (Vatican City, 1979), vol. 2: 929-33; *idem.,* "Florence Cathedral: The Design Stage," *Art Bulletin* 60 (1978):214-30; and *idem.,* "Arnolfo's S. Maria del Fiore: A Working Hypothesis," *Journal of the Society of Architectural Historians* 42 (1983): 101-20.

2. R. Davidsohn, *Geschichte von Florenz* (Frankfurt a.M., 1986-1927), 5 vols.; reprinted as *Storia di Firenze* (Florence, 1956-68), 8 vols.; *idem., Forschungen zur älteren Geschichte von Florenz* (Berlin, 1986-1927), 4 vols.

3. C. Hardie, "The Origin and Plan of Roman Florence," *Journal of Roman Studies* 55 (1965): 122-40.

4. G. Maetzke, "Osservazioni sulle recenti ricerche nel sottosuolo di Firenze," *Atti della Accademia Fiorentina La Colombaria* 2 (1951): 6-7.

5. E. Galli, "Dove sorse il 'bel S. Giovanni'," *Rivista d'Arte* 9 (1916-18): 81 ff., 161 ff.

6. G. Maetzke, "Firenze: resti di una basilica cimiteriale sotto Santa Felicita," *Notizie degli Scavi di Antichità* s. 8, XI (1957): 282-324.

7. F. Toker, "A Baptistery below the Baptistery of Florence," *Art Bulletin* 58 (1976): 157-67.

8. G. Maetzke, "Ricerche sulla topografia fiorentina nel periodo delle guerre gotobizantine," *Atti dell'Accademia Nazionale dei Lincei,* ser. 8, III (1948): 97-112.

Rewriting an Urban Text: The Ottomanization of Cretan Cities

DONALD PREZIOSI

This is an introduction to a research project begun in 1982 on the historical archaeology of the cities of Crete. Its overall aim is to reconstruct the urban fabric of the major cities of Herakleion, Rethymnon, and Khania during the period of Ottoman control (1669–1898), and to plot in detail the ways in which Ottoman planners transformed an abandoned stage-set of Venetian power to conform to Ottoman Islamic religious, political, and economic needs. Our interests are presently focused upon the creation and articulation of a symbolic architectonic morphology through the orchestration and manipulation of formal elements largely Venetian and Greek in origin. The present report describes some of the island's capital, Herakleion (the Venetian Candia and the Ottoman Kandiye). In part this study project had been motivated by the fact that under the onslaught of modern tourism, many of the signs of the Ottoman presence are being rapidly obliterated, and before long little will remain for the historian and urban archaeologist interested in the life and growth of these complex, multi-ethnic, strategic interfaces between Islam and the West in the early modern period.[1]

The island of Crete, the fourth largest Mediterranean island, has been inhabited continuously for the past 8000 years. Its history has only intermittently been peaceful, and the island has been the stage of power struggles among all of the major political forces in the Eastern Mediterranean. During this time, Crete had been settled by Minoans, Mycanaeans, Greeks, Romans, Byzantines, Arabs, Genoese, Venetians, Turks, Albanians, Jews, Armenians, and Egyptians (fig. 1).

Since World War II, the cities of Crete have undergone an unprecedented expansion which is threatening to obliterate the remaining monuments of the

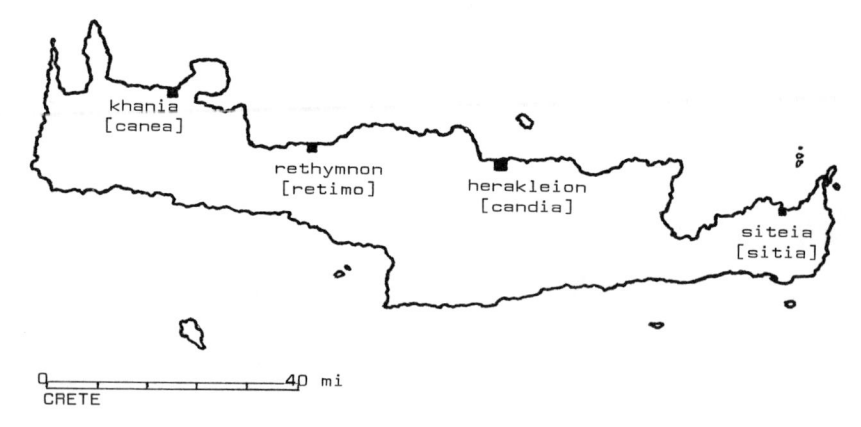

Fig. 1. Map of Crete, indicating major urban centers.

Ottoman and Venetian periods, which between them account for nearly all of the major urban public construction in Herakleion, Rethymnon, and Khania since the arrival of the Venetians in the thirteenth century, up to the time of the island's incorporation into the modern Greek nation at the beginning of the twentieth century.

The major city of Herakleion—known to the Venetians and Ottomans as Candia (Kandiye)—has since the 1960s become the fourth largest Greek metropolis, largely due to its touristic proximity to the ancient Minoan ruins of Knossos, the capital of the first European Bronze Age civilization [ca. 3000–ca. 1200 BC]. This expansion has all but eradicated its Ottoman and Venetian urban fabric as the city transforms itself into a multi-storied, glass and concrete cousin of scores of other cities along the Mediterranean littoral.

For the urban historian, historical archaeologist, and semiotician of visual and material culture, the situation has become critical, for within not many more years much of what still remains will be gone. From the seventeenth to the twentieth centuries, Herakleion was a polyglot, multi-ethnic mercantile city home to many diverse peoples from around the Eastern Mediterranean. Along with its smaller sister cities of Khania and Rethymnon (also situated along the north coast of the island), Herakleion embodied the political, ethnic and religious struggles of its resident groups in the formation and transformation of buildings, street layouts, places of worship, mercantile institutions and emporia, govern-mental offices, military works and fortifications. Having served for nearly a millennium as part of the interface between the Islamic and Western Christian worlds, the island and its history is of very great interest to scholars of Greek, Venetian, and Ottoman history, art history, and architecture.

The following is a preliminary report on a research project begun is 1982 whose general aim has been to reconstruct and map the details of the Cretan urban fabric since the medieval period, and in particular the transformations wrought under the two centuries of Ottoman control (ending in 1898). To date, this work has involved extensive photodocumentation of the three major cities, as well as documentary and archival work both in Crete and in Istanbul.[2] We have in addition been working with the text of the great seventeenth century Ottoman traveller and observer of world affairs, Evliya Celebi, whose writings describe in great detail the process of Ottomanization of the island, including the long, quarter-century conquest of Crete, as well as the inauguration of major building projects—mosques, religious schools, modifications of urban fortifications, governmental offices and residences, etc.[3] For evidence of the Greek and Venetian periods, we have relied upon the monumental volumes of the Venetian scholar of the turn of the century, Giuseppe Gerola; there exists no study of the Ottoman period comparable in scope and encyclopedic detail to that of Gerola for the Venetian, although important beginnings in this direction have very recently been made by several Turkish scholars.[4] Our focus in what follows will be upon the city of Herakleion (Kandiye), with occasional comparisons to its smaller sisters Rethymnon (Resmo) and Khania (Kaniye).

Until 824 the capital of Crete was the city of Gortyna in the south central part of the island. Founded originally by Doric-speaking Greek settlers, in AD 64 the Romans made the Cretan capital, replacing the older Minoan and Greek metropolis of Knossos (itself some 10 km inland from the site of present day Herakleion/Kandiye on the north central coast). Destroyed by Arab invaders under Abu Hafz Umar ibn Habib Andelusi in AD 824, the Roman and Byzantine city was largely abandoned.[5] The Arabs, having burnt their ships upon arriving in Crete, held sway on the island for a century and a half. They built a new capital city on the site of Herakleion, calling it Khandaq after the great defensive ditch excavated in semicircular fashion around the new port settlement.

Reconquered by the Byzantines in 961, Khandaq remained as Crete's capital under the Hellenized name of Khandax or Khandakos. Taken by Latin Christians with their conquest of Constantinople nearly two centuries later, and held for a time by the Genoese, the island became a Venetian colony beginning in AD 1204. For the next four and a half centuries, Crete served as Venice's major mercantile colony in the Eastern Mediterranean. Khandax became Candia, a name which the Venetians applied to the whole island (Shakespeare's "Isle of Candy"). Until the arrival of the Ottoman armies in the 1640s, Crete, mainly through the enlarged and fortified port city of Candia, exported substantial quantities of oil, wine, grain and timber to Europe, and was an important source of tax income for Venice during this period. Candia also became an important transshipment point for Near Eastern goods arriving in Venetian trading ships, and it seems likely that Candia passed on large quantities of spices and textiles to the European markets in Venetian ships.[6]

Under Venetian rule, the island came to be ringed by impressive fortified cities and coastal castles, and the fertile land was crossed by aqueducts and dotted with farming villages populated both by Greek natives and increasing numbers of Venetian settlers. The ports of Candia, Rethymnon and Khania (the Venetian Retimo and Canea) were continually expanded and crowded with warehouses opening directly onto their harbors for the speediest possible turn-around times for the loading and unloading of Venetian trading convoys. Despite ongoing antagonisms between the Latin and Greek religious communities, and periodic revolts against heavy taxation without representation in the Venetian Senate, the island flourished agriculturally and commercially.

After the fall of Constantinople to the Ottomans in 1453, however, various strong measures were taken to strengthen the island's fortifications against Ottoman incursions, and architects and engineers were brought from Italy to modify urban defenses and coastal forts according to the latest Western Renaissance planning theories. The effectiveness of these modern fortifications — and particularly those of Candia — was to be demonstrated in the seventeenth century when the Ottoman siege of Candia took nearly a quarter of a century to succeed.[7] After having conquered Canea and Retimo in the 1640s, the Ottoman Armies rapidly took control of all of the island except for Candia. After one of the longest sieges in the history of warfare, the Ottomans triumphed in 1669.

After the conquest, Crete became part of the Ottoman imperial network, and the exhausted Venetian and volunteer European forces — and most of the population of Candia itself — withdrew back to Venice under an amnesty granted by the equally exhausted conquerors. Crete remained part of the Ottoman Empire for nearly 230 years, until 1898. In 1912, the island became part of the new independent Greek state, and in the 1920s, an exchange of populations between Greece and the new Turkish nation founded by Ataturk caused an out-migration of moslem Cretans to Anatolia (principally to the area of Bodrum), and an influx of Anatolia Greek Christians to Crete. The latter group, mostly from Bodrum (the ancient Halikarnassos) settled on lands formerly owned by Cretan moslems, and in the vicinity of Candia (now renamed Herakleion) in a newly created suburb which was called Nea Alikarnassos.

When the Venetians and their European volunteer allies withdrew in 1669 back to Europe, they left behind a much-scarred but largely intact urban infrastructure. It was this "miniature Venice," this abandoned stage-set of Venetian power and commerce, which the Ottomans had to contend with.

But instead of levelling the monumental urban core, the Ottomans chose to transform it to their own religious, governmental, and economic needs. As we shall see, they accomplished this essentially through the manipulation of the formal signs of Western Christian presence. These transformations involved the conversion of Latin churches into mosques; the construction of religious establishments such as tekkes; the erection of public fountains, baths, market, and warehouse structures; the conversion of older seats of government into headquarters of the local representatives of the Sultan; the rebuilding of arsenals and military barracks and the repair and strengthening of fortifications; the housing of deliberately imported minority groups such as Albanians, Armenians, and Egyptians; and the construction of religious schools and libraries.

The visual and archival evidence has suggested to us that *the process of Ottomanization on Crete involved the pursuance of a policy aimed at the creation of an urban environment which repeated in a miniature and condensed form the major essential expressive architectonic features of the great capital on the Bosphorus, Istanbul.* It is our provisional thesis (subject to alteration and refinement as the project unfolds in coming years) that in this regard the Ottomans may have emulated an urban policy of their Venetian predecessors on the island, for whom the major Cretan cities were so organized as to echo the overall forms and relationships among buildings in the monumental core of Venice itself. At the present time, the evidence at hand is not sufficient to confirm or negate whether the Ottoman planners were consciously aware of this Venetian policy.[8]

Given this set of circumstances, in which nearly every Ottoman building of the early occupation was a palimpsest upon an older Venetian formation, few structures in our survey are formally or "stylistically" homogeneous. Nearly all embody an extremely complex history of conversion, alteration, and reconstruction over some two centuries. In attempting to understand the urban development of the island during the Ottoman period, it must be understood that we are dealing with a highly dynamic urban process over time, wherein both the formal and functional organization of buildings and their contexts underwent often dramatic changes several times in their history.

Our initial surveys in 1982 and 1983 have been devoted to learning how to disambiguate and "read" the history of given structures and neighborhoods by separating out the traces of different political and chronological periods as embodied in the buildings themselves. This above-ground archaeology has been guided by a growing amount of visual and archival documentation (Ottoman, Venetian, Greek), including maps, views and descriptions, tax-records, and other material.[9] Our preliminary sense is that a great deal may be learned about the urban policies of each of the major power groups controlling the island during its medieval and early modern history through a detailed examination of these often highly subtle architectonic modifications and transformations. And we have come to an early understanding of how the urban/architectonic/ideological programs of each group came to be reflected [i.e., produced] in the concrete ways in which each *reacted* to given sets of circumstances.

It is evident on architectural and archival grounds that the Venetians sought to make each of the three major cities—especially their capital, Candia—into a miniature Venice, complete with the primary distinctive visual features of the great imperial capital on the Adriatic.[10] This task involved the construc-

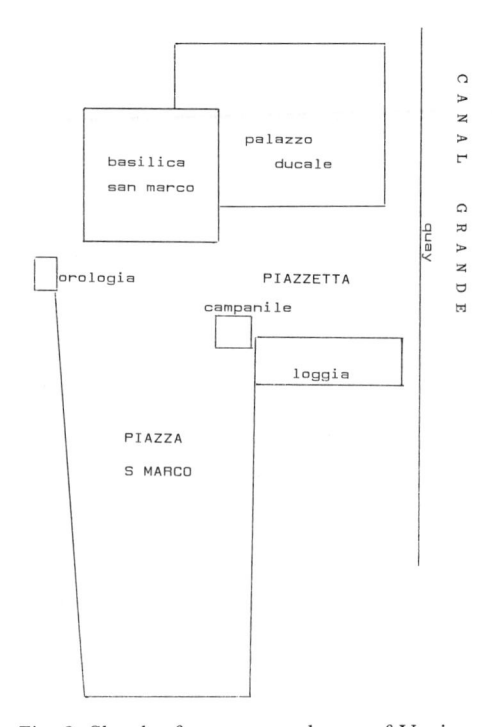

Fig. 2. Sketch of monumental core of Venice.

tion of buildings serving as concrete analogues for the Basilica San Marco, Palazzo Ducale, Loggia, Campanile, and Piazza San Marco in Venice. The corresponding structures in Candia were, to be sure, small-scale provincial versions of those at home. But what is of especial interest is the apparent fact that, given inevitable constraints of topography and relationships to the overall urban fabric, these elements of the public urban core were composed together in Candia (and Retimo) *according to spatial interrelationships which in the main replicated those of their prototypes in Venice.* In other words, the central monumental core of the cities was developed to echo that of Venice itself *in parvo* (fig. 2).

In Candia, the essential architectonic elements and relationships are marked in fig. 3 on the seventeenth century (pre-conquest) Venetian plan of the city (a comparison with fig. 4 will show corresponding elements in Retimo).[11] The Candian San Marco and its campanile stand on the east flank of its piazza (here known as the piazza delle biade,[12] to the south of the Loggia. The plan of Candia indicates the position of the Palazzo Ducale and palace of the Admiral to the west of the piazza; a major public fountain (built by Morosini[13]) near the center of the public square; the Fondaco and old city gate to the south[14]; and, further afield, the famous St. Francis church and monastery near the major

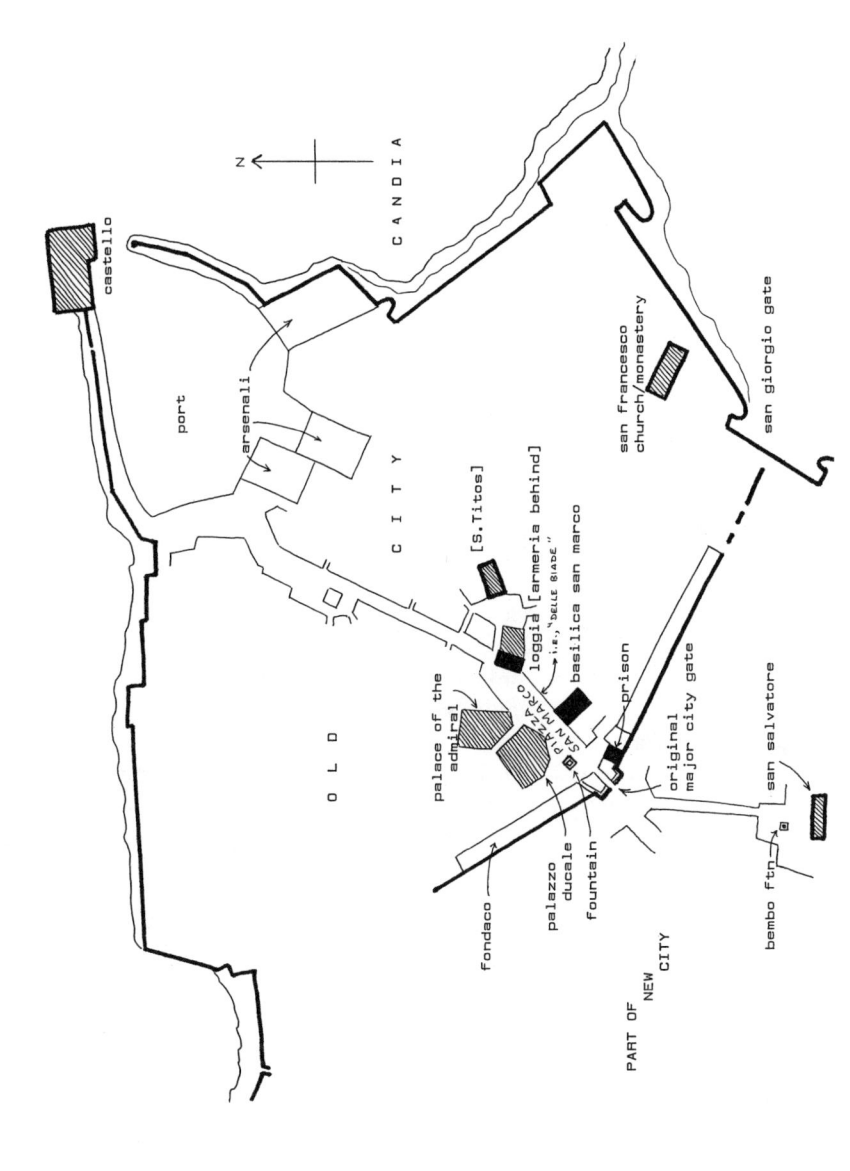

Fig. 3. Sketch of plan of Herakleion (Candia) during the Venetian period.

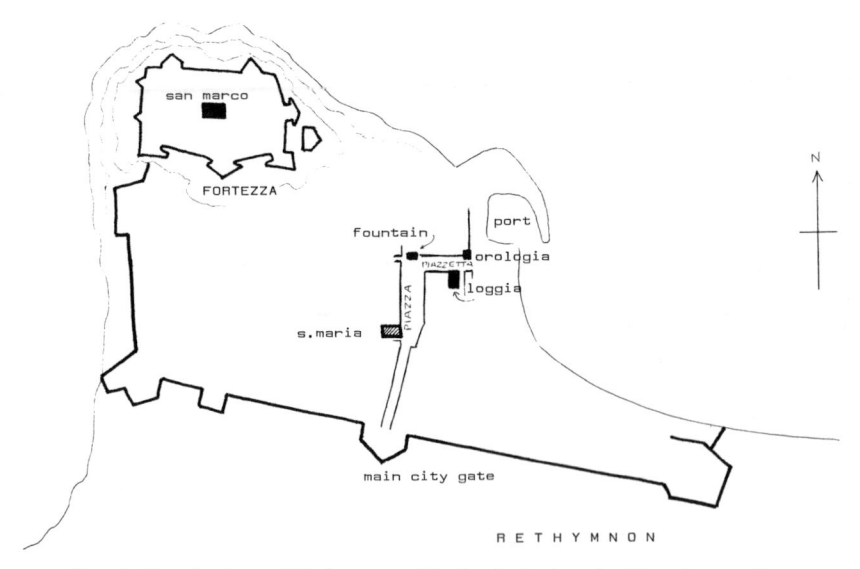

Fig. 4. Sketch plan of Rethymnon (Retimo) during the Venetian period.

city gate of San Giorgio on the east; the church of San Salvatore to the south, at the far end of the major market street near the terminus of which stands a public fountain (the Bembo fountain).[15]

A comparison with fig. 2 will indicate the similarities in the public monumental cores of Candia and Venice. It should be noted that the Candian central area is near to the earlier and original main Venetian city entrance gate, thus replicating the position of the Palazzo Ducale, San Marco, and Piazzetta of Venice itself vis-à-vis its major urban threshold on the Venetian Canal Grande. In the pre-conquest plan, the growth of Candia was to the south, and the new city walls enclosed these new "borghi," thereby relegating the monumental central core to the geographic center of the enlarged urban area.

A glance at the plan of Retimo in fig. 4 will reveal a somewhat different situation. There, the existence of a substantial inner citadel, the Fortezza, altered the ideal urban topography such that the basilica of San Marco is to be found away from the main piazza, up on the Fortezza (where we would postulate the earlier city center to have been[16]). The lower city of Retimo, on the flat land to the south of the citadel, came to constitute the major residential and commercial area of the settlement during the period before the Ottoman conquest. It is in this area, in the east-central part of the city fabric, that the major piazza and Loggia are to be found (along with the several other major religious establishments and commercial areas).

What is of interest in the organization of Retimo is the fact that its piazza is a miniature L-shaped version of the great Piazza-Piazzetta system in Venice: in both cases, the piazzetta section opens out to the water, on the east. Nearby, at the northeast side of the Retimo piazzetta, stood a tall clock tower (no longer extant but shown in old views,[17] recalling, if not the exact position, at least the relative size and prominence of the great Venetian Campanile.

It should be apparent, then, that in Candia and Retimo we are dealing with the articulation of urban fabrics in such a fashion as to echo on a small scale the elements and spatial relationships of Venice itself. Both forms and their interrelations within the urban center mark these cities as distinctly Venetian, obscuring the native Hellenic centers of religious power. Characteristically, the major Greek Orthodox church, that of St. Titos, stands in effect behind the public Venetian (Latin) urban core of Candia.[18]

Upon the assumption of control of Candia in 1669, the Ottomans embarked upon a rebuilding project which was to result in the transformation of the major Venetian structures of the city. The principal symbolic and religious act was the conversion of all the major Latin churches into mosques. It is not yet clear whether this policy included leaving Greek houses of worship intact,[19] although the following two centuries saw a number of appropriations of Orthodox buildings, largely, it seems, in reprisal against uprisings and popular revolts by the Greek population against their Ottoman rulers at the instigation of Orthodox priests and bishops.

The Ottoman transformations in Candia are of great interest in attempting to reconstruct Ottoman urban policies. The following conversions were made:[20]

Venetian structure	*into*	*Ottoman structure*
1. San Marco basilica		Mosque of Defterdar Ahmet Pasha
2. Loggia		Offices of Defterdar
3. Palazzo Ducale		Saray of Vizier/governor
4. Admiral's Palace		destroyed; site of religious school
5. Fondaco area		retained as shops
6. Morosini Fountain		rebuilt as Sebilhane; enlarged
7. San Salvatore church		Mosque of the Valide Sultana
8. Bembo Fountain		rebuilt as Sebilhane; enlarged
9. St. Francis church/monastery		Mosque of the Sultan

What is of especial interest here is the fact that the primary Venetian religious structure, San Marco, was *not* adapted for reuse as the primary Ottoman religious building (viz., the Mosque of the Sultan). Instead, the Sultan's mosque was constructed out of the shell of the St. Francis monastery church, just to the north of the major eastern city gate (the San Giorgio gate; see fig. 2). This contrasted with the situation in Retimo, where the church of San Marco, in the center of the Fortezza citadel, *was* transformed into a major mosque.[21]

Considering this curious anomaly, we have come to the tentative conclusion that the Ottoman planners chose to site their major Imperial house of worship at St. Francis because of the very prominent *topographical* position of the latter (rather than siting the Imperial mosque at San Marco, the most prominent internal *urban* position) precisely in order to create an *externally* visible emblem and symbol of Ottoman control. The St. Francis church stood on very high ground adjacent to the major eastern city gate. The church, visible for miles on land and sea, had come to stand as an emblem of the Venetian city both on Crete and abroad. It was a renowned treasury of precious religious objects, works of art, and important and unique manuscripts (all of which were removed by the Venetians in their retreat from the island in 1669).[22]

As far as our surveys have so far indicated, the church and its monastery were not prominently visible from within the urban core of Candia, but would have been the most prominent construction visible outside the city walls on land and sea, standing high above the massive urban fortification walls at this point; early maps and views from the Venetian period appear to sustain this impression.[23]

We may imagine, then, that the new Imperial Mosque served a similar symbolic visual function in the architectonic organization of the new Ottoman city, *marking* this city *as* Ottoman *and* Islamic to the external world. In this regard, the rebuilding of the Retimo San Marco church as a major mosque in the most prominent position (when seen from outside that city, and especially far out at sea) served an identical function. The characteristically large Ottoman dome and tall, slender minaret would have clearly identified the latter construction as emblematic of Ottoman control.

We might make an analogy here, then, with Ottoman practices elsewhere in the Near East where the Ottoman Empire extended itself into Arab lands; the most prominent parallel example would be the mosque of Muhammed Ali on the citadel of Cairo, whose distinctively Ottoman forms broadcast a distinctively political message to the city below and to the world externally.

Other analogies can be made here, but our sense is that all such parallels may be modelled after the central example of Istanbul itself, and the efforts made in the city over the centuries following 1453 to articulate a distinctively Ottoman *skyline* as an *architectonic and political symbol in its own right.* There, the major hills of the old city are capped by the most important Imperial Mosques, presenting an unmistakable visual profile embodying the power of the Islamic state.

The provincial mercantile city of Kandiye on Crete was thus transformed in such a way so as to broadcast and embody a similar message to the external world, both to the world of Islam and to the eyes of travellers and traders plying the waters of the Eastern Mediterranean from Christian Europe. What we see here is the articulation of an urban fabric so as to create a distinctively

Ottoman and Islamic skyline profile echoing that of the Imperial center on the Bosphorus; a rewriting of an urban "text" although the manipulation of forms so as to radically alter that text's meaning.

Much more may be said concerning the urban policies of the Ottomans in Crete and in Greece as a whole; our aim here has been to indicate in rough outline some of the directions of the present project in the light of our preliminary investigations. It is our sense that research in history, architectural history, and historical archaeology may well profit from a detailed and intensive focus upon the city as an analytic unit in its own right; as a framework wherein we may effectively study the ways in which societies orchestrate their built environments so as to embody and produce social or political power.

In the case of the present examples, it is our sense also that the production of ideologies may be examined in the ways in which one group alters and modifies formations engendered by other groups: measurements of such variations and transformations might serve as direct and indirect indices of social polices. One such area where inquiry may be fruitfully pursued is in the patient tracing of the fate of architectural members and pieces over time and geography. In the case of Candia, we have begun to be able to trace the movement of architectural pieces across the city and their use and re-use in differing contexts. We know, for example, that some of the architectural sculpted decor of the original St. Francis church was reused in the new Imperial mosque, and that some of this was dispersed elsewhere after a serious earthquake largely destroyed the latter in the mid-nineteenth century. It was incorporated into the design of entranceways of a new military barracks building erected in the third quarter of the nineteenth century nearby (a structure now serving as city offices of the city of Herakleion). At some point in this migration of members, pieces which were originally used as column capitals in the St. Francis church were *inverted* to serve as column bases (their present-day function). We suspect it to be the case that usable architectural members with some form of particular political, religious, or other symbolic reference were deliberately altered (such as by re-working or by inversion) so as to negate or neutralize or co-opt their original references.[24]

In dealing with complex urban fabrics such as those of the cities of Crete, we have come to appreciate that a great deal of information about a group's attitude and policies may be read in the ways in which older artifactual texts are edited and emended. We have also come to appreciate that a great deal may be learned about the essential principles of Ottoman urbanism through an understanding of the ways in which such principles were negotiated and compromised in foreign, multi-ethnic contexts. In such contexts, moreover, it becomes clear that the skills of the historian, architectural historian, and historical archaeologist are complementary and mutually illuminating.[25]

Notes

1. This paper is the first report based on preliminary surveys in Crete and Istanbul during 1982 and 1983, and is part of a larger ongoing project co-directed with Professor Irene A. Bierman of UCLA. We are grateful to the Research Foundation of SUNY Binghamton, the UCLA Academic Senate, and the UCLA Art Council for important initial funding. Edward Mitchell of UCLA is responsible for Ottoman translations used here, and all Greek translations are by the present author. We have received advice and invaluable help from a number of colleagues: Rifa'at Ali Abou-el-Haj, Oktay Aslanapa, Nurhan Atasoy, Jere Bacharach, Howard Crane, Pierre MacKay, Theo MacKay, Baha Talman, and Speros Vryonis. An earlier outline of the present report is scheduled to appear in print: Irene A. Bierman and Donald Preziosi, "Rereading an Urban Text: The Ottomanization of Crete," in *Semiotics 1983*, eds. John Deely and Margot Lenhart (New York: Plenum).

2. Photodocumentation of major monuments and streets in Herakleion, Rethymnon and Khania was done in the Summers of 1982 and 1983, and will continue in subsequent campaigns; archival research in Istanbul was made possible through the generous support of Dr. Nurhan Atasoy of the Topkapi Museums, and Drs. Oktay Aslanapa and Baha Talman of Istanbul University. In depth survey work in Khania remains to be completed, although an initial survey was begun there. Much is rapidly disappearing: even between 1982 and 1983, in Herakleion, several structures had disappeared, having been replaced by high-rise residences and tourist facilities.

3. Evliya Celebi, *Evliya Celebi Seyahatnamesi* (Istanbul: Turk Tarih Encumeni, 1928).

4. In 1900–1905, Giuseppi Gerola catalogued the Venetian religious, military, and civil architecture and inscriptions on the island: *Monumenti Veneti nell'Isola di Creta* (Bergamo: Reale Istituto Veneto di Scienze, Lettere ed Arti), 4 vols. in 5 parts. The then contemporary photographs and reproductions of 17th century maps and documents are invaluable today, as the island has suffered greatly during the two world wars of this century. More recent scholarship on Ottoman Crete has been published in Istanbul: Ekrem Hakki Ayverdi: *Avrup'da Osmanli Mimari Eserleri Bulgaristan, Yunanistan Arnavudluk*, vol. 4 (Istanbul: Gunuluk Ticaret Gazetesi Tesisleri, 1982). Regrettably, in this latter work there are confusions between the monuments of Khania and Candia, and all but one of Ayverdi's photographs are incorrectly captioned. We have also found useful Paul Hidiroglou, *Das Religiose Leben auf Kreta nach Ewlija Celebi* (Leiden: Brill, 1969).

5. A useful summary of the history of the island may be found in C. J. Haywood, *Encyclopedia of Islam*, 2nd edition, under the entry "Kandiye."

6. John Julius Norwich, *A History of Venice* (New York: Knopf, 1982), 237–39; 546–56.

7. Evliya Celebi was present in Crete at the time, describing in great detail the siege itself, as well as the topography of Kandiye and the constructions of the conquerors: Celebi, *op. cit.*, v.VIII.

8. Preliminary research in the Topkapi archives has not as yet uncovered any evidence in this direction. As discussed below, however, it is apparent that whether or not there was any conscious emulation of Venetian practice, the Ottomans pursued policies which on the whole were similar.

9. Gerola here is the major source [see above, n. 4]; see also S. Xanthoudhidhes, *Istoria tis Kritis* (Herakleion, 1980); A. Nenedhakis, *Rethemos: Trianda aiones politeia* (Athens, 1983); Markos Youmbakis, *Fortezza: The History of the Venetian Fortress at Rethymnon* (Rethymnon, 1970); S. Xanthoudhidhis, *O Naos tou Aghiou Titou*, 2nd ed. (Herakleion, 1974). Additional cartographic materials have been located in the city archives in Herakleion and Rethymnon. The most complete map of the city of Herakleion (Candia)

at the time of the Ottoman siege is that by Werdmüller (Gerola, tavola 3, vol. 1). Gerola [vol. 2, p. 112] gives a comprehensive list of religious foundations and their holdings in the three major cities of Candia, Rethymnon, and Khania, as well as Siteia.

10. Plans in Norwich, *A History of Venice*, xvi-xix.

11. Gerola, vol. I, tavola 3.

12. *Biade* = grain; the site of the original Venetian grain market dating from the time when this piazza's position was adjacent to the major [south] land gate in the old city wall. The name of the square remained long after its mercantile functions were transferred elsewhere.

13. Dedicated on April 25 (St. Mark's day), 1628, the foundation was the terminus of a 15 km. aqueduct. It was designed in a Renaissance manner, with relief sculpture based upon Greek mythology, topped by a large statue of Neptune (S. Spanakis, *Mnimeia Kritikis Istorias* [1940] 2:42). The structure was transformed into an Ottoman *sebilhane* a century later.

14. The trace of the older city wall and gate is shown clearly in the Werdmüller plan noted above (n. 11); the Fondaco served as a multistoried warehouse and emporium, running for at least five city blocks along the old wall. Finished in 1591, the Fondaco stood on the site of the modern city offices (themselves remodelled from the Ottoman military barracks): see S. Spanakis, *I Kriti*, (Herakleion: Sfakianakis, 1964) 1:146.

15. *Ibid.*, 155. Built in 1588 by Zuanne Bembo, the fountain was similarly decorated in a classical style, before which was a headless ancient torso unearthed in Ierapetra. It stood to the north of the church of San Salvatore, a building which during the Turkish period was transformed into the cami of the Valide Sultan.

16. A detailed discussion may be found in Youmbakis, esp. pp. 46-51.

17. See Nenedhakis, p. 17, for a reproduction of a painting by an anonymous Rethymniote showing a panoramic view of the city from the harbor. In this painting, the clock tower is clearly visible on the far right. A detailed view is also given on pp. 120-21. The most recent detailed study of the architecture of the city is I. Steriotou, *I Benetikes Okhyroseis tou Rethymnou (1540-1646): Symboli sti Frouriaki Arkhitektoniki tou 16ou k. 17 ou Aiona*, 2 Vols. (Thessaloniki: Graphosynthetiki O.E., 1979).

18. The history of the church of the (Greek) patron saint of the island, St. Titos, is complex. The best introduction remains that of S. Xanthoudhidhis, *O Naos tou Aghiou Titou*, 2nd ed. (Herakleion, 1974). The grand vizier took over the original St. Titos for his cami, but when the original structure was destroyed in the earthquake of 1856, the cami was rebuilt in the Ottoman style, with a central dome, by the local (Greek) architect Mousis. It functioned as a cami until 1923, to be transformed into the Orthodox Church of St. Titos in 1926. The church is invisible from the central piazza of the city, standing behind and to the northeast of the Venetian San Marco and Loggia.

19. Our initial sense is that the few remaining Greek churches after the Ottoman conquest continued in use, with the exception of St. Titos, appropriated by the grand vizier for his cami. The Ottomans transformed some Christian churches into camis and converted others to other functions. For example, in Istanbul, the Aghia Sophia and the Kariye Cami retained religious functions, whereas others, such as Aghia Irini, became secular buildings. F. W. Hasluck, in his two-volume work *Christianity and Islam under the Sultans* (Oxford: Clarendon Press, 1929) devotes a large section to expedient conversions of religious buildings.

20. Evliya Celebi's account of the conquest records the process of Ottomanization throughout the island the establishment of camis, mescids, hadith colleges, tekkes, sebils, cemeteries and fountains which transformed the cities from "infidel" to Ottoman (*Seyahatnamesi*, vol. 8). By comparing Evliya's listings with identifications given in Ger-

ola (vol. 1), the table shown here has been constructed. Of interest is the fact that there are a number of changes in function. The Venetian palace of the Admiral was torn down, to be replaced by a hadith college, and the Venetian Loggia became the offices of the chief financial administrator, the *defterdar,* adjacent to his cami (formerly San Marco).

21. Youmbakis, pp. 64–66. It is difficult to ascertain today how much of the original San Marco fabric remained in the new cami, apart from portions of the foundations on the southwest. Portions of the *mehrab* of this sultan's cami can still be made out today, along with traces of painted decoration within. We noticed a substantial deterioration in the state of this painted decor between 1982 and 1983. The structure's domed roof is intact, and the interior is occasionally used for musical events today.

22. Spanakis, *I Kriti,* 138 ff. The monastery was built in the late 14th–early 15th centuries. Its main gate was sent from Rome in 1409. Made of fine marble, it was taken from the monastery by the Ottomans and reused as part of the entranceway to their military barracks (the site of the Venetian Fondaco, and presently the city offices of Herakleion). One of our tasks has been to trace the often labyrinthine "migrations" of architectural elements within the cities, so as to begin reconstructing formal and functional changes in the urban fabric due to Ottomanization. The monastery church was said to be the tallest building in Herakleion, visible far away on land and sea.

23. The question as to whether the church was visible from the interior of the city — for example from the central piazza delle biade — is not easy to answer today, given the disappearance or overbuilding of the city fabric of the Venetian period in the areas between the church and the piazza. Judging from the Werdmüller map (see above, n. 11), it most likely was not visible at all.

24. See above, n. 22. The inverted column bases are clearly visible today, standing as they do on one of the major thoroughfares of the modern city.

25. This report is a preliminary one, and tentative in its conclusions. The views presented here will surely be modified over time, and we expect that this will be a long-term project. The next subject to be examined will be the history of Ottoman policies in other parts of the Empire during the 16th and 17th century. With Crete we are dealing with what in effect is the Empire's last colony, established at a time when building policies in Istanbul itself, and their systems of patronage and support, were already different from the century before, and substantially weaker with regard to imperial participation. Some of these changes in patronage may be reflected on Crete in the immediate post-conquest period in the increasing prominence of the valide sultan and non-imperial classes. It is our hope that the present project may help illuminate such historical transformations.

Subject Index

al-Bakri 117
al-Mukaddasi 117
agriculture 8, 29-30, 58, 60, 69-70, 199, 218, 219, 221, 223-27, 228, 288
architecture viii, 7, 8, 14, 16, 17, 23, 27, 28, 30-32, 34, 41, 44-50, 61, 63-70, 101, 102, 173, 188, 189-92, 197, 220, 221-26, 255-56, 267, 268, 271, 275, 277-78, 281, 282, 285-95
—design viii, 28, 31-32, 44, 61, 63-69, 188, 189-92, 220, 222, 223-26, 255-56, 271, 277-78, 281, 282, 288-89
—domestic 27, 28, 102, 197, 220, 221-23, 226
—monumental/public 7, 8, 14, 16, 17, 23, 30-32, 34, 41, 44-50, 63-69, 70, 173, 188, 189-92, 221-22, 256, 268, 271, 275, 277-78, 281, 297, 288-95
—technology viii, 7, 32, 34, 44, 49-50

barrow: see burials and monument
Britain 11, 25-27, 32, 35, 36, 41, 50, 156, 181, 187-200, 203-11
burials xi, 28, 32, 92, 120, 121, 158, 163-65, 171, 175, 180-81, 185, 196, 197, 198, 199, 272-73; see also cemeteries
Byzantium 8, 36, 140, 143-46, 147, 152-53, 275, 280, 287, 288; see also Constantinople

Carolingian period 3, 5, 6, 10-14, 17-18, 24, 41, 44, 47, 58, 59, 61-71, 176-77, 182, 262, 263, 271, 275, 281; see also Charlemaign and France
cemeteries 101, 119, 171-82, 197, 199, 268; see also burials
ceramic x, 16, 75-93, 97-116, 223, 225
—distribution 90-92, 103, 105
—production x, 75-89, 92-93, 102, 107, 115, 223; see also production
—types 16, 77, 103
Charlemaign 3, 6, 12-14, 18, 28, 263, 280; see also Carolingian period and France
chiefdoms 25, 27
China 16-17, 18, 24, 98
coins and coinage xi, 6, 10, 11-12, 17, 18, 25-27, 29, 32, 119-25, 188, 196, 199, 223, 226, 254, 256, 272, 279; see also economy and trade
colonization 25-27, 70, 277
commercial revolution: see economy
Constantinople 4-7, 287, 288, 294

Denmark 12, 23, 25, 30, 32-37, 155-56, 159, 161, 165; see also Jutland and Vikings
diversity measures xi, 97, 100-101, 103-15, 117-18

economy 8, 10-12, 17, 23, 29, 32, 36, 58-63, 70, 75-93, 97-98, 100, 103, 115, 121, 129-30, 159, 161, 203, 225-26, 229, 231, 239-40, 288; see also trade

Subject Index

—Baltic 10-12, 17
—North Africa 75-93, 97-98, 100, 103, 115
—Russia 129-30
—Scandinavian 23, 29, 32, 36
emporia 11-12, 28, 59, 286
ethnographic data 86-89

fauna xi, 153, 203-11, 222, 223, 225, 228
fortifications: *see* architecture—monumental; *and* military
France x, xi, 3-14, 24, 27, 41-51, 120, 169-83, 237-59; *see also* Charlemaign, Franks, Merovingians
Franks 24, 27, 46-47, 49, 171-83, 254; *see also* Charlemaign

geographic perspective ix, 49-50, 58, 61, 69, 97-98, 171, 176-77, 180-81, 185, 187, 195, 198, 224, 226, 288; *see also* settlement pattern
Germany 5, 6, 11, 18, 59, 156, 157, 260, 267, 281-82

intra-site organization viii, 7, 8, 27, 28, 29, 30-32, 61, 63-69, 101, 172, 174-75, 178-79, 181-82, 189-92, 219-20, 223, 226, 240-58, 265-75, 290-95
Islam 3, 4-5, 6, 14-18, 24, 27, 75-93, 97-116, 152, 217-32, 285-95
Istanbul: *see* Constantinople
Italy 6, 7, 9, 261-82, 286, 287-93

Jutland 29, 30-32

Magyars 24, 25, 32
markets: *see* economy *and* trade
Merovingians 10, 41, 48, 58, 119, 237, 254
migrations 24, 26, 29, 45, 46, 155, 231, 262, 272, 288
military 32, 34-36, 42-51, 173, 188-200, 221-27, 230, 231, 263, 267, 271, 287; *see also* raids
monasteries 42, 44, 46-49, 57, 61-70, 173, 175, 282, 290
monetary system: *see* coins
monumental architecture: *see* architecture—monumental
monuments viii, 10, 30, 157, 163, 181, 195, 267-68

nobility 12, 23, 30, 32-36, 46-50, 59, 70, 119, 128, 129, 159, 163, 218, 219
North Sea empire 35-36
Norway 35, 36

Ottoman: *see* Islam

population and demography 7, 27, 58, 62, 69, 70, 78, 228, 229-31
production x, 10, 57, 61, 98, 102-3, 119, 203

raids 24, 25, 27, 29, 36, 41, 43-51, 153, 156, 228, 281; *see also* military *and* Viking
regional perspective: *see* geographic perspective
Russia 14, 24, 27, 28, 29, 30, 127-34

settlement pattern xi, 10, 27, 30, 32-33, 44, 46, 50, 58, 60, 69, 174, 176-77, 180-82, 198, 199-200; *see also* geographic perspective
ship technology xi, 25, 26, 36, 139-53
specialized production xi, 86-87, 90-91, 93, 97, 107, 114-16
state formation 17, 24, 27, 30, 32, 101
subsistence: *see* agriculture, fauna, *and* trade—foodstuffs
Sweden 6, 12, 18, 24, 25, 27, 28, 35, 155-56, 161, 165

taxation 29, 30, 32, 35, 175-76, 180, 228, 229, 287, 288
technology xi, 29, 30, 36, 75-89, 92-93, 103, 120, 139
trade viii, 6, 7, 8, 9, 10-17, 18, 24, 25, 27, 28, 29, 35, 36, 46, 57-60, 70, 79, 90-92, 100, 103, 120, 140, 143-45, 152-53, 198, 223, 225-26, 228, 231, 286, 287
—Baltic 10-14, 36, 59-60, 120
—disruption of 6, 7, 9, 10, 231
—elite 58, 59-60, 70
—foodstuffs 8, 140, 228, 287
—gift exchange 11, 60
—maritime 14, 15, 90-92, 140, 143-45, 152-53, 286, 287
—Near East 14-17, 24, 27, 152-53, 287
—Scandinavian 6, 12-14, 18, 24, 25, 27, 28, 29, 36

tribute 25, 35, 36, 46, 158; *see also* taxation

Venetian: *see* Italy

Viking Age 23–37, 43, 51, 281; *see also* Denmark, Norway, *and* Sweden

World System 24

Author Index

Adams, R. McC. 24, 25, 37
Agache, R. 53, 54
Alain, D. 52
Albrechtsen, E. 25, 26, 37
Alcock, L. 187, 200
Alekseev, L. V. 137
Allen, D. F. 188, 200
Andersen, H. H. 30, 37
Amdren, A. 32, 37
Anzalone, R. 95
Arbman, H. 6, 18, 26, 37, 55
Arcixouskij, A. V. 134–35, 136
Aries, P. 185
Arnold, D. E. 116
Astill, G. 20
Atil, E. 94
Ayverd, E. H. 296

Baes, F. 52, 53, 56
Barcelo Tores, M. C. 232
Barker, G. 20
Bass, G. 154
Bautier, R. H. 55
Bel, A. 94
Benchekroun, M. B. A. 95
Benco, N. L. 94, 117
Beresford, M. W. 71
Bezanger, M. C. 52, 53
Biddle, M. 32, 37, 52, 56, 72
Bierman, I. A. 296
Binvenu, J. M. 185
Birnbaum, H. 135

Blackman, M. J. 93, 94, 95
Blake, H. McK. 20
Boessnek, J. 211, 215
Bolin, S. 21
Boone, J. 93
Booney, D. 181, 185, 195, 200
Born, E. 20, 72
Bottema, S. 19
Bourdillon, J. 212, 213
Boyle, L. E. 166
Brand, J. D. 125
Brown, P. 186
Brown, T. S. 20
Bruce-Milford, R. L. S. 20
Bur, M. 56
Burns, R. L. 232
Burrow, I. G. 187, 200
Butzer, E. K. 232, 233
Butzer, K. W. 232, 233

Caev, N. S. 135
Cameron, K. 213
Carandini, A. 19
Castelin, K. 125
Cavalli-Sforza, L. 166
Celebi, E. 296, 297
Chadwick, H. M. 165
Champion, T. 166
Chapelot, J. 71, 186
Chapman, B. 37
Charles-Edwards, T. M. 181, 186
Chase, C. 166

Chedeville, A. 184
Chejne, A. G. 232
Chenet, G. 125
Cherniss, M. D. 165
Christensen, A. E. 154
Clain-Stefanelli, E. E. 125
Clutton-Brock, J. 212, 213
Conkey, M. 115
Coolen, G. 55
Coy, J. 212, 213, 214
Creed, R. P. 166
Creswell, K. A. C. 21
Cunnison, I. 20

Davidsohn, R. 262, 265, 283
Deboer, W. 117
de Bourard, M. 55
de Broussillon, B. 184
de Jumieges, G. 54
Demolon, P. 52
Derville, A. 52, 53, 55, 56
de Slain, M. 117
Desportes, P. 55
Devisse, J. 186
d'Haenens, A. 52, 53, 55, 56
Dneprov, E. D. 135
Duby, G. 58, 61, 71, 72
Duclaux de Martin, T. 184
Duda, D. 94
Duparc, P. 184
Dyer, J. 195, 299

Eckstein, D. 20
Eiseman, C. J. 154
Elmqvist, M. 53
Engel, A. 125
Eennen E. 52
et Menjot d'Elbenne, R. C. 184
Eustache, D. 117
Evans-Pritchard, E. E. 20
Ewbamd, J. M. 212, 214

Fagerlie, J. M. 125
Federici, V. 72
Feinman, G. 116, 118
Feldman, M. W. 166
Fernandez-Sotelo, W. 94
Fevier, P. A. 20
Finberg, H. P. R. 188, 200
Foley, J. M. 166
Foote, P. G. 28, 37
Forde-Johnston, J. 188, 200

Fortnum, C. D. E. 94
Foss, C. 8, 19
Fossier, R. 71, 185, 186
Fowler, P. J. 187, 191, 200
Fox, C. 191, 201
Franken, H. J. 94
Franklin, S. 135
Frere, S. 213, 214
Frey, D. A. 154
Frydenberg, O. 27, 38
Fulford, M. 19

Galli, E. 283
Gamble, C. 166
Ganshof, F. L. 58, 72
Garcia Gomez, E. 232
Gelling, M. 201, 213, 214
Gerola, G. 296, 297
Glick, T. F. 95
Goitein, S. D. 95
Goodier, A. 185–86
Granja, F. de la 232
Grant, A. 211, 212, 214
Gregory, T. E. 20
Grenier de Cardinal, M. 94
Grierson, P. 11, 20, 72, 125, 126
Grongard Jeppesen, T. 30, 38
Guichard, P. 232
Guillotel, H. 184

Halperin, C. J. 135
Hamer, F. 94
Hamilton, J. 212, 214
Harcourt, R. 212, 214
Hardie, C. 267, 283
Harris, M. 71, 72
Haskova, J. 125
Hasluck, F. W. 297
Hawkal, I. 117
Hayes. J. D. 19
Haywood, C. J. 296
Helbaek, H. 30, 38
Heliot, P. 55
Herlihy, D. 72
Hermansen, G. 19
Herzen, A. 135
Herzfeld, E. 21
Hidiroglou, P. 296
Higgs, E. S. 212, 214
Hobley, B. 72
Hodder, B. W. 72

Hodges, R. 18, 20, 21, 24, 38, 59, 71, 72
Hogg, A. H. A. 191, 201
Holdsworth, P. 20, 211, 214
Holstein, E. 20
Holwerda, H. 18
Hood, S. 20
Horn, W. 20, 61, 72
Howard, H. 94
Hubert, J. 52
Humphrey, J. H. 19
Hurst, H. R. 19
Hurst, J. G. 71
Hvass, S. 29, 38

Ingstad, A. S. 26, 38
Isacenko, A. V. 135

Janin, V. L. 134, 135, 136, 137
Jankuhn, H. 20, 28, 38, 52
Johnson, G. A. 116
Jones, G. D. B. 20

Kalsbeek, J. 94
Karras, R. M. 125
Katze, S. 140
Katzev, M. 140, 154
Keenan, E. L. 135
Kent, J. P. C. 125
Kiernan, K. S. 166
King, D. J. C. 191, 201
Kinnes, I. 37
Kintigh, K. 117, 118
Klaeber, F. 166, 167
Kraus, P. 232
Krautheimer, R. 19
Kreutz, B. 154
Krogh, K. J. 30, 38

L'Africain, J. 95
Ladero Quesada, M. A. 232
Lapeyre, H. 232
Le Bras, G. 184
Lee, E. 72
Lejiksaar, J. 55
Lesne, E. 186
Lestocquoy, J. 55, 56
Levi-Provencal, E. 232
Levillain, L. 56
Levin, E. 136
Levy, J. E. 155, 159, 164, 165, 167
Lombard, M. 27, 38

Lorren, C. 185
Lot, F. 53
Lottin, A. 52, 55
Lusse, J. 55

Maetzke, G. 275, 277, 283
Malinowski, B. 11, 20
Malmer, B. 126
Malone, K. 166
Maltby, M. 212, 214
Malygina, P. D. 137
Mango, C. 8, 20
Mansi 184
Marsden, P. 153
Martensson, A. W. 38
Mateu, J. F. 232, 233
Mauss, M. 11, 20
May, J. 188, 201
Mayhew, N. J. 125
Meaney, A. 188, 201
Medvedev, A. F. 136, 137
Medynceva, A. A. 136
Metcalf, D. M. 125
Mikesell, M. 95
Miralles, I. 233
Mitchell, J. 72
Moore, J. A. 117
Moreland, J. 72
Morrozi, J. H. 283
Morris, C. 116
Morris, E. L. 94
Morris, W. 167
Muckelroy, K. 154
Musset, L. 184, 185
Myers, E. 93, 94, 95
Myers, J. L. 95

Nenedhakis, A. 296, 297
Noddle, B. 212, 213, 214
Noonan, T. S. 21, 135
Northedge, A. 21
Norwich, J. J. 296, 297

Okborn, M. 55
Olsen, O. 31, 38
Osborn, J. 19

Panella, C. 19
Parker, A. J. 19
Pastor de Togneri, R. 232
Patterson, H. 72

Peacock, D. P. S. 94
Pedley, J. G. 19
Peigne-Delacourt, M. 53, 54
Pellat, C. 117
Penarroja Torrejon, L. 232
Philipson, D. W. 212, 214
Picchio, R. 135, 136
Pielou, E. C. 117
Pietri, L. 52
Pirenne, H. 3-6, 18, 58, 60, 72
Platelle, H. 52, 53
Pohl, A. 125
Pokorny, J. 167
Pontal, O. 185
Pope, K. O. 20
Potter, T. W. 20
Preziosi, D. 296
Pulak, C. 151, 154

Rackow, E. 95
Ralph, E. 188, 201
Ramskou, T. 34, 38
Randsborg, K. 20, 30, 31, 32, 37, 38
Rasmusson, N. 125
Rau, R. 52, 53, 54
Redman, C. 93, 94, 95, 101, 117
Reichstein, H. 213, 214
Rhodes, D. 94
Rice, P. M. 116, 117
Riley, J. 116
Roblin, M. 55
Roesdahl, E. 31, 38
Rogers, J. M. 21
Rouche, M. 52, 53, 55, 56
Rubertone, P. 94
Runnels, C. N. 20
Rybina, A. 135, 136

Salin, E. 185, 186
Schietzel, K. 28, 38
Schlesinger, W. 52
Schlumberger, G. 125
Schmidt, H. 38
Serrure, R. 125
Shennan, S. 166
Sinopoli, C. 94
Skaare, K. 125
Skinner, G. W. 98, 116, 117
Smith, B. S. 188, 201
Smith, C. 72, 116, 117
Spanakis, S. 297, 298

Sparck, J. V. 27, 38
Spence, M. W. 116
Stalh, A. M. 125, 126
Steffy, J. R. 140, 147, 152, 154
Steriotou, I. 297
Stever, H. 52
Stoumann, T. 27, 39

Taylor, C. 213, 215
Terasse, H. 93, 94
Tessier, G. 55
Thompson, H. 19
Thompson, M. 126
Thorkelin, G. J. 166
Throckmorton, J. 154
Throckmorton, P. 147, 153, 154
Todd, M. 199, 201
Toker, I. 283
Tomasini, W. J. 126
Toynbee, J. 186
Trenard, L. 52, 55

Ucelli, G. 153
Ullmann, W. 72

Valk, S. N. 136
van Andel, T. H. 20
van der Leeuw, S. E. 94
van Doorninck, F. 143, 145, 147, 153, 154
van Es, W. A. 20, 72
van Gennep, A. 94
van Kirk Dobbie, E. 167
van Zeist, W. 19
Vercauteren, F. 52, 53, 54, 55
Verwers, W. J. H. 20, 72
Vielliard, R. 19
Villani, G. 262, 263, 264
Vita-Finzi, C. 9, 20
Vogel, W. 52
von Simson, B. 54
von deb Driesch 211, 215

Wade, K. 20
Wagstaffe, J. M. 20
Wallerstein, I. 117
Waquet, H. 54
Ward-Perkins, B. 19
Wattenbach, W. 52, 55
Werner, J. 18
West, S. 204, 211, 215
Whitehouse, D. 18, 19, 20, 21, 24, 38, 72, 212, 215

Whitehouse, R. D. 212, 214, 215
Whitelock, D. 26, 39
Whittaker, C. R. 19, 20
Whittle, A. 166
Wickham, C. J. 20, 71, 72
Wilkenson, C. 90, 95
Wilson, D. M. 28, 37, 39
Wilson, M. 188, 201
Wright, H. T. 116

Xanthoudhidis, S. 296, 297

Youmbakis, M. 296, 297, 298
Young, B. 125, 186

Zadora-Rio, E. 184
Zaliznjak, A. A. 136

The common theme of **Medieval Archeology** is the use of archeological information to solve central interpretive problems in medieval studies. Joint disciplinary approaches are emphasized and a broad range of data bases included, showing the variety of areas that can be addressed. The volume illustrates methodological issues that span the disciplines, as well as examples of research from diverse countries and as applied to diverse material. The volume demonstrates both the scope and vitality of medieval archeology — among the oldest and most respected branches of archeology in Europe and now beginning to generate great interest and excitement in North America.

Four sections examine the impact of the Viking conquest and trade on the growth of Europe; subjects and approaches employed by archeologists; excavations of rural and urban societies; and ideologies and organizations of various societies. Eighty-seven photographs illustrate these challenging studies.

Charles L. Redman is Professor and Chair of the Department of Anthropology at Arizona State University (Tempe), is the recipient of a Fulbright Fellowship in Islamic Civilization, and Chair of the Arizona Archeology Advisory Commission. He is author of *Qsar Es-Seghir: An Archaelogical View of Medieval Life* (1986); *Rise of Civilization* (1978), and editor or co-author of four other books on the subject of archeology.